MORAL AND POLITICAL PHILOSOPHY.

THE

PRINCIPLES

OF

MORAL AND POLITICAL

PHILOSOPHY.

BY WILLIAM PALEY, M.A.

ARCHDEACON OF CARLISLE.

―――――

THE SECOND EDITION CORRECTED.

―――――

LONDON:

PRINTED BY J. DAVIS,

FOR R. FAULDER, NEW BOND STREET.

M.DCC.LXXXVI.

TO

THE RIGHT REVEREND

EDMUND LAW, D. D.

LORD BISHOP OF CARLISLE.

MY LORD,

HAD the obligations which I owe to your Lordship's kindness been much less, or much fewer, than they are; had personal gratitude left any place in my mind for deliberation or for enquiry; in selecting a name which every reader might confess to be prefixed, with propriety, to a work, that, in many of its parts, bears no obscure relation to the general principles of natural and revealed religion, I should

should have found myself directed by many considerations to that of the Bishop of Carlisle. A long life, spent in the most interesting of all human pursuits, the investigation of moral and religious truth, in constant and unwearied endeavours to advance the discovery, communication, and success of both; a life so occupied, and arrived at that period which renders every life venerable, commands respect by a title, which no virtuous mind will dispute, which no mind sensible of the importance of these studies to the supreme concerns of mankind will not rejoice to see acknowledged. Whatever difference, or whatever opposition, some, who peruse your Lordship's writings, may perceive between your conclusions and their own, the good and wise of all

all persuasions will revere that industry, which has for its object the illustration or defence of our common Christianity. Your Lordship's researches have never lost sight of one purpose, namely, to recover the simplicity of the gospel from beneath that load of unauthorized additions, which the ignorance of some ages, and the learning of others, the superstition of weak, and the craft of designing men, have (unhappily for its interest) heaped upon it. And this purpose, I am convinced, was dictated by the purest motive; by a firm, and, I think, a just opinion, that whatever renders religion more rational, renders it more credible; that he, who, by a diligent and faithful examination of the original records, dismisses from the system one article, which contradicts the apprehension, the experience, or the reasoning of mankind, does more towards recommending the belief, and, with the belief, the influence of Christianity, to the understandings and consciences of serious enquirers, and through them to universal reception and authority, than can be effected by a thousand contenders for creeds and ordinances of human establishment.

When the doctrine of transubstantiation had taken possession of the Christian world, it was not without the industry of learned men that it came at length to be discovered, that no such doctrine was contained in the New Testament. But had those excellent persons done nothing more by their discovery, than

abolished

abolished an innocent superstition, or changed some directions in the ceremonial of public worship, they had merited little of that veneration, with which the gratitude of protestant churches remembers their services. What they did for mankind was this, they exonerated Christianity of a weight which sunk it. If indolence or timidity had checked these exertions, or suppressed the fruit and publication of these enquiries, is it too much to affirm, that infidelity would at this day have been universal?

I do not mean, my Lord, by the mention of this example, to insinuate, that any popular opinion which your Lordship may have encountered, ought to be compared with transubstantiation, or that the assurance with which

we

we reject that extravagant abfurdity, is attainable in the controverfies in which your Lordfhip has been engaged: but I mean, by calling to mind thofe great reformers of the public faith, to obferve, or rather to exprefs my own perfuafion, that to reftore the purity, is moft effectually to promote the progrefs of Chriftianity; and that the fame virtuous motive, which hath fanctified their labours, fuggefted yours. At a time when fome men appear not to perceive any good, and others to fufpect an evil tendency, in that fpirit of examination and refearch which is gone forth in Chriftian countries, this teftimony is become due not only to the probity of your Lordfhip's views, but to the general caufe of intellectual and religious liberty.

That your Lordship's life may be prolonged in health and honour; that it may afford whilst it continues an instructive proof, how serene and easy old age can be made, by the memory of important and well intended labours, by the possession of public and deserved esteem, by the presence of many grateful relatives; above all, by the resources of religion, by an unshaken confidence in the designs of a "faithful Creator," and a settled trust in the truth and in the promises of Christianity, is the fervent prayer of, my Lord,

Your Lordship's dutiful,

Most obliged,

And most devoted servant.

WILLIAM PALEY.

Carlisle,
Feb. 10, 1785.

PREFACE.

IN the treatises that I have met with upon the subject of *morals*, I appear to myself to have remarked the following imperfections—either that the principle was erroneous, or that it was indistinctly explained, or that the rules deduced from it were not sufficiently adapted to real life and to actual situations. The writings of Grotius, and the larger work of Puffendorff are of the *forensic* a cast, too much mixed up with the civil law, and with the jurisprudence of Germany, to answer precisely the design of a system of ethics—

the direction of private consciences in the general conduct of human life. Perhaps, indeed, they are not to be regarded as institutes of morality calculated to instruct an individual in his duty, so much as a species of law books and law authorities, suited to the practice of those courts of justice, whose decisions are regulated by general principles of natural equity in conjunction with the maxims of the Roman code: of which kind, I understand, there are many upon the continent. To which may be added concerning both these authors, that they are more occupied in describing the rights and usages of independent communities, than is necessary in a work which professes, not to adjust the correspondence of nations, but to delineate the offices of domestic life. The profusion also of classical quotations, with which many of their pages abound, seems to me a fault from which it will not be easy to excuse them. If these extracts be intended as decorations of style, the composition is overloaded with ornaments of one kind. To any thing more than ornament they can make no claim. To propose them as serious arguments; gravely to attempt to establish or fortify a moral duty by the testimony of a Greek or Roman poet, is to trifle with the attention of the reader, or rather to take it off from all just principles of reasoning in morals.

Of our own writers in this branch of philosophy, I find none that I think perfectly free from the three objections which I have stated. There is likewise a fourth property observable in almost all of them, namely, that they divide too much the law of nature from the precepts of revelation; some authors industriously declining the mention of scripture authorities, as belonging to a different province, and others reserving them for a separate volume: which appears to me much the same defect, as if a commentator on the laws of England should content himself with stating upon each head the common law of the land, without taking any notice of acts of parliament; or should choose to give his readers the common law in one book,

and the statute law in another. "When the obli-
"gations of morality are taught," says a pious and
celebrated writer, "let the sanctions of Christia-
"nity never be forgotten; by which it will be
"shewn that they give strength and lustre to each
"other; religion will appear to be the voice of
"reason, and morality the will of God." *

The *manner* also, in which modern writers have treated of subjects of morality, is, in my judgment, liable to much exception. It has become of late a fashion to deliver moral institutes in strings or series of detached propositions, without subjoining a continued argument or regular dissertation to any of them. This sententious, apothegmatizing style, by crowding propositions and paragraphs too fast upon the mind, and by carrying the eye of the reader from subject to subject in too quick a succession, gains not a sufficient hold upon the attention, to leave either the memory furnished, or the understanding satisfied.

* Preface to The Preceptor, by Dr. Johnson.

However useful a syllabus of topics, or a series of propositions may be in the hands of a lecturer, or as a guide to a student, who is supposed to consult other books, or to institute upon each subject researches of his own, the method is by no means convenient for ordinary readers; because few readers are such *thinkers* as to want only a hint to set their thoughts at work upon; or such as will pause and tarry at every proposition, till they have traced out its dependency, proof, relation, and consequences, before they permit themselves to step on to another. A respectable writer of this class * has comprized his doctrine of slavery in the three following propositions.

" No one is born a slave, because every one is
" born with all his original rights."

" No one can become a slave, because no one from
" being a person can, in the language of the Roman
" law, become a thing, or subject of property."

" The

---

* Dr. Ferguson, author of " Institutes of Moral Philosophy," 1767.

" The supposed property of the master in the slave, therefore, is matter of usurpation, not of right."

It may be possible to deduce from these few adages such a theory of the primitive rights of human nature, as will evince the illegality of slavery; but surely an author requires too much of his reader, when he expects him to make these deductions for himself; or to supply, perhaps from some remote chapter of the same treatise, the several proofs and explanations, which are necessary to render the meaning and truth of these assertions intelligible.

There is a fault, the opposite of this, which some moralists who have adopted a different, and, I think, a better plan of composition, have not always been careful to avoid; namely, the dwelling upon verbal and elementary distinctions, with a labour and prolixity, proportioned much more to the subtlety of the question, than to its value and

and importance in the prosecution of the subject. A writer upon the law of nature, * whose explications in every part of philosophy, though always diffuse, are often very successful, has employed three long sections in endeavouring to prove, that " permissions are not laws." The discussion of this controversy, however essential it might be to dialectic precision, was certainly not necessary to the progress of a work designed to describe the duties and obligations of civil life. The reader becomes impatient when he is detained by disquisitions which have no other object than the settling of terms and phrases; and, what is worse, they, for whose use such books are chiefly intended, will not be persuaded to read them at all.

I am led to propose these strictures, not by any propensity to depreciate the labours of my predecessors, much less to invite a comparison between the merits of their performances and my own; but solely by the consideration, that when a writer offers

---

* Dr. Rutherforth, author of " Institutes of Natural Law."

offers a book to the public upon a subject on which the public are already in possession of many others, he is bound by a kind of literary justice, to inform his readers distinctly and specifically, what it is he professes to supply, and what he expects to improve. The imperfections above enumerated are those which I have endeavoured to avoid or remedy. Of the execution the reader must judge: but this was the design.

Concerning the *principle* of morals it would be premature to speak; but concerning the manner of unfolding and explaining that principle, I have somewhat which I wish to be remarked. An experience of nine years in the office of a public tutor in one of the universities, and in that department of education to which these chapters relate, afforded me frequent occasion to observe, that, in discoursing to young minds upon topics of morality, it required much more pains to make them perceive the difficulty, than to understand the solution; that, unless the subject was so drawn up to a point, full force of an objection, or the exact place of a doubt, before any explanation was entered upon; in other words, unless some curiosity was excited before it was attempted to be satisfied, the labour of the teacher was lost. When information was not desired, it was seldom, I found, retained. I have made this observation my guide in the following work; that is, upon each occasion I have endeavoured, before I suffered myself to proceed in the disquisition, to put the reader in complete possession of the question; and to do it in the way that I thought most likely to stir up his own doubts and solicitude about it.

In pursuing the principle of morals through the detail of cases to which it is applicable, I have had in view to accommodate both the choice of the subjects, and the manner of handling them, to the situations which arise in the life of an inhabitant of this country in these times. This is the thing that I think to be principally wanting in former treatises; and, perhaps, the chief advantage which

will

will be found in mine. I have examined no doubts, I have discussed no obscurities, I have encountered no errors, I have adverted to no controversies, but what I have seen actually to exist. If some of the questions treated of appear to a more instructed reader minute or puerile, I desire such reader to be assured that I have found them occasions of difficulty to young minds; and what I have observed in young minds, I should expect to meet with in all who approach these subjects for the first time. Upon each article of human duty, I have combined with the conclusions of reason the declarations of scripture, when they are to be had, as of co-ordinate authority, and as both terminating in the same sanctions.

In the *manner* of the work, I have endeavoured so to attemper the opposite plans above animadverted upon, as that the reader may not accuse me either of too much haste, or of too much delay. I have bestowed upon each subject enough of dissertation

sertation to give a body and substance to the chapter in which it is treated of, as well as coherence and perspicuity: on the other hand, I have seldom, I hope, exercised the patience of the reader by the length and prolixity of my essays, or disappointed that patience at last by the tenuity and unimportance of the conclusion.

There are two particulars in the following work, for which it may be thought necessary that I should offer some excuse. The first of which is, that I have scarcely ever referred to any other book, or mentioned the name of the author whose thoughts, and sometimes, possibly, whose very expressions I have adopted. My method of writing has constantly been this; to extract what I could from my own stores and my own reflections in the first place; to put down that; and afterwards to consult upon each subject such reading as fell in my way: which order, I am convinced, is the only one whereby any person can keep his thoughts from sliding into other men's trains.

trains. The effect of such a plan upon the production itself will be, that whilst some parts in matter or manner may be new, others will be little else than a repetition of the old. I make no pretensions to perfect originality: I claim to be something more than a mere compiler. Much no doubt is borrowed: but the fact is, that the notes for this work having been prepared for some years, and such things having been from time to time inserted in them as appeared to me worth preserving, and such insertions made commonly without the name of the author from whom they were taken, I should, at this time, have found a difficulty in recovering these names with sufficient exactness to be able to render to every man his own. Nor, to speak the truth, did it appear to me worth while to repeat the search merely for this purpose. When authorities are relied upon, names must be produced: when a discovery has been made in science, it may be unjust to borrow the invention without ac-

knowledging

knowledging the author. But in an argumentative treatise, and upon a subject which allows no place for discovery or invention, properly so called; and in which all that can belong to a writer is his mode of reasoning, or his judgment of probabilities; I should have thought it superfluous, had it been easier to me than it was, to have interrupted my text, or crowded my margin with references to every author, whose sentiments I have made use of. There is, however, one work to which I owe so much, that it would be ungrateful not to confess the obligation: I mean the writings of the late Abraham Tucker, Esq. part of which were published by himself, and the remainder since his death, under the title of " The Light of Nature pursued, by Edward Search, Esq." I have found in this writer more original thinking and observation upon the several subjects that he has taken in hand, than in any other, not to say, than in all others put together. His talent also for illustration is unrivalled. But his thoughts are

diffused

diffused through a long, various, and irregular work. I shall account it no mean praise, if I have been sometimes able to dispose into method, to collect into heads and articles, or to exhibit in more compact and tangible masses, what, in that otherwise excellent performance, is spread over too much surface.

The next circumstance for which some apology may be expected, is the joining of moral and political philosophy together, or the addition of a book of politics to a system of ethics. Against this objection, if it be made one, I might defend myself by the example of many approved writers, who have treated *de officiis hominis et civis*, or, as some choose to express it, " of the rights and obli-
" gations of man, in his individual and social capa-
" city," in the same book. I might allege also, that the part a member of the commonwealth shall take in political contentions, the vote he shall give, the counsels he shall approve, the support he shall afford,

or

or the opposition he shall make, to any system of public measures, is as much a question of personal duty, as much concerns the conscience of the individual who deliberates, as the determination of any doubt which relates to the conduct of private life; that consequently political philosophy is, properly speaking, a continuation of moral philosophy; or rather indeed, a part of it, supposing moral philosophy to have for its aim the information of the human conscience in every deliberation that is likely to come before it. I might avail myself of these excuses, if I wanted them; but the vindication upon which I rely is the following. In stating the principle of morals, the reader will observe, that I have employed some industry in explaining the theory, and shewing the necessity of *general rules*; without the full and constant consideration of which, I am persuaded that no system of moral philosophy can be satisfactory or consistent. This foundation being laid, or rather, this habit being formed, the discussion of political subjects, to which, more than to almost any other, general rules are applicable, became clear and easy. Whereas, had these topics been assigned to a distinct work, it would have been necessary to have repeated the same rudiments, to have established over again the same principles as those which we had already exemplified, and rendered familiar to the reader, in the former parts of this. In a word, if there appear to any one too great a diversity, or too wide a distance between the subjects treated of in the course of the present volume, let him be reminded, that the doctrine of general rules pervades and connects the whole.

It may not be improper, however, to admonish the reader, that, under the name of *politics*, he is not to look for those occasional controversies, which the occurrences of the present day, or any temporary situation of public affairs may excite; and most of which, if not beneath the dignity

dignity, it is beside the purpose of a philosophical institution to advert to. He will perceive that the several disquisitions are framed with a reference to the condition of this country, and of this government: but it seemed to me to belong to the design of a work like the following, not so much to discuss each altercated point with the particularity of a political pamphlet upon the subject, as to deliver those universal principles, and to exhibit, as well as I was able, that mode and train of reasoning in politics, by the due application of which every man might be enabled to attain to just conclusions of his own.

I am not ignorant of an objection that has been advanced against all abstract speculations concerning the origin, principle, or limitation of civil authority; namely, that such speculations possess little or no influence upon the conduct either of the state or of the subject, of the governors or the governed; nor are attended with any useful consequences to either:

either: that in times of tranquillity they are not wanted; in times of confusion they are never heard. This representation however, in my opinion, is not just. Times of tumult, it is true, are not the times to learn; but the choice men make of their side and party, in the most critical occasions of the commonwealth, may neverthelefs depend upon the lessons they have received, the books they have read, and the opinions they have imbibed, in seasons of leisure and quietness. Some judicious persons, who were present at Geneva during the troubles which lately convulsed that city, thought they perceived in the contentions there carrying on, the operation of that political theory, which the writings of Rousseau, and the unbounded esteem in which these writings are held by his countrymen, had diffused amongst the people. Throughout the political disputes that have within these few years taken place in Great Britain, in her sister kingdom, and in her foreign dependencies, it was impossible not to observe, in the language

of

of party, in the resolutions of popular meetings, in debate, in conversation, in the general strain of those fugitive and diurnal addresses to the public, which such occasions call forth, the prevalency of those ideas of civil authority which are displayed in the works of Mr. Locke. The credit of that great name, the courage and liberality of his principles, the skill and clearness with which his arguments are proposed, no less than the weight of the arguments themselves, have given a reputation and currency to his opinions, of which, I am persuaded, in any unsettled state of public affairs, the influence would be felt. As this is not a place for examining the truth or tendency of these doctrines, I would not be understood, by what I have said, to express any judgment concerning either. I only mean to remark, that such doctrines are not without effect; and that it is of *practical* importance to have the principles from which the obligations of social union, and the extent of civil obedience are derived, rightly explained and well understood.

understood. Indeed, as far as I have observed, in political, beyond all other subjects, where men are without some fundamental and scientific principles to resort to, they are liable to have their understandings played upon by cant phrases and unmeaning terms, of which every party in every country possess a vocabulary. We appear astonished when we see the multitude led away by sounds; but we should remember that, if sounds work miracles, it is always upon ignorance. The influence of names is in exact proportion to the want of knowledge.

These are the observations with which I have judged it expedient to prepare the attention of my reader. Concerning the personal motives which engaged me in the following attempt, it is not necessary that I say much; the nature of my academical situation, a great deal of leisure since my retirement from it, the recommendation of an honoured and excellent friend, the authority of the venerable prelate to whom these labours are inscribed,

inscribed, the not perceiving in what way I could employ my time or talents better, and my disapprobation in literary men of that fastidious indolence, which sits still because it disdains to do *little*, were the considerations that directed my thoughts to this design. Nor have I repented of the undertaking. Whatever be the fate or reception of this work, it owes its author nothing. In sickness and in health I have found in it that which can alone alleviate the one, or give enjoyment to the other—occupation and engagement.

CONTENTS.

BOOK I.

PRELIMINARY CONSIDERATIONS.

CHAP.		PAGE.
I.	*Definition and Use of the Science*	1
II.	*The Law of Honour*	2
III.	*The Law of the Land*	3
IV.	*The Scriptures*	5
V.	*The Moral Sense*	8
VI.	*Human Happiness*	18
VII.	*Virtue*	35

BOOK II.

MORAL OBLIGATION.

I.	*The Question, Why am I obliged to keep my Word? considered*	47
II.	*What we mean, when we say a Man is obliged to do a Thing*	49

III. *The*

CONTENTS.

CHAP.		PAGE.
III.	The Question,—Why am I obliged to keep my Word? resumed	51
IV.	The Will of God	54
V.	The Divine Benevolence	57
VI.	Utility	61
VII.	The Necessity of General Rules	64
VIII.	The Consideration of General Consequences pursued	68
IX.	Of Right	72
X.	The Division of Rights	74
XI.	The General Rights of Mankind	82

BOOK III.

RELATIVE DUTIES.

PART I.

OF RELATIVE DUTIES WHICH ARE DETERMINATE.

I.	Of Property	91
II.	The Use of the Institution of Property	92
III.	The History of Property	96
IV.	In what the Right of Property is founded	98
V.	Promises	105
VI.	Contracts	121
VII.	Contracts of Sale	122
VIII.	Contracts of Hazard	127

IX. Contracts

CONTENTS.

CHAP.		PAGE.
IX.	Contracts of lending of inconsumable Property	130
X.	Contracts concerning the lending of Money	133
XI.	Contracts of Labour—Service	139
XII.	——————Commissions	144
XIII.	——————Partnership	147
XIV.	——————Offices	149
XV.	Lies	154
XVI.	Oaths	159
XVII.	Oaths in Evidence	167
XVIII.	Oaths of Allegiance	169
XIX.	Oath against Bribery in the Election of Members of Parliament	173
XX.	Oath against Simony	174
XXI.	Oaths to observe local Statutes	178
XXII.	Subscription to Articles of Religion	180
XXIII.	Wills	183

BOOK III.

PART II.

OF RELATIVE DUTIES WHICH ARE INDETERMINATE, AND OF THE CRIMES OPPOSED TO THESE.

I.	Charity	191
II.	Charity—The Treatment of our Domestics and Dependants	192
III.	Slavery	195

IV. *Charity*.

CONTENTS.

CHAP.		PAGE.
IV.	Charity.—*Professional Assistance*	199
V.	Charity.—*Pecuniary Bounty*	202
VI.	*Resentment*	215
VII.	*Anger*	216
VIII.	*Revenge*	219
IX.	*Duelling*	225
X.	*Litigation*	229
XI.	*Gratitude*	234
XII.	*Slander*	236

BOOK III.

PART III.

OF RELATIVE DUTIES WHICH RESULT FROM THE CONSTITUTION OF THE SEXES, AND OF THE CRIMES OPPOSITE TO THESE.

I.	*Of the public Use of Marriage Institutions*	241
II.	*Fornication*	243
III.	*Seduction*	250
IV.	*Adultery*	254
V.	*Incest*	260
VI.	*Polygamy*	262
VII.	*Of Divorce*	267
VIII.	*Marriage*	277
IX.	*Of the Duty of Parents*	282
X.	*The Rights of Parents*	301
XI.	*The Duty of Children*	304

CONTENTS.

BOOK IV.

DUTIES TO OURSELVES, AND THE CRIMES OPPOSITE TO THESE.

CHAP.		PAGE.
I.	*The Rights of Self-Defence*	312
II.	*Drunkenness*	315
III.	*Suicide*	323

BOOK V.

DUTIES TOWARDS GOD.

I.	*Division of these Duties*	333
II.	*Of the Duty, and of the Efficacy of Prayer, so far as the same appear from the Light of Nature*	335
III.	*Of the Duty and Efficacy of Prayer, as represented in Scripture*	343
IV.	*Of Private Prayer, Family Prayer, and Public Worship*	348
V.	*Of Forms of Prayer in Public Worship*	356
VI.	*Of the Use of Sabbatical Institutions*	364
VII.	*Of the Scripture Account of Sabbatical Institutions*	367
VIII.	*By what Acts and Omissions the Duty of the Christian Sabbath is violated*	384
IX.	*Of Reverencing the Deity*	388

BOOK VI.

ELEMENTS OF POLITICAL KNOWLEDGE.

CHAP.		PAGE.
I.	Of the Origin of Civil Government	399
II.	How Subjection to Civil Government is maintained	406
III.	The Duty of Submission to Civil Government explained	414
IV.	Of the Duty of Civil Obedience, as stated in the Christian Scriptures	431
V.	Of Civil Liberty	441
VI.	Of different Forms of Government	449
VII.	Of the British Constitution	463
VIII.	Of the Administration of Justice	497
IX.	Of Crimes and Punishments	526
X.	Of Religious Establishments, and of Toleration	554
XI.	Of Population and Provision; and of Agriculture and Commerce as subservient thereto	587
XII.	Of War and of Military Establishments	637

MORAL PHILOSOPHY.

BOOK I.

PRELIMINARY CONSIDERATIONS.

CHAP. I.

DEFINITION AND USE OF THE SCIENCE.

Moral Philosophy, Morality, Ethics, Casuistry, Natural Law, mean all the same thing; namely, *That science which teaches men their duty and the reasons of it.*

The use of such a study depends upon this, that, without it, the rules of life, by which men are ordinarily governed, oftentimes mislead them, thro' a defect either in the rule, or in the application.

These rules are, the Law of Honour, the Law of the Land, and the Scriptures.

CHAP. II.

THE LAW OF HONOUR.

THE Law of Honour is a system of rules constructed by people of fashion, and calculated to facilitate their intercourse with one another; and for no other purpose.

Consequently, nothing is adverted to by the Law of Honour, but what tends to incommode this intercourse.

Hence this law only prescribes and regulates the duties *betwixt equals*; omitting such as relate to the Supreme Being, as well as those which we owe to our inferiors.

For which reason, profaneness, neglect of public worship or private devotion, cruelty to servants, rigorous treatment of tenants or other dependants, want of charity to the poor, injuries done to tradesmen by insolvency or delay of payment, with numberless examples of the same kind, are accounted no breaches of honour; because a man is not a less agreeable companion for these vices, nor the worse to deal with, in those concerns which are usually transacted between one gentleman and another.

Again,

Again, the Law of Honour being conſtituted by men occupied in the purſuit of pleaſure, and for the mutual conveniency of ſuch men, will be found, as might be expected from the character and deſign of the law-makers, to be, in moſt inſtances, favourable to the licentious indulgence of the natural paſſions.

Thus it allows of fornication, adultery, drunkenneſs, prodigality, duelling, and revenge in the extreme; and lays no ſtreſs upon the virtues oppoſite to theſe.

CHAP. III.

THE LAW OF THE LAND.

THAT part of mankind, who are beneath the Law of Honour, often make the law of the land their rule of life; that is, they are ſatisfied with themſelves, ſo long as they do or omit nothing, for the doing or omitting of which the law can puniſh them.

Whereas every ſyſtem of human laws, conſidered as a rule of life, labours under the two following defects.

I. Human laws omit many duties, as not objects of compulſion; ſuch as piety to God, bounty to the poor, forgiveneſs

forgiveness of injuries, education of children, gratitude to benefactors.

The law never speaks but to command, nor commands but where it can compel; consequently those duties, which by their nature must be *voluntary*, are left out of the statute book, as lying beyond the reach of its operation and authority.

II. Human laws permit, or, which is the same thing, suffer to go unpunished, many crimes, because they are incapable of being defined by any previous description— Of which nature is luxury, prodigality, partiality in voting at those elections, where the qualification of the candidate ought to determine the success, caprice in the disposition of men's fortunes at their death; disrespect to parents; and a multitude of similar examples.

For this is the alternative, the Law must either define, beforehand and with precision, the offences which it punishes, or it must be left to the *discretion* of the magistrate, to determine upon each particular accusation, whether it constitutes that offence which the law designed to punish, or not; which is in effect leaving to the magistrate to punish or not to punish, at his pleasure, the individual who is brought before him: which is just so much tyranny. Where, therefore, as in the instances above-mentioned, the distinction between right and wrong is of too subtile or of too secret a nature, to be ascertained by any preconcerted language, the law of moſt countries, eſpecially of free ſtates, rather than commit the liberty of the ſubject to the diſcretion of the magiſtrate, leaves men in ſuch caſes to themſelves.

CHAP. IV.

THE SCRIPTURES.

WHOEVER expects to find in the Scriptures, particular directions for every moral doubt that ariſes, looks for more than he will meet with. And to what a magnitude ſuch a detail of particular precepts would have enlarged the ſacred volume, may be partly underſtood from the following conſideration. The laws of this country, including the acts of the legiſlature and the deciſions of our ſupreme courts of juſtice, are not contained in fewer than fifty folio volumes; and yet it is not once in ten attempts that you can find the caſe you look for, in any law-book whatever; to ſay nothing of thoſe numerous points of conduct, concerning which the law profeſſes not to preſcribe or determine any thing. Had then the ſame particularity, which obtains in human laws ſo far as they go, been attempted in the Scriptures,
throughout

throughout the whole extent of morality, it is manifest, they would have been by much too bulky to be either read or circulated; or rather, as St. John says, " even " the world itself could not contain the books that should " be written."

Morality is taught in Scripture in this wise. General rules are laid down of piety, justice, benevolence, and purity: such as worshiping God in spirit and in truth; doing as we would be done by; loving our neighbour as ourself; forgiving others, as we expect forgiveness from God; that mercy is better than sacrifice; that not that which entereth into a man, (nor by parity of reason, any ceremonial pollutions) but that which proceedeth from the heart, defileth him. Several of these rules are occasionally illustrated, either in *fictitious examples*, as in the parable of the good Samaritan; of the cruel servant, who refused to his fellow-servant that indulgence and compassion which his master had just shewn to him: *or in instances which actually presented themselves*, as the reproof of his disciples at the Samaritan village; the praise of the poor widow, who cast in her last mite; the censure of the Pharisees, who chose out the chief rooms—and of the tradition, whereby they evaded the command to sustain their indigent parents: *or lastly, in the resolution of questions, which those who were about our Saviour proposed to him*, as in his answer to the young man who asked him, " What lack I yet ?" and to the honest scribe, who had found out, even in that age and country,

country, that to love God and his neighbour was more than all whole burnt offerings and sacrifice.

And this is the way in which all practical sciences are taught, as Arithmetic, Grammar, Navigation, and the like.—Rules are laid down, and examples are subjoined; not that these examples are the cases, much less all the cases which will actually occur, but by way only of explaining the principle of the rule, and as so many specimens of the method of applying it. The chief difference is, that the examples in Scripture are not annexed to the rules with the didactic regularity to which we are now-a-days accustomed, but delivered dispersedly, as particular occasions suggested; which gave them however, especially to those who heard them, and were present to the occasions which produced them, an energy and persuasion, much beyond what the same or any instances would have appeared with, in their places in a system.

Besides this, the Scriptures commonly presuppose in the person they speak to, a knowledge of the principles of natural justice; and are employed not so much to teach *new* rules of morality, as to enforce the practice of it by *new* sanctions, and a *greater certainty*: which last part seems to be the proper business of a revelation from God, and what was most wanted.

Thus

Thus the " unjuſt, covenant breakers and extortioners" are condemned in Scripture, ſuppoſing it known, or leaving it, where it admits of doubt, to moraliſts to determine, what injuſtice, extortion, or breach of covenant are.

The above conſiderations are intended to prove that the Scriptures do not ſuperſede the uſe of the ſcience of which we profeſs to treat, and to acquit them of any charge of imperfection or inſufficiency on that account.

CHAP. V.

THE MORAL SENSE.

" THE father of *Caius Toranius* had been proſcribed
" by the triumvirate. *Caius Toranius*, coming over to
" the intereſts of that party, diſcovered to the officers, who
" were in purſuit of his father's life, the place where he
" concealed himſelf, and gave them withal a deſcription,
" by which they might diſtinguiſh his perſon, when they
" found him. The old man, more anxious for the ſafety
" and fortunes of his ſon, than about the little that might
" remain of his own life, began immediately to enquire of
" the officers who ſeized him, whether his ſon was well,
" whether he had done his duty to the ſatisfaction of his
" generals. That ſon, replied one of the officers, ſo dear to
" thy

"thy affections, betrayed thee to us; by his information thou art apprehended, and diest. The officer with this struck a poniard to his heart, and the unhappy parent fell, not so much affected by his fate, as by the means to which he owed it.*

Now the question is, whether, if this story were related to the wild boy, caught some years ago in the woods of Hanover, or to a savage, without experience and without instruction, cut off in his infancy from all intercourse with his species, and consequently, under no possible influence of example, authority, education, sympathy, or habit; whether, I say, such a one would feel upon the relation, any degree of *that sentiment of disapprobation of Toranius's conduct*, which we feel, or not.

They who maintain the existence of a moral sense—of innate maxims—of a natural conscience—that the love of virtue and hatred of vice are instinctive—or the perception

---

* "Caius Toranius triumvirum partes secutus, proscripti patris sui prætorii et ornati viri latebras, ætatem, notasque, corporis, quibus agnosci posset, centurionibus edidit, qui eum persecuti sunt. Senex de filii magis vita, et incrementis, quam de reliquo spiritu suo sollicitus; an incolumis esset, et an imperatoribus satisfaceret, interrogare eos coepit. E quibus unus: ab illo inquit, quem tantopere diligis, demonstratus, nostro ministerio, filii indicio occideris: protinusque pectus ejus gladio trajecit. Collapsus itaque est infelix, auctore cædis, quam ipsa cæde, miserior."

VALER. MAX. Lib. IX. Cap. 11.

of right and wrong intuitive, (all which are only different ways of expressing the same thing) affirm that he would.

They who deny the existence of a moral sense, &c. affirm that he would not.—

And upon this issue is joined.

As the experiment has never been made; and from the difficulty of procuring a subject (not to mention the impossibility of proposing the question to him, if we had one) is never likely to be made, what would be the event, can only be judged of from probable reasons.

Those who contend for the affirmative, observe, that we approve examples of generosity, gratitude, fidelity, &c. and condemn the contrary, instantly, without deliberation, without having any interest of our own concerned in them, ofttimes without being conscious of, or able to give, any reason for our approbation: that this approbation is uniform and universal; the same sorts of conduct being approved or disapproved in all ages and countries of the world—circumstances, say they, which strongly indicate the operation of an instinct or moral sense.

On the other hand, answers have been given to most of these arguments, by the patrons of the opposite system: and,

First,

First, as to the *uniformity* above alledged, they controvert the fact. They remark, from authentic accounts of historians and travellers, that there is scarce a single vice, which in some age or country of the world, has not been countenanced by public opinion: that in one country it is esteemed an office of piety in children to sustain their aged parents, in another to dispatch them out of the way; that suicide in one age of the world is heroism, in another felony; that theft, which is punished by most laws, by the laws of Sparta was not unfrequently rewarded; that the promiscuous commerce of the sexes, although condemned by the regulations and censure of all civilized nations, is practised by the savages of the tropical regions without reserve, compunction, or disgrace; that crimes, of which it is no longer permitted us even to speak, have had their advocates amongst the sages of very renowned times; that, if an inhabitant of the polished nations of Europe is delighted with the appearance, wherever he meets with it, of happiness, tranquillity, and comfort, a wild American is no less diverted with the writhings and contorsions of a victim at the stake; that even amongst ourselves, and in the present improved state of moral knowledge, we are far from a perfect consent in our opinions or feelings; that you shall hear duelling alternately reprobated and applauded, according to the sex, age, or station of the person you converse with; that the forgiveness of injuries and insults is accounted by one sort of people magnanimity, by another meanness: that in the above instances, and perhaps in most others, moral approbation follows the fashions and institutions of the country we live in; which fashions also, and institutions themselves have grown out of the exigencies, the climate, situation, or local circumstances of the country; or have been set up by the authority of an arbitrary chieftain, or the unaccountable caprice of the multitude—all which, they observe, looks very little like the steady hand and indelible character of nature. But,

Secondly, because, after these exceptions and abatements, it cannot be denied, but that some sorts of actions command and receive the esteem of mankind more than others; and that the approbation of them is general, though not universal: as to this they say, that the general approbation of virtue, even in instances where we have no interest of our own to induce us to it, may be accounted for, without the assistance of a moral sense; thus:

"Having experienced, in some instance, a particular
"conduct to be beneficial to ourselves, or observed that
"it would be so, a sentiment of approbation rises up in
"our minds, which sentiment afterwards accompanies the
"idea or mention of the same conduct, though the private
"advantage which first excited it be no more."

And this continuance of the passion, after the reason of it has ceased, is nothing else, say they, than what happens in other cases; especially in the love of money, which is in no person so strong and eager, as it is ofttimes found

found in a rich old miser, without family to provide for, or friend to oblige by it, and to whom consequently it is no longer (and he may be sensible of it too) of any real use or value: yet is this man as much overjoyed with gain, and mortified by losses, as he was the first day he opened his shop, and when his very subsistence depended upon his success in it.

By these means, the custom of approving certain actions *commenced;* and when once such a custom hath got footing in the world, it is no difficult thing to explain how it is transmitted and continued; for *then* the greatest part of those who approve of virtue, approve of it from authority, by imitation, and from a habit of approving such and such actions, inculcated in early youth, and receiving, as men grow up, continual accessions of strength and vigour, from censure and encouragement, from the books they read, the conversations they hear, the current application of epithets and turn of language, and the various other causes, by which it universally comes to pass, that a society of men, touched in the feeblest degree with the same passion, soon communicate to one another a great degree of it.*

This

---

* " From instances of popular tumults, seditions, factions, panics, and of
" all passions, which are shared with a multitude, we may learn the influence
" of society, in exciting and supporting any emotion; while the most un-
" governable disorders are raised, we find, by that means, from the slightest
" and most frivolous occasions.—He must be more or less than man, who kindles
" not in the common blaze. What wonder then, that moral sentiments are
" found

This is the case with most of us at present; and is the cause also, that the *process of association*, described in the last paragraph but one, is now-a-days little either perceived or wanted.

Amongst the causes assigned for the continuance and diffusion of the same moral sentiments amongst mankind, we have mentioned *imitation*. The efficacy of this principle is most observable in children; indeed, if there be any thing in them, which deserves the name of an *instinct*, it is their *propensity to imitation*. Now there is nothing which children imitate or apply more readily than expressions of affection and aversion, of approbation, hatred, resentment, and the like; and when these passions and expressions are once connected, which they soon will be by the same association which unites words with their ideas, the passion will follow the expression, and attach upon the object to which the child has been accustomed to apply the epithet. In a word, when almost every thing else is learned by *imitation*, can we wonder to find the same cause concerned in the generation of our moral sentiments?

Another considerable objection to the system of moral instincts is this, that there are no maxims in the science, which can well be deemed *innate*, as none perhaps can be assigned, which are absolutely and universally *true;* in

other

" found of such influence in life, though springing from principles, which may
" appear, at first sight, somewhat small and delicate?"
Hume's Enquiry concerning the Principles of Morals, Sect. IX. p. 326.

other words, which do not *bend* to circumstances. Veracity, which seems, if any be, a natural duty, is excused in many cases towards an enemy, a thief, or a madman. The obligation of promises, which is a first principle in morality, depends upon the circumstances under which they were made: they may have been unlawful, or become so since, or inconsistent with former promises, or erroneous, or extorted; under all which cases, instances may be suggested, where the obligation to perform the promise would be dubious or discharged: and so of most other general rules, when they come to be actually applied.

An argument has been also proposed on the same side of the question of this kind. Together with the instinct, there must have been implanted, it is said, a clear and precise idea of the object upon which it was to attach. The instinct and the idea of the object are inseparable even in imagination, and as necessarily accompany each other as any correlative ideas whatever: that is, in plainer terms, if we be prompted by nature to the approbation of particular actions, we must have received also from nature a distinct conception of the action we are thus prompted to approve; which we certainly have not received.

But as this argument bears alike against all instincts, and in brutes as well as in men, it will hardly, I suppose, produce conviction, though it may be difficult to find an answer to it.

Upon the whole, it seems to me, either that there exist no such instincts as compose what is called the moral sense, or that they are not now to be distinguished from prejudices and habits; on which account they cannot be depended upon in moral reasoning: I mean that it is not a safe way of arguing, to assume certain principles as so many dictates, impulses, and instincts of nature, and then to draw conclusions from these principles, as to the rectitude or wrongness of actions, independent of the tendency of such actions, or of any other consideration whatever.

Aristotle lays it down, as a fundamental and self-evident maxim, that nature intended barbarians to be slaves; and proceeds to deduce from this maxim a train of conclusions, calculated to justify the policy which then prevailed. And I question whether the same maxim be not still self-evident to the " company of merchants trading to the coast of " Africa."

Nothing is so soon made as a maxim; and it appears from the example of *Aristotle*, that authority and convenience, education, prejudice, and general practice, have no small share in the making of them; and that the laws of custom are very apt to be mistaken for the order of nature.

For which reason, I suspect, that a system of morality, built upon instincts, will only find out reasons and excuses for opinions and practices already established—will seldom correct or reform either.

Besides,

But further, suppose we admit the existence of these instincts, what is their authority? No man, you say, can act in deliberate opposition to them, without a secret remorse of conscience.—But this remorse may be borne with—and if the sinner choose to bear with it, for the sake of the pleasure or profit which he expects from his wickedness; or finds the pleasure of the sin to exceed the remorse of conscience, of which he alone is the judge, and concerning which, when he feels them both together, he can hardly be mistaken, the moral-instinct-man, so far as I can understand, has nothing more to offer.

For, if he alledge, that these instincts are so many indications of the will of God, and consequently presages of what we are to look for hereafter, this, I answer, is to resort to a rule and a motive, ulterior to the instincts themselves, and at which rule and motive we shall by and by arrive by a surer road—I say *surer*, so long as there remains a controversy whether there be any instinctive maxims at all; or any difficulty in ascertaining what maxims are instinctive.

This celebrated question therefore becomes in our system a question of pure curiosity; and as such we dismiss it to the determination of those who are more inquisitive, than we are concerned to be, about the natural history and constitution of the human species.

CHAP. VI.

HUMAN HAPPINESS.

THE word *happy* is a relative term; that is, when we call a man happy, we mean that he is happier than some others, with whom we compare him; than the generality of others; or than he himself was in some other situation: thus, speaking of one who has just compassed the object of a long pursuit, " now," we say, " he is " happy;" and in a like comparative sense, compared, that is, with the general lot of mankind, we call a man happy who possesses health and competency.

In strictness, any condition may be denominated happy, in which the amount or aggregate of pleasure exceeds that of pain; and the degree of happiness depends upon the quantity of this excess.

And the greatest quantity of it, ordinarily attainable in human life is what we mean by happiness, when we enquire or pronounce what human happiness consists in. *

---

* If any *positive* signification, distinct from what we mean by pleasure, can be affixed to the term " happiness," I should take it to denote a certain state of the nervous

In which enquiry I will omit much usual declamation upon the dignity and capacity of our nature; the superiority of the soul to the body, of the rational to the animal part of our constitution; upon the worthiness, refinement, and delicacy of some satisfactions, or the meanness, grossness, and sensuality of others: because I hold that pleasures differ in nothing, but in continuance and intensity; from a just computation of which, confirmed by what we observe of the apparent chearfulness, tranquillity, and contentment, of men of different tastes, tempers, stations, and pursuits, every question concerning human happiness must receive its decision.

nervous system in that part of the human frame in which we feel joy and grief, passions and affections. Whether this part be the heart, which the turn of most languages would lead us to believe, or the diaphragm, as Buffon, or the upper orifice of the stomach, as Van Helmont thought; or rather be a kind of fine network, lining the whole region of the præcordia, as others have imagined; it is possible, not only that every painful sensation may violently shake and disturb the fibres at the time, but that a series of such may at length so derange the very texture of the system, as to produce a perpetual irritation, which will shew itself by fretfulness, impatience, and restlessness. It is possible also, on the other hand, that a succession of pleasurable sensations may have such an effect upon this subtle organization, as to cause the fibres to relax, and return into their place and order, and thereby to recover, or, if not lost, to preserve that harmonious conformation which gives to the mind its sense of complacency and satisfaction. This state may be denominated happiness, and is so far distinguishable from pleasure, that it does not refer to any particular object of enjoyment, or consist, like pleasure, in the gratification of one or more of the senses, but is rather the secondary effect which such objects and gratifications produce upon the nervous system, or the state in which they leave it. These conjectures belong not, however, to our province. The comparative sense, in which we have explained the term happiness, is more popular, and is sufficient for the purpose of the present chapter.

It will be our business to show, if we can,

I. What Human Happiness does not consist in.

II. What it does consist in.

First, then, Happiness does not consist in the pleasures of sense, in whatever profusion or variety they be enjoyed—By the pleasures of sense I mean, as well the animal gratifications of eating, drinking, and that by which the species is continued, as the more refined pleasures of music, painting, architecture, gardening, splendid shews, theatric exhibitions, and the pleasures, lastly, of active sports, as of hunting, shooting, fishing, &c. For,

1*st*, These pleasures continue but a little while at a time. This is true of them all, especially of the grosser sort. Laying aside the preparation, and the expectation, and computing strictly the actual sensation, we shall be surprized to find, how inconsiderable a portion of our time they occupy, how few hours in the four and twenty they are able to fill up.

2*dly*, These pleasures, by repetition, lose their relish. It is a property of the machine, for which we know no remedy, that the organs, by which we perceive pleasure, are blunted and benumbed, by being frequently exercised in the same way. There is hardly any one who has not found the difference between a gratification, when new, and when familiar; or any pleasure which does not become indifferent as it grows habitual.

3dly, The eagerness for high and intense delights takes away the relish from all others; and as such delights fall rarely in our way, the greater part of our time becomes from this cause empty and uneasy.

There is hardly any delusion by which men are greater sufferers in their happiness, than by their expecting too much from what is called pleasure; that is, from those intense delights, which vulgarly engross the name of pleasure. The very expectation spoils them. When they do come, we are often engaged in taking pains to persuade ourselves how much we are pleased, rather than enjoying any pleasure, which springs naturally out of the object. And whenever we depend upon being vastly delighted, we always go home secretly grieved at missing our aim. Likewise, as hath been observed just now, when this humour of being prodigiously delighted, has once taken hold of the imagination, it hinders us from providing for, or acquiescing in, those gently soothing engagements, the due variety and succession of which, are the only things that supply a continued stream of happiness.

What I have been able to observe of that part of mankind, whose professed pursuit is pleasure, and who are withheld in the pursuit by no restraints of fortune, or scruples of conscience, corresponds sufficiently with this account.

account. I have commonly remarked in such men, a restless and inextinguishable passion for variety; a great part of their time to be vacant, and so much of it irksome; and that, with whatever eagerness and expectation they set out, they become by degrees, fastidious in their choice of pleasure, languid in the enjoyment, yet miserable under the want of it.

The truth seems to be that there is a limit, at which these pleasures soon arrive, and from which they ever afterwards decline. They are by necessity of short duration, as the organs cannot hold on their emotions beyond a certain length of time; and if you endeavour to compensate for this imperfection in their nature by the frequency with which you repeat them, you lose more than you gain, by the fatigue of the faculties, and the diminution of sensibility.

We have said nothing in this account of the loss of opportunities, or the decay of faculties, which, whenever they happen, leave the voluptuary, destitute and desperate; teased by desires that can never be gratified, and the memory of pleasures which must return no more.

It will also be allowed by those who have experienced it, and perhaps by those alone, that pleasure which is purchased by the incumbrance of our fortune, is purchased too dear; the pleasure never compensating for the perpetual irritation of embarrrassed circumstances.

These

These pleasures, after all, have their value: and, as the young are always too eager in their pursuit of them, the old are sometimes too remiss; that is, too studious of their ease, to be at the pains for them, which they really deserve.

Secondly, Neither does happiness consist in an exemption from pain, labour, care, business, suspense, molestation, and " those evils which are without;" such a state being usually attended not with ease, but with depression of spirits, a tastelessness in all our ideas, imaginary anxieties, and the whole train of hypochondriacal affections.

For which reason, it seldom answers the expectations of those, who retire from their shops and counting-houses, to enjoy the remainder of their days in leisure and tranquillity; much less of such, as in a fit of chagrin, shut themselves up in cloysters and hermitages, or quit the world and their stations in it, for solitude and repose.

Where there exists a known external cause of uneasiness, the cause may be removed, and the uneasiness will cease. But those imaginary distresses which men feel for want of real ones, (and which are equally tormenting, and so far equally real) as they depend upon no single or assignable subject of uneasiness, admit ofttimes of no application or relief.

Hence a moderate pain, upon which the attention may fasten and spend itself, is to many a refreshment; as a fit of the gout will sometimes cure the spleen. And the same of any moderate agitation of the mind, as a literary controversy, a law-suit, a contested election, and, above all, gaming; the passion for which, in men of fortune and liberal minds, is only to be accounted for on this principle.

Thirdly, Neither does happiness consist in greatness, rank, or elevated station.

Were it true that all superiority afforded pleasure, it would follow, that, by how much we were the greater, that is, the more persons we were superior to, in the same proportion, so far as depended upon this cause, we should be the happier; but so it is, that no superiority yields any satisfaction, save that which we possess or obtain over those with whom we immediately compare ourselves. The shepherd perceives no pleasure in his superiority over his dog; the farmer in his superiority over the shepherd; the lord in his superiority over the farmer; nor the king, lastly, in his superiority over the lord. Superiority, where there is no competition, is seldom contemplated; what most men indeed are quite unconscious of.

But if the same shepherd can run, fight, or wrestle better than the peasants of his village; if the farmer can show better cattle, if he keep a better horse, or be supposed to have a longer purse than any farmer in the hundred; if the lord have more interest in an election, greater favour at court, a better house, or larger estate, than any nobleman

man in the county; if the king poſſeſs a more extenſive territory, a more powerful fleet or army, a more ſplendid eſtabliſhment, more loyal ſubjects, or more weight and authority in adjuſting the affairs of nations, than any prince in Europe: in all theſe caſes the parties feel an actual ſatisfaction in their ſuperiority.

Now the concluſion that follows from hence is this—that the pleaſures of ambition, which are ſuppoſed to be peculiar to high ſtations, are in reality common to all conditions. The farrier who ſhoes a horſe better, and who is in greater requeſt for his ſkill than any man within ten miles of him, poſſeſſes, for all that I can ſee, the delight of diſtinction and of excelling, as truly and ſubſtantially as the ſtateſman, the ſoldier, and the ſcholar, who have filled Europe with the reputation of their wiſdom, their valour, or their knowledge.

No ſuperiority appears to be of any account but ſuperiority over a rival. This, it is manifeſt, may exiſt wherever rivalſhips do; and rivalſhips fall out amongſt men of all ranks and degrees. The object of emulation, the dignity or magnitude of this object, makes no difference; as it is not what either poſſeſſes that conſtitutes the pleaſure, but what one poſſeſſes more than the other.

Philoſophy ſmiles at the contempt with which the rich and great ſpeak of the petty ſtrifes and competitions of the poor; not reflecting that theſe ſtrifes and competitions are just as reasonable as their own, and the pleasure, which success affords, the same.

Our position is, that happiness does not consist in greatness. And this position we make out by shewing, that even what are supposed to be the peculiar advantages of greatness, the pleasures of ambition and superiority, are in reality common to all conditions. But whether the pursuits of ambition be ever wise, whether they contribute more to the happiness or misery of the pursuers is a different question; and a question concerning which we may be allowed to entertain great doubt. The pleasure of success is exquisite; so also is the anxiety of the pursuit, and the pain of disappointment—and what is the worst part of the account, the pleasure is short lived. We soon cease to look back upon those whom we have left behind; new contests are engaged in, new prospects unfold themselves; a succession of struggles is kept up, whilst there is a rival left within the compass of our views and profession; and when there is none, the pleasure with the pursuit, is at an end.

We have seen what happiness does not consist in. We are next to consider in what it does consist.

In the conduct of life, the great matter is, to know beforehand, what will please us, and what pleasures will hold out. So far as we know this, our choice will be justified by the event. And this knowledge is more scarce and difficult than at first sight it may seem to be: for sometimes,

times, pleasures, which are wonderfully alluring and flattering in the prospect, turn out in the possession extremely insipid; or do not hold out as we expected: at other times pleasures start up, which never entered into our calculation; and which we might have missed of by not foreseeing: from whence we have reason to believe, that we actually do miss of many pleasures from the same cause. I say, " to know beforehand," for after the experiment is tried, it is commonly impracticable to retreat or change; beside that, shifting and changing is apt to generate a habit of restlessness, which is destructive of the happiness of every condition.

By reason of the original diversity of taste, capacity, and constitution, observable in the human species, and the still greater variety, which habit and fashion have introduced in these particulars, it is impossible to propose any plan of happiness, which will succeed to all, or any method of life which is universally eligible or practicable.

All that can be said is, that there remains a presumption in favour of those conditions of life, in which men generally appear most cheerful and contented. For though the apparent happiness of mankind be not always a true measure of their real happiness, it is the best measure we have.

Taking this for my guide, I am inclined to believe that happiness consists,

I. In

I. In the exercise of the social affections.

Those persons commonly possess good spirits, who have about them many objects of affection and endearment, as wife, children, kindred, friends. And to the want of these may be imputed the peevishness of monks, and of such as lead a monastic life.

Of the same nature with the indulgence of our domestic affections, and equally refreshing to the spirits, is the pleasure which results from acts of bounty and beneficence, exercised either in giving money, or in imparting to those, who want it, the assistance of our skill and profession.

Another main article of human happiness is,

II. The exercise of our faculties, either of body or mind, in the pursuit of some engaging end.

It seems to be true, that no plenitude of present gratifications can make the possessor happy for a continuance, unless he have something in reserve—something to hope for, and look forward to. This I conclude to be the case, from comparing the alacrity and spirits of men, who are engaged in any pursuit which interests them, with the dejection and *ennui* of almost all, who are either born to so much that they want nothing more, or who have *used up* their satisfactions too soon, and drained the sources of them.

It is this intolerable vacuity of mind, which carries the rich and great to the horse-course and the gaming table; and often engages them in contests and pursuits, of which the success bears no proportion to the solicitude and expence, with which it is sought. An election for a disputed borough shall cost the parties twenty or thirty thousand pounds a piece, to say nothing of the anxiety, humiliation, and fatigue of the canvass; when a seat in the House of Commons, of exactly the same value, may be had for a tenth part of the money, and with no trouble. I do not mention this to blame the rich and great, (perhaps they cannot do better) but in confirmation of what I have advanced.

Hope, which thus appears to be of so much importance to our happiness, is of two kinds; where there is something to be done towards attaining the object of our hope, and where there is nothing to be done. The first alone is of any value; the latter being apt to corrupt into impatience, having nothing in its power but to sit still and wait, which soon grows tiresome.

The doctrine delivered under this head may be readily admitted; but how to provide ourselves with a succession of pleasurable engagements, is the difficulty. This requires two things; judgment in the choice of ends adapted to our opportunities; and a command of imagination, so as to be able, when the judgment has made choice of an end, to transfer

transfer a pleasure to the *means:* after which the end may be forgotten as soon as we will.

Hence those pleasures are most valuable, not which are most exquisite in the fruition, but most productive of engagement and activity in the pursuit.

A man who is in earnest in his endeavours after the happiness of a future state, has, in this respect, an advantage over all the world. For he has constantly before his eyes an object of supreme importance, productive of perpetual engagement and activity, and of which the pursuit (which can be said of no pursuit besides) lasts him to his life's end. Yet even he, must have many ends, beside the *far end:* but then they will conduct to that, be subordinate, and in some way or other capable of being referred to that, and derive their satisfaction, or an addition of satisfaction, from that.

Engagement is every thing: the more significant, however, our engagements are, the better; such as the planning of laws, institutions, manufactures, charities, improvements, public works, and the endeavouring, by our interest, address, solicitations, and activity, to carry them into effect: or, upon a smaller scale, the procuring of a maintenance and fortune for our families, by a course of industry and application to our callings, which forms and gives motion to the common occupations of life; training up a child; prosecuting a scheme for his future establishment; making
ourselves

ourselves masters of a language or a science; improving or managing an estate; labouring after a piece of preferment: and lastly, any engagement, wich is innocent, is better than none; as the writing of a book, the building of a house, the laying out of a garden, the digging of a fish-pond—even the raising of a cucumber or a tulip.

Whilst the mind is taken up with the objects or business before it, we are commonly happy, whatever the object or business be: when the mind is *absent*, and the thoughts are wandering to something else than what is passing in the place in which we are, we are often miserable.

III. Happiness depends upon the prudent constitution of the habits.

The art in which the secret of human happiness in a great measure consists, is to *set* the habits in such a manner, that every change may be a change for the better. The habits themselves are much the same; for whatever is made habitual, becomes smooth, and easy, and indifferent. The return to an old habit is likewise easy, whatever the habit be. Therefore the advantage is with those habits which allow of indulgence in the deviation from them. The luxurious receive no greater pleasure from their dainties, than the peasant does from his bread and cheese: but the peasant, whenever he goes abroad, finds a feast, whereas the epicure must be well entertained to escape disgust. Those who spend every day at cards, and those who go every day to plough, pafs their time much alike; intent upon what they are about, wanting nothing, regretting nothing, they are both in a ftate of eafe: but then, whatever fufpends the occupation of the card-player, diftreffes him; whereas to the labourer, every interruption is a refrefhment: and this appears in the different effect that Sunday produces upon the two, which proves a day of recreation to the one, but a lamentable burthen to the other. The man who has learned to live alone, feels his fpirits enlivened whenever he enters into company, and takes his leave without regret: another, who has long been accuftomed to a crowd, or continual fucceffion of company, experiences in company no elevation of fpirits, nor any greater fatisfaction, than what the man of a retired life finds in his chimney corner. So far their conditions are equal: but let a change of place, fortune, or fituation, feparate the companion from his circle, his vifitors, his club, common-room, or coffee-houfe, and the difference of advantage in the choice and conftitution of the two habits will fhew itfelf. Solitude comes to the one clothed with melancholy; to the other it brings liberty and quiet. You will fee the one fretful and reftlefs, at a lofs how to difpofe of his time, till the hour come round that he can forget himfelf in bed; the other eafy and fatisfied, taking up his book, or his pipe, as foon as he finds himfelf alone; ready to admit any little amufement that cafts up, or to turn his hands and attention to the firft bufinefs that prefents itfelf; or content without either to fit ftill, and let his trains of thought glide

indolently

indolently through his brain, without much use, perhaps, or pleasure, but without *hankering* after any thing better, and without irritation.—A reader, who has inured himself to books of science and argumentation, if a novel, a well written pamphlet, an article of news, a narrative of a curious voyage, or the journal of a traveller, fall in his way, sits down to the repast with relish; enjoys his entertainment while it lasts, and can return, when it is over, to his graver reading, without distaste. Another, with whom nothing will go down but works of humour and pleasantry, or whose curiosity must be interested by perpetual novelty, will consume a bookseller's window in half a forenoon; during which time he is rather in search of diversion than diverted; and as books to his taste are few, and short, and rapidly read over, the stock is soon exhausted, when he is left without resource from this principal supply of innocent amusement.

So far as circumstances of fortune conduce to happiness, it is not the income which any man possesses, but the increase of income that affords the pleasure. Two persons, of whom one begins with an hundred, and advances his income to a thousand pounds a year; and the other sets off with a thousand, and dwindles down to an hundred, may, in the course of their time, have the receipt and spending of the same sum of money: yet their satisfaction, so far as fortune is concerned in it, will be very different: the series and sum total of their incomes being the same, it makes a wide difference which end they begin at.

IV. Happiness consists in Health.

By health I understand, as well freedom from bodily distempers, as that tranquillity, firmness, and alacrity of mind, which we call good spirits; and which may properly enough be included in our notion of health, as depending commonly upon the same causes, and yielding to the same management, as our bodily constitution.

Health, in this sense, is the one thing needful. Therefore no pains, expence, self-denial, or restraint, which we submit to for the sake of it, is too much. Whether it require us to relinquish lucrative situations, to abstain from favourite indulgences, to control intemperate passions, or undergo tedious regimens; whatever difficulties it lays us under, a man, who pursues his happiness rationally and resolutely, will be content to submit to.

When we are in perfect health and spirits, we feel in ourselves a happiness independent of any particular outward gratification whatever, and of which we can give no account. This is an enjoyment which the Deity has annexed to life; and probably constitutes, in a great measure, the happiness of infants and brutes, especially of the lower and sedentary orders of animals, as of oysters, periwinkles, and the like; for which I have sometimes been at a loss to find out amusement.

The above account of human happinefs will juftify the two following conclufions, which, although found in moft books of morality, have feldom been fupported by any fufficient reafons:

First, that happinefs is pretty equally diftributed amongft the different orders of civil fociety.

Secondly, that vice has no advantage over virtue, even with refpect to this world's happinefs.

CHAP. VII.

VIRTUE.

VIRTUE is, "*the doing good to mankind, in obedience to the will of God, and for the sake of everlasting happiness.*"

According to which definition, "the good of mankind" is the subject, the "will of God" the rule, and "everlasting happiness" the motive of human virtue.

Virtue has been divided by some into *benevolence, prudence, fortitude,* and *temperance*. *Benevolence* proposes good ends; *prudence* suggests the best means of attaining them; *fortitude* enables us to encounter the difficulties, dangers, and discouragements, that stand in our way in the pursuit of these ends; *temperance* repels and overcomes the passions that obstruct it. *Benevolence*, for instance, prompts us to undertake the cause of an oppressed orphan; *prudence* suggests the best means of going about it; *fortitude* enables us to confront the danger, and bear up against the loss, disgrace, or repulse, that may attend our undertaking; and *temperance* keeps under the love of money, of ease, or amusement, which might divert us from it.

VIRTUE.

Virtue is distinguished by others into two branches only, *prudence* and *benevolence; prudence* attentive to our own interest; *benevolence* to that of our fellow creatures: both directed to the same end, the increase of happiness in nature; and taking equal concern in the future as in the present.

The four cardinal virtues are *prudence, fortitude, tempeance*, and *justice*.

But the division of Virtue, to which we are now-a-days most accustomed, is into duties,

Towards *God;* as piety, reverence, resignation, gratitude; &c.

Towards *other men;* (or relative duties) as justice, charity, fidelity, loyalty, &c.

Towards *ourselves;* as chastity, sobriety, temperance, preservation of life, care of health, &c.

There are more of these distinctions, which it is not worth while to set down.

I shall proceed to state a few observations, which relate to the general regulation of human conduct; unconnected indeed with each other, but very worthy of attention; and
which

which fall as properly under the title of this chapter as of any other.

I. Mankind act more from habit than reflection.

It is on few only and great occasions that men deliberate at all; on fewer still, that they institute any thing like a regular enquiry into the moral rectitude or depravity of what they are about to do; or wait for the result of it. We are for the most part determined at once; and by an impulse, which is the effect and energy of pre-established habits. And this constitution seems well adapted to the exigencies of human life, and to the imbecility of our moral principle. In the current occasions and rapid opportunities of life, there is ofttimes little leisure for reflection; and were there more, a man, who has to reason about his duty, when the temptation to transgress it is upon him, is almost sure to reason himself into an error.

If we are in so great a degree passive under our habits, where, it is asked, is the exercise of Virtue, the guilt of vice, or any use of moral and religious knowlede? I answer, in the *forming and contracting* of these habits.

And from hence results a rule of life of considerable importance, viz. that many things are to be done, and abstained from, solely for the sake of habit. We will explain ourselves by an example or two. A beggar, with the appearance of extreme distress, asks our charity. If we come to argue the matter, whether the diftrefs be real, whether it be not brought upon himfelf, whether it be of public advantage to admit fuch applications, whether it be not to encourage idlenefs and vagrancy, whether it may not invite impoftors to our doors, whether the money can be well fpared, or might not be better applied; when thefe confiderations are put together, it may appear very doubtful, whether we ought or ought not to give any thing. But when we reflect, that the mifery before our eyes excites our pity, whether we will or not, that it is of the utmoft confequence to us to cultivate this tendernefs of mind, that it is a quality, cherifhed by indulgence, and foon ftifled by oppofition; when this, I fay, is confidered, a wife man will do that for his own fake, which he would have hefitated to do for the petitioner's; he will give way to his compaffion, rather than offer violence to a habit of fo much general ufe.

A man of confirmed good habits will act in the fame manner without any confideration at all.

This may ferve for one inftance. Another is the following: A man has been brought up from his infancy with a dread of lying. An occafion prefents itfelf, where, at the expence of a little veracity, he may divert his company, fet off his own wit with advantage, attract the notice and engage the partiality of all about him. This is not a fmall temptation. And when he looks at the other fide of the queftion, he fees no mifchief that can enfue from this liberty, no flander of any man's reputation, no prejudice
likely

likely to arife to any man's intereft. Were there nothing farther to be confidered, it would be difficult to fhow why a man under fuch circumftances might not indulge his humour. But when he reflects that his fcruples about lying have hitherto preferved him free from this vice; that occafions like the prefent will return, where the inducement may be equally ftrong, but the indulgence much lefs innocent; that his fcruples will wear away by a few tranfgreffions, and leave him fubject to one of the meaneft and moft pernicious of all bad habits, a habit of lying whenever it will ferve his turn. When all this, I fay, is confidered, a wife man will forego the prefent, or a much greater pleafure, rather than lay the foundation of a character fo vicious and contemptible.

From what has been faid may be explained alfo the nature of habitual virtue. By the definition of Virtue, at the beginning of this chapter, it appears, that the good of mankind is the fubject, the will of God the rule, and everlafting happinefs the motive and end of all virtue. Yet a man fhall perform many an act of virtue, without having either the good of mankind, the will of God, or everlafting happinefs in his thoughts; juft as a man may be a very good fervant, without being confcious at every turn of a regard to his mafter's will, or of an exprefs attention to his intereft (and your beft old fervants are of this fort;) but then he muft have ferved for a length of time under the actual direction of thefe motives to bring it to this: in which fervice his merit and virtue confift.

There

There are *habits*, not only of drinking, swearing, and lying, and of some other things, which are commonly acknowledged to be habits, and called so; but of every modification of action, speech, and thought. Man is a bundle of habits. There are habits of industry, attention, vigilance, advertency; of a prompt obedience to the judgment occurring, or of yielding to the first impulse of passion; of extending our views to the future, or of resting upon the present; of apprehending, methodizing, reasoning; of indolence and dilatoriness; of vanity, self-conceit, melancholy, partiality; of fretfulness, suspicion, captiousness, censoriousness; of pride, ambition, covetousness; of over-reaching, intriguing, projecting. In a word, there is not a quality, or function, either of body or mind, which does not feel the influence of this great law of animated nature.

II. The Christian religion has not ascertained the precise quantity of virtue necessary to salvation.

This has been made an objection to Christianity; but without reason. For, as all revelation, however imparted originally, must be transmitted by the ordinary vehicle of language, it behoves those who make the objection to shew that any form of words could be devised, which might express this *quantity;* or that it is possible to constitute a standard of moral attainments, accommodated to the almost infinite diversity which subsists in the capacities and opportunities of different men.

It seems most agreeable to our conceptions of justice, and is consonant enough to the language of scripture, * to suppose, that there are prepared for us rewards and punishments, of all possible degrees, from the most exalted happiness down to extreme misery; so that " our labour is " never in vain;" whatever advancement we make in virtue, we procure a proportionable accession of future happiness; as, on the other hand, every accumulation of vice, is the " treasuring up of so much wrath against the day of " wrath." It has been said, that it can never be a just œconomy of providence, to admit one part of mankind into heaven, and condemn the other to hell, since there must be very little to choose, between the worst man who is received into heaven, and the best who is excluded. And how know we, it might be answered, but that there may be as little to choose in their conditions?

Without entering into a detail of scripture morality, which would anticipate our subject, the following general positions may be advanced, I think, with safety:

---

* " He which soweth sparingly shall reap also sparingly; and he which " soweth bountifully shall reap also bountifully," 2 Cor. ix. 6.—" And that " servant which knew his Lord's will, and prepared not himself, neither did " according to his will, shall be beaten with many stripes; but he that knew " not, shall be beaten with few stripes," Luke xii. 47, 48.—" Whosoever shall " give you a cup of water to drink in my name, because ye belong to Christ, " verily I say unto you, he shall not lose his reward;" to wit, intimating that there is in reserve a proportionable reward for even the smallest act of Virtue. Mark ix. 41.—See also the parable of the pounds, Luke xix. 16, &c. where he whose pound had gained ten pounds, was placed over ten cities; and he whose pound had gained five pounds, was placed over five cities.

1. That a state of happiness is not to be expected by those who are conscious of no moral or religious rule. I mean those, who cannot with truth say, that they have been prompted to one action, or withheld from one gratification, by any regard to virtue or religion, either immediate or habitual.

There need no other proof of this, than the consideration, that a brute would be as proper an object of reward as such a man; and that, if the case were so, the penal sanctions of religion could have no place. For whom would you punish, if you make such a one as this happy?—or rather indeed religion itself, both natural and revealed, would cease to have either use or authority.

2. That a state of happiness is not to be expected by those, who reserve to themselves the habitual practice of any one sin, or neglect of one known duty.

Because, no obedience can proceed upon proper motives which is not universal, that is, which is not directed to every command of God alike, as they all stand upon the same authority.

Because, such an allowance would in effect amount to a toleration of every vice in the world.

And because, the strain of scripture language excludes any such hope. When our *duties* are recited, they are put *collectively,*

collectively, that is, as all and every of them required in the Christian character. "*Add* to your faith virtue, and to "virtue knowledge, and to knowledge temperance, and to "temperance patience, and to patience godliness, and to "godliness brotherly kindness, and to brotherly kindness "charity."* On the other hand, when *vices* are enumerated, they are put *disjunctively*, that is, as separately and severally excluding the sinner from heaven. "*Neither* "fornicators, nor idolators, nor adulterers, nor effeminate, "nor abusers of themselves with mankind, nor thieves, "nor covetous, nor drunkards, nor revilers, nor extor- "tioners, shall inherit the kingdom of heaven."†

Those texts of scripture, which seem to lean a contrary way, as that "charity shall cover the multitude of sins"‡ that "he which converteth a sinner from the error of his "way shall hide a multitude of sins,"§ cannot, I think, for the reasons above-mentioned, be extended to sins deliberately and obstinately persisted in.

3. That a state of mere unprofitableness will not go unpunished.

This is expressly laid down by Christ in the parable of the talents, which supersedes all farther reasoning about the matter. "Then he which had received one talent, "came and said, Lord, I know thee that thou art an austere "man, reaping where thou hast not sown, and gathering "where

---

* 2 Pet. i. 5, 6, 7.   † 1 Cor. vi. 9, 10.   ‡ 1 Pet. iv. 8.   § James v. 20.

"where thou haſt not ſtrawed; and I was afraid, and hid "thy talent in the earth; lo, there thou haſt that is thine. "His lord anſwered and ſaid unto him, thou wicked and "*ſlothful* ſervant, thou kneweſt, (or kneweſt thou?) that I "reap where I ſowed not, and gather where I have not "ſtrawed; thou oughteſt therefore to have put my money "to the exchangers, and then at my coming I ſhould have "received mine own with uſury. Take therefore the talent "from him, and give it unto him which hath ten talents; "for unto every one that hath ſhall be given, and he ſhall "have abundance; but from him that hath not ſhall be "taken away even that which he hath; *and caſt ye the un-* "*profitable ſervant into outer darkneſs, there ſhall be weeping* "*and gnaſhing of teeth.*"*

III. In every queſtion of conduct where one ſide is doubtful, and the other ſide ſafe, we are bound to take the ſafe ſide.

This is beſt explained by an inſtance, and I know of none more to our purpoſe than that of ſuicide. Suppoſe, for example's ſake, that it appear doubtful to a reaſoner upon the ſubject, whether he may lawfully deſtroy himſelf. He can have no doubt, but that it is lawful for him to let it alone. Here therefore is a caſe, in which one ſide is doubtful, and the other ſide ſafe. By virtue therefore of our rule, he is bound to purſue the ſafe ſide, that is, to forbear from offering violence to himſelf, whilſt a doubt remains upon his mind concerning the lawfulneſs of ſuicide.

It

* Mat. xxv. 24, &c.

It is *prudent*, you allow, to take the safe side. But our observation means something more. We assert that the action, concerning which we doubt, whatever it may be in itself, or to another, would, in *us*, whilst this doubt remains upon our minds, be certainly sinful. The case is expressly so adjudged by St. Paul, with whose authority we will for the present rest contented. "I know and am persuaded "by the Lord Jesus, that there is nothing unclean of itself, "but *to him that esteemeth any thing to be unclean to him it is* "*unclean.* - - - - - - - - - Happy is he that condemneth not "himself in that thing which he alloweth; and he that "doubteth is damned *(condemned)* if he eat, for whatsoever "is not of faith (i. e. not done with a full persuasion of the "lawfulness of it) is sin."*

* Romans xiv. 14. 22, 23.

MORAL PHILOSOPHY.

BOOK II.

MORAL OBLIGATION.

CHAP. I.

THE QUESTION, WHY AM I OBLIGED TO KEEP MY WORD? CONSIDERED.

WHY am I *obliged* to keep my word?

Becaufe it is right, fays one.—Becaufe it is agreeable to the fitnefs of things, fays another.—Becaufe it is conformable to reafon and nature, fays a third.—Becaufe it is conformable to truth, fays a fourth.—Becaufe it promotes the public good, fays a fifth.—Becaufe it is required by the will of God, concludes a fixth.

Upon which different accounts, two things are obfervable:
FIRST,

First, that they all ultimately coincide.

The fitness of things means their fitness to produce happiness: the nature of things means that actual constitution of the world, by which some things, as such and such actions, for example, produce happiness, and others misery: reason is the principle, by which we discover or judge of this constitution: truth is this judgment expressed or drawn out into propositions. So that it necessarily comes to pass, that what promotes the public happiness, or happiness upon the whole, is agreeable to the fitness of things, to nature, to reason, and to truth; and such (as will appear by and by) is the divine character, that what promotes the general happiness is required by the will of God; and what has all the above properties must needs be *right:* for right means no more than conformity to the rule we go by, whatever that rule be.

And this is the reason that moralists, from whatever different principles they set out, commonly meet in their conclusions; that is, they enjoin the same conduct, prescribe the same rules of duty, and, with a few exceptions, deliver upon dubious cases the same determinations.

Secondly, it is to be observed, that these answers all leave the matter short; for the enquirer may turn round upon his teacher with a second question, in which he will expect to be satisfied, namely, *why* am I obliged to do what is right; to act agreeably to the fitness of things; to
con-

conform to reason, nature, or truth; to promote the public good, or to obey the will of God?

The proper method of conducting the enquiry is, FIRST, to examine what we mean, when we say a man is *obliged* to do any thing, and THEN to shew *why* he is obliged to do the thing which we have proposed as an example, namely, " to keep his word."

C H A P. II.

WHAT WE MEAN WHEN WE SAY A MAN IS OBLIGED TO DO A THING.

A MAN is said to be *obliged*, " *when he is urged by a violent motive resulting from the command of another.*"

I. " The motive must be violent." If a person, who has done me some little service, or has a small place in his disposal, ask me for my vote upon some occasion, I may possibly give it him, from a motive of gratitude or expectation; but I should hardly say, that I was *obliged* to give it him, because the inducement does not rise high enough. Whereas, if a father or a master, any great benefactor, or one on whom my fortune depends, require my vote, I give it him of course; and my answer to all who ask me why I voted so and so, is, that my father or my master *obliged* me; that I had received so many favours from, or had so great a dependence upon such a one, that I was *obliged* to vote as he directed me.

Secondly, "It must result from the command of "another." Offer a man a gratuity for doing any thing, for seizing, for example, an offender, he is not *obliged* by your offer to do it; nor would he say he is; though he may be *induced, persuaded, prevailed upon, tempted*. If a magistrate, or the man's immediate superior command it, he considers himself as *obliged* to comply, though possibly he would lose less by a refusal in this case, than in the former.

I will not undertake to say that the words *obligation* and *obliged* are used uniformly in this sense, or always with this distinction; nor is it possible to tie down popular phrases to any constant signification: but, wherever the motive is violent enough, and coupled with the idea of command, authority, law, or the will of a superior, there, I take it, we always reckon ourselves to be *obliged*.

And from this account of obligation it follows, that we can be obliged to nothing, but what we ourselves are to gain or lose something by; for nothing else can be a " vio- " lent motive" to us. As we should not be obliged to obey the laws, or the magistrate, unless rewards or punishments, pleasure or pain, some how or other depended upon our obedience; so neither should we, without the same reason, be obliged to do what is right, to practice virtue, or to obey the commands of God.

CHAP. III.

THE QUESTION, WHY I AM OBLIGED TO KEEP MY WORD? RESUMED.

LET it be remembered, that to be *obliged*, " is to be " urged by a violent motive, resulting from the com- " mand of another."

And then let it be asked, Why am I obliged to keep my word? and the answer will be, because I am " urged to do " so by a violent motive," (namely, the expectation of being after this life rewarded, if I do, or punished for it, if I do not) " resulting from the command of another," (namely, of God).

This solution goes to the bottom of the subject, as no farther question can reasonably be asked.

Therefore, private happiness is our motive, and the will of God our rule.

When I first turned my thoughts to moral speculations, an air of mystery seemed to hang over the whole subject; which arose, I believe, from hence—that I supposed, with many authors whom I had read, that to be *obliged* to do a thing, was very different from being *induced* only to do it; and that the obligation to practise virtue, to do what is right, just, &c. was quite another thing, and of another kind, than the obligation which a soldier is under to obey his officer, a servant his master, or any of the civil and ordinary obligations of human life. Whereas, from what has been said it appears, that moral obligation is like all other obligations; and that all *obligation* is nothing more than an *inducement* of sufficient strength, and resulting, in some way, from the command of another.

There is always understood to be a difference between an act of *prudence* and an act of *duty*. Thus, if I distrusted a man who owed me money, I should reckon it an act of prudence to get another bound with him; but I should hardly call it an act of duty. On the other hand, it would be thought a very unusual and loose kind of language, to say, that, as I had made such a promise, it was *prudent* to perform it; or that as my friend, when he went abroad, placed a box of jewels in my hands, it would be *prudent* in me to preserve it for him 'till he returned.

Now,

Now, in what, you will afk, does the difference confift? Inafmuch, as according to our account of the matter, both in the one cafe and the other, in acts of duty as well as acts of prudence, we confider folely what we fhall gain or lofe by the act?

The difference, and the only difference, is this; that, in the one cafe we confider what we fhall gain or lofe in the prefent world; in the other cafe, we confider alfo what we fhall gain or lofe in the world to come.

Thofe who would eftablifh a fyftem of morality, independent of a future ftate, muft look out for fome different idea of moral obligation; unlefs they can fhew that virtue conducts the poffeffor to certain happinefs in this life, or to a much greater fhare of it, than he could attain by a different behaviour.

To us there are two great queftions:

I. Will there be after this life any diftribution of rewards and punifhments at all?

II. If there be, what actions will be rewarded, and what will be punifhed?

The firft queftion comprizes the credibility of the Chriftian religion, together with the prefumptive proofs of a future retribution from the light of nature. The fecond
queftion

question composes the province of morality. Both questions are too much for one work. The affirmative therefore of the first, although we confess that it is the foundation upon which the whole fabric rests, must in this treatise be taken for granted.

CHAP. IV.

THE WILL OF GOD.

AS the will of God is our rule, to enquire what is our duty, or what we are obliged to do, in any instance, is, in effect, to enquire, what is the will of God in that instance? which consequently becomes the whole business of morality.

Now there are two methods of coming at the will of God on any point:

I. By his express declarations, when they are to be had; and which must be sought for in Scripture.

II. By what we can discover of his designs and disposition from his works, or, as we usually call it, the light of nature.

And here we may observe the absurdity of separating natural and revealed religion from each other. The object of both is the same—to discover the will of God—and, provided we do but discover it, it matters nothing by what means.

An ambassador, judging only from what he knows of his sovereign's disposition, and arguing from what he has observed of his conduct, or is acquainted with of his designs, may take his measures in many cases with safety; and presume with great probability how his master would have him act on most occasions that arise: but if he have his commission and instructions in his pocket, it would be strange never to look into them. He will naturally conduct himself by both rules: when his instructions are clear and positive, there is an end of all farther deliberation (unless indeed he suspect their authenticity): where his instructions are silent or dubious, he will endeavour to supply or explain them, by what he has been able to collect from other quarters of his master's general inclination or intentions.

Mr. HUME, in his fourth Appendix to his Principles of Morals, has been pleased to complain of the modern scheme of uniting Ethics with the Christian Theology. Those who find themselves disposed to join in this complaint will do well to observe what Mr. HUME himself has been able to make of morality without this union. And for that purpose, let them read the second part of the ninth

ninth section of the above essay; which part contains the practical application of the whole treatise—a treatise, which Mr. Hume declares to be "incomparably the best he "ever wrote." When they have read it over, let them consider, whether any motives there proposed are likely to be found sufficient to withhold men from the gratification of lust, revenge, envy, ambition, avarice, or to prevent the existence of these passions. Unless they rise up from this celebrated essay, with very different impressions upon their minds, than it ever left upon mine, they will acknowledge the necessity of additional sanctions. But the necessity of these sanctions is not now the question. If they be *in fact established*, if the rewards and punishments held forth in the gospel will actually come to pass, they *must* be considered. Those who reject the Christian religion are to make the best shift they can to build up a system, and lay the foundations of morality without it. But it appears to me a great inconsistency in those who receive Christianity, and expect something to come of it, to endeavour to keep all such expectations out of sight, in their reasonings concerning human duty.

The method of coming at the will of God concerning any action, by the light of nature, is to enquire into "the "tendency of the action to promote or diminish the general "happiness." This rule proceeds upon the presumption, that God Almighty wills and wishes the happiness of his creatures;

creatures; and consequently, that those actions, which promote that will and wish, must be agreeable to him; and the contrary.

As this presumption is the foundation of the whole system, it becomes necessary to explain the reasons upon which it rests.

CHAP. V.

THE DIVINE BENEVOLENCE.

WHEN God created the human species, either he wished their happiness, or he wished their misery, or he was indifferent and unconcerned about both.

If he had wished our misery, he might have made sure of his purpose, by forming our senses to be as many sores and pains to us, as they are now instruments of gratification and enjoyment; or by placing us amidst objects so ill suited to our perceptions, as to have continually offended us, instead of ministring to our refreshment and delight. He might have made, for example, every thing we tasted bitter; every thing we saw loathsome; every thing we touched a sting; every smell a stench; and every sound a discord.

If he had been indifferent about our happiness or misery, we must impute to our good fortune, (as all design by this supposition is excluded,) both the capacity of our senses to receive pleasure, and the supply of external objects fitted to excite it.

But either of these, and still more both of them, being too much to be attributed to accident, nothing remains but the first supposition, that God, when he created the human species, wished their happiness; and made for them the provision which he has made, with that view, and for that purpose.

The same argument may be proposed in different terms, thus: Contrivance proves design; and the predominant tendency of the contrivances indicates the disposition of the designer. The world abounds with contrivances; and all the contrivances which we are acquainted with, are directed to beneficial purposes. Evil no doubt exists; but it is never, that we can perceive, the object of contrivance. Teeth are contrived to eat, not to ache; their aching now and then is incidental to the contrivance, perhaps, inseparable from it; or even, if you will, let it be called a defect in the contrivance; but it is not the object of it. This is a distinction which well deserves to be attended to. In describing implements of husbandry, you would hardly say of a sickle, that it is made to cut the reaper's fingers, though from the construction of the instrument, and the manner of using it, this mischief often happens. But if you had

occasion

occasion to describe instruments of torture or execution, this, you would say, is to extend the sinews; this to dislocate the joints; this to break the bones; this to scorch the soles of the feet. Here pain and misery are the very objects of the contrivance. Now nothing of this sort is to be found in the works of nature. We never discover a train of contrivance to bring about an evil purpose. No anatomist ever discovered a system of organization, calculated to produce pain and disease; or, in explaining the parts of the human body, ever said this is to irritate; this to inflame; this duct is to convey the gravel to the kidneys; this gland to secrete the humour which forms the gout: if by chance he come at a part of which he knows not the use, the most he can say is, that it is useless; no one ever suspects that it is put there to incommode, to annoy, or torment. Since then God hath called forth his consummate wisdom, to contrive and provide for our happiness, and the world appears to have been constituted with this design at first, so long as this constitution is upheld by him, we must in reason suppose the same design to continue.

The contemplation of universal nature rather bewilders the mind than affects it. There is always a bright spot in the prospect, upon which the eye rests; a single example, perhaps, by which each man finds himself more *convinced* than by all others put together. I seem, for my own part, to see the benevolence of the Deity more clearly in the pleasures of very young children, than in any thing in the world. The pleasures of grown persons may be reckoned partly of their own procuring; especially if there has been any industry, or contrivance, or pursuit, to come at them; or if they are founded, like music, painting, &c. upon any qualification of their own acquiring. But the pleasures of a healthy infant are so manifestly provided for it by *another*, and the benevolence of the provision is so unquestionable, that every child I see at its sport affords to my mind a kind of sensible evidence of the finger of God, and of the disposition which directs it.

But the example, which strikes each man most strongly, is the true example for him; and hardly two minds hit upon the same; which shews the abundance of such examples about us.

We conclude therefore, that God wills and wishes the happiness of his creatures. And this conclusion being once established, we are at liberty to go on with the rule built upon it, namely, " that the method of coming at " the will of God, concerning any action, by the light of " nature, is, to enquire into the tendency of that action " to promote or diminish the general happiness."

CHAP. VI.

UTILITY.

SO then actions are to be estimated by their tendency to promote happiness*. Whatever is expedient is right. It is the utility of any moral rule alone which constitutes the obligation of it.

But to all this there seems a plain objection, viz. that many actions are useful, which no man in his senses will allow to be right. There are occasions, in which the hand of the assassin would be very useful. The present possessor of some great estate employs his influence and fortune, to annoy, corrupt, or oppress all about him. His estate would devolve, by his death, to a successor of an opposite character. It is useful, therefore, to dispatch such a one as

---

* Actions in the abstract are right or wrong, according to their *tendency*; the agent is virtuous or vicious, according to his *design*. Thus, if the question be, Whether relieving common beggars be right or wrong? we enquire into the *tendency* of such a conduct to the public advantage or inconvenience. If the question be, Whether a man, remarkable for this sort of bounty, is to be esteemed virtuous for that reason? we enquire into his *design*, whether his liberality sprung from charity or from ostentation. It is evident that our concern is with actions in the abstract.

soon as possible out of the way; as the neighbourhood would exchange thereby a pernicious tyrant for a wise and generous benefactor. It may be useful to rob a miser, and give the money to the poor; as the money, no doubt, would produce more happiness, by being laid out in food and cloathing for half a dozen distressed families, than by continuing locked up in a miser's chest. It may be useful to get possession of a place, a piece of preferment, or of a seat in parliament, by bribery or false swearing; as by means of them we may serve the public more effectually than in our private station. What then shall we say? Must we admit these actions to be right, which would be to justify assassination, plunder, and perjury; or must we give up our principle, that the criterion of right is utility?

It is not necessary to do either.

The true answer is this; that these actions, after all, are not useful, and for that reason, and that alone, are not right.

To see this point perfectly, it must be observed, that the bad consequences of actions are two-fold, *particular* and *general*.

The particular bad consequence of an action, is the mischief which that single action directly and immediately occasions.

The

The general bad confequence is, the violation of fome neceffary or ufeful *general rule*.

Thus the particular bad confequence of the affaffination above defcribed, is the fright and pain which the deceafed underwent; the lofs he fuffered of life, which is as valuable to a bad man, as to a good one, or more fo; the prejudice and affliction, of which his death was the occafion, to his family, friends, and dependents.

The general bad confequence is the violation of this neceffary general rule, that no man be put to death for his crimes, but by public authority.

Although, therefore, fuch an action have no particular bad confequence, or greater particular good confequences, yet it is not ufeful, by reafon of the general confequence, which is evil, and which is of more importance. And the fame of the other two inftances, and of a million more, which might be mentioned.

But as this folution fuppofes, that the moral government of the world muft proceed by general rules, it remains that we fhew the neceffity of this.

CHAP. VII.

THE NECESSITY OF GENERAL RULES.

YOU cannot permit one action and forbid another, without shewing a difference betwixt them. Therefore, the same sort of actions must be generally permitted or generally forbidden. Where, therefore, the general permission of them would be pernicious, it becomes necessary to lay down and support the rule which generally forbids them.

Thus, to return once more to the case of the assassin. The assassin knocked the rich villain on the head, because he thought him better out of the way than in it. If you allow this excuse in the present instance, you must allow it to all, who act in the same manner, and from the same motive; that is, you must allow every man to kill any one he meets, whom he thinks noxious or useless; which, in the event, would be to commit every man's life and safety to the spleen, fury, and fanaticism of his neighbour—a disposition of affairs which would presently fill the world with misery and confusion; and ere long put an end to human society, if not to the human species.

GENERAL RULES.

The neceſſity of general rules in human governments is apparent: but whether the ſame neceſſity ſubſiſt in the divine œconomy, in that diſtribution of rewards and puniſhments, to which a moraliſt looks forward, may be doubted.

I anſwer, that general rules are neceſſary to every moral government; and by moral government I mean any diſpenſation, whoſe object is to influence the conduct of reaſonable creatures. For if, of two actions perfectly ſimilar, one be puniſhed, and the other be rewarded or forgiven, which is the conſequence of rejecting general rules, the ſubjects of ſuch a diſpenſation would no longer know, either what to expect or how to act; rewards and puniſhments would ceaſe to be ſuch—would become accidents, like the ſtroke of a thunderbolt, or the diſcovery of a mine: like a blank or a benefit ticket in a lottery; they would occaſion pain or pleaſure when they happened; but following in no known order, from any particular courſe of action, they could have no previous influence or effect upon the conduct.

An attention to general rules, therefore, is included in the very idea of reward and puniſhment. Conſequently whatever reaſon there is to expect future reward and puniſhment at the hand of God, there is the ſame reaſon to believe, that he will proceed in the diſtribution of it by general rules.

Before we prosecute the consideration of general consequences any farther, it may be proper to anticipate a reflection, which will be apt enough to suggest itself in the progress of our argument.

As the general consequence of an action, upon which so much of the guilt of a bad action depends, consists in the example; it should seem, that, if the action be done with perfect secrecy, so as to furnish no bad example, that part of the guilt drops off. In the case of suicide, for instance, if a man can so manage matters, as to take away his own life, without being known or suspected to have done it, he is not chargeable with any mischief from the example; nor does his punishment seem necessary, in order to save the authority of any general rule.

In the first place, those who reason in this manner do not observe, that they are setting up a general rule, of all others the least to be endured; namely, that secrecy, whenever secrecy is practicable, will justify any action.

Were such a rule admitted, for instance, in the case above produced, is there not reason to fear that people would be *disappearing* perpetually?

In the next place, I would wish them to be well satisfied about the points proposed in the following queries:

1. Whether

GENERAL RULES

1. Whether the scriptures do not teach us to expect, that, at the general judgment of the world, the most secret actions will be brought to light*?

2. For what purpose can this be, but to make them the objects of reward and punishment?

3. Whether, being so brought to light, they will not fall under the operation of those equal and impartial rules, by which God will deal with his creatures?

They will then become examples, whatever they be now; and require the same treatment from the judge and governor of the moral world, as if they had been detected from the first.

---

* " In the day when God shall judge the secrets of men by Jesus Christ." Rom. xi. 16—" Judge nothing before the time until the Lord come, ho " will bring to light the hidden things of darkness, and will make manifest " the councils of the heart." 1 Cor. iv. 5.

CHAP. VIII.

THE CONSIDERATION OF GENERAL CONSEQUENCES PURSUED.

THE general confequence of any action may be eſtimated, by aſking what would be the confequence, if the fame fort of actions were generally permitted.—But ſuppoſe they were, and a thouſand ſuch actions perpetrated under this permiſſion; is it juſt to charge a ſingle action with the collected guilt and miſchief of the whole thouſand? I anſwer, that the reaſon for prohibiting and puniſhing an action (and this reaſon may be called the guilt of the action, if you pleaſe) will always be in proportion to the whole miſchief that would ariſe from the general impunity and toleration of actions of the fame fort.

" Whatever is expedient is right." But then it muſt be expedient upon the whole, at the long run, in all its effects collateral and remote, as well as in thoſe which are immediate and direct; as it is obvious, that, in computing conſequences, it makes no difference in what way or at what diſtance they enſue.

To impreſs this doctrine upon the minds of young readers, and to teach them to extend their views beyond the immediate miſchief of a crime, I ſhall here ſubjoin a ſtring

GENERAL CONSEQUENCES PURSUED.

a ſtring of inſtances, in which the particular conſequence is comparatively inſignificant; and where the malignity of the crime, and the ſeverity with which human laws purſue it, is almoſt entirely founded upon the general conſequence.

The particular conſequence of coining is, the loſs of a guinea, or of half a guinea, to the perſon who receives the counterfeit money; the general conſequence (by which I mean the conſequence that would enſue, if the ſame practice were generally permitted) is, to aboliſh the uſe of money.

The particular conſequence of forgery is, a damage of twenty or thirty pounds to the man who accepts the forged bill; the general conſequence is, the ſtoppage of paper currency.

The particular conſequence of ſheep-ſtealing, or horſe-ſtealing, is a loſs to the owner, to the amount of the value of the ſheep or horſe ſtolen; the general conſequence is, that the land could not be occupied, nor the market ſupplied with this kind of ſtock.

The particular conſequence of breaking into a houſe empty of inhabitants is, the loſs of a pair of ſilver candleſticks, or a few ſpoons; the general conſequence is, that nobody could leave their houſe empty.

The

The particular confequence of fmuggling may be a deduction from the national fund too minute for computation: the general confequence is, the deftruction of one entire branch of public revenue; a proportionable increafe of the burthen upon other branches; and the ruin of all fair and open trade in the article fmuggled.

The particular confequence of an officer's breaking his parole is, the lofs of a prifoner, who was poffibly not worth keeping; the general confequence is, that this mitigation of captivity would be refufed to all others.

And what proves inconteftably the fuperior importance of general confequences is, that crimes are the fame, and treated in the fame manner, though the particular confequence be very different. The crime and fate of the houfe-breaker is the fame, whether his booty be five pounds or fifty. And the reafon is, that the general confequence is the fame.

The want of this diftinction between particular and general confequences, or rather the not fufficiently attending to the latter, is the caufe of that perplexity we meet with in ancient moralifts. On the one hand, they were fenfible of the abfurdity of pronouncing actions good or evil, without regard to the good or evil they produced. On the other hand, they were ftartled at the conclufions to which a fteady adherence to confequences feemed fometimes to conduct them. To relieve this difficulty, they contrived the το πρεπον, or the *honeſtum*, by which terms they meant to conſtitute a meaſure of right, diſtinct from utility. Whilſt the *utile* ſerved them, that is, whilſt it correſponded with their habitual notions of the rectitude of actions, they went by *it*. When they fell in with ſuch caſes as thoſe mentioned in the ſixth chapter, they took leave of their guide, and reſorted to the *honeſtum*. The only account they could give of the matter was, that theſe actions might be uſeful; but, becauſe they were not at the ſame time *honeſta*, they were by no means to be deemed juſt or right.

From the principles delivered in this and the two preceding chapters, a maxim may be explained, which is in every man's mouth, and in moſt men's without meaning, viz. " not to do evil, that good may come :" that is, let us not violate a general rule, for the ſake of any particular good conſequence we may expect. Which is for the moſt part a ſalutary caution, the advantage ſeldom compenſating for the violation of the rule. Strictly ſpeaking, that cannot be " evil," from which " good comes ;" but in this way, and with a view to the diſtinction between particular and general conſequences, it may.

We will conclude this ſubject of *conſequences* with the following reflection. A man may imagine, that any action of his, with reſpect to the public, muſt be inconſiderable: ſo alſo is the agent. If his crime produce but a ſmall

effect

effect upon the univerfal intereft, his punifhment or deftruction bears a fmall proportion to the fum of happinefs and mifery in the creation.

CHAP. IX.

OF RIGHT.

RIGHT and obligation are reciprocal; that is, whereever there is a right in one perfon, there is a correfponding obligation upon others. If one man has a "right" to an eftate; others are "obliged" to abftain from it:—If parents have a "right" to reverence from their children; children are "obliged" to reverence their parents; and fo in all other inftances.

Now, becaufe moral *obligation* depends, as we have feen, upon the will of God, *right*, which is correlative to it, muft depend upon the fame. Right therefore fignifies, *the being confiflent with the will of God.*

If the divine will determines the diftinction of right and wrong, what elfe is it but an identical propofition, to fay of God, that he acts right, or how is it poffible even to conceive that he fhould act wrong; yet thefe affertions are intelligible and fignificant. The cafe is this: by virtue of the two principles, that God wills the happinefs of his creatures, and that the will of God is the meafure of
right

right and wrong, we arrive at certain conclusions; which conclusions become rules; and we soon learn to pronounce actions right or wrong, according as they agree or disagree with our rules, without looking any farther: and when the habit is once established of stopping at the rules, we can go back and compare with these rules, even the divine conduct itself, and yet it may be true (only not observed by us at the time) that the rules themselves are deduced from the divine will.

Right is a quality of persons or of actions.

Of persons; as when we say, such a one has a "right" to this estate; parents have a "right" to reverence from their children; the king to allegiance from his subjects; masters have a "right" to their servants labour; a man has not a "right" over his own life.

Of actions; as in such expressions as the following: it is "right" to punish murder with death; his behaviour on that occasion was "right;" it is not "right" to send an unfortunate debtor to jail; he did or acted "right," who gave up his place, rather than vote against his judgment.

In this latter set of expressions, you may substitute the definition of right above given for the term itself, v. g. it is "consistent with the will of God" to punish murder with death—his behaviour on that occasion, was "con-

"fiftent with the will of God"—it is not "confiftent with "the will of God" to fend an unfortunate debtor to jail— he did, or acted "confiftently with the will of God," who gave up his place, rather than vote againft his judgment.

In the former fet, you muft vary the phrafe a little, when you introduce the definition inftead of the term. Such a one has a "right" to this eftate, that is, it is "confiftent with the will of God," that fuch a one fhould have it—parents have a "right" to reverence from their children, that is, it is "confiftent with the will of God," that children fhould reverence their parents; and the fame of the reft.

CHAP. X.

THE DIVISION OF RIGHTS.

RIGHTS, when applied to perfons, are

Natural or adventitious.

Alienable or unalienable.

Perfect

Perfect or imperfect.

I. Rights are natural or adventitious.

Natural rights are such as would belong to a man, although there subsisted in the world no civil government whatever.

Adventitious rights are such as would not.

Natural rights are, a man's right to his life, limbs, and liberty; his right to the produce of his personal labour; to the use, in common with others, of air, light, water. If a thousand different persons, from a thousand different corners of the world, were cast together upon a desert island, they would from the first be every one entitled to these rights.

Adventitious rights are, the right of a King over his subjects; of a General over his soldiers; of a Judge over the life and liberty of a prisoner; a right to elect or appoint magistrates, to impose taxes, decide disputes, direct the descent or disposition of property; a right, in a word, in any one man, or particular body of men, to make laws and regulations for the rest. For none of these rights would exist in the newly inhabited island.

And here it will be asked how adventitious rights are created; or, which is the same thing, how any new rights can accrue, from the eſtabliſhment of civil ſociety; as rights of all kinds, we remember, depend upon the will of God, and civil ſociety is but the ordinance and inſtitution of man. For the ſolution of this difficulty, we muſt return to our firſt principles. God wills the happineſs of mankind, and the exiſtence of civil ſociety, as conducive to that happineſs. Conſequently, many things, which are uſeful for the ſupport of civil ſociety in general, or for the conduct and converſation of particular ſocieties already eſtabliſhed, are, for that reaſon, "conſiſtent with the will of God," or "right," which, without that reaſon, i. e. without the eſtabliſhment of civil ſociety, would not have been ſo.

From whence alſo it appears, that adventitious rights, though immediately derived from human appointment, are not, for that reaſon, leſs ſacred than natural rights, nor the obligation to reſpect them leſs cogent. They both ultimately rely upon the ſame authority, the will of God. Such a man claims a right to a particular eſtate. He can ſhew, it is true, nothing for his right, but a rule of the civil community to which he belongs; and this rule may be arbitrary, capricious, and abſurd. Notwithſtanding all this, there would be the ſame ſin in diſpoſſeſſing the man of his eſtate by craft or violence, as if it had been aſſigned to him, like the partition of the country amongſt the twelve tribes, by the immediate deſignation and appointment of heaven.

II. Rights

THE DIVISION OF RIGHTS.

II. Rights are alienable or unalienable.

Which terms explain themselves.

The right we have to most of those things, which we call property, as houses, lands, money, &c. is alienable.

The right of a prince over his people, of a husband over his wife, of a master over his servant, is generally and naturally unalienable.

The distinction depends upon the mode of acquiring the right. If the right originate from a contract; and be limited to the *person* by the express terms of the contract, or by the common interpretation of such contracts, (which is equivalent to an express stipulation) or by a *personal condition* annexed to the right, then it is unalienable. In all other cases it is alienable.

The right to civil liberty is alienable; though in the vehemence of men's zeal for it, and in the language of some political remonstrances, it has often been pronounced to be an unalienable right. The true reason why mankind hold in detestation the memory of those who have sold their liberty to a tyrant, is, that together with their own, they sold commonly, or endangered, the liberty of others; which certainly they had no right to dispose of.

III. Rights

III. Rights are perfect or imperfect.

Perfect rights may be asserted by force, or, what in civil society comes into the place of private force, by course of law.

Imperfect rights may not.

Examples of perfect rights. A man's right to his life, person, house; for if these be attacked, he may repel the attack by instant violence, or punish the aggressor by law; a man's right to his estate, furniture, clothes, money, and to all ordinary articles of property; for if they be injuriously taken from him, he may compel the author of the injury to make restitution or satisfaction.

Examples of imperfect rights. In elections or appointments to offices, where the qualifications are prescribed, the best qualified candidate has a right to success; yet, if he be rejected, he has no remedy. He can neither seize the office by force, nor obtain redress at law; his right therefore is imperfect. A poor neighbour has a right to relief; yet if it be refused him, he must not extort it. A benefactor has a right to returns of gratitude from the person he has obliged; yet if he meet with none, he must acquiesce. Children have a right to affection and education from their parents; and parents on their part, to duty and reverence from their children; yet if these rights

rights be on either side withholden, there is no compulsion to enforce them.

It may be at first view difficult to apprehend, how a person should have a right to a thing, and yet have no right to use the means necessary to obtain it. This difficulty, like most others in morality, is resolvable into the necessity of general rules. The reader recollects, that a person is said to have a "right" to a thing, when it is "consistent with the will of God" that he should possess it. So that the question is reduced to this; How it comes to pass, that it should be consistent with the will of God, that a person should possess a thing, and yet not be consistent with the same will that he should use force to obtain it? The answer is, that the permission of force in this case, because of the indeterminateness, either of the object, or of the circumstances of the right, would, in its consequence, lead to the permission of force in other cases, where there existed no right at all. The candidate above described has, no doubt, a right to success; but his right depends upon his qualifications: for instance, upon his comparative virtue, learning, &c. there must be somebody therefore to compare them. The existence, degree, and respective importance of these qualifications are all indeterminate; there must be somebody therefore to determine them. To allow the candidate to demand success by force, is to make him the judge of his own qualifications. You cannot do this, but you must make all other candidates the same; which would open a door to demands
without

without number, reaſon, or right. In like manner, a poor man has a right to relief from the rich; but the mode, ſeaſon, and quantum of that relief, who ſhall contribute to it, or how much, are not aſcertained. Yet theſe points muſt be aſcertained, before a claim to relief can be proſecuted by force. For to allow the poor to aſcertain them for themſelves, would be to expoſe property to ſo many of theſe claims, that it would loſe its value, or ceaſe indeed to be property. The ſame obſervation holds of all other caſes of imperfect rights; not to mention, that in the inſtances of gratitude, affection, reverence, and the like, force is excluded by the very idea of the duty, which muſt be voluntary, or not at all.

Wherever the right is imperfect, the correſponding obligation muſt be ſo too. I am obliged to prefer the beſt candidate, to relieve the poor, be grateful to my benefactors, take care of my children, and reverence my parents; but in all theſe caſes, my obligation, like their right, is imperfect.

I call theſe obligations "imperfect," in conformity to the eſtabliſhed language of writers upon the ſubject. The term however ſeems ill choſen, on this account, that it leads many to imagine, that there is leſs guilt in the violation of an imperfect obligation, than of a perfect one. Which is a groundleſs notion. For an obligation being perfect or imperfect, determines only whether violence may or may not be employed to enforce it; and determines nothing elſe.

THE DIVISION OF RIGHTS.

elſe. The degree of guilt incurred by violating the obligation is a different thing, and is determined by circumſtances altogether independent of this diſtinction. A man, who by a partial, prejudiced, or corrupt vote, diſappoints a worthy candidate of a ſtation in life, upon which his hopes, poſſibly, or livelihood depend, and thereby diſcourages merit and emulation in others, incurs, I am perſuaded, a much greater crime, than if he had filched a book out of a library, or picked a pocket of a handkerchief; though in the one caſe, he violates only an imperfect right, in the other a perfect one.

As poſitive precepts are often indeterminate in their extent, and as the indeterminateneſs of an obligation is that which makes it imperfect; it comes to paſs, that poſitive precepts commonly produce an imperfect obligation.

Negative precepts or prohibitions, being generally preciſe, conſtitute accordingly a perfect obligation.

The fifth commandment is poſitive, and the duty which reſults from it is imperfect.

The ſixth commandment is negative, and impoſes a perfect obligation.

Religion and virtue find their principal exerciſe amongſt the imperfect obligations; the laws of civil ſociety taking pretty good care of the reſt.

CHAP. XI.

THE GENERAL RIGHTS OF MANKIND.

BY the general Rights of Mankind, I mean the rights which belong to the species collectively; the original stock, as I may say, which they have since distributed among themselves.

These are,

I. A right to the fruits or vegetable produce of the earth.

The insensible parts of the creation are incapable of injury; and it is nugatory to enquire into the right, where the use can be attended with no injury. But it may be worth observing, for the sake of an inference which will appear below, that, as God has created us with a want and desire of food, and provided things suited by their nature to sustain and satisfy us, we may fairly presume, that he intended we should apply them to that purpose.

II. A right to the flesh of animals.

This is a very different claim from the former. Some excuse seems necessary for the pain and loss which we occasion to brutes, by restraining them of their liberty, mutilating their bodies, and, at last, putting an end to their lives, which we suppose to be their all, for our pleasure or conveniency.

The reasons alledged in vindication of this practice, are the following: that the several species of brutes being created to prey upon one another, affords a kind of analogy to prove, that the human species were intended to feed upon them; that, if let alone, they would over-run the earth, and exclude mankind from the occupation of it; that they are requited for what they suffer at our hands, by our care and protection.

Upon which reasons I would observe, that *the analogy contended for is extremely lame*; since brutes have no power to support life by any other means, and since we have: for the whole human species might subsist entirely upon fruit, pulse, herbs and roots, as many tribes of Hindoos actually do. The two other reasons may be valid reasons, as far as they go; for, no doubt, if man had been supported entirely by vegetable food, a great part of those animals, which die to furnish his table, would never have lived: but they by no means justify our right over the lives of brutes, to the extent in which we exercise it. What danger is there, for instance, of fish interfering with us, in the use of their element? Or what do *we* contribute to their support or preservation?

It seems to me that it would be difficult to defend this right, by any arguments which the light and order of nature afford; and that we are beholden for it, to the permission recorded in scripture, Gen. ix. 1, 2, 3, " And God " blessed Noah and his sons, and said unto them, be fruit- " ful, and multiply, and replenish the earth; and the fear " of you, and the dread of you, shall be upon every beast " of the earth, and upon every fowl of the air, and upon " all that moveth upon the earth, and upon all the fishes " of the sea; into your hand are they delivered: every " moving thing shall be meat for you; even as the green " herb, have I given you all things." To Adam and his posterity had been granted at the creation, " every green " herb for meat," and nothing more. In the last clause of the passage now produced, the old grant is recited, and extended to the flesh of animals, " even as the green " herb, have I given you all things." But this was not 'till after the flood; the inhabitants of the antediluvian world therefore had no such permission, that we know of. Whether they actually refrained from the flesh of animals, is another question. Abel, we read, was a keeper of sheep; and for what purpose he kept them, but for food, is difficult to say (unless it were for sacrifices): might not, however, some of the stricter sects among the antediluvians be scrupulous as to this point? and might not Noah and his family be of this description? for it is not probable that God would publish a permission, to authorize a practice which had never been disputed.

Wanton,

Wanton, and, what is worse, studied cruelty to brutes, is certainly wrong, as coming within none of these reasons.

From reason then, or revelation, or from both together, it appears to be God Almighty's intention, that the productions of the earth should be applied to the sustentation of human life. Consequently, all waste and misapplication of these productions, is contrary to the divine intention and will; and therefore wrong, for the same reason that any other crime is so. Such as what is related of William the Conqueror, the converting of twenty manors into a forest for hunting, or, what is not much better, suffering them to continue in that state; or the letting of large tracts of land lie barren, because the owner cannot cultivate them, nor will part with them to those who can; or destroying, or suffering to perish great part of an article of human provision, in order to enhance the price of the remainder, which is said to have been, 'till lately, the case with fish caught upon the English coast; or diminishing the breed of animals, by a wanton, or improvident consumption of the young, as of the spawn of shell-fish, or the fry of salmon, by the use of unlawful nets, or at improper seasons: to this head may also be referred, what is the same evil in a smaller way, the expending of human food on superfluous dogs or horses; and lastly, the reducing of the quantity, in order to alter the quality, and to alter it generally for the

worse;

worse; as the distillation of spirits from bread corn, the boiling down of solid meat for sauces, essences, &c.

This seems to be the lesson which our Saviour, after his manner, inculcates, when he bids his disciples " gather up " the fragments, that nothing be lost." And it opens indeed a new field of duty. Schemes of wealth or profit, prompt the active part of mankind to cast about, how they may convert their property to the most advantage: and their own advantage, and that of the public, commonly concur. But it has not as yet entered into the minds of mankind, to reflect that it is a *duty*, to add what we can to the common stock of provision, by extracting out of our estates the most they will yield; or that it is any sin to neglect this.

From the same intention of God Almighty, we also deduce another conclusion, namely, " that nothing ought " to be made exclusive property, which can be conveniently " enjoyed in common."

It is the general intention of God Almighty, that the produce of the earth be applied to the use of man. This appears from the constitution of nature, or, if you will, from his express declaration; and this is all that appears hitherto. Under this general donation, one man has the same right as another. You pluck an apple from a tree, or take a lamb out of a flock, for your immediate use and nourishment, and I do the same; and we both plead for what we do, the general intention of the Supreme Proprietor.

prietor. So far all is right; but you cannot claim the whole tree, or the whole flock, and exclude me from any share of them, and plead this general intention for what you do. The plea will not serve you: you must shew something farther. You must shew, by probable arguments at least, that it is God's intention, that these things should be parcelled out to individuals; and that the established distribution, under which you claim, should be upheld. Shew me this, and I am satisfied. But until this be shewn, the general intention, which has been made appear, and which is all that does appear, must prevail; and, under that, my title is as good as yours. Now there is no argument to induce such a presumption, but one, that the thing cannot be enjoyed at all, or enjoyed with the same, or with nearly the same advantage, while it continues in common, as when appropriated. This is true, where there is not enough for all, or where the article in question requires care or labour in the production or preservation: but where no such reason obtains, and the thing is in its nature capable of being enjoyed by as many as will, it seems an arbitrary usurpation upon the rights of mankind, to confine the use of it to any.

If a medicinal spring were discovered in a piece of ground which was private property, copious enough for every purpose it could be applied to, I would award a compensation to the owner of the field, and a liberal profit to the author of the discovery, especially, if he had bestowed pains or expence upon the search. But I question, whether any human laws would be justified, or would justify the owner, in prohibiting mankind from the use of the water, or setting such a price upon it, as would almost amount to a prohibition.

If there be fisheries, which are inexhaustible; as, for aught I know, the cod-fishery upon the Banks of Newfoundland, and the herring-fishery in the British seas are; then all those conventions, by which one or two nations claim to themselves, and guarantee to each other, the exclusive enjoyment of these fisheries, are so many encroachments upon the general rights of mankind.

Upon the same principle may be determined a question, which makes a great figure in books of natural law, *utrum mare sit liberum?* that is, as I understand it, whether the exclusive right of navigating particular seas, or a control over the navigation of these seas, can be claimed, consistently with the law of nature, by any nation. What is necessary for each nation's safety we allow; as their own bays, creeks, and harbours, the sea contiguous to, that is, within cannon shot, or three leagues of their coast; and, upon the same principle of safety, (if upon any principle) must be defended, the claim of the Venetian state to the Adriatic, of Denmark to the Baltic, of Great Britain to the seas which invest the island. But, when Spain asserts a right to the Pacific ocean, or Portugal to the Indian seas, or when any nation extends its pretensions much beyond the limits of its own territories, they erect a claim, which interferes
with

with the benevolent defigns of providence, and which no human authority can juftify.

III. Another right, which may be called a general right, as it is incidental to every man who is in a fituation to claim it, is the right of extreme neceffity: by which is meant, a right to ufe or deftroy another's property, when it is neceffary for our own prefervation to do fo; as a right to take, without or againft the owner's leave, the firft food, cloaths, or fhelter we meet with, when we are in danger of perifhing through want of them; a right to throw goods overboard, to fave the fhip; or to pull down a houfe, in order to ftop the progrefs of a fire; and a few other inftances of the fame kind. Of which right the foundation feems to be this, that, when property was firft inftituted, the inftitution was not intended to operate to the deftruction of any: therefore when fuch confequences would follow, all regard to it is fuperfeded. Or rather, perhaps, thefe are the few cafes, where the particular confequence exceeds the general confequence; where the mifchief refulting from the violation of the general rule, is over-balanced by the immediate advantage.

Reftitution however is due, when in our power; becaufe the laws of property are to be adhered to, fo far as confifts with fafety; and becaufe reftitution, which is one of thofe laws, fuppofes the danger to be over. But what is to be reftored? not the full value of the property deftroyed, but what it was worth at the time of deftroying it; which, confidering the danger it was in of perifhing, might be very little.

MORAL PHILOSOPHY.

BOOK III.
RELATIVE DUTIES.

PART I.
OF RELATIVE DUTIES WHICH ARE DETERMINATE.

CHAP. I.
OF PROPERTY.

IF you should see a flock of pigeons in a field of corn; and if (instead of each picking where, and what it liked, taking just as much as it wanted, and no more) you should see ninety-nine of them gathering all they got into a heap; reserving nothing for themselves, but the chaff and refuse; keeping this heap for one, and that the weakest perhaps and worst pigeon of the flock; sitting round, and looking on, all the winter, whilst this one was devouring, throwing about and wasting it; and, if a pigeon more hardy or hungry than the rest, touched a grain of the hoard, all the others instantly flying upon it, and tearing it to pieces: if you should see this, you would see nothing more, than what is every day practised and established among men. Among men you see the ninety and nine, toiling and scraping together a heap of superfluities for one; getting nothing for themselves all the while, but a little of the coarsest of the provision, which their own labour produces; and this one too, oftentimes the feeblest and worst of the whole set, a child, a woman, a madman, or a fool; looking quietly on, while they see the fruits of all their labour spent or spoiled; and if one of them take or touch a particle of it, the others join against him, and hang him for the theft.

CHAP. II.

THE USE OF THE INSTITUTION OF PROPERTY.

THERE must be some very important advantages to account for an institution, in one view of it so paradoxical and unnatural.

The principal of these advantages are the following:

I. It increases the produce of the earth.

INSTITUTION OF PROPERTY.

The earth, in climates like ours, produces little without cultivation; and none would be found willing to cultivate the ground, if others were to be admitted to an equal share of the produce. The same is true of the care of flocks and herds of tame animals.

Crabs and acorns, red deer, rabbits, game, and fish, are all we should have to subsist upon, if we trusted to the spontaneous productions of this country: and it fares not much better with other countries. A nation of North American savages, consisting of two or three hundred, will occupy, and be half-starved upon a tract of land, which, in Europe, and with European management, would be sufficient for the maintenance of as many thousands.

In some fertile soils, with great abundance of fish upon their coasts, and in regions where cloaths are unnecessary, a considerable degree of population may subsist without property in land; which is the case in the islands of Otaheite: but in less favoured situations, as in the country of New Zealand, though this sort of property obtain in a small degree, the inhabitants, for want of a more secure and regular establishment of it, are driven ofttimes by the scarcity of provision to devour one another.

II. It preserves the produce of the earth to maturity.

We may judge, what would be the effects of a community of right to the productions of the earth, from the

trifling

trifling specimens that we see of it at present. A cherry-tree in a hedge-row, nuts in a wood, the grass of an unstinted pasture, are seldom of much advantage to any body, because people do not wait for the proper season of reaping them. Corn, if any were sown, would never ripen; lambs and calves would never grow up to sheep and cows, because the first person that met with them would reflect, that he had better take them as they are, than leave them for another.

III. It prevents contests.

War and waste, tumult and confusion, must be unavoidable and eternal, where there is not enough for all, and where there are no rules to adjust the division.

IV. It improves the conveniency of living.

This it does two ways. It enables mankind to divide themselves into distinct professions; which is impossible, unless a man can exchange the productions of his own art for what he wants from others; and exchange implies property. Much of the advantage of civilized over savage life, depends upon this. When a man is from necessity his own taylor, tent-maker, carpenter, cook, huntsman, and fisherman, it is not probable that he will be expert at any of his callings. Hence the rude habitations, furniture, cloathing, and implements of savages; and the tedious length of time which all their operations require.

INSTITUTION OF PROPERTY.

It likewise encourages those arts, by which the accommodations of human life are supplied, by appropriating to the artist the benefit of his discoveries and improvements; without which appropriation, ingenuity will never be exerted with effect.

Upon these several accounts we may venture, with a few exceptions, to pronounce, that even the poorest and the worst provided in countries where property and the consequences of property prevail, are in a better situation, with respect to food, raiment, houses, and what are called the necessaries of life, than *any* are, in places where most things remain in common. The balance, therefore, upon the whole, must preponderate in favour of property with a great excess.

Inequality of property in the degree in which it exists in most countries of Europe, abstractedly considered, is an evil: but it is an evil, which flows from those rules concerning the acquisition and disposal of property, by which men are incited to industry, and by which the object of their industry is rendered secure and valuable. If there be any great inequality unconnected with this origin, it ought to be corrected.

CHAP. III.

THE HISTORY OF PROPERTY.

THE first objects of property were the fruits a man plucked, and the wild animals he caught; next to these, the tents or houses which he built, the tools he made use of to catch or prepare his food; and afterwards weapons of war and offence. Many of the savage tribes in North America have advanced no farther than this yet; for they are said to gather their harvest, and return the produce of their market with foreigners, into the common hoard or treasury of the tribe. Flocks and herds of tame animals soon became property; *Abel*, the second from *Adam*, was a keeper of sheep; sheep and oxen, and camels, and asses, composed the wealth of the *Jewish* patriarchs, as they do still of the modern *Arabs*. As the world was first peopled in the East, where there existed a great scarcity of water, wells probably were next made property; as we learn, from the frequent and serious mention of them in the Old Testament, the contentions and treaties about them,* and from its being recorded, among the most memorable atchievements of very eminent men, that they dug or discovered a well. Land, which is now so important a part of property, which alone our laws call *real* property, and regard upon all occasions with such peculiar attention, was probably not made property in any country, till long after the

* Gen. xxi. 25. xxvi. 18.

the inftitution of many other fpecies of property, that is, till the country became populous, and tillage began to be thought of. The firft partition of an eftate which we read of, was that which took place between *Abram* and *Lot*; and was one of the fimpleft imaginable: " If thou wilt take " the left hand, then I will go to the right; or if thou depart " to the right hand, then I will go to the left." There are no traces of property in land in *Cæsar's* account of *Britain*; little of it in the hiftory of the *Jewish* patriarchs; none of it found amongft the nations of *North America*; the *Scythians* are exprefsly faid to have appropriated their cattle and houfes, but to have left their land in common. Property in immoveables continued at firft no longer than the occupation; that is, fo long as a man's family continued in poffeffion of a cave, or his flocks depaftured upon a neighbouring hill, no one attempted, or thought he had a right, to difturb or drive them out: but when the man quitted his cave, or changed his pafture, the firft who found them unoccupied, entered upon them, by the fame title as his predeceffors; and made way in his turn for any one that happened to fucceed him. All more permanent property in land, was probably pofterior to civil government and to laws; and therefore fettled by thefe, or according to the will of the reigning chief.

CHAP. IV.

IN WHAT THE RIGHT OF PROPERTY IS FOUNDED.

WE now speak of Property in Land: and there is a difficulty in explaining the origin of this property, consistently with the law of nature; for the land was once no doubt common, and the question is, how any particular part of it could justly be taken out of the common, and so appropriated to the first owner, as to give him a better right to it than others; and, what is more, a right to exclude all others from it.

Moralists have given many different accounts of this matter; which diversity alone perhaps is a proof that none of them are satisfactory.

One tells us that mankind, when they suffered a particular person to occupy a piece of ground, by tacit consent relinquished their right to it; and, as the piece of ground belonged to mankind collectively, and mankind thus gave up their right to the first peaceable occupier, it thenceforward became his property, and no person afterwards had a right to molest him in it.

The objection to this account is, that confent can never be prefumed from filence, where the perfon whofe confent is required knows nothing about the matter; which muft have been the cafe with all mankind, except the neighbourhood of the place where the appropriation was made. And to fuppofe that the piece of ground previoufly belonged to the neighbourhood, and that they had a juft power of conferring a right to it upon whom they pleafed, is to fuppofe the queftion refolved, and a partition of land to have already taken place.

Another fays, that each man's limbs and labour are his own exclufively; that, by occupying a piece of ground a man infeparably mixes his labour with it; by which means the piece of ground becomes thenceforward his own, as you cannot take it from him, without depriving him at the fame time of fomething, which is indifputably *his*.

This is Mr. LOCKE's folution; and feems indeed a fair reafon, where the value of the labour bears a confiderable proportion to the value of the thing; or where the thing derives its chief ufe and value from the labour. Thus game and fifh, though they be common, whilft at large in the woods or water, inftantly become the property of the perfon that catches them; becaufe an animal, when caught, is much more valuable than when at liberty; and this increafe of value, which is infeparable from, and makes a great part of the whole value, is ftrictly the property of the fowler, being the produce of his personal labour. For the same reason, wood or iron, manufactured into utensils, become the property of the manufacturer; because the value of the workmanship far exceeds that of the materials. And upon a similar principle, a parcel of unappropriated ground, which a man should pare, burn, plow, harrow, and sow, for the production of corn, would justly enough be thereby made his own. But this will hardly hold, in the manner it has been applied, of taking a ceremonious possession of a tract of land, as navigators do of new discovered islands, by erecting a standard, engraving an inscription, or publishing a proclamation to the birds and beasts; or of turning your cattle into a piece of ground, setting up a landmark, digging a ditch, or planting a hedge round it. Nor will even the clearing, manuring, and plowing of a field, give the first occupier a right to it in perpetuity, and after this cultivation and all effects of it are ceased.

Another, and in my opinion a better account of the first right of ownership, is the following: that, as God has provided these things for the use of all, he has of consequence given each leave to take of them what he wants; by virtue therefore of this leave, a man may appropriate what he wants to his own use, without asking, or waiting for the consent of others; in like manner, as when an entertainment is provided for the freeholders of a county, each freeholder goes, and eats and drinks what he wants or chooses, without having or waiting for the consent of the other guests.

But

But then, this reason justifies property, as far as necessaries only, or, at the most, as far as a competent provision for our natural exigencies. For, in the entertainment we speak of (allowing the comparison to hold in all points), although every particular freeholder may sit down and eat till he be satisfied, without any other leave than that of the master of the feast, or any other proof of this leave, than the general invitation, or the manifest design with which the entertainment is provided; yet you would hardly permit any one to fill his pockets or his wallet, or to carry away with him a quantity of provision to be hoarded up, or wasted, or given to his dogs, or stewed down into sauces, or converted into articles of superfluous luxury; especially, if by so doing, he pinched the guests at the lower end of the table.

These are the accounts that have been given of the matter by the best writers upon the subject; but, were these accounts less exceptionable than they are, they would none of them, I fear, avail us in vindicating our present claims of property in land, unless it were more probable than it is, that our estates were actually acquired at first, in some of the ways which these accounts suppose; and that a regular regard had been paid to justice, in every successive transmission of them since: for if one link in the chain fail, every tittle posterior to it falls to the ground.

The real foundation of our right is THE LAW OF THE LAND.

It

It is the intention of God, that the produce of the earth be applied to the use of man; this intention cannot be fulfilled without establishing property; it is consistent therefore with his will, that property be established. The land cannot be divided into separate property, without leaving it to the law of the country to regulate that division; it is consistent therefore with the same will, that the law should regulate the division; and consequently, " consistent with " the will of God," or " right " that I should possess that share which these regulations assign me.

By whatever circuitous train of reasoning you attempt to derive this right, it must terminate at last in the will of God; the straightest therefore, and shortest way of coming at this will, is the best.

Hence it appears, that my right to an estate does not at all depend upon the manner or justice of the original acquisition; nor upon the justice of each subsequent change of possession. It is not, for instance, the less, nor ought it to be impeached, because the estate was taken possession of at first by a family of aboriginal Britons, who happened to be stronger than their neighbours; nor because the British possessor was turned out by a Roman, and the Roman by a Saxon invader; nor because it was seized, without colour of right or reason, by a follower of the Norman adventurer; from whom, after many interruptions of fraud and violence, it has at length devolved to me.

Nor does the owner's right depend upon the *expediency* of the law which gives it to him. On one side of a brook, an estate descends to the eldest son; on the other side, to all the children alike. The right of the claimants under both laws of inheritance is equal; though the expediency of such opposite rules must necessarily be different.

The principles we have laid down upon this subject apparently tend to a conclusion of which a bad use is apt to be made. As the right of property depends upon the law of the land, it seems to follow, that a man has a right to keep and take every thing, which the law will allow him to keep and take: which in many cases will authorise the most manifest and flagitious chicanery. If a creditor upon a simple contract neglect to demand his debt for six years, the debtor may refuse to pay it: would it be *right* therefore to do so, where he is conscious of the justice of the debt? If a person, who is under twenty-one years of age, contract a bargain (other than for necessaries,) he may avoid it, by pleading his minority: but would this be a fair plea, where the bargain was originally just?—The distinction to be taken in such cases is this. With the law, we acknowledge, resides the disposal of property: so long therefore as we keep within the design and intention of a law, that law will justify us, as well *in foro conscientiæ*, as *in foro humano*, whatever be the equity or expediency of the law itself. But when we convert to one purpose, a rule or expression of law, which is intended for another purpose; then, we plead in our justification, not the intention of the law,

law, but the words; that is, we plead a dead letter, which can fignify nothing: for words *without* meaning or intention have no force or effect in juftice, much lefs words taken *contrary* to the meaning and intention of the fpeaker or writer. To apply this diftinction to the examples juft now propofed: in order to protect men againft antiquated demands, from which it is not probable they fhould have preferved the evidence of their difcharge, the law prefcribes a limited time to certain fpecies of private fecurities, beyond which, it will not enforce them, or lend its affiftance to the recovery of the debt. If a man be ignorant, or dubious of the juftice of the demand made upon him, he may confcientioufly plead this limitation; becaufe *he applies the rule of law to the purpofe for which it was intended.* But when he refufes to pay a debt, of the reality of which he is confcious; he cannot, as before, plead the intention of the ftatute, and the fupreme authority of law, unlefs he could fhew, that the law *intended* to interpofe its fupreme authority, to acquit men of debts, of the exiftence and juftice of which they were themfelves fenfible. Again, to preferve youth from the practices and impofitions, to which their inexperience expofes them, the law compels the payment of no debts incurred within a certain age, nor the performance of any engagements, except for fuch neceffaries as are fuited to their condition and fortunes. If a young perfon therefore perceive that he has been practifed or impofed upon, he may honeftly avail himfelf of the privilege of his non-age to defeat the circumvention, But, if he fhelter himfelf under this privilege, to avoid a fair obligation,

tion, or an equitable contract, he extends the privilege to a case, in which it is not allowed by intention of law, and in which consequently it does not, in natural justice, exist.

As property is the principal subject of Justice, or " of " the determinate relative duties," we have put down what we had to say upon it in the first place: we now proceed to state these duties in the best order we can.

CHAP. V.

PROMISES.

I. *Whence the obligation to perform promises arises.*

II. *In what sense promises are to be interpreted.*

III. *In what cases promises are not binding.*

I. *Whence the obligation to perform promises arises.*

They who argue from innate moral principles, suppose a sense of the obligation of promises to be one of them;

but

but without assuming this, or any thing else, without proof, the obligation to perform promises, may be deduced from the necessity of such a conduct, to the well-being, or the existence, indeed, of human society.

Men act from expectation. Expectation is in most cases determined by the assurances and engagements which we receive from others. If no dependance could be placed upon these assurances, it would be impossible to know what judgment to form of many future events, or how to regulate our conduct with respect to them. Confidence therefore in promises is essential to the intercourse of human life; because, without it, the greatest part of our conduct would proceed upon chance. But there could be no confidence in promises, if men were not obliged to perform them: the obligation therefore to perform promises is essential, to the same end, and in the same degree.

Some may imagine, that, if this obligation were suspended, a general caution, and mutual distrust would ensue, which might do as well; but this is imagined, without considering, how every hour of our lives we trust to, and depend upon others; and how impossible it is, to stir a step, or, what is worse, to sit still a moment without such trust and dependance. I am now writing at my ease, not doubting (or rather never distrusting, and therefore never thinking about it) but that the butcher will send in the joint of meat, which I ordered; that his servant will bring it; that my cook will dress it; that my footman will serve it up;
and

and that I shall find it upon table at one o'clock. Yet have I nothing for all this, but the promise of the butcher, and the implied promise of his servant and mine. And the same holds of the most important, as well as the most familiar occurrences of social life. In the one the intervention of promises is formal, and is seen and acknowledged; our instance, therefore, is intended to show it in the other, where it is not so distinctly observed.

II. *In what sense promises are to be interpreted.*

Where the terms of a promise admit of more senses than one, the promise is to be performed " in that sense in which " the promiser apprehended at the time that the promisee " received it."

It is not the sense in which the promiser actually intended it, that always governs the interpretation of an equivocal promise; for, at that rate, you might excite expectations, which you never meant, nor would be obliged, to satisfy. Much less is it the sense, in which the promisee actually received the promise; according to that rule, you might be drawn into engagements which you never designed to undertake. It must therefore be the sense (for there is no other remaining) in which the promiser believed that the promisee accepted his promise.

This will not differ from the actual intention of the promiser, where the promise is given without collusion or reserve;

serve; but we put the rule in the above form, to exclude evasion in cases in which the popular meaning of a phrase, and the strict grammatical signification of the words differ, or, in general, wherever the promiser attempts to make his escape through some ambiguity in the expressions which he used.

Temures promised the garrison of *Sebastia*, that, if they would surrender, *no blood should be shed*. The garrison surrendered; and *Temures* buried them all alive. Now *Temures* fulfilled the promise, in one sense, and in the sense too in which he intended it at the time; but not in the sense in which the garrison of *Sebastia* actually received it, nor in the sense in which *Temures* himself knew that the garrison received it; which last sense, according to our rule, was the sense he was in conscience bound to have performed it in.

From the account we have given of the obligation of promises, it is evident, that this obligation depends upon the expectations which we *knowingly* and *voluntarily* excite. Consequently, any action or conduct towards another, which we are sensible excites expectations in that other, is as much a promise, and creates as strict an obligation, as the most express assurances. Taking, for instance, a relation's child, and educating him for a liberal profession, or in a manner suitable only for the heir of a large fortune, as much obliges us to place him in that profession, or to leave him such a fortune, as if we had given him a promise mife to do fo under our hands and feals. In like manner, a great man, who encourages an indigent retainer; or a minifter of ftate, who diftinguifhes and careffes at his levee, one who is in a fituation to be obliged by his patronage, engages, by fuch behaviour, to provide for him.—This is the foundation of *tacit promifes*.

You may either fimply declare your prefent intention, or you may accompany your declaration with an engagement to abide by it, which conftitutes a complete promife. In the firft cafe, the duty is fatisfied, if you were fincere, that is, if you entertained at the time the intention you expreffed, however foon, or for whatever reafon, you afterwards change it. In the latter cafe, you have parted with the liberty of changing. All this is plain; but it muft be obferved, that moft of thofe forms of fpeech, which, ftrictly taken, amount to no more than declarations of prefent intention, do yet, in the ufual way of underftanding them, excite the expectation, and therefore carry with them the force of abfolute promifes. Such as, " I " intend you this place."—" I defign to leave you this " eftate."—" I purpofe giving you my vote."—" I mean " to ferve you."—In which, although the " intention," the " defign," the " purpofe," the " meaning," be expreffed in words of the prefent time, yet you cannot afterwards recede from them, without a breach of good faith. If you choofe therefore to make known your prefent intention, and yet to referve to yourfelf the liberty of changing it, you muft guard your expreffions by an additional claufe, as " I intend *at present*"—*if I dont alter*—or the like—and after all, as there can be no reason for communicating your intention, but to excite some degree of expectation or other, a wanton change of an intention which is once disclosed, always disappoints somebody; and is always, for that reason, wrong.

There is, in some men, an infirmity with regard to promises, which often betrays them into great distress. From the confusion, or hesitation, or obscurity, with which they express themselves, especially when overawed, or taken by surprise, they sometimes encourage expectations, and bring upon themselves demands, which, possibly, they never dreamed of. This is a want, not so much of integrity, as of presence of mind.

III. *In what cases promises are not binding.*

1. Promises are not binding, where the performance is *impossible*.

But observe, that the promiser is guilty of a fraud, if he be privately aware of the impossibility, at the time of making the promise. For when any one promises a thing, he asserts his belief, at least, of the possibility of performing it; as no one can accept or understand the promise under any other supposition. Instances of this sort are the following. The minister promises a place, which he knows to be engaged, or not at his disposal—A father, in settling marriage

marriage articles, promises to leave his daughter an estate, which he knows to be entailed upon the heir male of his family—A merchant promises with his daughter a ship, or share of a ship, which he is privately advised is lost at sea—An incumbent promises to resign a living, being well assured that his resignation will not be accepted by the bishop. The promiser, as in these cases, with knowledge of the impossibility, is justly answerable in an equivalent; but otherwise not.

When the promiser himself occasions the impossibility, it is neither more nor less than a direct breach of the promise; as when a soldier maims, or a servant disables himself, to get rid of their engagements.

2. Promises are not binding, where the performance is *unlawful*.

There are two cases of this; one, where the unlawfulness is known to the parties, at the time of making the promise; as where an assassin promises to dispatch your rival or your enemy; a servant to betray his master; a pimp to procure a mistress; or a *friend* to give his assistance in a scheme of seduction. The parties in these cases are not obliged to perform what the promise requires, *because they were under a prior obligation to the contrary.* From which prior obligation what is there to discharge them? their promise—their own act and deed - - - but an obligation, from which a man can discharge himself, by his own act

act and deed, is no obligation at all. The guilt therefore of such promises is in the making, not in the breaking them; and if, in the interval betwixt the promise and the performance, a man so far recover his reflection, as to repent of his engagements, he ought certainly to break through them.

The other case is, where the unlawfulness did not exist, or was not known, at the time of making the promise; as where a merchant promises his correspondent abroad, to send him a ship load of corn, at a time appointed, and before the time arrives, an embargo is laid upon the exportation of corn—A woman gives a promise of marriage; before the marriage, she discovers that her intended husband is too near a-kin to her, or has a wife yet living. In all such cases, where the contrary does not appear, it must be presumed, that the parties supposed, what they promised to be lawful, and that the promise proceeded entirely upon this supposition. The lawfulness therefore becomes a condition of the promise; and where the condition fails, the obligation ceases. Of the same nature was Herod's promise to his daughter-in-law, " that he would give her what- " ever she asked, even to the half of his kingdom." The promise was not unlawful, in the terms in which Herod delivered it; and when it became so by the daughter's choice, by her demanding " JOHN the Baptist's head," Herod was discharged from the obligation of it, for the reason now laid down, as well as for that given in the last paragraph.

This

This rule, " that promises are void, where the performance is unlawful," extends also to imperfect obligations; for the reason of the rule holds of all obligations. Thus, if you promise a man a place, or your vote, and he afterwards render himself unfit to receive either, you are absolved from the obligation of your promise; or, if a better candidate appear, and it be a case in which you are bound by oath, or otherwise, to govern yourself by the qualification, the promise must be broken through.

And here I would recommend, to young persons especially, a caution, from the neglect of which, many involve themselves in embarrassment and disgrace; and that is, " never to give a promise which may interfere in the event " with their duty;" for if it do so interfere, the duty must be discharged, though at the expence of their promise, and not unusually of their good name.

The specific performance of promises is reckoned a perfect obligation. And many casuists have laid it down, in opposition to what has been here asserted, that, where a perfect and an imperfect obligation clash, the perfect obligation is to be preferred. For which opinion, however, there seems to be no reason, but what arises from the terms " perfect" and " imperfect," the impropriety of which has been remarked above. The truth is, of two contradictory obligations, that ought to prevail which is prior in point of crime.

It is the *performance* being unlawful, and not any unlawfulness in the subject or motive of the promise, which destroys its validity; therefore a bribe, after the vote is given; the wages of prostitution; the reward of any crime, after the crime is committed, ought, if promised, to be paid. For the sin and mischief, by this supposition, are over, and will be neither more nor less for the performance of the promise.

In like manner, a promise does not lose its obligation, merely because it proceeded from an *unlawful motive*. A certain person, in the life-time of his wife, who was then sick, paid his addresses, and promised marriage to another woman—the wife died; and the woman demanded performance of the promise. The man, who, it seems, had changed his mind, either felt or pretended doubts concerning the obligation of such a promise, and referred his case to bishop Sanderson, the most eminent in this kind of knowledge, of his time. Bishop Sanderson, after writing a dissertation upon the question, adjudged the promise to be void. In which however, upon our principles, he was wrong; for, however criminal the affection might be, which induced the promise, the performance, when it was demanded, was lawful; which is the only lawfulness required.

A promise cannot be deemed unlawful, where it produces, when performed, no effect beyond what would have taken place, had the promise never been made. And this is the single case, in which the obligation of a promise will justify a conduct, which, unless it had been promised, would be unjust. A captive may lawfully recover his liberty, by a promise of neutrality; for his conqueror takes nothing by the promise, which he might not have secured by his death or confinement: and neutrality would be innocent in him, although criminal in another. It is manifest, however, that promises which come into the place of coercion, can extend no farther than to passive compliances; for coercion itself could compel no more. Upon the same principle, promises of secrecy ought not to be violated, although the public would derive advantage from the discovery. Such promises contain no unlawfulness in them, to destroy their obligation; for, as the information would not have been imparted upon any other condition, the public lose nothing by the promise, which they would have gained without it.

3. Promises are not binding, where they contradict a former promise.

Because the performance is then unlawful, which resolves this case into the last.

4. Promises are not binding before acceptance; that is, before notice given to the promisee, for, where the promise is beneficial, if notice be given, acceptance may be presumed. Before the promise be communicated to the promisee, it is the same only as a resolution in the mind of the

promiser which may be altered at pleasure. For no expectation has been excited, therefore none can be disappointed.

But suppose I declare my intention to a third person, who, without any authority from me, conveys my declaration to the promisee; is that such a notice as will be binding upon me? It certainly is not: for I have not done that which constitutes the essence of a promise—I have not *voluntarily excited expectation.*

5. Promises are not binding which are released by the promisee.

This is evident; but it may be sometimes doubted who is the promisee. If I give a promise *to* A, of a place or vote for B; as to a father for his son; to an uncle for his nephew; to a friend of mine, for a relation or friend of his; then A is the promisee, whose consent I must obtain, to release me from the engagement.

If I promise a place or vote to B *by* A, that is, if A be a messenger to convey the promise, as if I should say, " you " may tell B, that he shall have this place, or may depend " upon my vote;" or if A be employed to introduce B's request, and I answer in any terms which amount to a compliance with it, then B is the promisee.

Promises to one person, for the benefit of another, are not released by the death of the promisee. For his death,
neither

PROMISES.

neither makes the performance impracticable, nor implies any consent to release the promiser from it.

6. *Erroneous* promises are not binding in certain cases; as,

1. Where the error proceeds from the mistake or misrepresentation of the promisee.

Because a promise evidently supposes the truth of the account, which the promisee relates in order to obtain it. A beggar solicits your charity by a story of the most pitiable distress—you promise to relieve him, if he will call again—in the interval you discover his story to be made up of lies—this discovery, no doubt, releases you from your promise. One who wants your service, describes the business or office for which he would engage you—you promise to undertake it—when you come to enter upon it, you find the profits less, the labour more, or some material circumstance different from the account he gave you—In such case you are not bound by your promise.

2. When the promise is understood by the promisee to proceed upon a certain supposition, or when the promiser thought he so understood it, and that supposition turns out to be false; then the promise is not binding.

This intricate rule will be best explained by an example. A father receives an account, from abroad, of the death of
his

his only son—soon after which he promises his fortune to his nephew—The account turns out to be false—the father, we say, is released from his promise; not merely because he never would have made it, had he known the truth of the case—for that alone will not do—but because the nephew also himself understood the promise to proceed upon the supposition of his cousin's death; or at least his uncle thought he so understood it; and could not think otherwise. The promise proceeded upon this supposition, in the promiser's own apprehension, and, as he believed, in the apprehension of both parties; and this belief of his is the precise circumstance which sets him free. The foundation of the rule is plainly this, a man is bound only to satisfy the expectation which he intended to excite; whatever condition therefore he intended to subject that expectation to, becomes an essential condition of the promise.

Errors, which come not within this description, do not annul the obligation of a promise. I promise a candidate my vote—presently another candidate appears, for whom I certainly would have reserved it, had I been acquainted with his design. Here therefore, as before, my promise proceeded from an error; and I never should have given such a promise, had I been aware of the truth of the case, as it has turned out—but the *promisee* did not know this—*he* did not receive the promise subject to any such condition, or as proceeding from any such supposition—nor did I at the time imagine he so received it—This error, therefore, of mine, must fall upon my own head, and the promise be
observed

obferved notwithstanding. A father promises a certain fortune with his daughter, supposing himself to be worth so much—his circumstances turn out, upon examination, worse than he was aware of. Here again the promise was erroneous, but, for the reason assigned in the last case, will nevertheless be obligatory.

The case of erroneous promises is attended with some difficulty; for to allow every mistake, or change of circumstances, to dissolve the obligation of a promise, would be to allow a latitude, which might evacuate the force of almost all promises: and, on the other hand, to gird the obligation so tight, as to make no allowances for manifest and fundamental errors, would, in many instances, be productive of great hardship and absurdity.

It has long been controverted amongst moralists, whether promises be binding, which are extorted by violence or fear. The obligation of all promises results, we have seen, from the necessity or the use of that confidence which mankind repose in them. The question, therefore, whether these promises are binding, will depend upon this, whether mankind, upon the whole, are benefited by the confidence placed in such promises? A highwayman attacks you—and being disappointed of his booty, threatens or prepares to murder you—you promise with many solemn asseverations, that, if he will spare your life, he shall find a purse of money left for him, at a place appointed—upon the faith of this promise, he forbears from farther violence. Now your

your life was saved by the confidence reposed in a promise extorted by fear; and the lives of many others may be saved by the same. This is a good consequence. On the other hand, a confidence in promises like these would greatly facilitate the perpetration of robberies. They might be made the instruments of almost unlimited extortion. This is a bad consequence; and in the question between the importance of these opposite consequences resides the doubt concerning the obligation of such promises.

There are other cases which are plainer; as where a magistrate confines a disturber of the public peace in jail, 'till he promise to behave better; or a prisoner of war promises, if set at liberty, to return within a certain time. These promises, say moralists, are binding, because the violence or duress is just; but, the truth is, because there is the same use of confidence in these promises, as of confidence in the promises of a person at perfect liberty.

Vows are promises to God. The obligation cannot be made out upon the same principle as that of other promises. The violation of them, nevertheless, implies a want of reverence to the Supreme Being; which is enough to make it sinful,

There appears no command or encouragement in the Christian scriptures to make vows; much less any authority to break through them, when they are made. The few instances inftances * of vows which we read of in the New Teftament were religioufly obferved.

The rules we have laid down concerning promifes are applicable to vows. Thus Jephthah's vow, taken in the fenfe in which that tranfaction is commonly underftood, was not binding; becaufe the performance, in that contingency, became unlawful.

CHAP. VI.

CONTRACTS.

A CONTRACT is a mutual promife. The obligation therefore of contracts; the fenfe in which they are to be interpreted; and the cafes where they are not binding, will be the fame as of promifes.

From the principle eftablifhed in the laft chapter, that the obligation of promifes is to be meafured by the expectation, which the promifer any how voluntarily and knowingly excites, refults a rule, which governs the conftruction of all contracts, and capable, from the fimplicity of it, of being applied with great eafe and certainty, viz. That,

Whatever

* Acts xviii. 18. xxi. 23.

Whatever is expected by one side, and known to be so expected by the other, is to be deemed a part or condition of the contract.

The several kinds of contracts, and the order in which we propose to consider them, may be exhibited at one view, thus:

Contracts of
- Sale.
- Hazard.
- Lending of
  - Inconsumable Property.
  - Money.
- Labour.
  - Service.
  - Commissions.
  - Partnership.
  - Offices.

CHAP. VII.

CONTRACTS OF SALE.

THE rule of justice, which wants most to be inculcated, in the making of bargains, is, that the seller is bound in conscience to disclose the faults of what he offers to sale. Amongst other methods of proving this, one may be the following:

I suppose it will be allowed, that to advance a direct falsehood in recommendation of our wares, by ascribing to them

them some quality which we know that they have not, is dishonest. Now compare with this the designed concealment of some fault, which we know that they have. The motives and the effects of actions are the only points of comparison, in which their moral quality can differ; but the motive in these two cases is the same, viz. to procure a higher price than we expect otherwise to obtain: the effect, that is, the prejudice to the buyer, is also the same; for he finds himself equally out of pocket by his bargain, whether the commodity, when he gets home with it, turn out worse than he had supposed, by the want of some quality which he expected, or the discovery of some fault which he did not expect. If therefore actions be the same as to all moral purposes, which proceed from the same motives, and produce the same effects; it is making a distinction without a difference, to esteem it a cheat, to magnify, beyond the truth, the virtues of what we have to sell; but none to conceal its faults.

It adds to the value of this kind of honesty, that the faults of many things are of a nature not to be known by any, but by the persons who have used them: so that the buyer has no security from imposition, but in the ingenuousness and integrity of the seller.

There is one exception, however, to this rule, namely, where the silence of the seller implies some fault in the thing to be sold, and where the buyer has a compensation in the price, for the risk which he runs: as where a horse, in a London repository, is sold by public auction, without warranty; the want of warranty is notice of some unsoundness, and produces a proportionable abatement in the price.

To this of concealing the faults of what we want to put off, may be referred the practice of passing bad money. This practice we sometimes hear defended by a vulgar excuse, that we have taken the money for good, and must therefore get rid of it. Which excuse is much the same, as if one, who had been robbed upon the highway, should imagine he had a right to reimburse himself out of the pocket of the first traveller he met; the justice of which reasoning the traveller possibly may not comprehend.

Where there exists no monopoly or combination, the market price is always a fair price; because it will always be proportionable to the use and scarcity of the article. Hence, there need be no scruple about demanding or taking the market price; and all those expressions, " provi-" sions are extravagantly dear," "corn bears an unreasonable " price," and the like, import no unfairness or unreasonableness in the seller.

If your taylor or your draper charge, or even ask of you more for a suit of cloaths, than the market price, you complain that you are imposed upon; you pronounce the tradesman who makes such a charge dishonest: although, as the man's goods were his own, and he had a right to prescribe the terms, upon which he would consent to part with

with them, it may be queftioned what difhonefty there can be in the cafe, and wherein the impofition confifts. Whoever opens a fhop, or in any manner expofes goods to public fale, virtually engages to deal with his cuftomers at a market price; becaufe it is upon the faith and idea of fuch an engagement, that any one comes within his fhop doors, or offers to treat with him. This is expected by the buyer; is known to be fo expected by the feller; which is enough, according to the rule delivered above, to make it a part of the contract between them, though not a fyllable be faid about it. The breach of this implied contract conftitutes the fraud enquired after.

Hence, if you difclaim any fuch engagement, you may fet what value you pleafe upon your property. If, upon being afked to fell a houfe, you anfwer that the houfe fuits your fancy or conveniency, and that you will not turn yourfelf out of it, under fuch a price; the price fixed may be double of what the houfe coft, or would fetch at a public fale, without any imputation of injuftice or extortion upon you.

If the thing fold be damaged, or perifh, between the fale and the delivery, ought the buyer to bear the lofs, or the feller? This will depend upon the particular conftruction of the contract. If the feller, either exprefsly, or by implication, or by cuftom, engage to *deliver* the goods; as if I buy a fet of china, and the china-man afk me whither he fhall bring or fend them to, and they are broken in the conveyance; the seller must abide by the loss. If the thing sold remain with the seller, at the instance, or for the conveniency of the buyer, then the buyer undertakes the risk; as if I buy a horse, and mention, that I will send for it on such a day, which is in effect desiring that it may continue with the seller till I do send for it; then, whatever misfortune befalls the horse in the mean time, must be at my cost.

And here, once for all, I would observe, that innumerable questions of this sort are determined solely by *custom;* not that custom possesses any proper authority to alter or ascertain the nature of right and wrong; but because the contracting parties are presumed to include in their stipulation, all the conditions which custom has annexed to contracts of the same sort; and when the usage is notorious, and no exception made to it, this presumption is generally agreeable to the fact.*

If I order a pipe of port from a wine merchant abroad; at what period the property passes from the merchant to me; whether upon delivery of the wine at the merchant's warehouse; upon its being put on shipboard at Oporto;

* It happens here, as in many cases, that what the parties ought to do, and what a judge or arbitrator would award to be done, may be very different. What the parties ought to do, by virtue of their contract, depends upon their consciousness, at the time of making it: whereas a third person finds it necessary to found his judgment upon presumptions, which presumptions may be false, although the most probable that he could proceed by.

upon the arrival of the ship in England; at its destin'd port; or not till the wine be committed to my servants, or deposited in my cellar; are all questions, which admit of no decision, but what custom points out. Whence, in justice, as well as law, what is called the *custom of merchants*, regulates the construction of mercantile concerns.

CHAP. VIII.

CONTRACTS OF HAZARD.

BY Contracts of Hazard, I mean gaming and insurance.

What some say of this kind of contracts, " that one side " ought not to have any advantage over the other," is neither practicable nor true. It is not practicable; for that perfect equality of skill and judgment, which this rule requires, is seldom to be met with. I might not have it in my power to play with fairness a game at cards, billiards, or tennis; lay a wager at a horse race; or underwrite a policy of insurance, once in a twelvemonth; if I must wait till I meet with a person, whose art, skill, and judgment, in these matters, is neither greater nor less than my own. Nor is this equality requisite to the justice of the contract. One party may give to the other the whole of the stake, if he please, and the other party may justly accept it, if it be given him; much more therefore may one give to the other a part of the stake, or, what is exactly the same thing, an advantage in the chance of winning the whole.

The proper restriction is, that neither side have an advantage, by means of which the other is not aware; for this is an advantage taken, without being *given*. Although the event be still an uncertainty, your advantage in the chance has a certain value; and so much of the stake, as that value amounts to, is taken from your adversary without his knowledge, and therefore without his consent. If I sit down to a game at whist, and have an advantage over the adversary, by means of a better memory, closer attention, or a superior knowledge of the rules and chances of the game, the advantage is fair; because it is obtained by means of which the adversary is aware; for he is aware, when he sits down with me, that I shall exert the skill that I possess, to the utmost. But if I gain an advantage by packing the cards, glancing my eye into the adversaries hands, or by concerted signals with my partner, it is a dishonest advantage; because it depends upon means, which the adversary never suspects that I make use of.

The same distinction holds of all contracts, into which chance enters. If I lay a wager at a horse race, founded upon the conjecture I form from the appearance, and character, and breed of the horse, I am justly entitled to any

CONTRACTS OF HAZARD.

advantage which my judgment gives me; but, if I carry on a clandestine correspondence with the jockies, and find out from them, that a trial has been actually made, or that it is settled before-hand which horse shall win the race; all such information is so much fraud, because derived from sources, which the other did not suspect, when he proposed or accepted the wager.

In speculations in trade, or in the stocks, if I exercise my judgment upon the general aspect and posture of public affairs, and deal with a person who conducts himself by the same sort of judgment; the contract has all the equality in it which is necessary: but, if I have access to secrets of state at home, or private advice of some decisive measure or event abroad, I cannot avail myself of these advantages with justice, because they are excluded by the contract, which proceeded upon the supposition, that I had no such advantage.

In insurances, where the underwriter computes his risk entirely from the account given by the person insured, it is absolutely necessary to the justice and validity of the contract, that this account be exact and complete.

CHAP. IX.

CONTRACTS OF LENDING OF INCONSUMABLE PROPERTY.

WHEN the identical loan is to be returned, as a book, a horſe, a harpſichord, it is called *inconſumable,* in oppoſition to corn, wine, money, and thoſe things which periſh, or are parted with in the uſe, and can therefore only be returned in kind.

The queſtions under this head are few and ſimple. The firſt is, if the thing lent be loſt or damaged, who ought to bear the loſs or damage? If it be damaged by the uſe, or by accident in the uſe for which it was lent, the lender muſt bear it; as if I hire a job-coach, the wear, tear, and ſoiling of the coach, muſt belong to the lender; or a horſe to go a particular journey, and in going the propoſed journey, the horſe die, or be lamed, the loſs muſt be the lender's: on the contrary, if the damage be occaſioned by the fault of the borrower, or by accident in ſome uſe for which it was not lent, then the borrower muſt make it good; as if the coach be overturned or broken to pieces by the careleſſneſs of your coachman; or the horſe be hired to take a morning's ride upon, and you go a hunting with him, or leap him over hedges, or put him into your cart, or

carriage,

INCONSUMABLE PROPERTY.

carriage, and he be strained, or staked, or galled, or accidentally hurt, or drop down dead, whilst you are thus using him; you must make satisfaction to the owner.

The two cases are distinguished by this circumstance, that in one case, the owner foresees the damage or risk, and therefore consents to undertake it; in the other case, he does not.

It is possible that an estate or a house may, during the term of a lease, be so increased or diminished in its value, as to become worth much more, or much less, than the rent agreed to be paid for it. In some of which cases, it may be doubted, to whom, of natural right, the advantage or disadvantage belongs. The rule of justice seems to be this: if the alteration might be expected by the parties, the hirer must take the consequence; if it could not, the owner. An orchard, or a vineyard, or a mine, or a fishery, or a decoy, may this year yield nothing, or next to nothing, yet the tenant shall pay his rent; and if they next year produce tenfold the usual profit, no more shall be demanded; because the produce is in its nature precarious, and this variation might be expected. If an estate in the fens of *Lincolnshire*, or the isle of *Ely*, be overflowed with water, so as to be incapable of occupation, the tenant, notwithstanding, is bound by his lease; because he entered into it with a knowledge and foresight of this danger. On the other hand, if by the irruption of the sea into a country where it was never known to have come before, by the change of the course of a river, the fall of a rock, the breaking out of a volcano, the bursting of a moss, the incursions of an enemy, or by a mortal contagion amongst the cattle; if by means like these, the estate change, or lose its value, the loss shall fall upon the owner; that is, the tenant shall either be discharged from his agreement, or be entitled to an abatement of rent. A house in *London*, by the building of a bridge, the opening of a new road or street, may become of ten times its former value; and by contrary causes, may be as much reduced in value: here also, as before, the owner, not the hirer, shall be affected by the alteration. The reason upon which our determination proceeds is this, that changes such as these, being neither foreseen, nor provided for, by the contracting parties, form no part or condition of the contract; and therefore ought to have the same effect as if no contract at all had been made, (for none was made with respect to *them*) that is, ought to fall upon the owner.

CHAP. X.

CONTRACTS CONCERNING THE LENDING OF MONEY.

THERE exists no reason, in the law of nature, why a man should not be paid for the lending of his money, as well as of any other property into which the money might be converted.

The scruples that have been entertained upon this head, and upon the foundation of which, the receiving of interest or usury (for they formerly meant the same thing) was once prohibited in almost all Christian countries, * arose from a passage in the law of MOSES, *Deuteronomy* xxiii, 19, 20, " Thou shalt not lend upon usury to thy brother; " usury of money, usury of victuals, usury of any thing, " that is lent upon usury: unto a stranger thou mayest lend " upon usury; but unto thy brother thou shalt not lend " upon usury."

This prohibition is now generally understood to have been intended for the Jews alone, as part of the civil or

---

By a statute of JAMES the First, interest above eight pounds per cent. was prohibited, (and consequently under that rate allowed) with this sage provision; *That this statute shall not be construed or expounded to allow the practice of usury in point of religion or conscience.*

political law of their nation, and calculated to preserve that distribution of property, to which many of their institutions were subservient; as the marriage of an heiress within her own tribe; of a widow, who was left childless, to her husband's brother; the year of jubilee, when alienated estates reverted to the family of the original proprietor—regulations, which were never thought to be binding upon any but the commonwealth of Israel.

This interpretation is confirmed, I think, beyond all controversy, by the distinction made in the law, between a Jew and a foreigner. " unto a stranger thou mayest lend upon " usury, but unto thy brother, thou mayest not lend upon " usury," a distinction, which could hardly have been admitted into a law, which the Divine Author intended to be of moral and of universal obligation.

The rate of interest has in most countries been regulated by law. The Roman law allowed of twelve pounds per cent. which *Justinian* reduced at one stroke to four pounds. A statute of the thirteenth year of Queen *Elizabeth*, which was the first that tolerated the receiving of interest in *England* at all, restrained it to ten pounds per cent. a statute of *James* the First to eight pounds; of *Charles* the Second, to six pounds; of Queen *Anne*, to five pounds, on pain of forfeiture of treble value of the money lent; at which rate and penalty the matter now stands. The policy of these regulations is, to check the power of accumulating wealth, without industry; to give encouragement to trade, by enabling

enabling adventurers in it to borrow money at a moderate price; and of late years, to enable the ſtate to borrow the ſubject's money itſelf.

Compound intereſt, though forbidden by the law of England, is agreeable enough to natural equity; for intereſt detained after it is due, becomes, to all intents and purpoſes, part of the ſum lent.

It is a queſtion which ſometimes occurs, how money borrowed in one country, ought to be paid in another, where the relative value of the precious metals is not the ſame. For example, ſuppoſe I borrow a hundred guineas in London, where each guinea is worth one and twenty ſhillings, and meet my creditor in the Eaſt Indies, where a guinea is worth no more perhaps than nineteen, is it a ſatisfaction of the debt to return a hundred guineas? or muſt I make up ſo many times one and twenty ſhillings? I ſhould think the latter: for it muſt be preſumed, that my creditor, had he not lent me his guineas, would have diſpoſed of them in ſuch a manner, as to have now had, in the place of them, ſo many one and twenty ſhillings; and the queſtion ſuppoſes, that he neither intended, nor ought to be a ſufferer, by parting with his money to me.

When the relative value of coin is altered by an act of the ſtate, if the alteration would have extended to the identical pieces which were lent, it is enough to return an equal number of pieces of the ſame denomination, or their

preſent

present value in any other. As if guineas were reduced by act of parliament to twenty shillings, so many twenty shillings, as I borrowed guineas, would be a just repayment. It would be otherwise, if the reduction was owing to a debasement of the coin; for then respect ought to be had, to the comparative value of the old guinea and the new.

Whoever borrows money is bound in conscience to repay it. This every man can see; but every man cannot see, or does not however reflect, that he is, in consequence, also bound, to use the means necessary to enable himself to repay it. "If he pay the money when he has it, or has it "to spare, he does all that an honest man can do," and all, he imagines, that is required of him; whilst the previous measures, which are necessary to furnish him with the money, he makes no part of his care, nor observes to be as much his duty as the other; such as selling a family seat, or a family estate, contracting his plan of expence, laying down his equipage, reducing the number of his servants, or any of those humiliating sacrifices, which justice requires of a man in debt, the moment he perceives that he has no reasonable prospect of paying his debts without them. An expectation, which depends upon the continuance of his own life, will not satisfy an honest man, if a better provision be in his power: for it is a breach of faith to subject a creditor, when we can help it, to the risk of our life, be the event what it will; that not being the security to which credit was given.

I know

I know few subjects which have been more misunderstood than the law which authorises the imprisonment of insolvent debtors. It has been represented as a gratuitous cruelty, which contributes nothing to the reparation of the creditor's loss, or to the advantage of the community. This prejudice arises principally from considering the sending of a debtor to jail, as an act of private satisfaction to the creditor, instead of a public punishment. As an act of satisfaction or revenge, it is always wrong in the motive, and often intemperate and undistinguishing in the exercise. Consider it as a public punishment, founded upon the same reason, and subject to the same rules, as other punishments; and the justice of it, together with the degree to which it should be extended, and the objects upon whom it may be inflicted will be apparent. There are frauds relating to insolvency, against which it is as necessary to provide punishment, as for any public crimes whatever: as where a man gets your money into his possession, and forthwith runs away with it; or, what is little better, squanders it in vicious expences; or stakes it at the gaming table; in the alley; or upon wild adventures in trade; or is conscious at the time he borrows it, that he can never repay it; or wilfully puts it out of his power by profuse living; or conceals his effects, or transfers them by collusion to another: not to mention the obstinacy of some debtors, who had rather rot in a jail, than deliver up their estates; for, to say the truth, the first absurdity is in the law itself, which leaves it in a debtor's power to withhold any part of his property from the claim of his creditors. The only question

question is, whether the punishment be properly placed in the hands of an exasperated creditor; for which it may be said, that these frauds are so subtile and versatile, that nothing but a discretionary power can overtake them; and that no discretion is likely to be so well informed, so vigilant, and so active, as that of the creditor.

It must be remembered, however, that the confinement of a debtor in jail is a punishment; and that every punishment supposes a crime. To pursue therefore, with the extremity of legal rigour, a sufferer, whom the fraud or failure of others, his own want of capacity, or the disappointments and miscarriages to which all human affairs are subject, have reduced to ruin, merely because we are provoked by our loss, and seek to relieve the pain we feel by that which we inflict, is repugnant not only to humanity, but to justice; for it is to pervert a provision of law, designed for a different and a salutary purpose, to the gratification of private spleen and resentment. Any alteration in these laws, which could distinguish the degrees of guilt, or convert the service of the insolvent debtor to some public profit, might be an improvement; but any considerable mitigation of their rigour, under colour of relieving the poor, would increase their hardships. For whatever deprives the creditor of his power of coercion, deprives him of his security: and as this must add greatly to the difficulty of obtaining credit, the poor, especially the lower sort of tradesmen, are the first who would suffer by such a regulation. As tradesmen must buy *before* they sell, you would

exclude

exclude from trade two thirds of thofe who now carry it on, if none were enabled to enter into it without a capital fufficient for prompt payments. An advocate, therefore, for the interefts of this important clafs of the community, will deem it more eligible, that one out of a thoufand fhould be fent to jail by his creditor, than that the nine hundred and ninety-nine fhould be ftraitened, and embarraffed, and many of them lie idle, by the want of credit.

CHAP. XI.

CONTRACTS OF LABOUR.

SERVICE.

SERVICE in this country is, as it ought to be, voluntary, and by contract; and the mafter's authority extends no farther than the terms, or equitable conftruction of the contract will juftify.

The treatment of fervants, as to diet, difcipline and accommodation, the kind and quantity of work to be required of them, the intermiffion, liberty and indulgence to be allowed them, muft be determined in a great meafure by cuftom; for where the contract involves fo many particulars, the contracting parties exprefs a few perhaps of the principal, and by mutual underftanding refer the reft to the known cuftom of the country in like cafes.

A fervant is not bound to obey the unlawful commands of his mafter; to minifter, for inftance, to his unlawful pleafures; or to affift him in unlawful practices in his profeffion; as in fmuggling or adulterating the articles which he deals in. For the fervant is bound by nothing but his own promife; and the obligation of a promife extends not to things unlawful.

For the fame reafon, the mafter's authority is no juftification of the fervant in doing wrong; for the fervant's own promife, upon which that authority is founded, would be none.

Clerks and apprentices ought to be employed entirely in the profeffion or trade which they are intended to learn. Inftruction is their wages, and to deprive them of the opportunities of inftruction, by taking up their time with occupations foreign to their bufinefs, is to defraud them of their wages.

The mafter is refponfible for what a fervant does in the ordinary courfe of his employment; for it is done under a general authority committed to him, which is in juftice equivalent to a fpecific direction. Thus, if I pay money to a banker's clerk, the banker is accountable; but not if I had paid it to his butler or his footman, whofe bufinefs
it

it is not to receive money. Upon the fame principle, if I once fend a fervant to take up goods upon credit, whatever goods he afterwards takes up at the fame fhop, fo long as he continues in my fervice, are juftly chargeable to my account.

The law of this country goes great lengths in intending a kind of concurrence in the mafter, fo as to charge him with the confequences of his fervant's conduct. If an inn-keeper's fervant rob his guefts, the inn-keeper muft make reftitution; if a farrier's fervant lame your horfe, the farrier muft anfwer for the damage; and ftill farther, if your coachman or carter drive over a paffenger in the road, the paffenger may recover from you a fatisfaction for the hurt he fuffers. But thefe determinations ftand, I think, rather upon the authority of the law, than any principle of natural juftice.

There is a careleffnefs and facility in giving characters, as it is called, of fervants, efpecially when given in writing, or according to fome eftablifhed form, which, to fpeak plainly of it, is a cheat upon thofe who accept them. They are given with fo little referve and veracity, " that I fhould as foon depend " fays the author of the Rambler, " upon an acquittal at the Old Bailey, by way " of recommendation of a fervant's honefty, as upon one " of thefe characters." It is fometimes careleffnefs; and fometimes alfo to get rid of a bad fervant without the uneasiness of a dispute; for which nothing can be pleaded, but the most ungenerous of all excuses, that the person we deceive is a stranger.

There is a conduct, the reverse of this, but more injurious, because the injury falls where there is no remedy. I mean the obstructing of a servant's advancement, because you are unwilling to spare his service. To stand in the way of your servant's interest, is a poor return for his fidelity; and affords slender encouragement for good behaviour, in this numerous, and therefore important, part of the community. It is a piece of injustice, which, if practised towards an equal, the law of honour would lay hold of; as it is, it is neither uncommon nor disreputable.

A master of a family is culpable, if he permit any vices among his domestics, which he might restrain by due discipline and a proper interference. This results from the general obligation to prevent misery when in our power; and the assurance which we have, that vice and misery at the long run go together. Care to maintain in his family a sense of virtue and religion, received the divine approbation in the person of ABRAHAM, *Gen.* xviii, 19, " I know him, that he will command his children, " and *his household* after him; and they shall keep the " way of the LORD, to do justice and judgment." And indeed no authority seems so well adapted to this purpose, as that of masters of families; because none operates upon
the

the subjects of it, with an influence so immediate and constant.

What the Christian Scriptures have delivered, concerning the relation and reciprocal duties of masters and servants, breathes a spirit of liberality, very little known in ages when servitude was slavery; and which flowed from a habit of contemplating mankind under the common relation in which they stand to their Creator, and with respect to their interest in another existence.* " Servants
" be obedient to them that are your masters, according to
" the flesh, with fear and trembling; in singleness of
" your heart, as unto Christ; not with eye service, as
" men pleasers, but as the servants of Christ, doing the
" will of God from the heart; *with good will, doing service*
" *as to the Lord, and not to men:* knowing that whatsoever
" good thing any man doth, the same shall he receive of
" the Lord, whether he be bond or free. And ye mas-
" ters do the same thing unto them, forbearing threaten-
" ing; knowing that your master also is in heaven;
" neither is there respect of persons with him." The idea of referring their service to God, of considering *him* as having appointed them their task, that they were doing *his* will, and were to look to *him* for their reward, was new, and affords a greater security to the master than any inferior principle; because it tends to produce a steady and cordial obedience in the place of that constrained service, which can never be trusted out of sight, and which is justly
enough

Eph. vi. 5——9.

enough called eye-service. The exhortation to masters, to keep in view their own subjection and accountableness, was no less seasonable.

CHAP. XII.

CONTRACTS OF LABOUR.

COMMISSIONS.

WHOEVER undertakes another man's business, makes it his own, that is, promises to employ upon it the same care, attention, and diligence, that he would do if it were actually his own; for he knows that the business was committed to him with that expectation. And he promises no more than this: therefore an agent is not obliged to wait, enquire, solicit, ride about the country, toil, or study, whilst there remains a possibility of benefiting his employer. If he exert so much of his activity, and use such caution, as the value of the business, in his judgment, deserves, that is, as he would have thought sufficient, if the same interest of his own had been at stake, he has discharged his duty, although it should afterwards turn out, that by more activity, and longer perseverance, he might have concluded the business with greater advantage.

This rule defines the duty of factors, stewards, attornies, advocates.

One of the chief difficulties of an agent's situation is, to know how far he may depart from his instructions, when he sees reason to believe, from some change or discovery in the circumstances of his commission, that his employer, if he were present, would alter his intention. The latitude allowed to agents in this respect will be different, according as the commission was confidential or ministerial; and according as the general rule and nature of the service require a prompt and precise obedience to orders or not. An attorney sent to treat for an estate, if he found out a flaw in the title, would desist from proposing the price he was directed to propose; and very properly. On the other hand, if the commander in chief of an army detach an officer under him upon a particular service, which service turns out more difficult, or less expedient, than was supposed; in so much that the officer is convinced that his commander, if he were acquainted with the true state in which the affair is found, would recall his orders; yet, if he cannot wait for fresh directions, without prejudice to the expedition he is sent upon, he must at all hazards pursue those which he brought out with him.

What is trusted to an agent may be lost or damaged in his hands by misfortune. An agent who acts without pay is clearly not answerable for the loss; for, if he give his labour for nothing, it cannot be presumed, that he gave also security for the success of it. If the agent be hired to the business, the question will depend upon the apprehension of the parties at the time of making the contract; which apprehension of theirs must be collected chiefly from custom, by which probably it was guided. Whether a public carrier ought to account for goods sent by him; the owner or master of a ship for the cargo; the post-office for letters or bills inclosed in letters, where the loss is not imputed to any fault or neglect of theirs; are questions of this sort. Any expression, which by implication amounts to a promise, will be binding upon the agent, without custom; as where the proprietors of a stage-coach advertise, that they will not be accountable for money, plate, or jewels; this makes them accountable for every thing else; or where the price is too much for the labour, part of it may be considered as a premium for insurance. On the other hand, any caution on the part of the owner to guard against danger, is evidence that he considers the risk to be his; as cutting a bank bill in two, to send by the post at different times.

Universally, unless a *promise*, either express or tacit, can be proved against the agent, the loss must fall upon the owner.

The agent may be a sufferer in his own person or property by the business which he undertakes; as where one goes a journey for another, and lames his horse, by a fall upon the road, or is hurt himself, can the agent in such case claim a compensation for the misfortune? Unless the same be provided for by express stipulation, the agent is not entitled to any compensation from his employer on that account: for where the danger is not foreseen, there can be no reason to believe, that the employer engaged to indemnify the agent against it; much less where it is foreseen: for whoever knowingly undertakes a dangerous employment, in common construction takes upon himself the danger and the consequences; as where a fireman undertakes for a reward to rescue a box of writings from the flames; or a sailor to bring off a passenger from a ship in a storm.

CHAP. XIII.

CONTRACTS OF LABOUR.

PARTNERSHIP.

I KNOW of nothing upon the subject of partnership that requires explanation, but how the profits are to be divided, where one partner contributes money, and the other labour; which is a common case.

Rule. From the stock of the partnership deduct the sum advanced, and divide the remainder between the monied partner and the labouring partner, in the proportion of the interest of the money to the wages of the labour, allowing such a rate of interest as money might be borrowed for upon the same security, and such wages as a journeyman would require for the same labour and trust.

Example. A advances a thousand pounds, but knows nothing of the business; B produces no money, but has been brought up to the business and undertakes to conduct it. At the end of the year the stock and effects of the partnership amount to twelve hundred pounds; consequently there are two hundred pounds to be divided. Now nobody would lend money upon the event of the business succeeding, which is A's security, under six per cent.—Therefore A must be allowed sixty pounds for the interest of his money. B, before he engaged in the partnership, earned thirty pounds a year in the same employment: his labour therefore, ought to be valued at thirty pounds, and the two hundred pounds must be divided between the partners, in the proportion of sixty to thirty; that is, A must receive one hundred and thirty-three pounds six shillings and eight pence, and B sixty-six pounds thirteen shillings and four pence.

If there be nothing gained, A loses his interest, and B his labour, which is right. If the original stock be diminished, by this rule B loses only his labour as before; whereas A loses his interest, and part of the principal: for which eventual disadvantage A is compensated, by having the interest of his money computed at six per cent, in the division of the profits, when there is any.

It is true, that the division of the profit is seldom forgotten in the constitution of the partnership; and is therefore commonly settled by express agreement: but these agreements, to be equitable, should pursue the principle of the rule here laid down.

All the partners are bound by what any one of them does in the course of the business; for, *quoad hoc*, each partner is considered as an authorised agent for the rest.

CHAP. XIV.

CONTRACTS OF LABOUR.

OFFICES.

IN many offices, as schools, fellowships of colleges, professorships of the universities. and the like, there is a twofold contract, one with the founder, the other with the electors.

The contract with the founder obliges the incumbent of the office to discharge every duty appointed by the charter, statutes, deed of gift, or will of the founder; because the endowment was given, and consequently accepted for that purpose, and upon these conditions.

The

The contract with the electors extends this obligation to all duties that have been customarily connected with and reckoned a part of the office, though not prescribed by the founder: for the electors expect from the person they choose, all the duties which his predecessors have discharged, and as the person elected, cannot be ignorant of their expectation, if he mean to refuse this condition, he ought to apprise them of his objection.

And here let it be observed that the permission of the electors is, in conscience, an excuse from this last class of duties only; because this class results from a contract, to which the electors and the person elected are the only parties. The other class of duties results from a different contract.

It is a question of some magnitude and difficulty, what offices may be conscientiously supplied by a deputy.

We will state the several objections to the substitution of a deputy; and then it will be understood that a deputy may be allowed in all cases, to which these objections do not apply.

An office may not be discharged by deputy,

1. Where a particular confidence is reposed in the person appointed to it; as the office of a steward, guardian, judge, commander in chief by land or sea.

2. Where

2. Where the custom hinders; as in the case of school-masters, tutors, and of commissions in the army and navy.

3. Where the duty cannot, from its nature, be so well performed by a deputy; as the deputy governor of a province may not possess the legal authority, or the actual influence of his principal.

4. When some inconveniency would result to the service in general from the permission of deputies in such cases: for example, it is probable that military merit would be much discouraged, if the duties belonging to commissions in the army were generally allowed to be executed by substitutes.

The non-residence of the parochial clergy, who supply the duty of their benefices by curates, is worthy of a more distinct consideration. And, in order to draw the question upon this case to a point, we will suppose the officiating curate to discharge every duty, which his principal, were he present, would be bound to discharge, and in a manner equally beneficial to the parish; under which circumstances, the only objection to the absence of the principal, at least the only one of the foregoing objections is the last.

And, in my judgment, the force of this objection will be much diminished, if the absent rector or vicar be, in the meantime

meantime engaged in any function or employment, of equal importance to the general interest of religion, or of greater. For the whole revenue of the national church may properly enough be considered as a common fund for the support of the national religion; and, if a clergyman be serving the cause of Christianity and protestantism, it can make little difference, out of what particular portion of this fund, that is, by the tithes and glebe of what particular parish his service be requited; any more than it can prejudice the king's service, that an officer who has signalized his merit in America, should be rewarded with the government of a fort or castle in Ireland, which he never saw; but for the custody of which proper provision is made, and care taken.

Upon the principle thus explained, this indulgence is due to none more than to those who are occupied in cultivating, or communicating religious knowledge, or the sciences subsidiary to religion.

This way of considering the revenues of the church, as a common fund for the same purpose, is the more equitable, as the value of particular preferments bears no proportion to the particular charge or labour.

But when a man draws upon this fund, whose studies and employments bear no relation to the object of it; and who is no farther a minister of the Christian religion, than as a cockade mades a soldier, it seems a misapplication little better than robbery.

And to those who have the management of such matters I submit this question, whether the impoverishing of the fund, by converting the best share of it into *annuities* for the gay and illiterate youth of great families, threatens not to starve and stifle the little clerical merit that is left amongst us?

All legal dispensations from residence proceed upon the supposition, that the absentee is detained from his living, by some engagement of equal or of greater public importance. Therefore, if in a case, where no such reason can with truth be pleaded, it be said that this question regards a right of property, and that all right of property awaits the disposition of law; that, therefore, if the law, which gives a man the emoluments of a living, excuse him from residing upon it, he is excused in conscience; we answer, that the law does not excuse him *by intention*, and that all other excuses are fraudulent.

CHAP. XV.

LIES.

A LIE is a breach of promise: for whoever seriously addresses his discourse to another, tacitly promises to speak the truth, because he knows that the truth is expected.

Or the obligation of veracity may be made out from the direct ill consequences of lying to social happiness. Which consequences consist, either in some specific injury to particular individuals, or in the destruction of that confidence, which is essential to the intercourse of human life: for which latter reason, a lie may be pernicious in its general tendency, and therefore criminal, though it produce no particular or visible mischief to any one.

There are falsehoods which are not lies; that is, which are not criminal; as,

1. Where no one is deceived; which is the case in parables, fables, novels, jests, tales to create mirth, ludicrous embellishments of a story, where the declared design of the speaker is not to inform, but to divert; compliments in the subscription

subscription of a letter, a servant's *denying* his master, a prisoner's pleading not guilty, an advocate asserting the justice, or his belief of the justice of his client's cause. In such instances no confidence is destroyed, because none was reposed; no promise to speak the truth is violated, because none was given, or understood to be given.

2. Where the person you speak to has no right to know the truth, or more properly, where little or no inconveniency results from the want of confidence, and in such cases; as where you tell a falsehood to a madman, for his own advantage; to a robber, to conceal your property; to an assassin, to defeat, or to divert him from, his purpose. The particular consequence is by the supposition beneficial; and, as to the general consequence, the worst that can happen is, that the madman, the robber, the assassin, will not trust you again; which (beside that the first is incapable of deducing regular conclusions from having been once deceived, and the two last not likely to come a second time in your way) is sufficiently compensated by the immediate benefit which you propose by the falsehood.

It is upon this principle, that, by the laws of war, it is allowed to deceive an enemy by feints, false colours, spies,*

---

* There have been two or three instances of late, of English ships decoying an enemy into their power, by counterfeiting signals of distress; an artifice, which ought to be reprobated by the common indignation of mankind: for

false intelligence, and the like; but, by no means, in treaties, truces, signals of capitulation, or surrender: and the difference is, that the former suppose hostilities to continue, the latter are calculated to terminate or suspend them. In the *conduct* of war, and whilst the war continues, there is no use, or rather no place for confidence, betwixt the contending parties; but in whatever relates to the *termination* of war, the most religious fidelity is expected, because without it wars could not cease, nor the victors be secure, but by the entire destruction of the vanquished.

Many people indulge in serious discourse a habit of fiction and exaggeration, in the accounts they give of themselves, of their acquaintance, or of the extraordinary things which they have seen or heard; and so long as the facts they relate are indifferent, and their narratives, though false, are inoffensive, it may seem a superstitious regard to truth, to censure them merely for truth's sake.

In the first place, it is almost impossible to pronounce beforehand, with certainty, concerning any lie, that it is inoffensive. *Volat irrevocabile*; and collects ofttimes accretions in its flight, which entirely change its nature. It may owe possibly its mischief to the officiousness or misrepresentation of those who circulate it; but the mischief is

---

a few examples, of captures effected by this stratagem, would put an end to that promptitude, in affording assistance to ships in distress, which is the best virtue in a seafaring character, and by which the perils of navigation are diminished to all.

nevertheless, in some degree, chargeable upon the original editor.

In the next place, this liberty in conversation defeats its own end. Much of the pleasure, and all the benefit of conversation, depends upon our opinion of the speaker's veracity; for which this rule leaves no foundation. The faith indeed of a hearer must be extremely perplexed, who considers the speaker, or believes that the speaker considers himself, as under no obligation to adhere to truth, but according to the particular importance of what he relates.

But beside and above both these reasons, *white* lies always introduce others of a darker complexion. I have seldom known any one who deserted truth in trifles, that could be trusted in matters of importance. Nice distinctions are out of the question, upon occasions, which, like those of speech, return every hour. The habit therefore, when once formed, is easily extended to serve the designs of malice or interest; like all habits, it spreads indeed of itself.

Pious frauds, as they are improperly enough called, pretended inspirations, forged books, counterfeit miracles, are impositions of a more serious nature. It is possible that they may sometimes, though seldom, have been set up and encouraged, with a design to do good; but the good they aim at, requires that the belief of them should be perpetual, which is hardly possible: and the detection of the fraud

fraud is sure to disparage the credit of all pretensions of the same nature. Christianity has suffered more injury from this cause, than from all other causes put together.

As there may be falsehoods which are not lies, so there may be lies without literal or direct falsehood. An opening is always left for this species of prevarication, when the literal and grammatical signification of a sentence is different from the popular and customary meaning. It is the wilful deceit that makes the lie; and we wilfully deceive, when our expressions are not true, in the sense in which we believe the hearer apprehends them. Besides, it is absurd to contend for any sense of words, in opposition to usage, for all senses of all words are founded upon usage, and upon nothing else.

Or a man may *act* a lie; as by pointing his finger in a wrong direction, when a traveller enquires of him his road; or when a tradesman shuts up his windows, to induce his creditors to believe that he is abroad: for to all moral purposes, and therefore as to veracity, speech and action are the same; speech being only a mode of action.

Or lastly, there may be lies of *omission*. A writer of *English* history, who, in his account of the reign of *Charles* the First, should wilfully suppress any evidence of that prince's despotic measures and designs, might be said to lie; for, by entitling his book a *history of England*, he engages to relate the whole truth of the history, or, at least, all he knows of it.

CHAP. XVI.

OATHS.

I. *Forms of Oaths.*

II. *Signification.*

III. *Lawfulness.*

IV. *Obligation.*

V. *What oaths do not bind.*

VI. *In what sense oaths are to be interpreted.*

I. The forms of oaths, like other religious ceremonies, have been always various; but consisting, for the most part, of some bodily action,* and of a prescribed form of words. Amongst the *Jews*, the juror held up his right hand towards heaven, which explains a passage in the cxlivth Psalm, " whose mouth speaketh vanity, and *their right-hand is a* " *right-hand of falsehood.* The same form is retained in *Scotland* still. An oath of fidelity was taken, by the servant's putting his hand under the thigh of his lord, as *Eliezer* did

* It is commonly thought that oaths are denominated *corporal* oaths from the bodily action which accompanies them of laying the right hand upon a book containing the four gospels. This opinion, however, appears to be a mistake; for the term is borrowed from the ancient usage of touching, upon these occasions, the *corporale*, or cloth which covered the consecrated elements.

to *Abraham*, *Gen.* xxiv. 2. from whence, with no great variation, is derived perhaps the form of doing homage at this day, by putting the hands between the knees, and within the hands of the liege.

Amongſt the *Greeks* and *Romans*, the form varied with the ſubject and occaſion of the oath. In private contracts, the parties took hold of each other's hand, whilſt they ſwore to the performance; or they touched the altar of the God, by whoſe divinity they ſwore. Upon more ſolemn occaſions, it was the cuſtom to ſlay a victim; and the beaſt being *ſtruck down*, with certain ceremonies and invocations, gave birth to the expreſſions τεμνειν ορκον, *ferire pactum*, and to our *Engliſh* phraſe, tranſlated from theſe, of " ſtriking a bargain."

The forms of oaths in Chriſtian countries are alſo very different; but in none, I believe, worſe contrived, either to convey the meaning, or impreſs the obligation of an oath, than in our own. The juror, with us, after repeating the promiſe or affirmation, which the oath is intended to confirm, adds, " ſo help me God:" or more frequently the ſubſtance of the oath is repeated to the juror, by the officer or magiſtrate who adminiſters it, adding in the concluſion " ſo help you God." The energy of the ſentence reſides in the particle *ſo*; *ſo*, that is, *hâc lege*, upon condition of my ſpeaking the truth, or performing this promiſe, may God help me, and not otherwiſe. The juror, whilſt he hears or repeats the words of the oath, holds

OATHS.

holds his right-hand upon a bible, or other book, containing the four gospels. The conclusion of the oath sometimes runs, " ita me Deus adjuvet et hæc sancta evangelia," or " so help me God, and the contents of this book;" which last clause forms a connection between the words and action of the juror, which before was wanting. The juror then kisses the book: the kiss, however, seems rather an act of reverence to the contents of the book, as, in the popish ritual, the priest kisses the gospel before he reads it, than any part of the oath.

This obscure and elliptical form, together with the levity and frequency with which it is administered, has brought about a general inadvertency to the obligation of oaths, which, both in a religious and political view, is much to be lamented: and it merits public consideration, whether the requiring of oaths on so many frivolous occasions, especially in the customs, and in the qualification for petty offices, has any other effect, than to make them cheap in the minds of the people. A pound of tea cannot travel regularly from the ship to the consumer, without costing half a dozen oaths at the least; and the same security for the due discharge of their office, namely, that of an oath, is required from a churchwarden and an archbishop, from a petty constable and the chief justice of England. Let the law continue its own sanctions, if they be thought requisite; but let it spare the solemnity of an oath. And where it is necessary, from the want of something better to depend upon, to accept men's own word or own account, let it annex to prevarication penalties proportioned to the public consequence of the offence.

II. But whatever be the form of an oath, the *signification* is the same. It is " the calling upon God to witness, *i. e.* " to take notice of what we say, and invoking his ven- " geance, or renouncing his favour, if what we say be false, " or what we promise be not performed."

III. Quakers and Moravians refuse to swear upon any occasion; founding their scruples concerning the *lawfulness* of oaths, upon our Saviour's prohibition, *Matth.* v. 34. " I say unto you swear not at all."

The answer which we give to this objection cannot be understood, without first stating the whole passage; " Ye " have heard, that it hath been said by them of old time " thou shalt not forswear thyself, but shalt perform unto " the Lord thine oaths: but I say unto you, swear not " at all; neither by heaven, for it is God's throne; nor " by the earth, for it is his footstool; neither by *Jerusalem*, " for it is the city of the great King; neither shalt thou " swear by thy head, because thou can'st not make one " hair white or black: but let your communication be yea " yea, nay nay, for whatsoever is more than these cometh " of evil.

To reconcile with this passage of scripture, the practice of swearing, or of taking oaths, when required by law, the following observations must be attended to.

1. It

OATHS.

1. It does not appear, that swearing " by heaven," " by the earth," " by *Jerusalem*," or " by their own head," was a form of swearing ever made use of amongst the *Jews* in judicial oaths: and consequently, it is not probable that they were judicial oaths, which Christ had in his mind when he mentioned those instances.

2. As to the seeming universality of the prohibition, " swear not at all," the emphatic clause " not at all" is to be read in connection with what follows; " not at all," *h. e.* " neither by the heaven," nor " by the earth," nor by " *Jerusalem*, nor by thy " head:" " *not at all*" does not mean upon no occasion, but by none of these forms. Our Saviour's argument seems to suppose, that the people, to whom he spake, made a distinction between swearing directly by the " name of God," and swearing by those inferior objects of veneration, " the heavens," " the earth," " *Jerusalem*," " or their own head." In opposition to which distinction he tells them, that, on account of the relation which these things bore to the supreme Being, to swear by any of them, was in effect and substance to swear by *him*; " by heaven, for it is his throne; by the earth, for it is his " footstool; by *Jerusalem*, for it is the city of the great " King; by thy head," for it is *his* workmanship, not thine, " thou canst not make one hair white or black:" for which reason, he says, " swear *not at all*," that is, neither directly by God, nor indirectly by any thing related to him. This interpretation is greatly confirmed, by a passage in the twenty-third chapter of the same gospel, where a similar

distinction, made by the Scribes and Pharisees, is replied to in the same manner.

3. Our Saviour himself being "adjured by the living "God," to declare whether he was the Christ, the son of God, or not, condescended to answer the high priest, without making any objection to the oath, (for such it was) upon which he examined him. "*God is my witness,*" says St. *Paul* to the *Romans*, " that without ceasing, I make men- " tion of you in my prayers:" and to the *Corinthians* still more strongly, " *I call God for a record upon my soul*, that, " to spare you, I came not as yet to *Corinth*." Both these expressions contain the nature of oaths. The epistle to the *Hebrews* speaks of the custom of swearing judicially, without any mark of censure or disapprobation; " men verily " swear by the greater, and an oath, for confirmation, is " to them an end of all strife."

Upon the strength of these reasons, we explain our Saviour's words to relate, not to judicial oaths, but to the practice of vain, wanton, and unauthorised swearing, in common discourse. St. *James's* words, chap. v. 12, are not so strong as our Saviour's, and therefore admit the same explanation with more ease.

IV. Oaths are nugatory, that is, carry with them no *proper* force or *obligation*, unless we believe, that God will punish false swearing with more severity than a simple lie,

OATHS.

lie, or breach of promise; for which belief there are the following reasons:

1. Perjury is a sin of greater deliberation. The Juror has, I believe, in fact, the thoughts of God and of religion upon his mind at the time; at least, there are very few who can shake them off entirely. He offends, therefore, if he do offend, with a high hand, in the face, that is, and in defiance of the sanctions of religion. His offence implies a disbelief or contempt of God's knowledge, power, and justice; which cannot be said of a lie, where there is nothing to carry the mind to any reflection upon the Deity, or the divine attributes at all.

2. Perjury violates a superior confidence. Mankind must trust to one another; and they have nothing better to trust to than one another's oath. Hence legal adjudications, which govern and affect every right and interest on this side the grave, of necessity proceed and depend upon oaths. Perjury, therefore, in its general consequence, strikes at the security of reputation, property, and even of life itself. A lie cannot do the same mischief, because the same credit is not given to it.*

---

* Except, indeed, where a Quaker's or Moravian's affirmation is accepted in the place of an oath; in which case, a lie partakes, so far as this reason extends, of the nature and guilt of perjury.

3. God directed the *Israelites* to swear by his name;* and was pleased, "in order to show the immutability of "his own council," † to confirm his covenant with that people by an oath: neither of which it is probable he would have done, had he not intended to represent oaths, as having some meaning and effect, beyond the obligation of a bare promise; which effect must be owing to the severer punishment, with which he will vindicate the authority of oaths.

V. Promissory oaths are *not binding*, where the promise itself would not be so: for the several cases of which, see the Chapter of Promises.

VI. As oaths are designed for the security of the imposer, it is manifest they must be performed, and *interpreted*, in the sense in which the imposer intends them; otherwise, they afford no security to *him*. And this is the meaning and reason of the rule, "jurare in animum imponentis;" which rule, the reader is desired to carry along with him, whilst we proceed to consider certain particular oaths, which are, either of greater importance, or more likely to fall in our way than others.

* Deut. vi. 13. x. 20. † Heb. vi. 17.

CHAP.

CHAP. XVII.

OATH IN EVIDENCE.

THE witnefs fwears, " to fpeak the truth, the whole " truth, and nothing but the truth, touching the " matter in queftion."

Upon which it may be obferved, that the defigned concealment of any truth, which relates to the matter in agitation, is as much a violation of the oath, as to teftify a pofitive falfehood; and this, whether the witnefs be interrogated to that particular point or not. For when the perfon to be examined is fworn upon a *voir dire*, that is, in order to enquire, whether he ought to be admitted to give evidence in the caufe at all, the form runs thus, " You " fhall true anfwer make to all fuch queftions as fhall be " afked you;" but, when he comes to be fworn in chief, he fwears, " to fpeak the whole truth," without reftraining it, as before, to the queftions that fhall be afked: which difference fhews, that the law intends, in this latter cafe, to require of the witnefs, that he give a complete and unreferved account of what he knows of the fubject of the trial, whether the queftions propofed to him reach the extent of his knowledge or not. So that if it be enquired of the witnefs afterwards, why he did not inform the court fo and fo, it is no fufficient, though a very common anfwer to fay, " becaufe it was never afked me."

I know but one exception to this rule; which is, when a full difcovery of the truth tends to accufe the witnefs himfelf of fome legal crime. The law of *England* conftrains no man to become his own accufer; confequently, impofes the oath of teftimony with this tacit refervation. But the exception muft be confined to *legal* crimes. A point of honour, of delicacy, or of reputation, may make a witnefs backward to difclofe fome circumftance with which he is acquainted; but is no excufe for concealment, unlefs it could be fhewn, that the law which impofes the oath, intended to allow this indulgence to fuch motives. The exception is alfo withdrawn by compact between the magiftrate and the witnefs, when an accomplice is admitted to give evidence againft the partners of his crime.

Tendernefs to the prifoner is a fpecious apology for concealment, but no juft excufe; for if this plea be thought fufficient, it takes the adminiftration of penal juftice out of the hands of judges and juries, and makes it depend upon the temper of profecutors and witneffes.

Queftions may be afked which are irrelative to the caufe, which affect the witnefs himfelf, or fome third perfon; in which, and in all cafes, where the witnefs doubts of the pertinency and propriety of the queftion, he ought to refer his doubts to the court. The anfwer of the court, in relaxation of the oath, is authority enough to the witnefs: for the law which impofes the oath may remit what it will of the obligation; and it belongs to the court to declare

clare what the mind of the law is. Neverthelefs, it cannot be faid univerfally, that the anfwer of the court is conclufive upon the confcience of the witnefs: for his obligation depends upon what he apprehended, at the time of taking the oath, to be the defign of the law in impofing it; and no after requifition or explanation by the court, can carry the obligation beyond that.

CHAP. XVIII.

OATH OF ALLEGIANCE.

"I DO fincerely promife, and fwear, that I will be faithful and bear true allegiance to his Majefty King GEORGE." Formerly the oath of allegiance ran thus: " I do promife to be true and faithful to the King " and his heirs, and truth and faith to bear, of life, and " limb, and terrene honour; and not to know or hear of " any ill or damage intended him, without defending him " therefrom:" and was altered at the Revolution to the prefent form. So that the prefent oath is a relaxation of the old one. And as the oath was intended to afcertain, not fo much the extent of the fubject's obedience, as to whom it was due, the legiflature feems to have wrapped up its meaning upon the former point, in a word purpofely made choice of for its general and indeterminate fignification.

It will be most convenient to consider, first, what the oath excludes, as inconsistent with it; secondly, what it permits.

1. The oath excludes all intention to support the claim or pretensions of any other person or persons than the reigning sovereign, to the crown and government. A *Jacobite*, who is persuaded of the *Pretender*'s right to the crown, and who moreover designs to join with the adherents of that cause, to assert this right, whenever a proper opportunity, with a reasonable prospect of success, presents itself, cannot take the oath of allegiance; or, if he could, the oath of abjuration follows, which contains an express renunciation of all opinions in favour of the claim of the exiled family.

2. The oath excludes all design, at the time, of attempting to depose the reigning prince, for any reason whatever. Let the justice of the Revolution be what it would, no honest man could have taken even the present oath of allegiance to *James the Second*, who entertained at the time of taking it a design of joining in the measures that were entered into to dethrone him.

3. The oath forbids the taking up arms against the reigning prince, with views of private advancement, or from motives of personal resentment or dislike. It is possible to happen in this, what frequently happens in despotic governments, that an ambitious general, at the head of the military force

force of the nation, by a conjuncture of fortunate circumstances, and a great ascendency over the minds of the soldiery, might depose the prince upon the throne, and make way to it for himself, or for some creature of his own. A person in this situation would be withheld from such an attempt by the oath of allegiance, if he paid any regard to it. If there were any who engaged in the rebellion of the year forty-five, with the expectation of titles, estates, or preferment; or because they were disappointed, and thought themselves neglected and ill used at court; or because they entertained a family animosity, or personal resentment against the king, the favourite, or the minister; if any were induced to take up arms by these motives, they added to the many crimes of an unprovoked rebellion, that of wilful and corrupt perjury. If the same motives determined others lately to connect themselves with the American opposition; their part in it was chargeable with perfidy and falsehood to their oath, whatever was the justice of the opposition itself, or however well founded their particular complaint might be of private injuries.

We are next to consider what the oath of allegiance permits, or does not require.

1. It permits resistance to the king, when his ill behaviour, or imbecility is such, as to make resistance beneficial to the community. It may fairly be presumed, that the convention Parliament, which introduced the oath in its present form, did not intend, by imposing it, to exclude

all resistance; since the members of that legislature had many of them recently taken up arms against *James the Second;* and the very authority by which they sat together, was itself the effect of a successful opposition to an acknowledged sovereign. Some resistance, therefore, was meant to be allowed; and if any, it must be that which has the public interest for its object.

2. The oath does not require obedience to such commands of the king, as are unauthorised by law. No such obedience is implied by the terms of the oath: the *fidelity* there promised, is intended of fidelity in opposition to his enemies, and not in opposition to law; and *allegiance*, at the utmost, signifies only obedience to lawful commands. Therefore, if the king should issue a proclamation, levying money, or imposing any service or restraint upon the subject, beyond what the crown is impowered by law to enjoin, there would exist no sort of obligation to obey such a proclamation, in consequence of having taken the oath of allegiance.

3. The oath does not require that we should continue our allegiance to the king, after he is actually and absolutely deposed, driven into exile, carried away captive, or otherwise rendered incapable of exercising the regal office. The promise of allegiance implies, and is understood by all parties to suppose, that the person to whom the promise is made continues king; continues, that is, to exercise the power, and afford the protection, which belongs to the

office

office of king: for it is the poffeffion of this power, which makes fuch a particular perfon the object of the oath; without it, why fhould I fwear allegiance to this man, rather than to any other man in the kingdom? Befides, the contrary doctrine is burthened with this confequence, that every conqueft, revolution of government, or difafter which befalls the perfon of the prince, muft be followed by public and perpetual anarchy.

CHAP. XIX.

OATH AGAINST BRIBERY IN THE ELECTION OF MEMBERS OF PARLIAMENT.

" I DO fwear, I have not received, or had, by myfelf, or any perfon whatfoever, in truft for me, or for my ufe and benefit, directly or indirectly, any fum or fums of money, office, place, or employment, gift, or reward, or any promife or fecurity, for any money, office, employment, or gift, in order to give my vote at this election."

The feveral contrivances to evade this oath, fuch as the electors accepting money under colour of borrowing, and giving

giving a promissory note, or other security for it, which is cancelled after the election; receiving money from a stranger, or a person in disguise, or out of a drawer, or purse, left open for the purpose; or promises of money to be paid after the election; or stipulating for a place, living, or other private advantage of any kind; if they escape the legal penalties of perjury, incur the moral guilt: for they are manifestly within the mischief and design of the statute which imposes the oath; and within the terms indeed of the oath itself; for the word " indirectly " is inserted on purpose to comprehend such cases as these.

CHAP. XX.

OATH AGAINST SIMONY.

FROM an imaginary resemblance between the purchase of a benefice and *Simon Magus*'s attempt to purchase the gift of the Holy Ghost, *Acts* viii. 19, the obtaining of a presentation by pecuniary considerations has been called *Simony*.

The sale of advowsons is inseparable from the right of private patronage; as patronage would otherwise devolve to the most indigent, and for that reason, the most improper hands it could be placed in. Nor did the law ever intend to prohibit the passing of advowsons from one patron to another; but to restrain the patron, who possesses the right of presenting at the vacancy, from being influenced, in the choice of his presentee, by a bribe, or benefit to himself. It is the same distinction with that which obtains in a freeholder's vote for his representative in parliament. The right of voting, that is the freehold, to which the right pertains, may be bought and sold, as freely as any other property; but the exercise of that right, the vote itself, may not be purchased, or influenced by money.

For this purpose, the law imposes upon the presentee, who is generally concerned in the simony, if there be any, the following oath: " I do swear, that I have made no
" *simoniacal* payment, contract, or promise, directly or in-
" directly, by myself, or by any other to my knowledge,
" or with my consent, to any person or persons whatso-
" ever, for or concerning the procuring and obtaining of
" this ecclesiastical place, &c. nor will, at any time here-
" after, perform, or satisfy, any such kind of payment,
" contract, or promise, made by any other without my
" knowledge or consent: So help me God, through Jesus
" Christ."

It is extraordinary, that bishop *Gibson* should have thought this oath to be against all promises whatsoever, when the terms of the oath expresly restrain it to *simo-*
niacal

niacal promises; and the law alone must pronounce what promises, as well as what payments, and contracts, are simoniacal, and consequently, come within the oath; and what are not so.

Now the law adjudges to be simony,

1. All payments, contracts, or promises, made by any person, for a benefice already vacant. The advowson of a void turn, by law cannot be transferred from one patron to another: therefore, if the void turn be procured by money, it must be by a pecuniary influence upon the then subsisting patron in the choice of his presentee; which is the very practice the law condemns.

2. A clergyman's purchasing of the next turn of a benefice for himself, " directly or indirectly," that is, by himself, or by another person with his money. It does not appear, that the law prohibits a clergyman from purchasing the perpetuity of a patronage, more than any other person; but purchasing the perpetuity, and forthwith selling it again, with a reservation of the next turn, and with no other design than to possess himself of the next turn, is in *fraudem legis*, and inconsistent with the oath.

3. The procuring of a piece of preferment, by ceding to the patron, any rights, or probable rights, belonging to it. This is simony of the worst kind; for it is not only buying preferment, but robbing your successor to pay for it.

4. Promises

4. Promises to the patron of a portion of the profit, of a remission of tythes and dues, or other advantage out of the produce of the benefice: which kind of compact is a pernicious condescension in the clergy, independent of the oath; for it tends to introduce a practice, which may very soon become general, of giving the revenues of churches to the lay patrons, and supplying the duty by indigent stipendaries.

5. General bonds of resignation, that is, bonds to resign upon demand.

I doubt not but that the oath is binding upon the consciences of those who take it, though I question much the expediency of requiring it. It is very fit to debar public patrons, such as the king, the lord chancellor, bishops, ecclesiastical corporations, and the like, from this kind of traffic; because, from them may be expected some regard to the qualifications of the persons whom they promote. But the oath lays a snare for the integrity of the clergy; and I do not perceive, that the requiring of it, in cases of private patronage, produces any good effect, sufficient to compensate for this danger.

Where advowsons are holden along with manors, or other principal estates, it would be an easy regulation to forbid that they should ever hereafter be separated; and would, at least, keep church preferment out of the hands of brokers.

CHAP. XXI.

OATHS TO OBSERVE LOCAL STATUTES.

MEMBERS of colleges in the univerfities, and of other ancient foundations, are required to fwear to the obfervance of their refpective ftatutes; which obfervance is become in fome cafes unlawful, in others impracticable, in others ufelefs, in others inconvenient.

Unlawful directions are countermanded by the authority which made them unlawful.

Impracticable directions are difpenfed with by the neceffity of the cafe.

The only queftion is, how far the members of thefe focieties may take upon themfelves to judge of the *inconveniency* of any particular direction, and make that a reafon for laying afide the obfervation of it.

The *animus imponentis*, which is the meafure of the juror's duty, feems to be fatisfied, when nothing is omitted, but what, from fome change in the reafon and circumftances

under

under which it was prescribed, it may fairly be presumed that the founder himself would have dispensed with.

To bring a case within this rule, the *inconveniency* must,

1. Be manifest; concerning which there is no doubt.

2. It must arise from some change in the circumstances of the institution; for let the inconveniency be what it will, if it existed at the time of the foundation, it must be presumed, that the founder did not deem the avoiding of it of sufficient importance to alter his plan.

3. It must not only be inconvenient in the general, for so may the institution itself be, but prejudicial to the particular end proposed by the institution; for it is this last circumstance which proves that the founder would have dispensed with it in pursuance of his own purpose.

The statutes of some colleges forbid the speaking of any language but *Latin*, within the walls of the college; direct that a certain number, and not fewer than that number, be allowed the use of an apartment amongst them; that so many hours of each day be employed in public exercises, lectures, or disputations; and some other articles of discipline adapted to the tender years of the students, who in former times resorted to universities. Were colleges to retain such rules, nobody now-a-days would come near them. They are laid aside therefore, though parts of the statutes, and as such included within the oath, not merely because they are inconvenient, but because there is sufficient reason to believe, that the founders themselves would have dispensed with them, as subversive of their own designs.

CHAP. XXII.

SUBSCRIPTION TO ARTICLES OF RELIGION.

SUBSCRIPTION to Articles of Religion, though no more than a *declaration* of the subscriber's assent, may properly enough be considered in connection with the subject of oaths, because it is governed by the same rule of interpretation:

Which rule is the *animus imponentis*.

The enquiry therefore concerning subscription will be, *quis imposuit, et quo animo*.

The bishop who receives the subscription, is not the imposer, any more than the cryer of a court, who administers the oath to the jury and witnesses, is the person that imposes it; nor consequently is the private opinion or interpretation of the bishop of any signification to the subscriber, one way or other.

The compilers of the thirty-nine articles are not to be considered as the imposers of subscription, any more than the framer or drawer up of a law is the person that enacts it.

The legislature of the 13th *Eliz.* is the imposer, whose intention the subscriber is bound to satisfy.

They who contend, that nothing less can justify subscription to the thirty-nine articles, than the actual belief of each and every separate proposition contained in them, must suppose, that the legislature expected the consent of ten thousand men, and that in perpetual succession, not to one controverted proposition, but to many hundreds. It is difficult to conceive how this could be expected by any, who observed the incurable diversity of human opinion upon all subjects short of demonstration.

If the authors of the law did not intend this, what did they intend?

They intended to exclude from offices in the church,

1. All abettors of popery.

2. Anabaptists, who were at that time a powerful party on the continent.

3. The Puritans, who were hostile to the episcopal constitution; and in general the members of such leading sects or foreign establishments, as threatened to overthrow our own.

Whoever finds himself comprehended within these descriptions, ought not to subscribe.

During the present state of ecclesiastical patronage, in which private individuals are permitted to impose teachers upon parishes, with which they are often little or not at all connected, some limitation of the patron's choice may be necessary, to prevent unedifying contentions between neighbouring teachers, or between the teachers and their respective congregations. But this danger, if it exist, may be provided against with equal effect, by converting the articles of faith into articles of peace.

CHAP. XXIII.

WILLS.

THE fundamental question upon this subject is, whether Wills are of natural or of adventitious right? that is, whether the right of directing the disposition of property after his death belongs to a man in a state of nature, and by the law of nature, or whether it be given him entirely by the positive regulations of the country he lives in?

The immediate produce of each man's personal labour, as the tools, weapons, and utensils, which he manufactures, the tent or hut he builds, and perhaps the flocks and herds which he breeds and rears, are as much his own as the labour was which he employed upon them, that is, are his property naturally and absolutely; and consequently he may give or leave them to whom he pleases, there being nothing to limit the continuance of his right, or to restrain the alienation of it.

But every other species of property, especially property in land, stands upon a different foundation.

We have seen in the Chapter upon Property, that, in a state of nature, a man's right to a particular spot of ground arises from his using it, and wanting it; consequently ceases with the use and want; so that at his death the estate reverts to the community, without any regard to the last owner's will, or even any preference of his family, farther than as they become the first occupiers after him, and succeed to the same want and use.

Moreover, as natural rights cannot, like rights created by act of parliament, expire at the end of a certain number of years; if the testator have a right by the law of nature, to dispose of his property one moment after his death, he has the same right to direct the disposition of it, for a million of ages after him; which is absurd.

The ancient apprehensions of mankind upon the subject were conformable to this account of it: for wills have been introduced into most countries by a positive act of the state, as by the laws of *Solon* into *Greece*, by the twelve tables into *Rome*; and that, not till after a considerable progress had been made in legislation, and in the œconomy of civil life. *Tacitus* relates, that amongst the *Germans* they were disallowed; and, what is more remarkable, since the conquest, lands in this country could not be devised by will, till within little more than two hundred years ago, when this privilege was restored to the subject, by an act of parliament in the latter end of the reign of *Henry* the Eighth.

No doubt many beneficial purposes are attained by extending the owner's power over his property beyond his life,

life, and beyond his natural right. It invites to industry; it encourages marriage; it secures the dutifulness and dependency of children. But a limit must be assigned to the duration of this power. The utmost extent to which, in any case, entails are allowed by the laws of *England* to operate, is during the lives in existence at the death of the testator, and one and twenty years beyond these: after which, there are ways and means of setting them aside.

From the consideration that wills are the creatures of the municipal law which gives them their efficacy, may be deduced a determination of the question, whether the intention of the testator in an *informal* will be binding upon the conscience of those, who, by operation of law, succeed to his estate. By an *informal* will, I mean a will void in law, for want of some requisite formality, though no doubt be entertained of its meaning or authenticity: as suppose a man make his will, devising his freehold estate to his sister's son, and the will be attested by two only, instead of three subscribing witnesses; would the brother's son, who is heir at law to the testator, be bound in conscience, to resign his claim to the estate, out of deference to his uncle's intention? Or, on the contrary, would not the devisee under the will be bound, upon discovery of this flaw in it, to surrender the estate, suppose he had gained possession of it, to the heir at law?

Generally speaking, the heir at law is not bound by the intention of the testator. For the intention can signify nothing,

thing, unless the person intending have a right to govern the descent of the estate. That is the first question. Now this right the testator can only derive from the law of the land; but the law confers the right upon certain conditions, which conditions he has not complied with. Therefore, the testator can lay no claim to the power which he pretends to exercise, as he hath not entitled himself to the benefit of that law, by virtue of which alone the estate ought to attend his disposal. Consequently, the devisee under the will, who, by concealing this flaw in it, keeps possession of the estate, is in the situation of any other person, who avails himself of his neighbour's ignorance to detain from him his property. The will is so much waste paper, from the defect of right in the person who made it. Nor is this catching at an expression of law to pervert the substantial design of it, for I apprehend it to be the deliberate mind of the legislature, that no will should take effect upon real estates, unless authenticated in the precise manner which the statute describes. Had testamentary dispositions been founded in any natural right, independent of positive constitutions, I should have thought differently of this question. For then I should have considered the law, rather as refusing its assistance to enforce the right of the devisee, than as extinguishing, or working any alteration in the right itself.

And after all, I should choose to propose a case, where no consideration of pity to distress, of duty to a parent, or of gratitude

gratitude to a benefactor, interfered with the general rule of justice.

The regard due to kindred in the disposal of our fortune, (except the case of lineal kindred, which is different) arises, either from the respect we owe to the presumed intention of the ancestor from whom we received our fortunes, or from the expectations which we have encouraged. The intention of the ancestor is presumed with greater certainty, as well as entitled to more respect, the fewer degrees he is removed from us, which makes the difference in the different degrees of kindred. It may be presumed to be a father's intention and desire, that the inheritance he leaves, after it has served the turn and generation of one son, should remain a provision for the families of his other children, equally related and dear to him as the eldest. Whoever therefore, without cause, gives away his patrimony from his brother's or sister's family, is guilty not so much of an injury to them, as of ingratitude to his parent. The deference due from the possessor of a fortune to the presumed desire of his ancestor will also vary with this circumstance, whether the ancestor earned the fortune by his personal industry, acquired it by accidental successes, or only transmitted the inheritance which he received.

Where a man's fortune is acquired by himself, and he has done nothing to excite expectation, but rather has refrained from those particular attentions which tend to cherish expectation, he is perfectly disengaged from the force of the above reasons, and at liberty to leave his fortune to his friends, to charitable or public purposes, or to whom he will; the same blood, proximity of blood, and the like, are merely modes of speech, implying nothing real, nor any obligation of themselves.

There is always, however, a reason for providing for our poor relations, in preference to others who may be equally necessitous, which is, that if we do not, no body else will; mankind, by an established consent, leaving the reduced branches of good families to the bounty of their wealthy alliances.

The not making a will is a very culpable omission, where it is attended with the following effects: where it leaves daughters or younger children at the mercy of the eldest son; where it distributes a personal fortune equally amongst the children, although there be no equality in their exigencies or situations; where it leaves an opening for litigation; or lastly, and principally, where it defrauds creditors; for by a defect in our laws, which has been long and strangely overlooked, real estates are not subject to the payment of debts by simple contract, unless made so by will; although credit is in fact generally given to the possession of such estates. He therefore, who neglects to make the necessary appointments for the payment of his debts, as far as his effects extend, sins, as it has been justly said, in his grave; and, if he omits this on purpose to defeat the
demands

demands of his creditors, he dies with a deliberate fraud in his heart.

Anciently, when any one died without a will, the bishop of the diocese took possession of his personal fortune, in order to dispose of it for the benefit of his soul, that is, to pious or charitable uses. It became necessary therefore, that the bishop should be satisfied of the authenticity of the will, when there was any, before he resigned the right he had to take possession of the dead man's fortune, in case of intestacy. In this way, wills, and controversies relating to wills, came within the cognizance of ecclesiastical courts; under the jurisdiction of which, wills of personals (the only wills that were made formerly) still continue, though, in truth, no more now-a-days connected with religion, than any other instruments of conveyance. This is a peculiarity in the English law.

Succession to intestates must be regulated by positive rules of law, there being no principle of natural justice whereby to ascertain the proportion of the different claimants; not to mention that the claim itself, especially of collateral kindred, seems to have little foundation in the law of nature. These regulations should be guided by the duty and presumed inclination of the deceased, so far as these considerations can be consulted by general rules. The statutes of *Charles* the Second, commonly called the statutes of distribution, which adopt the rule of the *Roman* law in the distribution of personals, are sufficiently equitable. They assign

assign one third to the widow, and two thirds to the children; in case of no children, one half to the widow, and the other half to the next of kin; where neither widow nor lineal descendants survive, the whole to the next of kin, and to be equally divided amongst kindred of equal degrees; without distinction of whole blood and half blood, or of consanguinity by the father's or mother's side.

The descent of real estates, of houses, that is, and land, having been settled in more remote and in ruder times, is less reasonable. There never can be much to complain of in a rule, which every person may avoid by so easy a provision as that of making his will; otherwise, our law in this respect is chargeable with some flagrant absurdities; such as that an estate shall in no wise go to the brother or sister of the half blood, though it came to the deceased from the common parent; that it shall go to the remotest relation the intestate has in the world, rather than to his own father or mother, or even be forfeited for want of an heir, though both parents survive; that the most distant paternal relation shall be preferred to an uncle or own cousin by the mother's side, notwithstanding the estate was purchased and acquired by the intestate himself.

Land not being so divisible as money, may be a reason for making a difference in the course of inheritance; but there ought to be no difference but what is founded upon that reason. The *Roman* law made none.

BOOK

BOOK III.

PART II.

OF RELATIVE DUTIES WHICH ARE INDETERMINATE.

CHAP. I.

CHARITY.

I USE the term Charity neither in the common sense of bounty to the poor, nor in St. *Paul*'s sense of benevolence to all mankind, but I apply it at present, in a sense more commodious to my purpose, to signify *the promoting the happiness of our inferiors.*

Charity in this sense I take to be the principal province of virtue and religion: for whilst worldly prudence will direct our behaviour towards our superiors, and politeness towards our equals, there is little beside the consideration of duty, or an habitual humanity which comes into the place of consideration, to produce a proper conduct towards those who are beneath us, and dependent upon us.

There are three principal methods of promoting the happiness of our inferiors:

1. By the treatment of our domestics and dependants.

2. By professional assistance.

3. By pecuniary bounty.

CHAP. II.

CHARITY.

THE TREATMENT OF OUR DOMESTICS AND DEPENDANTS.

A PARTY of friends setting out together upon a journey, soon find it to be the best for all sides, that while they are upon the road, one of the company should wait upon the rest; another ride forward to seek out lodging and entertainment; a third carry the portmanteau; a fourth take charge of the horses; a fifth bear the purse, conduct and direct the rout: not forgetting however, that as they were equal and independent when they set out, so they are all to return to a level again at their journey's end. The same regard and respect; the same forbearance, lenity, and tenderness in using their service; the same mildness in delivering commands; the same study to make their journey comfortable and agreeable to them, which he, whose lot it was to direct the rest, would in common decency think himself bound to observe towards them; ought we to shew to those, who, in the casting of the parts of human society, happen to be placed within our power, or to depend upon us.

Another reflection of a like tendency with the former is, that our obligation to them is much greater than theirs to us. It is a mistake to suppose, that the rich man maintains his servants, tradesmen, tenants, and labourers: the truth is, they maintain him. It is their industry which supplies his table, furnishes his wardrobe, builds his houses, adorns his equipage, provides his amusements. It is not his estate, but the labour employed upon it, that pays his rent. All that he does, is to distribute what others produce; which is the least part of the business.

Nor do I perceive any foundation for an opinion, which is often handed round in genteel company, that good usage is thrown away upon low and ordinary minds; that they are insensible of kindness, and incapable of gratitude. If by "low and ordinary minds" are meant the minds of men in low and ordinary stations, they seem to be affected by benefits in the same way that all others are; and to be no less ready to requite them: and it would be a very unaccountable law of nature, if it were otherwise.

Whatever uneasiness we occasion to our domestics, which neither promotes our service, nor answers the just ends of punishment, is manifestly wrong; were it only upon the general principle of diminishing the sum of human happiness.

By which rule we are forbidden,

1. To injoin unnecessary labour or confinement, from the mere love and wantonness of domination.

2. To insult them by harsh, scornful, or opprobrious language.

3. To refuse them any harmless pleasures.

And by the same principle are also forbidden causeless or immoderate anger, habitual peevishness, and groundless suspicion.

CHAP. III.

SLAVERY.

THE prohibitions of the last chapter extend to the treatment of slaves, being founded upon a principle independent of the contract between masters and servants.

I define slavery to be " an obligation to labour for the " benefit of the master, without the contract or consent of " the servant."

This obligation may arise, consistently with the law of nature, from three causes.

1. From crimes.

2. From captivity.

3. From debt.

In the first case, the continuance of the slavery, as of any other punishment, ought to be proportioned to the crime; in the second and third cases, it ought to cease, as soon as the demand of the injured nation or private creditor is satisfied.

The slave-trade upon the coast of Africa is not excused by these principles. When slaves are in that country brought to market, no questions, I believe, are asked about the origin or justice of the vendor's title. It may be presumed therefore, that this title is not always, if it be ever, founded in any of the causes above assigned.

But defect of right in the first purchase is the least crime, with which this traffic is chargeable. The natives are excited to war and mutual depredation, for the sake of supplying their contracts, or furnishing the market with slaves. With this the wickedness begins: the slaves, torn away from parents, wives, children, from their friends and companions, their fields and flocks, their home and country, are transported to the European settlements in America, with no other accommodation on shipboard, than what is provided for brutes. This is the second stage of cruelty: from which the miserable exiles are delivered only to be placed, and that for life, in subjection to a dominion and system of laws, the most merciless and tyrannical that ever were tolerated upon the face of the earth: and from all that can be learned by the accounts of people upon the spot, the inordinate authority, which the plantation laws confer upon the slave-holder, is exercised, by the *English* slave-holder especially, with rigor and brutality.

But *necessity* is pretended; the name under which all enormities are attempted to be excused. And after all, what is the necessity? It has never been proved that the land could not be cultivated there, as it is here, by hired fervants. It is faid that it could not be cultivated with quite the fame conveniency and cheapnefs, as by the labour of flaves: by which means, a pound of fugar, which the planter now fells for fixpence, could not be afforded under fixpence halfpenny—and this is the *neceffity*.

The great revolution which has taken place in the Weftern world may probably conduce, and who knows but that it was defigned, to accelerate the fall of this abominable tyranny: and now that this conteft, and the paffions which attend it are no more, there may fucceed perhaps a feafon for reflecting, whether a legiflature, which had fo long lent its affiftance to the fupport of an inftitution replete with human mifery, was fit to be trufted with an empire, the moft extenfive that ever obtained in any age or quarter of the world.

Slavery was a part of the civil conftitution of moft countries, when Chriftianity appeared; yet no paffage is to be found in the Chriftian fcriptures, by which it is condemned or prohibited. This is true; for Chriftianity, foliciting admiffion into all nations of the world, abftained, as behoved it, from intermeddling with the civil inftitutions of any. But does it follow from the filence of fcripture concerning them, that all the civil inftitutions which then prevailed, were right? or that the bad fhould not be exchanged for better?

Beside this, the discharging slaves from all obligation to obey their masters, which is the consequence of pronouncing slavery to be unlawful, would have had no better effect, than to let loose one half of mankind upon the other. Slaves would have been tempted to embrace a religion, which asserted their right to freedom. Masters would hardly have been persuaded to consent to claims founded upon such authority. The most calamitous of all contests, a *bellum servile*, might probably have ensued, to the reproach, if not the extinction of the Christian name.

The truth is, the emancipation of slaves should be gradual; and be carried on by provisions of law, and under the protection of civil government. Christianity can only operate as an alterative. By the mild diffusion of its light and influence, the minds of men are insensibly prepared to perceive and correct the enormities, which folly, or wickedness, or accident, have introduced into their public establishments. In this way the *Greek* and *Roman* slavery, and since these, the feudal tyranny, has declined before it. And we trust that, as the knowledge and authority of the same religion advance in the world, they will banish what remains of this odious institution.

CHAP.

CHAP. IV.

CHARITY.

PROFESSIONAL ASSISTANCE.

THIS kind of beneficence is chiefly to be expected from members of the legiflature, magiftrates, medical, legal, and facerdotal profeffions.

1. The care of the poor ought to be the principal object of all laws, for this plain reafon, that the rich are able to take care of themfelves.

Much has been, and more might be done, by the laws of this country, towards the relief of the impotent, and the protection and encouragement of the induftrious poor. Whoever applies himfelf to collect obfervations upon the ftate and operation of the poor laws, and to contrive remedies for the imperfections and abufes which he obferves, and digefts thefe remedies into acts of parliament, and conducts them by argument or influence through the two branches of the legiflature, or communicates his ideas to thofe, who are more likely to carry them into effect; deferves well of a clafs of the community fo numerous, that their

their happiness makes no inconsiderable part of the whole. The study and activity thus employed is charity, in the most meritorious sense of the word.

2. The care of the poor is entrusted in the first instance to overseers and contractors, who have an interest in opposition to that of the poor, inasmuch as whatever they allow them comes in part out of their own pocket. For this reason, the law has deposited with justices of the peace, a power of superintendence and control; and the judicious interposition of this power is a most useful exertion of charity, and ofttimes within the ability of those, who have no other way of serving their generation. A country gentleman, of very moderate education, and who has little to spare from his fortune, by learning so much of the poor law as is to be found in Dr. *Burn's Justice*, and furnishing himself with a knowledge of the prices of labour and provision, so as to be able to estimate the exigencies of a family, and what is to be expected from their industry, may, in this way, place out the one talent committed to him, to great account.

3. Of all private professions, that of medicine puts it in a man's power to do the most good at the least expence. Health, which is precious to all, is to the poor invaluable; and their complaints, as agues, rheumatisms, &c. are often such as yield to medicine. And with respect to the expence, drugs at first hand cost little, and advice nothing, where it is only bestowed upon those who could not afford to pay for it.

4. The rights of the poor are not so important or intricate as their contentions are violent and ruinous. A Lawyer or Attorney, of tolerable knowledge in his profession, has commonly judgment enough to adjust these disputes, with all the effect, and without the expence, of a law suit; and he may be said to give a poor man twenty pounds, who prevents his throwing it away upon law. A *legal* man, whether of the profession or not, who, together with a spirit of conciliation, possesses the confidence of his neighbourhood, will be much resorted to for this purpose, especially since the great increase of costs has produced a general dread of going to law.

Nor is this line of beneficence confined to *arbitration*. Seasonable counsel, coming with the weight which the reputation of the adviser gives it, will often keep or extricate the rash and uninformed out of great difficulties.

I know not a more exalted charity than that which presents a shield against the rapacity or persecution of a tyrant.

5. Betwixt argument and authority (I mean that authority which flows from voluntary respect, and attends upon sanctity and disinterestedness of character) something may be done amongst the lower orders of mankind, towards the regulation of their conduct, and the satisfaction of their thoughts. This office belongs to the ministers of religion; or rather whoever undertakes it becomes a mi-

nifter of religion. The inferior clergy, who are nearly upon a level with the common fort of their parifhioners, and who on that account gain an eafier admiffion to their fociety and confidence, have in this refpect more in their power than their fuperiors: the difcreet ufe of this power conftitutes one of the moft refpectable functions of human nature.

CHAP. V.

CHARITY.

PECUNIARY BOUNTY.

I. *The obligation to beftow relief upon the poor.*
II. *The manner of beftowing it.*
III. *The pretences by which men excufe themfelves from it.*

I. *The obligation to beftow relief upon the poor.*

THEY who rank pity amongft the original impulfes of our nature rightly contend, that when it prompts us to the relief of human mifery, it indicates fufficiently the divine intention, and our duty. Indeed, the fame conclufion is deducible from the exiftence of the paffion, whatever account be given of its origin. Whether it be an inftinct or a habit, it is in fact a property of our nature, which

which God appointed: and the final cause, for which it was appointed, is to afford to the miserable, in the compassion of their fellow creatures, a remedy for those inequalities and distresses, which God foresaw that many must be exposed to, under every general rule for the distribution of property.

Beside this, the poor have a claim founded in the law of nature, which may be thus explained. All things were originally common. No one being able to produce a charter from Heaven, had any better title to a particular possession, than his next neighbour. There were reasons for mankind's agreeing upon a separation of this common fund; and God for these reasons is presumed to have ratified it. But this separation was made and consented to, upon the expectation and condition, that every one should have left a sufficiency for his subsistence, or the means of procuring it: and as no fixed laws for the regulation of property can be so contrived, as to provide for the relief of every case and distress which may arise, these cases and distresses, when their right and share in the common stock was given up or taken from them, were supposed to be left to the voluntary bounty of those, who might be acquainted with the exigencies of their situation, and in the way of affording assistance. And therefore, when the partition of property is rigidly maintained against the claims of indigence and distress, it is maintained in opposition to the intention of those who made it, and to *his*, who is the Supreme Proprietor of every thing, and who has filled the world with plenteousness for the sustentation and comfort of all whom he sends into it.

The Christian scriptures are more copious and explicit upon this duty than almost any other. The description which Christ hath left us of the proceedings of the last day establishes the obligation of bounty, beyond controversy. "When the Son of man shall come in his glory, "and all the holy angels with him, then shall he sit upon "the throne of his glory, and before him shall be gathered "all nations; and he shall separate them one from ano- "ther.—Then shall the king say unto them on his right "hand, Come ye blessed of my father, inherit the king- "dom prepared for you from the foundation of the world: "For I was an hungred, and ye gave me meat: I was "thirsty, and ye gave me drink: I was a stranger, and ye "took me in: naked, and ye clothed me: I was sick, and "ye visited me: I was in prison, and ye came unto me.— "And inasmuch as ye have done it to one of the least "of these my brethren, ye have done it unto me."* It is not necessary to understand this passage as a literal account of what will actually pass on that day. Supposing it only a scenical description of the rules and principles, by which the Supreme Arbiter of our destiny will regulate his decisions, it conveys the same lesson to us; it equally demonstrates of how great value and importance these duties in the sight of God are, and what stress will be laid upon them. The Apostles also describe this virtue as propitiating

* Matt. xxv. 31.

ing the divine favour in an eminent degree. And thefe recommendations have produced their effect. It does not appear that, before the times of Chriftianity, an infirmary, hofpital, or public charity of any kind, exifted in the world; whereas, moft countries in Chriftendom have long abounded with thefe inftitutions. To which may be added, that a fpirit of private liberality feems to flourifh amidft the decay of many other virtues: not to mention the legal provifion for the poor, which obtains in this country, and which was unknown and unthought of by the moft polifhed nations of antiquity.

St. Paul adds upon the fubject an excellent direction; and which is practicable by all who have any thing to give. "Upon the firft day of the week (or any other ftated "time) let every one of you lay by in ftore, as God hath "profpered him." By which I underftand St. Paul to recommend, what is the very thing wanting with moft men, *the being charitable upon a plan;* that is, from a deliberate comparifon of our fortunes with the reafonable expences and expectations of our families, to compute what we can fpare, and to lay by fo much for charitable purpofes, in fome mode or other. The *mode* will be a confideration afterwards.

The effect, which Chriftianity produced upon fome of its firft converts was fuch as might be looked for from a divine religion coming with full force and miraculous evidence upon the confciences of mankind. It overwhelmed

whelmed all worldly confiderations in the expectation of a more important exiftence. " And the multitude of them "that believed were of one heart and of one foul; neither "faid any of them that aught of the things, which he "poffeffed, was his own; but they had all things in com-"mon.—Neither was there any among them that lacked; "for as many as were poffeffors of lands or houfes fold "them, and brought the prices of the things that were "fold, and laid them down, at the Apoftles feet; and "diftribution was made unto every man, according as he "had need." Acts iv. 32.

Neverthelefs, this community of goods, however it manifefted the fincere zeal of the primitive Chriftians, is no precedent for our imitation. It was confined to the church at *Jerufalem;* continued not long there; was never enjoined upon any (Acts. v. 4); and, although it might fuit with the particular circumftances of a fmall and felect fociety, is altogether impracticable in a large and mixed community.

The conduct of the Apoftles upon the occafion deferves to be noticed. Their followers laid down their fortunes at their feet: but fo far were they from taking advantage of this unlimited confidence to enrich themfelves or eftablifh their authority, that they foon after got rid of this bufinefs, as inconfiftent with the main object of their miffion, and transferred the cuftody and management of the

public

public fund to deacons, elected to that office by the people at large. (Acts vi.)

II. *The manner of beſtowing bounty—or the different kinds of charity.*

Every queſtion between the different kinds of charity ſuppoſes the ſum beſtowed to be the ſame.

There are three kinds of charity which prefer a claim to attention.

The firſt, and in my judgment one of the beſt, is to give ſtated and conſiderable ſums, by way of penſion or annuity, to individuals or families, with whoſe behaviour and diſtreſs we ourſelves are acquainted. When I ſpeak of *conſiderable* ſums, I mean only, that five pounds, or any other ſum, given at once, or divided amongſt five or fewer families, will do more good than the ſame ſum diſtributed amongſt a greater number in ſhillings or half crowns; and that, becauſe it is more likely to be properly applied by the perſons who receive it. A poor fellow, who can find no better uſe for a ſhilling than to drink his benefactor's health, and purchaſe half an hour's recreation for himſelf, would hardly break into a guinea for any ſuch purpoſe, or be ſo improvident, as not to lay it by for an occaſion of importance, for his rent, his cloathing, fuel, or ſtock of winter's proviſion. It is a ſtill greater recommendation of this kind of charity, that penſions and annuities, which are paid regularly, and can be expected at the time, are the only way by which we can prevent one part of a poor man's sufferings, the dread of want.

2. But as this kind of charity supposes that proper objects of such expensive benefactions fall within our private knowledge and observation, which does not happen to all, a second method of doing good, which is in every one's power who has the money to spare, is by subscription to public charities. Public charities admit of this argument in their favour, that your money goes farther towards attaining the end for which it is given, than it can do by any private and separate beneficence. A guinea, for example, contributed to an infirmary, becomes the means of providing one patient at least, with a physician, surgeon, apothecary, with medicine, diet, lodging, and suitable attendance; which is not the tenth part, of what the same assistance, if it could be procured at all, would cost to a sick person or family in any other situation.

3. The last, and compared with the former, the lowest exertion of benevolence, is in the relief of beggars. Nevertheless, I by no means approve the indiscriminate rejection of all who implore our alms in this way. Some may perish by such a conduct. Men are sometimes overtaken by distress, for which all other relief would come too late. Beside which, resolutions of this kind compel us to offer such violence to our humanity, as may go near, in a little while, to suffocate the principle itself; which is a very

serious

ferious confideration. A good man, if he do not furrender himfelf to his feelings without referve, will at leaft lend an ear to importunities which come accompanied with outward atteftations of diftrefs, and after a patient hearing of the complaint, will direct himfelf by the circumftances and credibility of the account that he receives.

There are other fpecies of charity well contrived to make the money expended *go far;* fuch as keeping down the price of fuel or provifion, in cafe of a monopoly or temporary fcarcity, by purchafing the articles at the beft market, and retailing them at prime coft, or at a fmall lofs; or the adding a bounty to particular fpecies of labour, when the price is accidentally depreffed.

The proprietors of large eftates have it in their power to facilitate the maintenance, and thereby encourage the eftablifhment of families (which is one of the nobleft purpofes to which the rich and great can convert their endeavours) by building cottages, fplitting farms, erecting manufactures, cultivating waftes, embanking the fea, draining marfhes, and other expedients, which the fituation of each eftate points out. If the profits of thefe undertakings do not repay the expence, let the authors of them place the difference to the account of charity. It is true of almoft all fuch projects that the public is a gainer by them, whatever the owner be. And where the lofs can be fpared, this confideration is fufficient.

It is become a queftion of fome importance, under what circumftances works of charity ought to be done in private, and when they may be made public without detracting from the merit of the action: if indeed they ever may, the Author of our religion having delivered a rule upon this fubject, which feems to enjoin univerfal fecrecy. " When thou " doeft alms, let not thy left hand know what thy right " hand doth; that thy alms may be in fecret, and thy " father which feeth in fecret, himfelf fhall reward thee " openly." (Mat. vi. 3, 4.) From the preamble to this prohibition I think it, however, plain, that our Saviour's fole defign was to forbid *oftentation*, and all publifhing of good works which proceeds from that motive. " Take heed " that ye do not your alms before men, *to be feen of them;* " otherwife ye have no reward of your father, which is " in Heaven: therefore, when thou doeft thine alms, do " not found a trumpet before thee, as the hypocrites do, " in the fynagogues and in the ftreets, *that they may have* " *glory of men.* Verily I fay unto thee they have their " reward." v. 2. There are motives for the doing our alms in public befide thofe of *oftentation*; with which therefore our Saviour's rule has no concern: fuch as to teftify our approbation of fome particular fpecies of charity, and to recommend it to others; to take off the prejudice, which the want, or which is the fame thing, the fuppreffion of our name in the lift of contributors might excite againft the charity, or againft ourfelves. And, fo long as thefe motives are free from any mixture of vanity, they are in no danger of invading our Saviour's prohibition:

tion: they rather seem to comply with another direction, which he has left us: "Let your light so shine before men, "that they may see your good works, and glorify your "father which is in Heaven." If it be necessary to propose a precise distinction upon the subject, I can think of none better than the following. When our bounty is *beyond* our fortune or station, that is, when it is more than could be expected from us, our charity should be private, if privacy be practicable; when it is not more than might be expected, it may be public: for we cannot hope to influence others to the imitation of *extraordinary* generosity, and therefore want, in the former case, the only justifiable reason for making it public.

Having thus described several different exertions of charity, it may not be improper to take notice of a species of liberality, which is not *charity* in any sense of the word: I mean the giving of entertainments or liquor, for the sake of popularity; or the rewarding, treating, and maintaining, the companions of our diversions, as hunters, shooters, fishers, and the like. I do not say that this is criminal: I only say that it is not charity; and that we are not to suppose, because we *give*, and give to the *poor*, that it will stand in the place, or supersede the obligation, of more meritorious and disinterested bounty.

IV. *The pretences by which men excuse themselves from giving to the poor.*

1. "That

1. "That they have nothing to spare," i. e. nothing, for which they have not some other use; nothing, which their plan of expence, together with the savings they have resolved to lay by, will not exhaust: never reflecting whether it be in their *power*, or that it is their *duty* to retrench their expences, and contract their plan, " that they may " have to give to them that need;" or rather that this ought to have been part of their plan originally.

2. "That they have families of their own, and that " charity begins at home." The extent of this plea will be considered, when we come to explain the duty of parents.

3. "That charity does not consist in giving money, but in " benevolence, philanthropy, love to all mankind, goodness " of heart, &c." Hear St. James. " If a brother or sister " be naked, and destitute of daily food, and one of you " say unto them, depart in peace, be you warmed and filled, " notwithstanding *ye give them not those things which are need-* " *ful to the body*, what doth it profit?" (James ii. 15, 16.)

4. "That giving to the poor is not mentioned in St. " Paul's description of charity, in the thirteenth chapter of " his first Epistle to the Corinthians." This is not a description of charity, but of good-nature; and it is not necessary that every duty be mentioned in every place.

5. "That they pay the poor rates." They might as well alledge that they pay their debts; for the poor have

the fame right to that portion of a man's property, which the laws affign them, that the man himfelf has to the remainder.

6. " That they employ many poor perfons:"—for their own fake, not the poor's—otherwife it is a good plea.

7. " That the poor do not fuffer fo much as we imagine;
" that education and habit have reconciled them to the
" evils of their condition, and make them eafy under it."
Habit can never reconcile human nature to the extremities of cold, hunger, and thirft, any more than it can reconcile the hand to the touch of a red-hot iron: befides, the queftion is not, how unhappy any one is, but how much more happy we can make him.

8. " That thefe people, give them what you will, will
" never thank you, or think of you for it." In the firft place, this is not true: in the fecond place, it was not for the fake of their thanks that you relieved them.

9. " That we are fo liable to be impofed upon." If a due enquiry be made, our motive and merit is the fame: befide that, the diftrefs is generally real, whatever has been the caufe of it.

10. " That they fhould apply to their parifhes." This is not always practicable: to which we may add, that there are many requifites to a comfortable fubfiftence, which

parifh

parish relief does not always supply; and that there are some, who would suffer almost as much from receiving parish relief, as by the want of it; and lastly, that there are many modes of charity, to which this answer does not relate at all.

11. "That giving money encourages idleness and va-"grancy." This is true only of injudicious and indiscriminate generosity.

12. "That we have too many objects of charity at "home, to bestow any thing upon strangers; or that there "are other charities, which are more useful, or stand in "greater need." The value of this excuse depends entirely upon the *fact*, whether we actually relieve those neighbouring objects, and contribute to those other charities.

Beside all these excuses, pride, or prudery, or delicacy, or love of ease, keep one half of the world out of the way of observing what the other half suffer.

CHAP. VI.

RESENTMENT.

RESENTMENT may be distinguished into *anger* and *revenge*.

By *anger*, I mean the pain we suffer upon the receipt of an injury or affront, with the usual effects of that pain upon ourselves.

By *revenge*, the inflicting of pain upon the person who has injured or offended us, farther than the just ends of punishment or reparation require.

Anger prompts to revenge; but it is possible to suspend the effect, when we cannot altogether quell the principle. We are bound also to endeavour to qualify and correct the principle itself. So that our duty requires two different applications of the mind: and for that reason anger and revenge should be considered separately.

CHAP. VII.

ANGER.

"BE ye angry and sin not;" therefore all anger is not sinful: I suppose, because some degree of it, and upon some occasions, is inevitable.

It becomes sinful, or contradicts however the rule of scripture, when it is conceived upon slight and inadequate provocations, and when it continues long.

1. When it is conceived upon slight provocations; for " charity suffereth long, is not easily provoked." "Let every " man be slow to anger." Peace, long suffering, gentleness, meekness, are enumerated among the fruits of the Spirit Gal. v. 22, and compose the true Christian temper, as to this article of duty.

2. When it continues long; for " let not the sun go " down upon your wrath."

These precepts, and all reasoning indeed upon the subject, suppose the passion of anger to be within our power: and this power consists not so much in any faculty we have of appeasing our wrath at the time, for we are passive under the smart which an injury or affront occasions, and all we can then do is to prevent its breaking out into action) as in so mollifying our minds by habits of just reflexion, as to be less irritated by impressions of injury, and to be sooner pacified.

Reflexions proper for this purpose, and which may be called the *sedatives* of anger, are the following: the possibility of mistaking the motives from which the conduct that offends us proceeded; how often *our* offences have been the effect of inadvertency, when they were mistaken for malice; the inducement which prompted our adversary to act as he did, and how powerfully the same inducement has, at one time or other, operated upon ourselves; that he is suffering perhaps under a contrition, which he is ashamed, or wants opportunity, to confess; and how ungenerous it is to triumph by coldness or insult over a spirit already humbled in secret; that the returns of kindness are sweet, and that there is neither honour, nor virtue, nor use in resisting them—for some persons think themselves bound to cherish and keep alive their indignation, when they find it dying away of itself. We may remember that others have their passions, their prejudices, their favourite aims, their fears, their cautions, their interests, their sudden impulses, their varieties of apprehension, as well as we: we may recollect what hath sometimes passed in our own minds, when we have got on the wrong side of a quarrel, and imagine the same to be passing in our adversary's mind now; when we became senſible of our miſbehaviour, what palliations we perceived in it, and expected others to perceive; how we were affected by the kindneſs, and felt the ſuperiority of a generous reception and ready forgiveneſs; how perſecution revived our ſpirits with our enmity, and ſeemed to juſtify the conduct in ourſelves, which we before blamed. Add to this, the indecency of extravagant anger; how it renders us, whilſt it laſts, the ſcorn and ſport of all about us, of which it leaves us, when it ceaſes, ſenſible and aſhamed; the inconveniencies, and irretrievable miſconduct into which our iraſcibility has ſometimes betrayed us; the friendſhips it has loſt us; the diſtreſſes and embarraſſments in which we have been involved by it; and the ſore repentance which on one account or other it always coſts us.

But the reflection calculated above all others to allay that haughtineſs of temper which is ever finding out provocations, and which renders anger ſo impetuous, is that which the goſpel propoſes; namely, that we ourſelves are, or ſhortly ſhall be, ſuppliants for mercy and pardon at the judgment ſeat of God. Imagine our ſecret ſins all diſcloſed and brought to light; imagine us thus humbled and expoſed; trembling under the hand of God; caſting ourſelves on his compaſſion; crying out for mercy—imagine ſuch a creature to talk of ſatisfaction and revenge; refuſing to be entreated, diſdaining to forgive; extreme to mark and to reſent, what is done amiſs; imagine I ſay this, and you can hardly feign to yourſelf an inſtance of more impious and unnatural arrogance.

The

The point is to habituate ourselves to these reflections, till they rise up of their own accord, when they are wanted, that is, instantly upon the receipt of an injury or affront, and with such force and colouring, as both to mitigate the paroxysms of our anger at the time, and at length to produce an alteration in the temper and disposition itself.

CHAP. VIII.

REVENGE.

ALL pain occasioned to another in consequence of an offence, or injury received from him, farther than what is calculated to procure reparation, or promote the just ends of punishment, is so much revenge.

There can be no difficulty in knowing when we occasion pain to another; nor much in distinguishing whether we do so, with a view only to the ends of punishment, or from revenge; for in the one case we proceed with reluctance, in the other with pleasure.

It is highly *probable* from the light of nature, that a passion, which seeks its gratification immediately and expressly in giving pain, is disagreeable to the benevolent will and counsels of the Creator. Other paffions and pleafures may, and often do, produce pain to fome one; but then pain is not, as it is here, the object of the paffion, and the direct caufe of the pleafure. This *probability* is converted into certainty, if we give credit to the authority which dictated the feveral paffages of the Chriftian fcriptures that condemn revenge, or what is the fame thing, which enjoin forgivenefs.

We will fet down the principal of thefe paffages; and endeavour to collect from them, what conduct upon the whole is allowed towards an enemy, and what is forbidden.

" If ye forgive men their trefpaffes, your heavenly
" Father will alfo forgive you; but if ye forgive not men
" their trefpaffes, neither will your father forgive your
" trefpaffes." " And his Lord was wroth, and delivered him
" to the tormentors, till he fhould pay all that was due unto
" him: fo likewife, fhall my heavenly Father do alfo unto
" you, if ye from your hearts forgive not every one his
" brother their trefpaffes." " Put on bowels of mercy,
" kindnefs, humblenefs of mind, meeknefs, long fuffering,
" forbearing one another, forgiving one another, if any
" man have a quarrel againft any, even as Chrift forgave
" you, fo alfo do ye." " Be patient towards all men; fee
" that none render evil for evil unto any man." " Avenge
" not yourfelves, but rather give place unto wrath: for it is
" written, vengeance is mine, I will repay faith the Lord.
" Therefore if thine enemy hunger, feed him; if he thirft,
" give him drink; for in fo doing, thou fhalt heap coals of
" fire

REVENGE.

"fire on his head. Be not overcome of evil, but overcome
"evil with good." *

I think it evident from some of these passages taken separately, and still more so, from all of them together, that *revenge*, as described in the beginning of this chapter, is forbidden in every degree, under all forms, and upon any occasion. We are likewise forbidden to refuse to an enemy even the most imperfect right; " if he hunger, feed " him, if he thirst give him drink," † which are examples of imperfect rights. If one who has offended us, solicit from us a vote to which his qualifications entitle him, we may not refuse it from motives of resentment, or the remembrance of what we have suffered at his hands. His right, and our obligation which follows the right, is not altered by his enmity to us, or ours to him.

On the other hand, I do not conceive, that these prohibitions were intended to interfere with the punishment or prosecution of public offenders. In the eighteenth chapter of St. Matthew, our Saviour tells his disciples, " if thy bro-
" ther who has trespassed against thee, neglect to hear the

---

* Mat. vi. 14, 15. xviii. 34, 35. Col. iii. 12, 13. Thess. v. 14, 15. Rom. xii. 19. i.

† See also Exodus xxiii. 4. " If thou meet thine enemy's ox, or his ass, " going astray thou shalt surely bring it back to him again: if thou see the ass of " him that hateth thee lying under his burden, and wouldest forbear to help him, " thou shalt surely help with him."

"church, let him be unto thee as an heathen man, and a "publican." Immediately after this, when St. Peter asked him, "how oft shall my brother sin against me, and I "forgive him? till seven times?" Christ replied, "I say "not unto thee until seven times; but until seventy times "seven;" that is as often as he repeats the offence. From these two passages compared together, we are authorized to conclude that the forgiveness of an enemy is not inconsistent with the proceeding against him as a public offender; and that the discipline established in religious or civil societies, for the restraint or punishment of criminals, ought to be upheld.

As the magistrate is not tied down by these prohibitions from the execution of his office, so neither is the prosecutor; for the office of the prosecutor is as necessary as that of the magistrate.

Nor by parity of reason, are private persons withheld from the correction of vice, when it is in their power to exercise it; provided they be assured that it is the guilt which provokes them, and not the injury; and that their motives are pure from all mixture and every particle of that spirit which delights and triumphs in the pain and humiliation of an adversary.

Thus it is no breach of Christian charity, to withdraw our company or civility, when the same tends to discountenance any vicious practice. This is one branch of that extrajudicial discipline, which supplies the defects and remissness of law; and is expressly authorized by St. Paul (1 Cor. v. 11.) " But now I have written unto you, not to " keep company, if any man, that is called a brother, be " a fornicator, or covetous, or an idolator, or a railer, or " a drunkard, or an extortioner; with such an one no not " to eat." The use of this association against vice continues to be experienced in one remarkable instance, and might be extended with good effect to others. The confederacy amongst women of character, to exclude from their society kept mistresses and prostitutes, contributes more perhaps to discourge that condition of life, and prevents greater numbers from entering into it, than all the considerations of prudence and religion put together.

We are likewise allowed to practise so much caution, as not to put ourselves in the way of injury, or invite the repetition of it. If a servant or tradesman has cheated us, we are not bound to trust him again; for this is to encourage him in his dishonest practices, which is doing him much harm.

Where a benefit can be conferred only upon one or few, and the choice of the person, upon whom it is conferred, is a proper object of favour, we are at liberty to prefer those who have not offended us to those who have; the contrary being no where required.

Christ

Chrift, who, as hath been well demonftrated, * eftimated virtues by their folid utility, and not by their fafhion or popularity, prefers this of the forgivenefs of injuries to every other, He injoins it oftener; with more earneftnefs; under a greater variety of forms; and with this weighty and peculiar circumftance, that the forgivenefs of others is the condition, upon which alone we are to expect, or even afk. from God, forgivenefs for ourfelves. And this preference is juftified by the fuperior importance of the virtue itfelf. The feuds and animofities in families and between neighbours, which difturb the intercourfe of human life, and collectively compofe half the mifery of it, have their foundation in the want of a forgiving temper, and can never ceafe, but by the exercife of this virtue, on one fide, or on both.

---

* See a View of the internal Evidence of the Chriftian Religion.

CHAP. IX.

DUELLING.

DUELLING as a punishment is absurd; because it is an equal chance, whether the punishment fall upon the offender, or the person offended. Nor is it much better as a reparation; it being difficult to explain what the *satisfaction* consists in, or how it tends to undo the injury, or to afford a compensation for the damage already sustained.

The truth is, it is not considered as either. A law of honour having annexed the imputation of cowardice to patience under an affront, challenges are given and accepted with no other design than to prevent or wipe off this suspicion; without malice against the adversary, generally without a wish to destroy him, or any concern but to preserve the duellist's own reputation and reception in the world.

The unreasonableness of this rule of manners is one consideration; the duty and conduct of individuals, whilst such a rule exists, is another.

As to which, the proper and single question is this, whether a regard for our own reputation is or is not sufficient to justify the taking away the life of another.

Murder is forbidden; and wherever human life is deliberately taken away, otherwise than by public authority, there is murder. The value and security of human life make this rule necessary; for I do not see what other idea or definition of murder can be admitted, which will not let in so much private violence, as to render society a scene of peril and bloodshed.

If unauthorized laws of honour be allowed to create exceptions to divine prohibitions, there is an end of all morality as founded in the will of the Deity; and the obligation of every duty may at one time or other be discharged by the caprice and fluctuations of fashion.

" But a sense of shame is so much torture; and no relief
" presents itself otherwise than by an attempt upon the life
" of our adversary." What then? The distress which men suffer by the want of money is oftentimes extreme, and no resource can be discovered but that of removing a life, which stands between the distressed person and his inheritance. The motive in this case is as urgent, and the means much the same, as in the former: yet this case finds no advocates.

Take away the circumstance of the duellist's exposing his own life, and it becomes assassination: add this circumstance, and what difference does it make? none but this, that fewer perhaps will imitate the example, and human life will be somewhat more safe, when it cannot be attacked without
equal

equal danger to the aggressor's own. Experience, however, proves that there is fortitude enough in most men to undertake this hazard; and were it otherwise, the defence, at best, would be only that which a highwayman or housebreaker might plead, whose attempt had been so daring and desperate, that few were likely to repeat the same.

In expostulating with the duellist I all along suppose his adversary to *fall*. Which supposition I am at liberty to make, because, if he have no right to kill his adversary, he has none to attempt it.

In return, I forbear from applying to the case of duelling the Christian principle of the forgiveness of injuries; because it is possible to suppose the injury to be forgiven, and the duellist to act entirely from a concern for his own reputation: where this is not the case, the guilt of duelling is manifest, and greater.

In this view it seems unnecessary to distinguish, between him who gives, and him who accepts a challenge: for they incur an equal hazard of destroying life; and both act upon the same persuasion, that what they do is necessary in order to recover or preserve the good opinion of the world.

Public opinion is not easily controlled by civil institutions: for which reason I question whether any regulations can be contrived of sufficient force to suppress or change the rule of honour which ſtigmatiſes all ſcruples about duelling with the reproach of cowardice.

The inadequate redreſs which the law of the land affords, for thoſe injuries which chiefly affect a man in his ſenſibility and reputation, tempts many to redreſs themſelves. Proſecutions for ſuch offences, by the trifling damages that are recovered, ſerve only to make the ſufferer more ridiculous.—This ought to be remedied.

For the army, where the point of honour is cultivated with exquiſite attention and refinement, I would eſtabliſh a Court of Honour, with a power of awarding thoſe ſubmiſſions and acknowledgments, which it is generally the object of a challenge to obtain; and it might grow into a faſhion, with perſons of rank of all profeſſions, to refer their quarrels to the ſame tribunal.

Duelling, as the law now ſtands, can ſeldom be overtaken by legal puniſhment. The challenge, appointment, and other previous circumſtances, which indicate the intention with which the combatants met, being ſuppreſſed, nothing *appears* to a court of juſtice, but the actual reincounter. And if a perſon be ſlain when actually fighting with his adverſary, the law deems his death nothing more than manſlaughter.

CHAP. X.

LITIGATION.

"IF it be *possible* live peaceably with all men;" which precept contains an indirect confession that this is not always *possible*.

The instances * in the fifth chapter of St. Matthew are rather to be understood as proverbial methods of describing the general duties of forgiveness and benevolence, and of the temper we ought to aim at acquiring, than as directions to be specifically observed; or of themselves of any great importance to be observed. The first of these is, " if thine enemy smite thee on thy right cheek, turn to " him the other also;" yet, when one of the officers struck Jesus with the palm of his hand, we find Jesus rebuking him for the outrage with becoming indignation; " if I " have spoken evil, bear witness of the evil; but if well,

---

* " Whosoever shall smite thee on thy right cheek, turn to him the other " also; and if any man will sue thee at the law, and take away thy coat, let " him have thy cloak also; and whosoever shall compel thee to go a mile, go " with him twain."

"why smitest thou me?" (John xviii. 22.) It may be observed likewise, that all the examples are drawn from instances of small and tolerable injuries. A rule which forbad all opposition to injury, or defence against it, could have no other effect, than to put the good in subjection to the bad, and deliver one half of mankind to the depredation of the other half: which must be the case, so long as some considered themselves as bound by such a rule, whilst others despised it. *St. Paul*, though no one inculcated forgiveness and forbearance, with a deeper sense of the value and obligation of these virtues, did not interpret either of them to require an unresisting submission to every contumely, or a neglect of the means of safety and self-defence. He took refuge in the laws of his country, and in the privileges of a *Roman* citizen, from the conspiracy of the *Jews*, (Acts xxv. 11.) and from the clandestine violence of the chief Captain. (Acts xxii. 25.) And yet this is the same Apostle who reproved the litigiousness of his *Corinthian* converts with so much severity. "Now therefore, "there is utterly a fault among you, because ye go to law "one with another; why do you not rather take wrong? "why do ye not rather suffer yourselves to be defrauded?"

On the one hand, therefore, Christianity excludes all vindictive motives, and all frivolous causes of prosecution; so that where the injury is small, where no good purpose of public example is answered, where forbearance is not likely to invite a repetition of the injury, or where the expence

LITIGATION.

expence of an action becomes a punishment too severe for the offence; there the Christian is withholden by the authority of his religion from going to law.

On the other hand, a law-suit is inconsistent with no rule of the gospel, when it is instituted,

1. For the establishing of some important right.

2. For the procuring a compensation for some considerable damage.

3. For the preventing of future injury.

But since it is supposed to be undertaken simply with a view to the ends of justice and safety, the prosecutor of the action is bound to confine himself to the cheapest process that will accomplish these ends, as well as to consent to any peaceable expedient for the same purpose; as *a reference*, in which the arbitrators can do, what the law cannot, divide the damage, when the fault is mutual; or *a compounding of the dispute*, by accepting a compensation in the gross, without entering into articles and items which it is often very difficult to adjust separately.

As to the rest, the duty of the contending parties may be expressed in the following directions.

Not

Not to prolong a suit by appeals against your own conviction.

Not to undertake or defend a suit against a poor adversary, or render it more dilatory or expensive than necessary, with the hope of intimidating or wearying him out by the expence.

Not to influence *evidence* by authority or expectation.

Nor to stifle any in your possession, although it make against you.

Hitherto we have treated of civil actions. In criminal prosecutions the private injury should be forgotten, and the prosecutor proceed with the same temper, and upon the same motives, as the magistrate; the one being a necessary minister of justice as well as the other; and both bound to direct their conduct by a dispassionate care of the public welfare.

In whatever degree the punishment of an offender is conducive, or his escape dangerous, to the interest of the community, in the same degree is the party against whom the crime was committed bound to prosecute, because such prosecutions must in their nature originate from the sufferer.

Therefore

Therefore, great public crimes, as robberies, forgeries, &c. ought not to be spared, from an apprehension of trouble or expence in carrying on the prosecution, or from false shame or misplaced compassion.

There are many offences, such as nuisances, neglect of public roads, forestalling, engrossing, smuggling, sabbath breaking, profaneness, drunkenness, prostitution, the keeping of lewd or disorderly houses, the writing, publishing, or exposing to sale lascivious books or prints, with some others, the prosecution of which, being of equal concern to the whole neighbourhood, cannot be charged as a peculiar obligation upon any.

Nevertheless, there is great merit in the person who undertakes such prosecutions upon proper motives; which amounts to the same thing.

The character of an *informer* is in this country undeservedly odious. But where any public advantage is likely to be attained by informations, or other activity in promoting the execution of the laws, a good man will despise a prejudice founded in no just reason, or will acquit himself of the imputation of interested designs by giving away his share of the penalty.

On the other hand, prosecutions for the sake of the reward, or for the gratification of private enmity, where the offence produces no public mischief, or where it arises from ignorance or inadvertency, are reprobated under the general description of *applying a rule of law to a purpose for which it was not intended.* Under which description may be ranked an officious revival of the laws against popish priests, and dissenting teachers.

CHAP. XI.

GRATITUDE.

EXAMPLES of ingratitude check and discourage voluntary beneficence: And in this the mischief of ingratitude consists. Nor is the mischief small; for after all is done that can be done, by prescribing general rules of justice, and enforcing the observation of them by penalties or compulsion, much must be left to those offices of kindness, which men remain at liberty to exert or withhold. Now not only the choice of the objects, but the quantity and even the existence of this sort of kindness in the world depends, in a great measure, upon the return which it receives; and this is a consideration of public importance.

A second reason for cultivating a grateful temper in ourselves is the following: the same principle which is touched

touched with the kindness of a human benefactor, is capable of being affected by the divine goodness, and of becoming, under the influence of that affection, a source of the purest and most exalted virtue. The love of God is the sublimest gratitude. It is a mistake, therefore, to imagine, that this virtue is omitted in the Christian scriptures, for every precept, which commands us " to love God, " because he first loved us," presupposes the principle of gratitude, and directs it to its proper object.

It is impossible to particularise the several expressions of gratitude, which vary with the character and situation of the benefactor, and with the opportunities of the person obliged; for this variety admits of no bounds.

It may be observed, however, that gratitude can never oblige a man to do what is wrong, and what by consequence he is previously obliged not to do. It is no ingratitude to refuse to do, what we cannot reconcile to any apprehensions of our duty; but it is ingratitude and hypocrisy together, to pretend this reason, when it is not the real one: and the frequency of such pretences has brought this apology for noncompliance with the will of a benefactor into unmerited disgrace.

It has long been accounted a violation of delicacy and generosity to upbraid men with the favours they have received; but it argues a total destitution of both these

qualities,

qualities, as well as of moral probity, to take advantage of that afcendency, which the conferring of benefits juftly creates, to draw or drive thofe whom we have obliged into mean or difhoneft compliances.

CHAP. XII.

SLANDER.

SPEAKING is acting, both in philofophical ftrictnefs, and as to all moral purpofes; for, if the mifchief and motive of our conduct be the fame, the means we ufe make no difference.

And this is in effect what our Saviour declares, *Matt.* xii. 37. " By thy words thou fhalt be juftified, and by " thy words thou fhalt be condemned:" by thy words, as well, that is, as by thy actions; the one fhall be taken into the account, as well as the other, for they both poffefs the fame property of voluntarily producing good or evil.

Slander may be diftinguifhed into two kinds, *malicious* flander, and *inconfiderate* flander.

Malicious flander, is the relating of either truth or falfehood, with a confcious purpofe of creating mifery.

I acknow-

I acknowledge that the truth or falsehood of what is related varies the degree of guilt considerably; and that slander, in the ordinary acceptation of the term, signifies the circulation of mischievous *falsehoods:* but truth may be made instrumental to the success of malicious designs as well as falsehood; and if the end be bad, the means cannot be innocent.

I think the idea of slander ought to be confined to the production of *gratuitous* mischief. When we have an end or interest of our own to serve, if we attempt to compass it by falsehood, it is *fraud;* if by a publication of the truth, it is not without some additional circumstance of breach of promise, betraying of confidence, or the like, to be deemed criminal.

Sometimes the pain is intended for the person to whom we are speaking; at other times an enmity is to be gratified by the prejudice or disquiet of a third person. To infuse suspicions, to kindle or continue disputes; to avert the favour and esteem of benefactors from their dependents, to render some one we dislike contemptible or obnoxious in the public opinion, are all offices of slander; of which the guilt must be measured by the intensity and extent of the misery produced.

The disguises under which slander is conveyed, whether in a whisper, with injunctions of secresy, by way of caution, or with affected reluctance, are all so many aggravations

vations of the offence, as they manifest a more concerted and deliberate design.

Inconsiderate slander is a different offence, although the same mischief actually follow, and although it might have been foreseen. The not being conscious of that mischievous design, which we have hitherto attributed to the slanderer, makes the difference.

The guilt here consists in the want of that regard to the consequences of our conduct, which a just affection for human happiness and concern for our duty would not have failed to have produced in us. And it is no answer to this crimination to say, that we entertained no evil *design*. A servant may be a very bad servant, and yet seldom or never *design* to act in opposition to his master's interest or will; and his master may justly punish such servant for a thoughtlessness and neglect nearly as prejudicial as deliberate disobedience. I accuse you not, he may say, of any express intention to hurt me; but had not the fear of my displeasure, the care of my interest, and indeed all the qualities which constitute the merit of a good servant, been wanting in you, they would not only have excluded every direct purpose of giving me uneasiness, but have been so far present to your thoughts, as to have checked that unguarded licentiousness, by which I have suffered so much, and inspired you in its place with an habitual solicitude about the effects and tendency of what you did or said. This very much resembles the case of all sins

of

of inconsideration; and, amongst the foremost of these, that of inconsiderate slander.

Information communicated for the real purpose of warning or cautioning is not slander.

Indiscriminate praise is the opposite of slander, but it is the opposite extreme; and, however it may affect to be thought excess of candour, is commonly the production of a frivolous understanding, and sometimes of a settled contempt of all moral distinctions.

BOOK III.

PART III.

OF RELATIVE DUTIES WHICH RESULT FROM THE CONSTITUTION OF THE SEXES.

THE constitution of the sexes is the foundation of *marriage*.

Collateral to the subject of marriage, are fornication, seduction, adultery, incest, polygamy, divorce.

Consequential to marriage, is the relation and reciprocal duty of parent and child.

We will treat of these subjects in the following order: first, of the public use of marriage institutions; secondly, of the subjects collateral to marriage, in the order in which we have here proposed them; thirdly, of marriage itself; and lastly, of the relation and reciprocal duties of parents and children.

CHAP. I.

OF THE PUBLIC USE OF MARRIAGE INSTITUTIONS.

THE public use of marriage inſtitutions conſiſts in their promoting the following beneficial effects:

1. The private comfort of individuals, eſpecially of the female ſex. It may be true, that all are not intereſted in this reaſon: nevertheleſs, it is a reaſon to all for abſtaining from any conduct which tends in its general conſequence to obſtruct marriage; for whatever promotes the happineſs of the majority is binding upon the whole.

2. The production of the greateſt number of healthy children, their better education, and the making of due proviſion for their ſettlement in life.

3. The peace of human ſociety, in cutting off a principal ſource of contention, by aſſigning one or more women to one man, and protecting his excluſive right by ſanctions of morality and law.

4. The better government of ſociety, by diſtributing the community into ſeparate families, and appointing over

each the authority of a master of a family, which has more actual influence than all civil authority put together.

5. The same end, in the additional security which the state receives for the good behaviour of its citizens, from the solicitude they feel for the welfare of their children, and from their being confined to permanent habitations.

6. The encouragement of industry.

Some ancient nations appear to have been more sensible of the importance of marriage institutions than we are. The Spartans obliged their citizens to marry by penalties, and the Romans encouraged theirs by the *jus trium liberorum.* A man who had no child was entitled by the Roman law only to one half of any legacy that should be left him, that is, at the most, could only receive one half of the testator's fortune.

CHAP. II.

FORNICATION.

THE first and great mischief, and by consequence the guilt, of promiscuous concubinage, consists in its tendency to diminish marriages, and thereby to defeat the several public and beneficial purposes enumerated in the preceding chapter.

Promiscuous concubinage discourages marriage by abating the chief temptation to it. The male part of the species will not undertake the incumbrance, expence, and restraint of married life, if they can gratify their passions at a cheaper price; and they will undertake any thing, rather than not gratify them.

The reader will learn to comprehend the magnitude of this mischief, by attending to the importance and variety of the uses to which marriage is subservient; and by recollecting withal, that the malignity and moral quality of each crime is not to be estimated by the particular effect of one offence, or of one person's offending, but by the general tendency and consequence of crimes of the same nature. The libertine may not be conscious that these irregularities hinder his own marriage, from which he is deterred, he may alledge, by many different considerations; much less does he perceive how *his* indulgencies can hinder other men from marrying: but what, will he say, would be the consequence, if the same licentiousness were universal? or what should hinder its becoming universal, if it be innocent or allowable in him?

2. Fornication supposes prostitution; and prostitution brings and leaves the victims of it to almost certain misery. It is no small quantity of misery in the aggregate, which, between want, disease, and insult, is suffered by those outcasts of human society, who infest populous cities; the whole of which is a *general consequence* of fornication, and to the increase and continuance of which, every act and instance of fornication contributes.

3. Fornication produces habits of ungovernable lewdness, which introduce the more aggravated crimes of seduction, adultery, violation, &c.* Likewise, however it be accounted for, the criminal commerce of the sexes corrupts and depraves the mind and moral character more than any single species of vice whatsoever. That ready perception of guilt, that prompt and decisive resolution against it, which constitutes a virtuous character, is seldom

* " Of this passion it has been truly said, that irregularity has no limits; that " one excess draws on another; that the most easy, therefore, as well as the ". most excellent way of being virtuous, is to be so entirely." Ogden. Ser. xvi.

found in perfons addicted to thefe indulgencies. They prepare an eafy admiffion for every fin that feeks it; are, in low life, ufually the firft ftage in men's progrefs to the moft defperate villanies; and, in high life, to that lamented diffolutenefs of principle, which manifefts itfelf in a profligacy of public conduct, and a contempt of the obligations of religion and moral probity. Add to this, that habits of libertinifm incapacitate and indifpofe the mind for all intellectual, moral, and religious pleafures, which is a great lofs to any man's happinefs.

4. Fornication perpetuates a difeafe, which may be accounted one of the foreft maladies of human nature; and the effects of which are faid to vifit the conftitution of even diftant generations.

The paffion being natural proves that it was intended to be gratified; but under what reftrictions, or whether without any, muft be collected from different confiderations.

The Chriftian fcriptures condemn fornication abfolutely and peremptorily. " Out of the heart," fays our Saviour, " proceed evil thoughts, murders, adulteries, *fornication*, " thefts, falfe witnefs, blafphemies, thefe are the things " which defile a man." Thefe are Chrift's own words, and one word from him upon the fubject is final. It may be obferved with what fociety fornication is claffed; with murders, thefts, falfe witnefs, blafphemies. I do not mean that thefe crimes are all equal, becaufe they are all mentioned

tioned together; but it proves that they are all crimes. The Apostles are more full upon this topic. One well known passage in the Epistle to the Hebrews may stand in the place of all others; because, admitting the authority by which the Apostles of Christ spake and wrote, it is decisive; " Marriage and the bed undefiled is honourable " amongst all men, but whoremongers and adulterers God " will judge;" which was a great deal to say, at a time when it was not agreed even amongst philosophers that fornication was a crime.

The scriptures give no sanction to those austerities, which have been since imposed upon the world under the name of Christ's religion, as the celibacy of the clergy, the praise of perpetual virginity, the *prohibitio concubitûs cum gravidâ uxore*; but with a just knowledge of, and regard to the condition and interest of the human species, have provided in the marriage of one man with one woman an adequate gratification for the propensities of their nature, and have *restrained* them to that gratification.

The avowed toleration, and in some countries the licensing, taxing, and regulating of public brothels, has appeared to the people an authorizing of fornication, and has contributed with other causes, so far to vitiate the public opinion, that there is no practice of which the immorality is so little thought of or acknowledged, although there are few, in which it can more plainly be made out. The legislators who have patronized receptacles of prostitution

tution ought to have foreseen this effect, as well as considered, that whatever facilitates fornication, diminishes marriages. And as to the usual apology for this relaxed discipline, the danger of greater enormities if access to prostitutes were too strictly watched and prohibited, it will be time enough to look to that, after the laws and the magistrates have done their utmost. The greatest vigilance of both will do no more, than oppose some bounds and some difficulties to this intercourse. And after all, these pretended fears are without foundation in experience. The men are in all respects the most virtuous, in countries where the women are most chaste.

There is a species of cohabitation, distinguishable, no doubt, from promiscuous concubinage, and which by reason of its resemblance to marriage may be thought to participate of the sanctity and innocence of that estate; I mean the case of *kept mistresses*, under the favourable circumstance of mutual fidelity. This case I have heard defended by some such apology as the following:

" That the marriage rite being different in different
" countries, and in the same country amongst different sects,
" and with some, scarce any thing; and moreover, not
" being prescribed or even mentioned in scripture, can be
" accounted of only as of a form and ceremony of human
" invention: that consequently, if a man and woman betroth and confine themselves to each other, their intercourse must be the same, as to all moral purposes, as if they
" were

"were legally married: for the addition or omission of a mere form and ceremony can make no difference in the sight of God, or in the actual nature of right and wrong."

To all which it may be replied,

1. If the situation of the parties be the same thing as marriage, why do they not marry?

2. If the man choose to have it in his power to dismiss the woman at his pleasure, or to retain her in a state of humiliation and dependence inconsistent with the rights which marriage would confer upon her, it is not the same thing.

3. It is not at any rate the same thing to the children.

Again, as to the marriage rite being a mere form, and that also variable, the same may be said of signing and sealing of bonds, wills, deeds of conveyance, and the like, which yet make a great difference in the rights and obligations of the parties concerned in them.

And with respect to the rite not being appointed in scripture—the scriptures forbid fornication, that is cohabitation without marriage, leaving it to the law of each country to pronounce what is, or what makes a marriage, in like manner as they forbid theft, that is, the taking away of another's property, leaving it to the municipal law to fix what makes the thing property, or whose it is, which

which also, like marriage, depends on arbitrary and mutable forms.

Laying aside the injunctions of scripture, the plain account of the question seems to be this: it is immoral, because it is pernicious, that men and women should cohabit, without undertaking certain irrevocable obligations, and mutually conferring certain civil rights; if, therefore, the law has annexed these rights and obligations to certain forms, so that they cannot be secured or undertaken by any other means, which is the case here (for whatever the parties may promise to each other, nothing but the marriage ceremony can make their promise irrevocable) it becomes in the same degree immoral, that men and women should cohabit without the interposition of these forms.

If fornication be criminal, all those incentives which lead to it are accessaries to the crime, as lascivious conversation, whether expressed in obscene or disguised under modest phrases; also wanton songs, pictures, books; the writing, publishing, and circulating of which, whether out of frolic, or for some pitiful profit, is productive of so extensive a mischief from so mean a temptation, that few crimes, within the reach of private wickedness, have more to answer for, or less to plead in their excuse.

Indecent conversation, and by parity of reason all the rest, are forbidden by St. Paul, Eph. iv. 29. " Let no " corrupt communication proceed out of your mouth;"

and again, Col. iii. 8. " put off - - - filthy communication
" out of your mouth."

The invitation, or voluntary admission, of impure thoughts, or the suffering them to get possession of the imagination, falls within the same description, and is condemned by *Christ, Matt.* v. 28. " Whosoever looketh on a " woman to lust after her, hath committed adultery with " her already in his heart." *Christ*, by thus enjoining a regulation of the thoughts, strikes at the root of the evil.

CHAP. III.

SEDUCTION.

THE *seducer* practises the same stratagems to draw a woman's person into his power, that a *swindler* does, to get possession of your goods, or money; yet the *law of honour*, which abhors deceit, applauds the address of a successful intrigue: so much is this capricious rule guided by names, and with such facility does it accomodate itself to the pleasures and conveniency of higher life.

Seduction is seldom accomplished without fraud; and the fraud is by so much more criminal than other frauds,

as

as the injury effected by it is greater, continues longer, and less admits of reparation.

This injury is three-fold; to the woman, to her family, and to the public.

1. The injury to the woman is made up, of the *misery* she suffers from shame, of the *loss* she sustains in her reputation and prospects of marriage, and of the *depravation of her moral principle*.

This *misery* must be extreme, if we may judge of it from those barbarous endeavours to conceal their disgrace, to which women, under such circumstances, sometimes have recourse; and compare this barbarity with their passionate fondness for their offspring, in other cases. Nothing but an agony of mind the most insupportable can induce a woman to forget her nature, and the pity which even a stranger would show to a helpless and imploring infant. It is true, that all are not urged to this extremity; but if any are, it affords an indication of how much all suffer from the same cause. What shall we say to the authors of such mischief.

The *loss* which a woman sustains by the ruin of her reputation almost exceeds computation. Every person's happiness depends in part upon the respect and reception they meet with in the world; and it is no inconsiderable mortification even to the firmest tempers to be rejected from the society of their equals, or received there with neglect and disdain. But this is not all, nor the worst. By a rule of life, which it is not easy to blame, and which it is impossible to alter, a woman loses with her chastity the chance of marrying at all, or in any manner equal to the hopes she had been accustomed to entertain. Now marriage, whatever it be to a man, is that, from which every woman expects her chief happiness. And this is still more true in low life, of which condition the women are, who are most exposed to solicitations of this sort. Add to this, that where a woman's maintenance depends upon her character, as it does, in a great measure, with those who are to support themselves by service, little sometimes is left to the forsaken sufferer, but to starve for want of employment, or to have recourse to prostitution for food and raiment.

As a woman collects her virtue into this point, the loss of her chastity is generally the *destruction of her moral principle;* and this consequence is to be apprehended, whether the criminal intercourse be discovered or not.

2. The injury to the family may be understood, by the application of that infallible rule ," of doing to others what " we would that others should do unto us." Let a father, or a brother say, for what they would suffer this injury in a daughter or a sister; and whether any, or even a total loss of fortune would create equal affliction and distress. And when they reflect upon this, let them distinguish, if they can, between a robbery committed upon their property

perty by fraud or forgery, and the ruin of their happiness by the treachery of a Seducer.

3. The public at large lose the benefit of the woman's service in her proper place and destination, as a wife and parent. This to the whole community may be little; but it is often more than all the good, which the seducer does to the community, can recompense. Moreover, prostitution is supplied by seduction, and in proportion to the danger there is of the woman's betaking herself after her first sacrifice to a life of public lewdness, the seducer is answerable for the multiplied evils to which his crime gives birth.

Upon the whole, if we pursue the effects of seduction through the complicated misery which it occasions; and if it be right to estimate crimes by the mischief they knowingly produce, it will appear something more than mere invective to assert, that not one half of the crimes, for which men suffer death by the laws of England, are so flagitious as this.*

* Yet the law has provided no punishment for this offence beyond a pecuniary satisfaction to the injured family; and this can only be come at, by one of the quaintest fictions in the world, by the father's bringing his action against the seducer, for the loss of his daughter's service, during her pregnancy and nurturing.

CHAP. IV.

ADULTERY.

A NEW sufferer is introduced, the injured husband, who receives a wound in his sensibility and affections, the most painful and incurable that human nature knows. In all other respects, adultery on the part of the man who solicits the chastity of a married woman, includes the crime of seduction, and is attended with the same mischief.

The infidelity of the woman is aggravated by cruelty to her children, who are generally involved in their parents shame, and always made unhappy by their quarrel.

If it be said that these consequences are chargeable not so much upon the crime, as the discovery, we answer, first, that the crime could not be discovered unless it were committed, and that the commission is never secure from discovery; and secondly, that if we allow of adulterous connections, whenever they can hope to escape detection, which is the conclusion to which this argument conducts us, us, we leave the husband no other security for his wife's chastity, than in her want of opportunity or temptation, which would probably deter most men from marrying, or render marriage a state of jealousy and continual alarm to the husband, which would end in the slavery and confinement of the wife.

The vow, by which married persons mutually engage their fidelity is "witnessed before God," and accompanied with circumstances of solemnity and religion, which approach to the nature of an oath. The married offender therefore incurs a crime little short of perjury, and the seduction of a married woman is little less than subornation of perjury:—and this guilt is independent of the discovery.

All behaviour, which is designed, or which knowingly tends, to captivate the affection of a married woman, is a barbarous intrusion upon the peace and virtue of a family, though it fall short of adultery.

The usual and only apology for adultery is the prior transgression of the other party. There are degrees no doubt in this, as in other crimes; and so far as the bad effects of adultery are anticipated by the conduct of the husband or wife who offends first, the guilt of the second offender is extenuated. But this can never amount to a justification; unless it could be shewn that the obligation of the marriage vow depends upon the condition of reciprocal

procal fidelity; for which construction, there appears no foundation, either in expediency, or in the terms of the promise, or in the design of the legislature which prescribed the marriage rite. Moreover, the rule contended for by this plea has a manifest tendency to multiply the offence, but none to reclaim the offender.

The way of considering the offence of one party as a *provocation* to the other, and the other as only *retaliating* the injury by repeating the crime, is a childish trifling with words.

" Thou shalt not commit adultery," was an interdict delivered by God himself. By the Jewish law adultery was capital to both parties in the crime; " Even he that " committeth adultery with his neighbour's wife, the adul- " terer and adulteress shall surely be put to death." Lev. xx. 10. which passages prove, that the divine legislator placed a great difference between adultery and fornication. And with this agree the Christian scriptures; for in almost all the catalogues they have left us of crimes and criminals, they enumerate " fornication, adultery," " whoremongers, " adulterers," (Matt. xv. 19. 1 Cor. vi. 9. Gal. v. 9. Heb. xiii. 4.) by which mention of both, they shew that they did not consider them as the same; but that the crime of adultery was, in their apprehension, distinct from, and accumulated upon that of fornication.

The history of the woman taken in adultery, recorded in

ADULTERY.

in the eighth chapter of *St. John's Gospel*, has been thought by some to give countenance to that crime. As Christ told the woman, "neither do *I condemn* thee," we must believe, it is said, that he deemed her conduct either not criminal, or not a crime however of the heinous nature we represent it to be. A more attentive examination of the case will, I think, convince us, that nothing can be concluded from it, as to Christ's opinion concerning adultery, either one way or the other. The transaction is thus related. " Early in the morning Jesus came again into
" the temple, and all the people came unto him; and he
" sat down and taught them; and the Scribes and Pharisees
" brought unto him a woman taken in adultery; and when
" they had set her in the midst, they say unto him, Master,
" this woman was taken in adultery, in the very act; now
" Moses in the law commanded that such should be stoned,
" but what sayest thou? This they said tempting him, that
" they might have to accuse him: but Jesus stooped down,
" and with his finger wrote on the ground, as though he
" heard them not. So when they continued asking him,
" he lift up himself, and said unto them, he that is without
" sin amongst you, let him first cast a stone at her; and
" again he stooped down and wrote on the ground: and
" they which heard it, being convicted by their own con-
" science, went out one by one, beginning at the eldest,
" even unto the last; and Jesus was left alone, and the
" woman standing in the midst. When Jesus had lift up
" himself, and saw none but the woman, he said unto her,
" woman where are those thine accusers? hath no man

"condemned thee? She said unto him, no man, Lord;
"and he said unto her, *neither do I condemn thee*, go and sin
"no more."

"This they said tempting him, that they might have to
"accuse him," to draw him, that is, into an exercise of
judicial authority, that they might have to accuse him
before the Roman governor of usurping or intermeddling
with the civil government. This was their design; and
Christ's behaviour throughout the whole affair proceeded
from a knowledge of this design, and a determination to
defeat it. He gives them at first a cold and sullen reception,
well suited to the insidious intention with which they came:
"he stooped down, and with his finger wrote on the
"ground, as though he heard them not." "When they
"*continued* asking him," when they teazed him to speak,
he dismissed them with a rebuke, which the impertinent
malice of their errand, as well as the secret character of
many of them deserved: "he that is without sin (that is
"this sin) among you, let him first cast a stone at her."
This had its effect. Stung with the reproof, and disappointed of their aim, they stole away one by one, and left
Jesus and the woman alone. And then follows the conversation, which is the part of the narrative most material
to our present subject. "Jesus saith unto her, woman,
"where are those thine accusers? hath no man condemned
"thee? She said, no man, Lord. And Jesus said unto her,
"neither do I condemn thee; go and sin no more." Now,
when Christ asked the woman, "hath no man *condemned*
"thee,"

ADULTERY.

"thee," he certainly spoke, and was understood by the woman to speak, of a legal and judicial condemnation; otherwise, her answer, "no man, Lord," was not true. In every other sense of condemnation, as blame, censure, reproof, private judgment, and the like, many had condemned her; all those indeed who brought her to Jesus. If then a judicial sentence was what Christ meant by *condemning* in the question, the common use of language requires us to suppose that he meant the same in his reply, "neither do I condemn thee," *i.e.* I pretend to no judicial character or authority over thee; it is no office or business of mine to pronounce or execute the sentence of the law.

When Christ adds, "go and sin no more," he in effect tells her, that she had sinned already; but as to the degree or quality of the sin, or Christ's opinion concerning it, nothing is declared, or can be inferred, either way.

Adultery, which was punished with death during the usurpation, is now regarded by the law of England as only a civil injury; for which the imperfect satisfaction that money can afford, may be recovered by the husband.

CHAP. V.

INCEST.

IN order to preserve chastity in families, and between persons of different sexes, brought up and living together in a state of unreserved intimacy, it is necessary by every method possible to inculcate an abhorrence of incestuous conjunctions; which abhorrence can only be upheld by the absolute reprobation of all commerce of the sexes between near relations. Upon this principle, the *marriage* as well as other cohabitation of brothers and sisters, of lineal kindred, and of all who usually live in the same family, may be said to be forbidden by the law of nature.

Restrictions which extend to remoter degrees of kindred than what this reason makes it necessary to prohibit from intermarriage, are founded in the authority of the positive law which ordains them, and can only be justified by their tendency to diffuse wealth, to connect families, or promote some political advantage.

The *Levitical* law, which is received in this country, and from which the rule of the *Roman* law differs very little, prohibits

prohibits * marriage between relations within *three* degrees of kindred; computing the generations through the common anceſtor, and accounting affinity the ſame as conſanguinity. The iſſue, however, of ſuch marriages are not baſtardized, unleſs the parents be divorced during their life-time.

The *Egyptians* are ſaid to have allowed of the marriage of brothers and ſiſters. Amongſt the *Athenians* a very ſingular regulation prevailed; brothers and ſiſters of the half blood, if related by the father's ſide, might marry; if by the mother's ſide, they were prohibited from marrying. The ſame cuſtom alſo probably obtained in Chaldæa ſo early as the age in which Abraham left it; for he and Sarah his wife ſtood in this relation to each other. " And yet " indeed, ſhe is my ſiſter, ſhe is the daughter of my father, " but not of my mother, and ſhe became my wife." Gen. xx. 12.

* The *Roman* law continued the prohibition without limits to the deſcendants of brothers and ſiſters. In the *Levitical* or *Engliſh* law, there is nothing to hinder a man from marrying his *great* niece.

CHAP. VI.

POLYGAMY.

THE equality* in the number of males and females born into the world intimates the intention of God, that one woman should be assigned to one man; for if to one man be allowed an exclusive right to five or more women, four or more men must be deprived of the exclusive possession of any: which could never be the order intended.

It seems also a pretty significant indication of the divine will, that he at first created only one woman to one man. Had God intended polygamy for the species, it is probable he would have begun with it; especially as by giving to Adam more wives than one, the multiplication of the human race would have proceeded with a quicker progress.

Polygamy not only violates the constitution of nature, and the apparent design of the Deity, but produces to the parties themselves, and to the public, the following bad effects—contests and jealousies amongst the wives of the same husband—distracted affections, or the loss of all affec-

---

* This equality is not exact. The number of male infants exceeds that of females in the proportion of nineteen to eighteen, or thereabouts; which excess provides for the greater consumption of males by war, seafaring, and other dangerous or unhealthy occupations.

tion in the husband himself—a voluptuousness in the rich which dissolves the vigour of their intellectual as well as active faculties, producing that indolence and imbecility both of mind and body, which have long characterized the nations of the East—the abasement of one half of the human species, who, in countries where polygamy obtains, are degraded into mere instruments of physical pleasure to the other half—neglect of children—and the manifold, and sometimes unnatural mischiefs, which arise from a scarcity of women. To compensate for these evils, polygamy does not offer a single advantage. In the article of population, which it has been thought to promote, the community gain nothing:* for the question is not, whether one man will have more children by five or more wives than by one, but whether these five wives would not bear the

---

* Nothing, I mean, compared with a state in which marriage is nearly universal. Where marriages are less general, and many women unfruitful from the want of husbands, polygamy might at first add a little to population; and but a little: for as a variety of wives would be sought chiefly from temptations of voluptuousness, it would rather increase the demand for female beauty, than for the sex at large. And this *little* would soon be made less, by many deductions. For firstly, as none but the opulent can maintain a plurality of wives, where polygamy obtains, the rich indulge in it, while the rest take up with a vague and barren incontinency. And secondly, women would grow less jealous of their virtue, when they had nothing for which to reserve it, but a chamber in the *Haram*; when their chastity was no longer to be rewarded with the rights and happiness of a wife, as enjoyed under the marriage of one woman to one man. These considerations may be added to what is mentioned in the text, concerning the easy and early settlement of children in the world.

same, or a greater number of children, to five separate husbands. And as to the care of the children when produced, and the sending of them into the world in situations in which they may be likely to form and bring up families of their own, upon which the increase and succession of the human species in a great degree depends; this is less provided for, and less practicable, where twenty or thirty children are to be supported by the attention and fortunes of one father, than if they were divided into five or six families, to each of which were assigned the industry and inheritance of two parents.

Whether simultaneous polygamy was permitted by the law of *Moses*, seems doubtful:* but whether permitted or not, it was certainly practised by the *Jewish* patriarchs, both before that law, and under it. The permission, if there was any, might be like that of divorce, " for the " hardness of their heart," in condescension to their established indulgencies, rather than from the general rectitude or propriety of the thing itself. The state of manners in *Judæa* had probably undergone a reformation in this respect before the time of *Christ*, for in the New Testament we meet with no trace or mention of any such practice being tolerated.

For which reason, and because it was likewise forbidden amongst the Greeks and Romans, we cannot expect to find any express law upon the subject in the Christian code.

The

---

* See Deut. xvii. 16. xxi. 15.

POLYGAMY.

The words of Chrift * Matt. xix. 9, may be conftrued by an eafy implication to prohibit polygamy; for, if "who-"ever putteth away his wife, and *marrieth* another, com-"mitteth adultery," he who marrieth another *without* putting away the firft, is no lefs guilty of adultery; becaufe the adultery does not confift in the repudiation of the firft wife, (for however unjuft or cruel that may be, it is not adultery) but in entering into a fecond marriage, during the legal exiftence and obligation of the firft. The feveral paffages in *St. Paul's* writings, which fpeak of marriage, always fuppofe it to fignify the union of one man with one woman. Upon this fuppofition he argues, Rom. vii. 2, 3. "Know ye not, brethren, for I fpeak to them that "know the law, how that the law hath dominion over "a man, as long as he liveth; for the woman which hath "an hufband, is bound by the law to her hufband fo long "as he liveth; but if the hufband be dead, fhe is loofed "from the law of her hufband; fo then, if while her "hufband liveth fhe be married to another man, fhe fhall "be called an adulterefs." When the fame Apoftle permits marriage to his Corinthian converts (which, "for the "prefent diftrefs," he judges to be inconvenient) he reftrains the permiffion to the marriage of one hufband with one wife; "it is good for a man not to touch a woman, "neverthelefs, to avoid fornication, let every man have his "own wife, and let every woman have her own hufband."

* "I fay unto you, whofoever fhall put away his wife, except it be for forni-"nication, and fhall marry another, committeth adultery."

The manners of different countries have varied in nothing more than in their domestic constitutions. Less polished and more luxurious nations have either not perceived the bad effects of polygamy, or, if they did perceive them, they who in such countries possessed the power of reforming the laws, have been unwilling to resign their own gratifications. Polygamy is retained at this day among the *Turks*, and throughout every part of *Asia*, in which Christianity is not professed. In Christian countries it is universally prohibited. In *Sweden* it is punished with death. In *England*, beside the nullity of the second marriage, it subjects the offender to imprisonment and branding for the first offence, and to capital punishment for the second. And whatever may be said in behalf of polygamy, when it is authorised by the law of the land, the marriage of a second wife, during the life-time of the first, in countries where such a second marriage is void, must be ranked with the most dangerous and cruel of those frauds, by which a woman is cheated out of her fortune, her person, and her happiness.

The ancient *Medes* compelled their citizens, in one canton, to take seven wives; in another, each woman to receive five husbands: according as war had made, in one quarter of their country, an extraordinary havock among the men, or the women had been carried away by an enemy from another. This regulation, so far as it was adapted to the proportion which subsisted between the numbers of males and females, was founded in the reason upon which the most improved nations of *Europe* proceed at present.

Cæsar

Cæsar found amongst the inhabitants of this island a species of polygamy, if it may be so called, which was perfectly singular. *Uxores*, says he, *habent deni duodenique inter se communes, et maxime fratres cum fratribus, parentesque cum liberis: sed si qui sunt ex his nati, eorum habentur liberi, quo primum virgo quæque deducta est.*

CHAP. VII.

OF DIVORCE.

BY *Divorce*, I mean, the dissolution of the marriage contract, by the act, and at the will, of the husband.

This power was allowed to the husband, among the *Jews*, the *Greeks*, and later *Romans;* and is at this day exercised by the *Turks* and *Persians*.

The congruity of such a right with the law of nature, is the question before us.

And in the first place, it is manifestly inconsistent with the duty, which the parents owe to their children; which duty can never be so well fulfilled as by their cohabitation and united care. It is also incompatible with the right which the mother possesses, as well as the father, to the gratitude of her children and the comfort of their society; of both which she is almost necessarily deprived, by her dismission from her husband's family.

Where this objection does not interfere, I know of no principle of the law of nature applicable to the question, beside that of general expediency.

For, if we say, that arbitrary divorces are excluded by the terms of the marriage contract, it may be answered, that the contract might be framed so as to admit of this condition.

If we argue with some Moralists, that the obligation of a contract naturally continues, so long as the purpose, which the contracting parties had in view, requires its continuance, it will be difficult to show what purpose of the contract (the care of children excepted) should confine a man to a woman, from whom he seeks to be loose.

If we contend with others, that a contract cannot, by the law of nature, be dissolved, unless the parties be replaced in the situation, which each possessed before the contract was entered into; we shall be called upon to prove this to be an universal or indispensible property of contracts.

I confess

DIVORCE.

I confess myself unable to assign any circumstance in the marriage contract, which essentially distinguishes it from other contracts, or which proves that it contains, what many have ascribed to it, a natural incapacity of being dissolved by the consent of the parties, at the option of one of them, or either of them. But if we trace the effects of such a rule upon the general happiness of married life, we shall perceive reasons of expediency, that abundantly justify the policy of those laws, which refuse to the husband the power of divorce, or restrain it to a few extreme and specific provocations: and our principles teach us to pronounce that to be contrary to the law of nature, which can be proved to be detrimental to the common happiness of the human species.

A lawgiver, whose counsels were directed by views of general utility, and obstructed by no local impediment, would make the marriage contract indissoluble during the joint lives of the parties, for the sake of the following advantages.

I. Because this tends to preserve peace and concord between married persons, by perpetuating their common interest, and by inducing a necessity of mutual compliance.

There is great weight and substance in both these considerations. An earlier termination of the union would produce a separate interest. The wife would naturally
look

look forward to the diffolution of the partnerfhip, and endeavour to draw to herfelf a fund, againft the time when fhe was no longer to have accefs to the fame refources. This would beget peculation on one fide, and miftruft on the other; evils which at prefent very little difturb the confidence of married life. The fecond effect of making the union determinable only by death, is not lefs beneficial. It neceffarily happens, that adverfe tempers, habits, and taftes, oftentimes meet in marriage. In which cafe, each party muft take pains to give up what offends, and practife what may gratify the other. A man and woman in love with each other, do this infenfibly: but love is neither general nor durable; and where that is wanting, no leffons of duty, no delicacy of fentiment, will go half fo far with the generality of mankind and womankind, as this one intelligible reflection, that they muft each make the beft of their bargain; and that feeing they muft either both be miferable, or both fhare in the fame happinefs, neither can find their own comfort but in promoting the pleafure of the other. Thefe compliances, though at firft extorted by neceffity, become in time eafy and mutual; and though lefs endearing than affiduities which take their rife from affection, generally procure to the married pair a repofe and fatisfaction fufficient for their happinefs.

II. Becaufe new objects of defire would be continually fought after, if men could, at will, be releafed from their fubfifting engagements. Suppofe the hufband to have once preferred his wife to all other women, the duration of this preference cannot be trusted to. Possession makes a great difference: and there is no other security against the invitations of novelty, than the known impossibility of obtaining the object. Did the cause, which brings the sexes together, hold them together by the same force with which it first attracted them to each other, or could the woman be restored to her personal integrity, and to all the advantages of her virgin estate; the power of divorce might be deposited in the hands of the husband, with less danger of abuse or inconveniency. But constituted as mankind are, and injured as the repudiated wife generally must be, it is necessary to add a stability to the condition of married women, more secure than the continuance of their husband's affection; and to supply to both sides, by a sense of duty and of obligation, what satiety has impaired of passion and of personal attachment. Upon the whole, the power of divorce is evidently and greatly to the disadvantage of the woman; and the only question appears to be, whether the real and permanent happiness of one half of the species should be surrendered to the caprice and voluptuousness of the other?

We have considered divorces as depending upon the will of the husband, because that is the way in which they have actually obtained in many parts of the world: but the same objections apply, in a great degree, to divorces by mutual consent; especially when we consider the indelicate situation and small prospect of happiness, which remains to the

party,

party, who opposed his or her dissent to the liberty and desires of the other.

The law of nature admits of an exception in favour of the injured party, in cases of adultery, of obstinate desertion, of attempts upon life, of outrageous cruelty, of incurable madness, and, perhaps, of personal imbecility; but by no means indulges the same privilege to mere dislike, to opposition of humours and inclinations, to contrariety of taste and temper, to complaints of coldness, neglect, severity, peevishness, jealousy: not that these reasons are trivial, but because such objections may always be alledged, and are impossible by testimony to be ascertained; so that to allow implicit credit to them, and to dissolve marriages whenever either party thought fit to pretend them, would lead in its effect to all the licentiousness of arbitrary divorces.

Milton's story is well known. Upon a quarrel with his wife, he paid his addresses to another woman, and set forth a public vindication of his conduct, by attempting to prove, that confirmed dislike was as just a foundation for dissolving the marriage contract, as adultery; to which position, and to all the arguments by which it can be supported, the above consideration affords a sufficient answer. And if a married pair, in actual and irreconcileable discord, complain that their happiness would be better consulted, by permitting them to determine a connection, which is become odious to both, it may be told them, that the same

same permiſſion, as a general rule, would produce libertiniſm, diſſenſion, and miſery, amongſt thouſands, who are now virtuous, and quiet, and happy, in their condition: and it ought to ſatisfy them to reflect, that when their happineſs is ſacrificed to the operation of an unrelenting rule, it is ſacrificed to the happineſs of the community.

The ſcriptures ſeem to have drawn the obligation tighter than the law of nature left it. " Whoſoever," ſaith *Chriſt*, " ſhall put away his wife, except it be for fornication, " and ſhall marry another, committeth adultery; and " whoſo marrieth her which is put away, doth commit " adultery." Matt. xix. 9. The law of *Moſes*, for reaſons of local expediency, permitted the *Jewiſh* huſband to put away his wife; but whether for every cauſe, or for what cauſes, appears to have been controverted amongſt the interpreters of thoſe times. *Chriſt*, the precepts of whoſe religion were calculated for more general uſe and obſervation, revokes this permiſſion, as given to the *Jews* " for " the hardneſs of their hearts," and promulges a law which was thenceforward to confine divorces to the ſingle cauſe of adultery in the wife. And I ſee no ſufficient reaſon to depart from the plain and ſtrict meaning of the words. The rule was new. It both ſurpriſed and offended his diſciples; yet *Chriſt* added nothing to relax or explain it.

Inferior cauſes may juſtify the ſeparation of huſband and wife, although they will not authoriſe ſuch a diſſolution of the marriage contract, as would leave either at liberty to marry again: for it is that liberty in which the danger and mischief of divorces principally consist. If the care of children does not require that they should live together, and it is become, in the serious judgment of both, necessary for their mutual happiness that they should separate, let them separate by consent. Nevertheless this necessity can hardly exist, without guilt and misconduct on one side or on both. Moreover cruelty, ill usage, extreme violence, or moroseness of temper, or other great and continued provocations, make it lawful for the party aggrieved to withdraw from the society of the offender, without his or her consent. The law which imposes the marriage vow, whereby the parties promise to " keep each other," or, in other words, to live together, must be understood to impose it with a silent reservation of these cases; because the same law has constituted a judicial relief from the tyranny of the husband, by the divorce *a mensâ et toro*, and by the provision which it makes for the separate maintenance of the injured wife. St. *Paul* likewise distinguishes between a wife's merely separating herself from the family of her husband, and her marrying again. " Let not the wife " depart from her husband; but, and if she do depart, " let her remain unmarried."

The law of this country, in conformity to our Saviour's injunction, confines the dissolution of the marriage contract, to the single case of adultery in the wife; and a divorce even in that case can only be brought about by the operation of an act of parliament, founded upon a previous

DIVORCE.

sentence in the spiritual court, and a verdict against the adulterer at common law: which proceedings taken together compose as complete an investigation of the complaint as a cause can receive. It has lately been proposed to the legislature to annex a clause to these acts, restraining the offending party from marrying with the companion of her crime, who by the course of proceeding is always known and convicted; for there is reason to fear, that adulterous connections are often formed with the prospect of bringing them to this conclusion; at least, when the seducer has once captivated the affection of a married woman, he may avail himself of this tempting argument to subdue her scruples, and complete his victory; and the legislature, as the business is managed at present, assists by its interposition, the criminal design of the offenders, and confers a privilege where it ought to inflict a punishment. The proposal deserved an experiment; but something more penal, will, I apprehend, be found necessary, to check the progress of this alarming depravity. Whether a law might not be framed directing *the fortune of the adulteress to descend as in case of her natural death*, reserving, however, a certain proportion of the produce of it, by way of annuity, for her subsistence, (such annuity in no case to exceed a certain sum,) and also so far suspending the estate in the hands of the heir, as to preserve the inheritance to any children she might bear to a second marriage, in case there was none to succeed in the place of their mother by the first; whether, I say, such a law would not render female virtue in higher life less vincible, as well as the seducers of that virtue less urgent in their suit, we recommend to the deliberation of those, who are willing to attempt the reformation of this important, but most incorrigible class of the community. A passion for splendor, for expensive amusements and distinctions, is commonly found in that description of women who would become the subjects of such a law, not less inordinate than their other appetites. A severity of the kind we propose applies immediately to that passion. And there is no room for any complaint of injustice, since the provisions above stated, with others which might be contrived, confine the punishment, so far as it is possible, to the person of the offender; suffering the estate to remain to the heir, or within the family of the ancestor from whom it came, or to attend the appointments of his will.

Sentences of the ecclesiastical courts, which release the parties *a vinculo matrimonii* by reason of impuberty, frigidity, consanguinity within the prohibited degrees, prior marriage, or want of the requisite consent of parents or guardians, are not dissolutions of the marriage contract, but judicial declarations, that there never was any marriage; such impediment subsisting at the time, as rendered the celebration of the marriage rite a mere nullity. And the rite itself contains an exception of these impediments. The man and woman to be married are charged, " if they know " any impediment why they may not be lawfully joined " together, to confess it;" and assured " that so many as are " coupled together, otherwise than God's word doth allow, " are not joined together by God, neither is their matri-
" mony

"mony lawful;" all which is intended by way of solemn notice to the parties, that the vow they are about to make will bind their consciences and authorise their cohabitation, only upon the supposition that no legal impediment exist.

CHAP. VIII.

MARRIAGE.

WHETHER it hath grown out of some tradition of the divine appointment of marriage in the persons of our first parents, or merely from a design to impress the obligation of the marriage contract with a solemnity suited to its importance, the marriage rite, in almost all countries of the world, has been made a religious ceremony;[*] although marriage in its own nature, and abstracted from the rules and declarations, which the Jewish and Christian scriptures deliver concerning it, be properly a civil contract and nothing more.

As to one main article in matrimonial alliances, an alteration has taken place in the fashion of the world; the

[*] It was not, however, in Christian countries required that marriages should be celebrated in churches 'till the thirteenth century of the Christian æra. Marriages in *England* during the usurpation were solemnized before justices of the peace, but for what purpose this novelty was introduced, except to degrade he clergy, does not appear.

wife

wife now brings money to her husband, whereas anciently, the husband paid money to the family of the wife; as was the case among the *Jewish* patriarchs, the *Greeks*, and the old inhabitants of *Germany*.* This alteration has proved of no small advantage to the female sex; for their importance in point of fortune procures to them in modern times, that assiduity and respect which are wanted to compensate for the inferiority of their strength, but which their personal attractions would not always secure.

Our business is with marriage, as it is established in this country. And in treating thereof, it will be necessary to state the terms of the marriage vow, in order to discover,

1. What duties this vow creates.

2. What situation of mind at the time is inconsistent with it.

3. By what subsequent behaviour it is violated.

The husband promises on his part, " to love, comfort, " honour and keep his wife;" the wife on her's, " to obey, " serve, love, honour, and keep her husband;" in every

---

* The ancient *Assyrians* sold their *beauties* by an annual auction. The prices were applied by way of portions to the more homely. By this contrivance all of both sorts were disposed of in marriage.

variety

MARRIAGE.

variety of health, fortune, and condition; and both stipulate "to forsake all others, and to keep only unto one another, so long as they both shall live." This promise is called the marriage vow; is witnessed before God and the congregation; accompanied with prayers to Almighty God for his blessing upon it; and attended with such circumstances of devotion and solemnity, as place the obligation of it, and the guilt of violating it, nearly upon the same foundation with that of oaths.

The parties by this vow engage their personal fidelity expressly and specifically: they engage likewise to consult and promote each other's happiness: the wife, moreover, promises *obedience* to her husband. Nature may have made and left the sexes of the human species nearly equal in their faculties, and perfectly so in their rights; but to guard against those competitions which equality, or a contested superiority is almost sure to produce, the Christian scriptures enjoin upon the wife that obedience which she here promises, and in terms so peremptory and absolute, that it seems to extend to every thing not criminal, or not entirely inconsistent with the woman's happiness. "Let the wife," says St. Paul, "be subject to her own husband in every thing." "The ornament of a meek and quiet spirit, (says the same Apostle, speaking of the duty of wives,) is in the sight of God of great price." No words ever expressed the true merit of the female character so well as these.

The

The condition of human life will not permit us to say, that no one can conscientiously marry, who does not prefer the person at the altar, to all other men or women in the world: but we can have no difficulty in pronouncing, (whether we respect the end of the institution, or the plain terms in which the contract is conceived) that whoever is conscious, at the time of his marriage, of such a dislike to the woman he is about to marry, or of such a subsisting attachment to some other woman, that he cannot reasonably, nor does in fact, expect ever to entertain an affection for his future wife, is guilty, when he pronounces the marriage vow, of a direct and deliberate prevarication; and that too, aggravated by the presence of those ideas of religion, and of the Supreme Being, which the place, the ritual, and the solemnity of the occasion, cannot fail of bringing to his thoughts. The same likewise of the woman. This charge must be imputed to all, who, from mercenary motives, marry the objects of their aversion and disgust; and likewise to those who desert, from any motive whatever, the object of their affection, and, without being able to subdue that affection, marry another.

The crime of falsehood is also incurred by the man, who intends, at the time of his marriage, to commence, renew, or continue a personal commerce with any other woman. And the parity of reason, if a wife be capable of so much guilt, extends to her.

The marriage vow is violated.

I. By adultery.

II. By any behaviour, which, knowingly, renders the life of the other miserable; as desertion, neglect, prodigality, drunkenness, peevishness, penuriousness, jealousy, or any levity of conduct, which may administer occasion of jealousy.

A late regulation in the law of marriages in this country, has made the consent of the father, if he be living, of the mother, if she survive the father, and remain unmarried, or of guardians, if both parents be dead, necessary to the marriage of a person under twenty-one years of age. By the *Roman* law, the consent *et avi et patris* was required so long as they lived. In *France*, the consent of parents is necessary to the marriage of sons, until they attain to thirty years of age; of daughters, until twenty-five. In *Holland*, for sons, 'till twenty-five; for daughters, 'till twenty. And this distinction between the sexes appears to be well founded, for a woman is usually as well qualified for the domestic and interior duties of a wife or mother at eighteen, as a man is for the business of the world, and the more arduous care of providing for a family, at twenty-one.

The constitution also of the human species indicates the same distinction.*

CHAP. IX.

OF THE DUTY OF PARENTS.

THAT virtue, which confines its beneficence within the walls of a man's own house, we have been accustomed to consider as little better than a more refined selfishness; and yet it will be confessed, that the subject and matter of this class of duties are inferior to none, in utility and importance: and where, it may be asked, is virtue the most valuable, but where it does the most good? What duty is the most obligatory, but that, on which the most depends? And where have we happiness and misery so much in our power, or liable to be so affected by our conduct, as in our own families? It will also be acknowledged, that the good order and happiness of the world is better upheld, whilst each man applies himself to his own concerns and the care of his own family, to which

* Cum vis prolem procreandi diutius hæreat in mare quam in fœminâ, populi numerus nequaquam minuetur, si serius venerem colere inceperint viri.

he is present, than if every man, from an excess of mistaken generosity, should leave his own business, to undertake his neighbour's, which he must always manage with less knowledge, conveniency, and success. If, therefore, the low estimation of these virtues be well founded, it must be owing, not to their inferior importance, but to some defect or impurity in the motive. And indeed it cannot be denied, but that it is in the power of *association*, so to unite our children's interest with our own, as that we shall often pursue both from the same motive, place both in the same object, and with as little sense of duty in one pursuit as in the other. Where this is the case, the judgment above stated is not far from the truth. And so often as we find a solicitous care of a man's own family, in a total absence or extreme penury of every other virtue, or interfering with other duties, or directing its operation solely to the temporal happiness of the children, placing that happiness in amusement and indulgence whilst they are young, or in advancement of fortune when they grow up, there is reason to believe that this is the case. In this way the common opinion concerning these duties may be accounted for and defended. If we look to the subject of them, we perceive them to be indispensible: if we regard the motive, we find them often not very meritorious. Wherefore, although a man seldom rises high in our esteem, who has nothing to recommend him beside the care of his own family, yet we always condemn the neglect of this duty with the utmost severity; both by reason of the manifest and immediate mischief which we see arising from

this neglect, and because it argues a want not only of parental affection, but of those moral principles, which ought to come in aid of that affection, where it is wanting. And if, on the other hand, our praise and esteem of these duties be not proportioned to the good they produce, or to the indignation with which we resent the absence of them, it is for this reason, that virtue is the most valuable, not where in strictness it produces the most good, but where it is the most wanted; which is not the case here; because its place is often supplied by instincts, or involuntary associations. Nevertheless, the offices of a parent may be discharged from a consciousness of their obligation, as well as other duties; and a sense of this obligation is sometimes necessary to assist the stimulus of parental affection; especially in stations of life, in which the wants of a family cannot be supplied without the continual hard labour of the father, nor without his refraining from many indulgencies and recreations, which unmarried men of like condition are able to purchase. Where the parental affection is sufficiently strong, or has fewer difficulties to surmount, a principle of duty may still be wanted to direct and regulate its exertions; for otherwise, it is apt to spend and waste itself in a womanish fondness for the person of the child; an improvident attention to his present ease and gratification; a pernicious facility and compliance with his humours; an excessive and superfluous care to provide the externals of happiness, with little or no attention to the internal sources of virtue and satisfaction. Universally, wherever a parent's conduct is
prompted

prompted or directed by a sense of duty, there is so much virtue.

Having premised thus much concerning the place which parental duties hold in the scale of human virtues, we proceed to state and explain the duties themselves.

When moralists tell us, that parents are bound to do *all they can* for their children, they tell us more than is true; for, at that rate, every expence which might have been spared, and every profit omitted, which might have been made, would be criminal.

The duty of parents has its limits, like other duties; and admits, if not of perfect precision, at least of rules definite enough for application.

These rules may be explained under the several heads of *maintenance, education,* and *a reasonable provision for the child's happiness* in respect of outward condition.

I. *Maintenance.*

The wants of children make it necessary that some person maintain them; and, as no one has a right to burthen others by his act, it follows, that the parents are bound to undertake this charge themselves. Beside this plain inference, the affection of parents to their children, if it be instinctive, and the provision which God has prepared in the perſon of the mother for the ſuſtentation of the infant, concerning the exiſtence and deſign of which there can be no doubt, are manifeſt indications of the divine will.

From hence we learn the guilt of thoſe, who run away from their families, or, (what is much the ſame) in conſequence of idleneſs or drunkenneſs throw them upon a pariſh; or who leave them deſtitute at their death, when, by diligence and frugality, they might have laid up a proviſion for their ſupport: alſo of thoſe, who refuſe or neglect the care of their baſtard offspring, abandoning them to a condition in which they muſt either periſh or become burthenſome to others; for the duty of maintenance, like the reaſon upon which it is founded, extends to baſtards, as well as to legitimate children.

The Chriſtian ſcriptures, although they concern themſelves little with maxims of prudence or œconomy, and much leſs authorize worldly mindedneſs or avarice, have yet declared in explicit terms their judgment of the obligation of this duty: " if any provide not for his own, " eſpecially for thoſe of his own houſehold, he hath denied " the faith, and is worſe than an infidel," (1 Tim. v. 8.) he hath diſgraced the Chriſtian profeſſion, and fallen ſhort in a duty which even infidels acknowledge.

II. *Education.*

Education, in the most extensive sense of the word, may comprehend every preparation that is made in our youth for the sequel of our lives: and in this sense I use it.

Some such preparation is necessary for children of all conditions, because, without it they must be miserable, and probably will be vicious, when they grow up, either from want of the means of subsistence, or from want of rational and inoffensive occupation. In civilized life, every thing is effected by art and skill. Whence a person who is provided with neither (and neither can be acquired without exercise and instruction) will be useless; and he that is useless, will generally be at the same time mischievous to the community. So that to send an uneducated child into the world is injurious to the rest of mankind; it is little better than to turn out a mad dog, or a wild beast into the streets.

In the inferior classes of the community, this principle condemns the neglect of parents, who do not inure their children betimes to labour and restraint, by providing them with apprenticeships, services, or other regular employment, but suffer them to waste their youth in idleness and vagrancy, or to betake themselves to some lazy, trifling, and precarious calling: for the consequence of having thus tasted the sweets of natural liberty, at an age when their passion and relish for it are at the highest, is, that they become incapable for the remainder of their lives of continued industry, or of persevering attention to any thing; spend their time in a miserable struggle between the importunity of want, and the irksomeness of regular application; and are prepared to embrace every expedient, which presents a hope of supplying their necessities, without confining them to the plough, the loom, the shop, or the counting-house.

In the middle orders of society, those parents are most reprehensible, who neither qualify their children for a profession, nor enable them to live without one*: and those in the highest, who, from indolence, indulgence, or avarice, omit to procure their children those liberal attainments, which are necessary to make them useful in the stations to which they are destined. A man of fortune, who permits his son to consume the season of education, in hunting, shooting, or in frequenting horse-races, assemblies, or other unedifying, though not vicious diversions, defrauds the community of a benefactor, and bequeaths them a nuisance.

Some, though not the same, preparation for the sequel of their lives, is necessary for youth of every description; and therefore for bastards, as well as for children of better expectations. Consequently, they who leave the education of their bastards to chance, contenting themselves

---

* Amongst the Athenians, if the parent did not put his child into a way of getting a livelihood, the child was not bound to make provision for the parent when old and necessitous.

with

with making provision for their subsistence, desert half their duty.

III. A reasonable provision for the happiness of a child in respect of outward condition, requires three things: a situation suited to his habits and reasonable expectations; a competent provision for the exigencies of that situation; and a probable security for his virtue.

The two first articles will vary with the condition of the parent. A situation somewhat approaching in rank and condition to the parent's own; or, where that is not practicable, similar to what other parents of like condition provide for their children, bounds the reasonable, as well as, (generally speaking,) the actual expectations of the child, and therefore contains the extent of the parent's obligation.

Hence, a peasant satisfies his duty, who sends out his children, properly instructed for their occupation, to husbandry, or to any branch of manufacture. Clergymen, lawyers, physicians, officers in the army or navy, gentlemen possessing moderate fortunes of inheritance, or exercising trade in a large or liberal way, are required by the same rule to provide their sons with learned professions, commissions in the army or navy, places in public offices, or reputable branches of merchandise. Providing a child with a situation, includes a competent supply for the expences of that situation, until the profits of it enable the child to support himself. Noblemen, and gentlemen of high rank and fortune, may be bound to transmit an inheritance to the representatives of their family, sufficient for their support without the aid of a trade or profession, to which there is little hope that a youth, who has been flattered with other expectations, will apply himself with diligence or success. In these parts of the world, public opinion has assorted the members of the community into four or five general classes, each class comprizing a great variety of employments and professions, the choice of which must be committed to the private discretion of the parent.* All that can be expected from parents as a *duty*, and

* The health and virtue of a child's future life are considerations so superior to all others, that whatever is likely to have the smallest influence upon these, deserves the parent's first attention. In respect of health, agriculture, and all active, rural, and out-of-door employments, are to be preferred to manufactures, and sedentary occupations. In respect of virtue, a course of dealings in which the advantage is mutual, in which the profit on one side is connected with the benefit of the other (which is the case in trade, and all serviceable art or labour) is more favourable to the moral character, than callings in which one man's gain is another man's loss, in which, what you acquire, is acquired without equivalent, and parted with in distress; as in gaming, and whatever partakes of gaming, and in the predatory profits of war. The following distinctions also deserve notice. A business, like a retail trade, in which the profits are small and frequent, and accruing from the employment, furnishes a moderate and constant engagement to the mind, and so far, suits better with the general disposition of mankind, than professions which are supported by fixed salaries, as stations in the church, army, navy, revenue, public offices, &c. or wherein the profits are made in large sums, by a few great concerns, or fortunate adventures; as in many branches of wholesale and foreign merchandize, in which the occupation is neither so constant, nor the activity so kept alive

and therefore the only rule which a moralist can deliver upon the subject is, that they endeavour to preserve their children in the *class* in which they are born, that is to say, in which others of similar expectations are accustomed to be placed; and that they be careful to confine their hopes and habits of indulgence to objects which will continue to be attainable.

It is an ill-judged thrift in some rich parents, to bring up their sons to mean employments, for the sake of saving the charge of a more expensive education: for these sons, when they become masters of their liberty and fortune, will hardly continue in occupations, by which they think themselves degraded, and are seldom qualified for any thing better.

An attention, in the first place, to the exigencies of the children's respective conditions in the world; and a regard, in the second place, to their reasonable expectations, always postponing the expectations to the exigencies, when both cannot be satisfied, ought to guide parents in the disposal of their fortunes after their death. And these exigencies and expectations must be measured by the standard which custom has established; for there is a certain appearance,

---

alive by immediate encouragement. For security, manual arts exceed merchandize, and such as supply the wants of mankind are better than those which minister to their pleasure. Situations which promise an early settlement in marriage, are on many accounts to be chosen before those, which require a longer waiting for a larger establishment.

attendance, establishment, and mode of living, which custom has annexed to the several ranks and orders of civil life, (and which compose what is called *decency*,) together with a certain society, and particular pleasures belonging to each class; and a young person, who is with-held from sharing in these by want of fortune, can scarcely be said to have a fair chance for happiness; the indignity and mortification of such a seclusion being what few tempers can bear, or bear with contentment. And as to the second consideration, of what a child may reasonably expect from his parent, he will expect, what he sees all or most others in similar circumstances receive; and we can hardly call expectations unreasonable, which it is impossible to suppress.

By virtue of this rule, a parent is justified in making a difference between his children, according as they stand in greater or less need of the assistance of his fortune, in consequence of the difference of their age or sex, or of the situations in which they are placed, or the various success which they have met with.

On account of the few lucrative employments which are left to the female sex, and by consequence the little opportunity they have of adding to their income, daughters ought to be the particular objects of a parent's care and foresight: and as an option of marriage, from which they can reasonably expect happiness, is not presented to every woman who deserves it, especially in the present times,

times, in which a licentious celibacy seems to have grown into fashion with the men, a father should endeavour to enable his daughters to lead a single life with independency and decorum, even though he substract more for that purpose from the portions of his sons, than is agreeable to modern usage, or than they expect.

But when the exigencies of their several situations are provided for, and not before, a parent ought to admit the second consideration, the satisfaction of his children's expectations; and upon that principle to prefer the eldest son to the rest, and sons to daughters: which constitutes the right, and the whole right of primogeniture, as well as the only reason for the preference of one sex to the other. The preference, indeed, of the first born has one public good effect, that if the estate were divided equally amongst the sons, it would probably make them all idle; whereas, by the present rule of descent, it makes only one so; which is the less evil of the two. And it must farther be observed on the part of sons, that if the rest of the community make it a rule to prefer sons to daughters, an individual of that community ought to guide himself by the same rule, upon principles of mere equality. For as the son suffers by the rule in the fortune he may expect in marriage, it is but reasonable that he should receive the advantage of it in his own inheritance. Indeed, whatever the rule be, as to the preference of one sex to the other, marriage restores the equality. And as money is generally more convertible to profit, and more likely to promote industry,

industry, in the hands of men than of women, the custom of this country may properly be complied with, when it does not interfere with the weightier reason explained in the last paragraph.

The point of the children's actual expectations, together with the expediency of subjecting the illicit commerce of the sexes to every discouragement which it can receive, makes the difference between the claims of legitimate children and of bastards. But neither reason will in any case justify the leaving of bastards to the world, without provision, education, or profession; or, what is more cruel, without the means of continuing in the situation to which the parent has introduced them: which last, is to leave them to inevitable misery.

After the first requisite, namely, a provision for the exigencies of his situation, is satisfied, a parent may diminish a child's portion, in order to punish any flagrant crime, or to punish contumacy and want of filial duty in instances not otherwise criminal: for a child who is conscious of bad behaviour, or of contempt of his parent's will and happiness, cannot reasonably expect the same instances of his munificence.

A child's vices may be of that sort, and his vicious habits so incorrigible, as to afford much the same reason for believing that he will waste or misemploy the fortune put into his power, as if he were mad or idiotish, in which case a parent may treat him as a madman or an idiot; that is, may deem it sufficient to provide for this support, by an annuity equal to his wants and innocent enjoyments, and which he may be restrained from alienating. This seems to be the only case, in which a disinherison, nearly absolute, is justifiable.

Let not a father hope to excuse an officious disposition of his fortune, by alleging, that " every man may do " what he will with his own." All the truth which this expression contains, is, that his discretion is under no controul of law; and that his will, however capricious, will be valid. This, by no means, absolves his conscience from the obligations of a parent, or imports that he may neglect, without injustice, the several wants and expectations of his family, in order to gratify a whim or a pique, or indulge a preference founded in no reasonable distinction of merit and situation. Although, in his intercourse with his family, and the lesser endearments of domestic life, a parent may not always resist his partiality to a favourite child, (which, however, should be both avoided and concealed, as oftentimes productive of lasting jealousies and discontents) yet when he sits down to make his will, these tendernesses must give place to more manly deliberations.

A father of a family is bound to adjust his œconomy with a view to these demands upon his fortune; and until a sufficiency for these ends is acquired, or in due time

probably

probably will be acquired, (for in human affairs *probability* is enough) frugality and exertions of industry are duties: he is also justified in declining expensive liberality; for to take from those who want, in order to give to those who want, adds nothing to the stock of public happiness. Thus far, therefore, and no farther, the plea of " children," " of large " families," " charity begins at home," &c. is an excuse for parsimony, and an answer to those who solicit our bounty. Beyond this point, as the use of riches becomes less, the desire of *laying up* should abate proportionably. The truth is, our children gain not so much as we imagine, in the chance of this world's happiness, or even of its external prosperity, by setting out in it with large capitals. Of those who die rich, a great part began with little. And, in respect of enjoyment, there is no comparison between a fortune, which a man acquires himself by a fruitful industry, or a series of successes in his business, and one found in his possession, or received from another.

A principal part of the parent's duty is still behind, viz. the using of proper precautions and expedients, in order to form and preserve his children's virtue.

To us, who believe that in one stage or other of our existence virtue will conduct to happiness, and vice terminate in misery; and who observe withal, that men's virtues and vices are, to a certain degree, produced or affected by the management of their youth, and the situations in which they are placed; to all who attend to these reafons, the obligation to confult a child's virtue will appear to differ in nothing from that, by which the parent is bound to provide for his maintenance or fortune. The child's intereft is concerned in the one means of happinefs as well as in the other; and both means are equally, and almoft exclufively, in the parent's power.

The firft point to be endeavoured after is to imprefs upon children the idea of *accountablenefs*, that is, to accuftom them to look forward to the confequences of their actions in another world; which can only be brought about by the parents vifibly acting with a view to thefe confequences themfelves. Parents, to do them juftice, are feldom fparing in leffons of virtue and religion; in admonitions which coft little and profit lefs, whilft their *example* exhibits a continual contradiction of what they teach. A father, for inftance, will, with much folemnity and apparent earneftnefs, warn his fon againft idlenefs, excefs in drinking, debauchery, and extravagance, who himfelf loiters about all day without employment; comes home every night drunk; is made infamous in his neighbourhood by fome profligate connection; and waftes the fortune which fhould fupport or remain a provifion for his family, in riot, or luxury, or oftentation. Or he will difcourfe gravely before his children of the obligation and importance of revealed religion, whilft they fee the moft frivolous and oftentimes feigned excufes detain him from its reafonable and folemn ordinances. Or he will fet before them, perhaps, the fupreme and tremendous authority of Almighty God;

that such a being ought not to be named, or even thought upon, without sentiments of profound awe and veneration. This may be the lecture he delivers to his family one hour; when the next, if an occasion arise to excite his anger, his mirth, or his surprise, they will hear him treat the name of the Deity with the most irreverent profanation, and sport with the terms and denunciations of the Christian religion, as if they were the language of some ridiculous and long exploded superstition. Now even a child is not to be imposed upon by such mockery. He sees through the grimace of this counterfeited concern for virtue. He discovers that his parent is acting a part; and receives his admonitions, as he would hear the same maxims from the mouth of a player. And when once this opinion has taken possession of the child's mind, it has a fatal effect upon the parent's influence in all subjects; even in those, in which he himself may be sincere and convinced. Whereas a silent, but observable regard to the duties of religion, in the parent's own behaviour, will take a sure and gradual hold of the child's disposition, much beyond formal reproofs and chidings, which, being generally prompted by some present provocation, discover more of anger than of principle, and are always received with a temporary alienation and disgust.

A good parent's first care is to be virtuous himself; his second, to make his virtues as easy and engaging to those about him, as their nature will admit. Virtue itself offends, when coupled with forbidding manners. And some

virtues

virtues may be urged to such excess, or brought forwards so unseasonably, as to discourage and repel those, who observe and who are acted upon by them, instead of exciting an inclination to imitate and adopt them. Young minds are particularly liable to these unfortuuate impressions. For instance, if a father's œconomy degenerate into a minute and teasing parsimony, it is odds, but that the son, who has suffered under it, set out a sworn enemy to all rules of order and frugality. If a father's piety be morose, rigorous, and tinged with melancholy, perpetually breaking in upon the recreations of his family, and surfeiting them with the language of religion upon all occasions, there is danger, lest the son carry from home with him a settled prejudice against seriousness and religion, as inconsistent with every plan of a pleasureable life, and turn out, when he mixes with the world, a character of levity or dissoluteness.

Something likewise may be done towards the correcting or improving of those early inclinations which children discover by disposing them into situations the least dangerous to their particular characters. Thus I would make choice of a retired life for young persons addicted to licentious pleasures; of private stations for the proud and passionate; of liberal professions, and a town life, for the mercenary and sottish: and not, according to the general practice of parents, send dissolute youths into the army; pernurious tempers to trade; or make a crafty lad an attorney; or flatter a vain and haughty temper with elevated

vated names, or situations, or callings, to which the fashion of the world has annexed precedency and distinction, but in which his disposition, without at all promoting his success, will serve both to multiply and exasperate his disappointments. In the same way, that is, with a view to the particular frame and tendency of the pupil's character, I would make choice of a public or private education. The reserved, timid, and indolent will have their faculties called forth, and their nerves invigorated by a public education. Youths of strong spirits and passions will be safer in a private education. At our public schools, as far as I have observed, more literature is acquired, and more vice: quick parts are cultivated, slow ones are neglected. Under private tuition, a moderate proficiency in juvenile learning is seldom exceeded, but oftener attained.

CHAP. X.

THE RIGHTS OF PARENTS.

THE Rights of Parents refult from their duties. If it be the duty of a parent to educate his children, to form them for a life of ufefulnefs and virtue, to provide for them fituations needful for their fubfiftence, and fuited to their circumftances, and to prepare them for thofe fituations; he has a right to fuch authority, and, in fupport of that authority, to exercife fuch difcipline, as may be neceffary for thefe purpofes. The law of nature acknowledges no other foundation of a parent's right over his children, befide his duty towards them, (I fpeak now of fuch rights as may be enforced by coercion). This relation confers no property in their perfons, or natural dominion over them, as is commonly fuppofed.

Since it is, in general, neceffary to determine the deftination of children, before they are capable of judging of their own happinefs, parents have a right to elect profeffions for them.

As the mother herfelf owes obedience to the father, her authority muft fubmit to his. In a competition, therefore, of commands, the father is to be obeyed. In case of the death of either, the authority, as well as duty, of both parents devolves upon the survivor.

These rights, always following the duty, belong likewise to guardians; and so much of them, as is delegated by the parents or guardians, belongs to tutors, schoolmasters, &c.

From this principle, " that the rights of parents result " from their duty," it follows, that parents have no natural right over the lives of their children, as was absurdly allowed to *Roman* fathers; nor any to exercise unprofitable severities; nor to command the commission of crimes: for these rights can never be wanted for the purposes of a parent's duty.

Nor, for the same reason, have parents any right to sell their children into slavery. Upon which, by the way, we may observe, that the children of slaves are not, by the law of nature, born slaves; for, as the master's right is derived to him through the parent, it can never be greater than the parent's own.

Hence also it appears, that parents not only pervert, but exceed their just authority, when they consult their own ambition, interest, or prejudice, at the manifest expence of their children's happiness. Of which abuse of parental power, the following are instances: the shutting up up of daughters and younger sons in nunneries and monasteries, in order to preserve entire the estate and dignity of the family; or the using of any arts, either of kindness or unkindness, to induce them to make choice of this way of life themselves; or, in countries where the clergy are prohibited from marriage, putting sons into the church for the same end, who are never likely either to do or receive any good in it, sufficient to compensate for this sacrifice; the urging of children to marriages, from which they are averse, with the view of exalting or enriching the family, or for the sake of connecting estates, parties, or interests; or the opposing of a marriage, in which the child would probably find his happiness, from a motive of pride or avarice, of family hostility or personal pique.

CHAP. XI.

THE DUTY OF CHILDREN.

THE Duty of Children may be considered,

I. During childhood.

II. After they have attained to manhood, but continue in their father's family.

III. After they have attained to manhood, and have left their father's family.

I. *During childhood.*

Children must be supposed to have attained to some degree of discretion before they are capable of any duty. There is an interval of eight or nine years, between the dawning and the maturity of reason, in which it is necessary to subject the inclination of children to many restraints, and direct their application to many employments, of the tendency and use of which they cannot judge; for which cause, the submission of children during this period must be ready and implicit, with an exception, however, of any manifest crime, which may be commanded him.

II. *After they have attained to manhood, but continue in their father's family.*

If children, when they are grown up, voluntarily continue members of their father's family, they are bound, beside the general duty of gratitude to their parents, to observe such regulations of the family as the father shall appoint; contribute their labour to its support, if required; and confine themselves to such expences as he shall allow. The obligation would be the same, if they were admitted into any other family, or received support from any other hand.

III. *After they have attained to manhood, and have left their father's family.*

In this state of the relation, the duty to parents is simply the duty of gratitude; not different *in kind,* from that which we owe to any other benefactor; *in degree,* just so much exceeding other obligations, by how much a parent has been a greater benefactor than any other friend. The services and attentions, by which filial gratitude may be testified, can be comprised within no enumeration. It will shew itself in compliances with the will of the parents, however contrary to the child's own taste or judgment, provided it be neither criminal, nor totally inconsistent

consistent with his happiness; in a constant endeavour to promote their enjoyments, prevent their wishes, and soften their anxieties, in small matters as well as in great; in assisting them in their business; in contributing to their support, ease, or better accommodation, when their circumstances require it; in affording them our company, in preference to more amusing engagements; in waiting upon their sickness or decrepitude; in bearing with the infirmities of their health or temper, with the peevishness and complaints, the unfashionable, negligent, austere manners, and offensive habits, which often attend upon advanced years; for where must old age find indulgence, if it do not meet with it in the piety and partiality of children?

The most serious contentions between parents and their children, are those commonly, which relate to marriage, or to the choice of a profession.

A parent has, in no case, a right to destroy his child's happiness. If it be true therefore, that there exist such personal and exclusive attachments between individuals of different sexes, that the possession of a particular man or woman in marriage be really necessary to the child's happiness; or if it be true, that an aversion to a particular profession may be involuntary and unconquerable; then it will follow, that parents, where this is the case, ought not to urge their authority, and that the child is not bound to obey it.

The

The point *is*, to discover how far, in any particular instance, this *is* the case. Whether the fondness of lovers ever continues with such intensity, and so long, that the success of their desires constitutes, or the disappointment affects, any considerable portion of their happiness, compared with that of their whole life, it is difficult to determine; but there can be no difficulty in pronouncing, that not one half of those attachments, which young people conceive with so much haste and passion, are of this sort. I believe it also to be true, that there are few aversions to a profession, which resolution, perseverance, activity in going about the duty of it, and above all, despair of changing, will not subdue: yet there are some such. Wherefore, a child who respects his parent's judgment, and is, as he ought to be, tender of his happiness, owes, at least, so much deference to his will, as to try fairly and faithfully, in one case, whether time and absence will not quench his affection; and in the other, whether a longer continuance in his profession may not reconcile him to it. The whole depends upon the experiment being made on the child's part with sincerity, and not merely with a design of compassing his purpose at last, by means of a simulated and temporary compliance. It is the nature of love and hatred, and of all violent affections, to delude the mind with a persuasion, that we shall always continue to feel them, as we feel them at present. We cannot conceive that they will either change or cease. Experience of similar or greater changes in ourselves, or a habit of giving credit to what our parents or tutors or books teach us, may control this perfuasion; otherwife it renders youth very untractable: for they fee clearly and truly, that it is impoffible they fhould be happy under the circumftances propofed to them, in their prefent ftate of mind. After a fincere, but ineffectual endeavour, by the child, to accommodate his inclination to his parent's pleafure, he ought not to fuffer in his parent's affection, or in his fortunes. The parent, when he has reafonable proof of this, fhould acquiefce: at all events, the child is *then* at liberty to provide for his own happinefs.

Parents have no right to urge their children upon marriages, to which they are averfe; nor ought, in any fhape, to refent the children's difobedience to fuch commands. This is a different cafe from oppofing a match of inclination, becaufe the child's mifery is a much more probable confequence; it being eafier to live without a perfon that we love, than with one whom we hate. Add to this, that compulfion in marriage neceffarily leads to prevarication; as the reluctant party promifes an affection, which neither exifts, nor is expected to take place: and parental, like all human authority ceafes, at the point, where obedience becomes criminal.

In the above-mentioned, and in all contefts between parents and children, it is the parent's duty to reprefent to the child the confequences of his conduct; and it will be

found

found his best policy to represent them with fidelity. It is usual for parents to exaggerate these descriptions beyond probability, and by exaggeration to lose all credit with their children; thus, in a great measure, defeating their own end.

Parents are forbidden to interfere, where a trust is reposed personally in the son; and where, consequently, the son was expected, and by virtue of that expectation is obliged, to pursue his own judgment, and not that of any other; as is the case with judicial magistrates, in the execution of their office; with members of the legislature in their votes; with electors, where preference is to be given to certain prescribed qualifications. The son may assist his own judgment by the advice of his father, or of any one whom he chooses to consult: but his own judgment, whether it proceed upon knowledge or authority, ought finally to determine his conduct.

The duty of children to their parents was thought worthy to be made the subject of one of the ten commandments; and, as such, is recognized by *Christ*, together with the rest of the moral precepts of the decalogue, in various places of the gospel.

The same divine teacher's sentiments concerning the relief of indigent parents, appear sufficiently from that manly and deserved indignation, with which he reprehended ed the wretched cafuiftry of the *Jewifh* expofitors, who, under the name of a tradition, had contrived a method of evading this duty, by converting, or pretending to convert, to the treafury of the temple, fo much of their property, as their diftreffed parent might be entitled by their law to demand.

Agreeably to this law of nature and Chriftianity, children are, by the law of *England*, bound to fupport, as well their immediate parents, as their grandfathers and grandmothers, or remoter anceftors, who ftand in need of fupport.

Obedience to parents is injoined by St. *Paul* to the *Ephefians*, " Children obey your parents in the Lord, for this " is right;" and to the *Coloffians*, " Children obey your pa" rents inall things, for this is well pleafing unto the Lord."*

By the *Jewifh* law, difobedience to parents was, in fome extreme cafes, capital. Deut. xxi. 18.

---

* Upon which two phrafes, " this is right," and " for this is well pleafing " unto the Lord," being ufed by St. *Paul* in a fenfe perfectly parallel, we may obferve, that moral rectitude and conformity to the divine will, were, in his apprehenfion, the fame.

MORAL PHILOSOPHY.

BOOK IV.

DUTIES TO OURSELVES.

THIS division of the subject is merely for the sake of *method*, by which the writer and the reader are equally assisted. To the subject itself it imports nothing; for the obligation of all duties being fundamentally the same, it matters little under what class or title any of them are considered. In strictness, there are few duties or crimes, which terminate in a man's self; and, so far as others are affected by their operation, they have been treated of in some article of the preceding book. We have reserved to this head the *rights of self-defence;* also the consideration of *drunkenness* and *suicide*, as offences against that care of our faculties, and preservation of our person, which we account duties, and call *duties to ourselves*.

CHAP.

CHAP. I.

THE RIGHTS OF SELF-DEFENCE.

IT has been asserted, that in a state of nature we might lawfully defend the most insignificant right, provided it were a perfect determinate right, by any extremities which the obstinacy of the aggressor made necessary. Of this I doubt; because I doubt whether the general rule be worth sustaining at such an expence, and because, apart from the general consequence of yielding to the attempt, it cannot be contended to be for the augmentation of human happiness, that one man should lose his life or a limb, rather than another a pennyworth of his property. Nevertheless, perfect rights can only be distinguished by their value; and it is impossible to ascertain the value, at which the liberty of using extreme violence begins. The person attacked must balance, as well as he can, between the general consequence of yielding, and the particular effect of resistance.

However, this right, if it exist in a state of nature, is suspended by the establishment of civil society; because *thereby* other remedies are provided against attacks upon our property, and because it is necessary to the peace and safety of the community, that the prevention, punishment, and redress of injuries be adjusted by public laws. Moreover, as the individual is assisted in the recovery of his right, or of a compensation for it, by the public strength, it is no less equitable than expedient, that he should submit to public arbitration, the manner as well as the measure of the satisfaction which he is to obtain.

There is one case in which all extremities are justifiable, namely, when our life is assaulted, and it becomes necessary for our preservation to kill the assailant. This is evident in a state of nature; unless it can be shown, that we are bound to prefer the aggressor's life to our own, that is to say, to love our enemy *better than* ourselves, which can never be a debt of justice, nor any where appears to be a duty of charity. Nor is the case altered by our living in civil society; because, by the supposition, the laws of society cannot interpose to protect us, nor by the nature of the case compel restitution. This liberty is restrained to cases, in which no other probable means of preserving our life remain, as flight, calling for assistance, disarming the adversary, &c. The rule holds, whether the danger proceed from a voluntary attack, as by an enemy, robber, or assassin; or from an involuntary one, as by a madman, or person sinking in the water, and dragging us after him; or where two persons are reduced to a situation, in which one or both of them must perish; as in a ship-wreck, where two seize upon a plank, which will support only one: although, to say the truth, these extreme cases, which happen seldom, and hardly, when they do happen, admit of moral agency, are scarcely worth mentioning, much less debating.

The instance, which approaches the nearest to the preservation of life, and which seems to justify the same extremities, is the defence of chastity.

In all other cases, it appears to me the safest to consider the taking away of life as authorised by the law of the land; and the person who takes it away, as in the situation of a minister or executioner of the law.

In which view, homicide, in *England*, is justifiable:

1. To prevent the commission of a crime, which, when committed, would be punishable with death. Thus it is lawful to shoot a highwayman, or one attempting to break into a house by night; but not by day: which particular distinction, by a consent that is remarkable, obtained also in the *Jewish* law, as well as in the laws both of *Greece* and *Rome*.

2. In necessary endeavours to carry the law into execution, as in suppressing riots, apprehending malefactors, preventing escapes, &c.

I do not know, that the law holds forth its authority to any cases beside those which fall within one or other of the above descriptions; or that after the exception of
immediate

immediate danger to life or chastity, the destruction of a human being can be innocent without that authority.

The rights of war are not here taken into the account.

CHAP. II.

DRUNKENNESS.

DRUNKENNESS is either actual or habitual; just as it is one thing to be drunk, and another to be a drunkard. What we shall deliver upon the subject, must principally be understood of a *habit* of intemperance; although *part* of the guilt and danger described may be applicable to casual excesses; and *all* of it, in a certain degree, forasmuch as every habit is only a repetition of single instances.

The mischief of drunkenness, from which we are to compute the guilt of it, consists in the following bad effects:

1. It betrays most constitutions either into extravagancies of anger, or sins of lewdness.

2. It disqualifies men for the duties of their station, both by the temporary disorder of their faculties, and at length by a constant incapacity and stupefaction.

3. It is attended with expences, which can often be ill spared.

4. It is sure to occasion uneasiness to the family of the drunkard.

5. It shortens life.

To these consequences of drunkenness must be added the peculiar danger and mischief of the *example*. Drunkenness is a social festive vice; apt, beyond any vice I can mention, to draw in others by the example. The drinker collects his circle; the circle naturally spreads; of those who are drawn within it, many become the corrupters and centers of sets and circles of their own; every one countenancing, and, perhaps, emulating the rest, 'till a whole neighbourhood be infected from the contagion of a single example. This account is confirmed by what we often observe of drunkenness, that it is a *local* vice; found to prevail in certain countries, in certain districts of a country, or in particular towns, without any reason to be given for the fashion, but that it had been introduced by some popular examples. With this observation upon the spreading quality of drunkenness, let us connect a remark which belongs to the several evil effects above recited. The consequences of a vice, like the symptoms of a disease, though they be all enumerated in the description, seldom all meet in the same subject. In the instance under consideration, the age and temperature of one drunkard may have little to fear from inflammations of lust or anger; the fortune of a second may not be injured by the expence; a third may have no family to be disquieted by his irregularities; and a fourth may possess a constitution fortified against the poison of strong liquors. But if, as we always ought to do, we comprehend within the consequences of our conduct the mischief and tendency of the example, the above circumstances, however fortunate for the individual, will be found to vary the guilt of his intemperance, less, probably, than he supposes. Although the waste of time and money may be of small importance to you, it may be of the utmost to some one or other whom your society corrupts. Repeated, or long continued excesses, which hurt not *your* health, may be fatal to your companion. Although you have neither wife nor child, nor parent, to lament your absence from home, or expect your return to it with terror; other families, whose husbands and fathers have been invited to share in your ebriety, or encouraged to imitate it, may justly lay their misery or ruin at your door. This will hold good, whether the person seduced, be seduced immediately by you, or the vice be propagated from you to him, through several intermediate examples. A moralist must assemble all these considerations, to judge truly of a vice, which usually meets with milder names, and more indulgence than it deserves.

I omit those outrages upon one another, and upon the peace and safety of the neighbourhood, in which drunken revels often end; and also those deleterious and maniacal effects, which strong liquors produce upon particular constitutions; because, in general propositions concerning drunkenness, no consequences should be included, but what are constant enough to be generally expected.

Drunkenness is repeatedly forbidden by St. *Paul*, " Be " not drunk with wine, wherein is excess." " Let us " walk honestly as in the day, not in rioting and drunken- " ness." " Be not deceived, neither fornicators————nor " *drunkards*, nor revilers, nor extortioners, shall inherit the " kingdom of God." *Eph.* v. 18. *Rom.* xiii. 13. 1 *Cor.* vi. 9, 10. The same Apostle likewise condemns drunkenness, as peculiarly inconsistent with the Christian profession; " They that be drunken, are drunken in the night; but let " us, who are of the day, be sober." 1 *Thess.* v. 7, 8. We are not concerned with the argument; the words amount to a prohibition of drunkenness; and the authority is conclusive.

It is a question of some importance, how far drunkenness is an excuse for the crimes which the drunken person commits.

In the solution of this question, we will first suppose the drunken person to be altogether deprived of moral agency, that is to say, of all reflection and foresight. In this condition, it is evident that he is no more capable of guilt than a madman; although, like him, he may be extremely mischievous. The only guilt, with which he is chargeable, was incurred at the time when he voluntarily brought himself into this situation. And as every man is responsible for the consequences which he foresaw, or might have foreseen, and for no other, this guilt will be in proportion to the probability of such consequences ensuing. From which principle results the following rule, viz. that the guilt of any action in a drunken man bears the same proportion to the guilt of the like action in a sober man, that the probability of its being the consequence of drunkenness bears to absolute certainty. By virtue of this rule, those vices, which are the *known* effects of drunkenness, either in general, or upon particular constitutions, are, in all, or in men of such constitutions, nearly as criminal, as if committed with all their faculties and senses about them.

If the privation of reason be only partial, the guilt will be of a mixt nature. For so much of his self-government as the drunkard retains, he is as responsible then, as at any other time. He is entitled to no abatement, beyond the strict proportion in which his moral faculties are impaired. Now I call the guilt of the crime, if a sober man had committed it, the *whole* guilt. A person in the condition we describe, incurs part of this at the instant of perpetration; and by bringing himself into this condition, he incurred such a fraction of the remaining part, as the danger of this consequence was of an integral certainty. For the sake of illustration, we are at liberty to suppose, that a man loses half his moral faculties by drunkenness: this
leaving

leaving him but half his responsibility, he incurs, when he commits the action, half of the whole guilt. We will also suppose that it was known before-hand, that it was an even chance, or half a certainty, that this crime would follow his getting drunk. This makes him chargeable with half of the remainder; so that altogether, he is responsible in three fourths of the guilt, which a sober man would have incurred by the same action.

I do not mean that any real case can be reduced to numbers, or the calculation made with arithmetical precision: but these are the principles, and this the rule, by which our general admeasurement of the guilt of such offences, should be regulated.

The appetite for intoxicating liquors appears to me to be almost always *acquired*. One proof of which is, that it is apt to return only at particular times and places; as after dinner, in the evening, on the market day, at the market town, in such a company, at such a tavern. And this may be the reason, that if a habit of drunkenness be ever overcome, it is upon some change of place, situation, company, or profession. A man sunk deep in a habit of drunkenness, will upon such occasions as these, when he finds himself loosened from the associations which held him fast, sometimes make a plunge, and get out. In a matter of such great importance, it is well worth while, where it is tolerably

DRUNKENNESS.

convenient, to change our habitation and society, for the sake of the experiment.

Habits of drunkenness commonly take their rise either from a fondness for and connection with some company, or some companion, already addicted to this practice; which affords an almost irresistible invitation to take a share in the indulgencies, which those about us are enjoying with so much apparent relish and delight: or from want of regular employment, which is sure to let in many superfluous cravings and customs, and often this amongst the rest: or lastly, from grief or fatigue, both which strongly solicit that relief which inebriating liquors administer for the present, and furnish a specious excuse for complying with the inclination. But the habit, when once set in, is continued by different motives from those to which it owes its origin. Persons addicted to excessive drinking suffer, in the intervals of sobriety, and near the return of their accustomed indulgence, a faintness and oppression *circa præcordia*, which it exceeds the ordinary patience of human nature to endure. This is usually relieved, for a short time, by a repetition of the same excess: and to this relief, as to the removal of every long continued pain, they who have once experienced it, are urged almost beyond the power of resistance. This is not all: as the liquor loses its *stimulus*, the dose must be increased, to reach the same pitch of elevation, or ease; which increase proportionably accelerates the progress of all the maladies that drunkenness brings on. Whoever reflects upon the violence

lence of the craving in the advanced stages of the habit, and the fatal termination to which the gratification of it leads, will, the moment he perceives the least tendency in himself of a growing inclination to intemperance, collect his resolution to this point; or, (what perhaps he will find his best security), arm himself with some peremptory rule, as to the times and quantity of his indulgencies. I own myself a friend to the laying down of rules to ourselves of this sort, and rigidly abiding by them. They may be exclaimed against as stiff, but they are often salutary. Indefinite resolutions of abstemiousness are apt to yield to *extraordinary* occasions; and *extraordinary* occasions to occur perpetually. Whereas, the stricter the rule is, the more tenacious we grow of it; and many a man will abstain rather than break his rule, who would not easily be brought to exercise the same mortification from higher motives. Not to mention, that when our rule is once known, we are provided with an answer to every importunity.

There is a difference, no doubt, between convivial intemperance, and that solitary sottishness, which waits neither for company nor invitation. But the one, I am afraid, commonly ends in the other: and this last is the basest degradation, to which the faculties and dignity of human nature can be reduced.

CHAP. III.

SUICIDE.

THERE is no subject inmorality, in which the consideration of *general consequences* is more necessary than in this of suicide. Particular and extreme cases of suicide may be feigned, and may happen, of which it would be difficult to assign the particular harm, or demonstrate from that consideration alone the guilt. And these cases have chiefly occasioned confusion and doubtfulness in the question. Albeit, this is no more, than what is sometimes true of the most acknowledged vices. I could propose many possible cases even of murder, which, if they were detached from the general rule, and governed by their own particular consequences alone, it would be no easy undertaking to prove criminal.

The true question in the argument is no other than this— may every man who pleases to destroy his life, innocently do so? Twist, limit, and distinguish the subject as you can, it will come at last to this question.

For, shall we say, that we are then only at liberty to commit suicide, when we find our continuance in life become useless to mankind? Any one, who pleases, may make himself useless; and melancholy minds are prone to think themselves useless, when they really are not so. Suppose a law were promulged, allowing each private person to destroy every man he met, whose longer continuance in the world he judged to be *useless*; who would not condemn the latitude of such a rule? Who does not perceive that it amounts to a permission to commit murder at pleasure? A similar rule, regulating the right over our own lives, would be capable of the same extention. Beside which, no one is *useless* for the purpose of this plea, but he who has lost every capacity and opportunity of being useful, together with the possibility of recovering any degree of either; which is a state of such complete destitution and despair, as cannot, I belief, be predicated of any man living.

Or rather, shall we say, that to depart voluntarily out of life, is lawful for those alone, who leave none to lament their death? If this consideration is to be taken into the account at all, the subject of debate will be, not whether there are any to sorrow for us, but whether their sorrow for our death will exceed that which we should suffer by continuing to live. Now this is a comparison of things, so indeterminate in their nature, capable of so different a judgment, and concerning which the judgment will differ so much, according to the state of the spirits, or the pressure of any present anxiety, that it would vary little in hypocondriacal constitutions from an unqualified licence to commit suicide, whenever the distresses men
felt

felt or fancied, rose high enough to overcome the pain and dread of death. Men are never tempted to destroy themselves, but when under the oppression of some grievous uneasiness. The restrictions of the rule, therefore, ought to apply to these cases. But what effect can we look for from a rule, which proposes to weigh our own pain, against that of another; the misery that is felt against that which is only conceived; and in so corrupt a balance as the party's own distempered imagination.

In like manner, whatever other rule you assign, it will ultimately bring us to an indiscriminate toleration of suicide, in all cases in which there is danger of its being committed.

It remains, therefore, to enquire what would be the effect of such a toleration—evidently, the loss of many lives to the community, of which some might be useful or important; the affliction of *many* families, and the consternation of *all*; for mankind must live in continual alarm for the fate of their friends and dearest relations, when the restraints of religion and morality are withdrawn; when every disgust, which is powerful enough to tempt men to suicide, shall be deemed sufficient to justify it; and when the follies and vices, as well as the inevitable calamities of human life, so often make existence a burthen.

A second consideration, and perfectly distinct from the former,

former, is this. By continuing in the world, and in the exercise of those virtues which remain within our power, we retain the opportunity of meliorating our condition in a future state. This argument, it is true, does not in strictness prove suicide to be a crime; but if it supply a motive to dissuade us from committing it, it amounts to much the same thing. Now there is no condition in human life which is not capable of some virtue, active or passive. Even piety and resignation under the sufferings to which we are called, testify a trust and acquiescence in the divine counsels more acceptable, perhaps, than the most prostrate devotion; afford an edifying example to all who observe them, and may hope for a recompence among the most arduous of human virtues. These qualities are always in the power of the miserable; indeed of none but the miserable.

The two considerations above stated, belong to all cases of suicide whatever. Beside which general reasons, each case will be aggravated by its own proper and particular consequences; by the duties that are deserted; by the claims that are defrauded; by the loss, affliction, or disgrace, which our death, or the manner of it, causes to our family, kindred, or friends; by the occasion we give to many to suspect the sincerity of our moral and religious professions, and, together with ours, those of all others; by the reproach we draw upon our order, calling, or sect; in a word, by a great variety of evil consequences, attending upon peculiar situations, with some or other of which every actual case of suicide is chargeable.

I refrain

I refrain from the common topics of "deserting our "post," "throwing up our trust," "rushing uncalled into "the presence of our maker," with some others of the same sort, not because they are *common*, (for that rather affords a presumption in their favour (but because I do not perceive in them much argument, to which an answer may not easily be given.

Hitherto we have pursued upon the subject the light of nature alone, taking into the account, however, the expectation of a future existence, without which our reasoning upon this, as indeed all reasoning upon moral questions, is vain. We proceed to enquire, whether any thing is to be met with in scripture, which may add to the probability of the conclusions we have been endeavouring to support. And here, I acknowledge, that there is to be found neither any express determination of the question, nor sufficient evidence to prove, that the case of suicide was in the contemplation of the law which prohibited murder. Any inference, therefore, which we deduce from scripture, can be sustained only by construction and implication; that is to say, although they, who were authorized to instruct mankind, have not decided a question, which never, so far as appears to us, came before them; yet, I think, they have left enough to constitute a presumption, how they would have decided it, had it been proposed or thought of.

What occurs to this purpose is contained in the following observations:

1. Human

1. Human life is spoken of as a *term* assigned or prescribed to us. "Let us run with patience the race that is "set before us."—"I have finished my course."—"That "I may finish my course with joy."—"You have need of "patience, that after ye have done the will of God, ye "might receive the promise." These expressions appear to me inconsistent with the opinion, that we are at liberty to determine the duration of our lives for ourselves. If this were the case, with what propriety could life be called a race, *that is set before us*, or which is the same thing, "*our course;*" that is, the course set out, or appointed to us? The remaining quotation is equally strong: "that "after ye have done the will of God, ye might receive "the promises." The most natural meaning that can be given to the words, "after ye have done the will of "God," is, after ye have discharged the duties of life so long as God is pleased to continue you in it. According to this interpretation, the text militates strongly against suicide; and they who reject this paraphrase, will please to propose a better.

2. There is not one quality, which *Christ* and his Apostles inculcate upon their followers so often, or so earnestly, as that of patience under affliction. Now this virtue would have been in a great measure superseded, and the exhortations to it might have been spared, if the disciples of his religion had been at liberty to quit the world, as soon as they grew weary of the ill usage which they received in it. When the evils of life pressed sore, they were to look

look forward to a "far more exceeding and eternal weight "of glory;" they were to receive them "as the chastening "of the Lord," as intimations of his care and love: by these and the like reflections, they were to support and improve themselves under their sufferings, but not a hint has any where escaped of seeking relief in a voluntary death. The following text, in particular, strongly combats all impatience of distress, of which the greatest is that which prompts to acts of suicide: "Consider him that "endured such contradiction of sinners against himself, "lest ye be wearied and faint in your minds." I would offer my comment upon this passage in these two queries; first, whether a Christian convert, who had been impelled by the continuance and urgency of his sufferings, to destroy his own life, would not have been thought by the author of this text, "to have been weary," "to have "fainted in his mind," to have fallen off from that example, which is here proposed to the meditation of Christians in distress? And yet, secondly, whether such an act would not have been attended with all the circumstances of mitigation, which can excuse or extenuate suicide at this day?

3. The *conduct* of the Apostles, and of the Christians of the apostolic age, affords no obscure indication of their sentiments upon this point. They lived, we are sure, in a confirmed persuasion of the existence, as well as of the happiness, of a future state. They experienced in this world every extremity of external injury and distress. To die was gain. The change which death brought with it

was, in their expectation, infinitely beneficial. Yet it never, that we can find, entered into the intention of one of them, to haften this change by an act of fuicide: from which it is difficult to fay, what motive could have fo univerfally withheld them, except an apprehenfion of fome unlawfulnefs in the expedient.

Having ftated what we have been able to collect, in oppofition to the lawfulnefs of fuicide, by way of direct proof, it feems unneceffary to open a feparate controverfy with all the arguments, which are made ufe of to defend it; which would only lead us into a repetition of what has been offered already. The following argument, however, being fomewhat more artificial and impofing than the reft, as well as diftinct from the general confideration of the fubject, cannot fo properly be paffed over. If we deny to the individual a right over his own life, it feems impoffible, it is faid, to reconcile with the law of nature that right which the ftate claims and exercifes over the lives of its fubjects, when it ordains or inflicts capital punifhments. For this right, like all other juft authority in the ftate, can only be derived from the compact and virtual confent of the citizens which compofe the ftate; and it feems felf-evident, if any principle in morality be fo, that no one, by his confent, can transfer to another a right which he does not poffefs himfelf. It will be equally difficult to account for the power of the ftate to commit its fubjects to the dangers of war, and to expofe their lives without fcruple in the field of battle; efpecially in offenfive

hoftihostilities, in which the privileges of self-defence cannot be pleaded with any appearance of truth: and still more difficult to explain, how in such, or in any circumstances, prodigality of life can be a virtue, if the preservation of it be a duty of our nature.

This whole reasoning sets out from one error, namely, that the state acquires its right over the life of the subject from the subject's own consent, as a part of what originally and personally belonged to himself, and which he has made over to his governors. The truth is, the state derives this right, neither from the consent of the subject, nor through the medium of that consent, but, as I may say, immediately from the donation of the Deity. Finding that such a power in the sovereign of the community is expedient, if not necessary, for the community itself, it is justly presumed to be the will of God, that the sovereign should possess and exercise it. It is this *presumption* which constitutes the right; it is the same indeed which constitutes every other; and if there were the like reasons to authorize the presumption in the case of private persons, suicide would be as justifiable as war, or capital executions. But, until it can be shown, that the power over human life may be converted to the same advantage in the hands of individuals over their own, as in those of the state over the lives of the subjects, and that it may be entrusted with equal safety to both, there is no room for arguing from the existence of such a right in the latter, to the toleration of it in the former.

MORAL PHILOSOPHY.

BOOK V.

DUTIES TOWARDS GOD.

CHAP. I.

DIVISION OF THESE DUTIES.

IN one sense, every duty is a duty towards God, since it is his will which makes it a duty: but there are some duties, of which God is the object, as well as the author; and these are peculiarly, and in a more appropriated sense, called *duties towards God*.

That silent piety, which consists in a habit of tracing out the Creator's wisdom and goodness in the objects around

around us, or in the hiſtory of his diſpenſations; of referring the bleſſings we enjoy to his bounty, and of reſorting to his ſuccour in our diſtreſs, may poſſibly be more acceptable to the Deity, than any viſible expreſſions of devotion whatever. Yet theſe latter, which, although they may be excelled, are not ſuperſeded by the former, compoſe the only part of the ſubject which admits of direction or diſquiſition from a moraliſt.

Our duty towards God, ſo far as it is external, is divided into *worſhip* and *reverence*. God is the immediate object of both: and the difference between them is, that the one conſiſts in action, the other in forbearance. When we go to church on the Lord's day, led thither by a ſenſe of duty towards God, we perform an act of worſhip: when we reſt in a journey upon that day, from the ſame motive, we diſcharge a duty of reverence.

Divine worſhip is made up of adoration, thankſgiving, and prayer. But, as what we have to offer concerning the two former, may be obſerved of prayer, we ſhall make that the title of the following chapters, and the direct ſubject of our conſideration.

CHAP. II.

OF THE DUTY AND OF THE EFFICACY OF PRAYER, SO FAR AS THE SAME APPEAR FROM THE LIGHT OF NATURE.

WHEN one man desires to obtain any thing of another, he betakes himself to intreaty: and this may be observed of mankind in all ages and countries of the world. Now what is universal, may be called natural; and it seems probable, that God, as our supreme governor, should expect that towards himself, which, by a natural impulse, or by the irresistible order of our constitution, he has prompted us to pay to every other being on whom we depend.

The same may be said of thanksgiving.

Again, prayer is necessary to keep up in the minds of mankind a sense of God's agency in the universe, and of their dependency upon him.

But after all, the duty of prayer depends upon its efficacy: for I confess myself unable to conceive, how any man can pray, or be obliged to pray, who expects nothing from his prayer, but who is persuaded at the time he utters

utters his requeſt, that it cannot poſſibly produce the ſmalleſt impreſſion upon the being to whom it is addreſſed, or advantage to himſelf. Now the efficacy of prayer imports, that we obtain ſomething in conſequence of praying, which we ſhould not have received without prayer; againſt all expectation of which, the following objection has been often and ſeriouſly alledged. "If it be moſt "agreeable to perfect wiſdom and juſtice, that we ſhould "receive what we deſire, God, as perfectly wiſe and juſt, "will give it to us without aſking: if it be not agreeable to "theſe attributes of his nature, our intreaties cannot move "him to give it us; and it were impious to expect they "ſhould." In fewer words, thus; "If what we requeſt "be fit for us, we ſhall have it without praying; if it be "not fit for us, we cannot obtain it by praying." This objection admits but of one anſwer, namely, that it may be agreeable to perfect wiſdom, to grant that to our prayers, which it would not have been agreeable to the ſame wiſdom to have given us without praying for. But what virtue, you will aſk, is there in prayer, which ſhould make a favour conſiſtent with wiſdom, which would not have been ſo without it? To this queſtion, which contains the whole difficulty attending the ſubject, the following poſſibilities are offered in reply.

1. A favour granted to prayer may be more apt, on that very account, to produce good effects upon the perſon obliged. It may hold in the divine bounty, what experience has raiſed into a proverb in the collation of human

benefits,

benefits, that what is obtained without asking, is ofttimes received without gratitude.

2. It may be consistent with the wisdom of the Deity to withhold his favours till they be asked for, as an expedient to encourage devotion in his rational creation, in order thereby to keep up and circulate a knowledge and sense of their dependency upon *him*.

3. Prayer has a natural tendency to amend the petitioner himself; and thus to bring him within the rules, which the wisdom of the Deity has prescribed to the dispensation of his favours.

If these, or any other assignable suppositions, serve to remove the apparent repugnancy between the success of prayer and the character of the Deity, it is enough; for the question with the petitioner is not from which, out of many motives, God may grant his petition, or in what particular manner he is moved by the supplications of his creatures; but whether it be consistent with his nature to be moved at all, and whether there be any conceivable motives, which may dispose the divine will to grant the petitioner what he wants, in consequence of his praying for it. It is sufficient for the petitioner, that he gain his end. It is not necessary to devotion, perhaps not very consistent with it, that the circuit of causes, by which his prayers prevail, should be known to the petitioner, much less that they should be present to his imagination at the time. All that is necessary is, that there be no impossibility apprehended in the matter.

Thus much must be conceded to the objection; that prayer cannot reasonably be offered to God with all the same views, with which we oftentimes address our intreaties to men (views which are not commonly or easily separated from it), viz. to inform them of our wants or desires; to tease them out by importunity; to work upon their indolence or compassion, to persuade them to do what they ought to have done before, or ought not to do at all.

But suppose there existed a prince, who was known by his subjects to act of his own accord, always and invariably for the best; the situation of a petitioner, who solicited a favour or pardon from such a prince, would sufficiently resemble our's; and the question with him, as with us, would be, whether, the character of the prince being considered, there remained any chance that he should obtain from him by prayer, what he would not have received without it. I do not conceive, that the character of such a prince would necessarily exclude the effect of his subjects prayers; for when that prince reflected, that the earnestness and humility of the supplication had generated in the suppliant a frame of mind, upon which the pardon or favour asked, would produce a permanent and active sense of gratitude; that the granting of it to prayer would put others upon praying to him, and by that means preserve the love and submission of his subjects, upon which love and submission, their own happiness, as well as his glory, depended; that beside that the memory of the particular kindness would be heightened and prolonged by the anxiety with which it had been sued for, prayer had

in

in other refpects fo difpofed and prepared the mind of the petitioner, as to render capable of future fervices him who before was unqualified for any: might not that prince, I fay, although he proceeded upon no other confiderations than the ftrict rectitude and expediency of the meafure, grant a favour or pardon to *this man*, which he did not grant to *another*, who was too proud, too lazy, or too bufy, too indifferent whether he received it or not, or too infenfible of the fovereign's abfolute power to give or to withhold it, ever to afk for it; or even to the *philofopher*, who, from an opinion of the fruitleffnefs of all addreffes to a prince of the character which he had formed to himfelf, refufed in his own example, and difcouraged in others, all outward returns of gratitude, acknowledgements of duty, or application to the fovereign's mercy or bounty; the difufe of which (feeing affections do not long fubfift which are never expreffed) was followed by a decay of loyalty and zeal amongft his fubjects, and threatened to end in a forgetfulnefs of his rights, and a contempt of his authority? Thefe, together with other affignable confiderations, and fome perhaps infcrutable, and even inconceivable by the perfons upon whom his will was to be exercifed, might pafs in the mind of the prince, and move his counfels; whilft nothing, in the mean time, dwelt in the petitioner's thoughts but a fenfe of his own grief and wants; of the power and goodnefs from which alone he was to look for relief; and of his obligation to endeavour, by future obedience, to render that perfon propitious to his happinefs in whofe hands, and at the difpofal of whofe mercy, he found himfelf to be.

The objection to prayer supposes, that a perfectly wise being must necessarily be inexorable: but where is the proof, that *inexorability* is any part of perfect wisdom; especially of that wisdom, which is explained to consist in bringing about the most beneficial ends by the wisest means?

The objection likewise assumes another principle, which is attended with considerable difficulty and obscurity, namely, that upon every occasion, there is *one*, and only *one* mode of action *for the best;* and that the divine will is necessarily determined and confined to that mode: both which positions presume a knowledge of universal nature, much beyond what we are capable of attaining. Indeed when we apply to the divine nature such expressions as these, " God *must* always do what is right," " God *can-* " *not*, from the moral perfection and necessity of his nature, " act otherwise than for the best," we ought to apply them with much indeterminateness and reserve; or rather, we ought to confess, that there is something in the subject out of the reach of our apprehension: for to our apprehension, to be under a necessity of acting according to any rule, is inconsistent with free agency; and it makes no difference, which we can understand, whether the necessity be internal or external, or that the rule is the rule of perfect rectitude.

But efficacy is ascribed to prayer without the proof, we are told, which can alone in such a subject produce conviction,

viction, the confirmation of experience. Concerning the appeal to experience, I shall content myself with this remark, that if prayer were suffered to disturb the order of second causes appointed in the universe too much, or to produce its effect with the same regularity that they do, it would introduce a change into human affairs, which in some important respects would be evidently for the worse. Who, for example, would labour, if his necessities could be supplied with equal certainty by prayer? How few would contain within any bounds of moderation those passions and pleasures, which at present are checked only by disease or the dread of it, if prayer would infallibly restore health? In short, if the efficacy of prayer were so constant and observable as to be relied upon *before hand*, it is easy to foresee that the conduct of mankind would, in proportion to that reliance, become careless and disorderly. It is possible in the nature of things, that our prayers may, in many instances, be efficacious, and yet our experience of their efficacy be dubious and obscure. Therefore, if the light of nature instruct us by any other arguments to hope for effect from prayer; still more, if the scriptures authorize these hopes by promises of acceptance; it seems not a sufficient reason for calling in question the reality of such effects, that our observations of them are ambiguous: especially since it appears probable, that this very ambiguity is necessary to the happiness and safety of human life.

But some, whose objections do not exclude all prayer, are offended with the mode of prayer in use amongst us,

and

and with many of the subjects, which are almost universally introduced into public worship, and recommended to private devotion. To pray for particular favours by name, is to dictate, it has been said, to divine wisdom and goodness: to intercede for others, especially for whole nations and empires, is still worse: it is to presume that we possess such an interest with the Deity, as to be able, by our applications, to bend the most important of his counsels; and that the happiness of others, and even the prosperity of whole communities, is to depend upon this interest and upon our choice. Now how unequal soever our knowledge of the divine œconomy may be to the solution of this difficulty, which may require a comprehension of the entire plan, and of all the ends of God's moral government, to explain satisfactorily, we can understand one thing concerning it, that it is after all nothing more than the making of one man the instrument of happiness and misery to another; which is perfectly of a piece with the course and order that obtain, and which we must believe were intended to obtain, in human affairs. Why may we not be assisted by the prayers of other men, who are beholden *for our support to their labour?* Why may not our happiness be made in some cases to depend upon the intercession, as it certainly does in many upon the good offices of our neighbours? The happiness and misery of great numbers we see oftentimes at the disposal of one man's choice, or liable to be much affected by his conduct: what greater difficulty is there in supposing, that the prayers of an individual may avert a calamity from multitudes, or be accepted to the benefit of whole communities?

CHAP. III.

OF THE DUTY AND EFFICACY OF PRAYER, AS REPRESENTED IN SCRIPTURE.

THE reader will have observed, that the reflections stated in the preceding chapter, whatever truth and weight they may be allowed to contain, rise many of them no higher, than to negative arguments in favour of the propriety of addressing prayer to God. To prove that the efficacy of prayers is not inconsistent with the attributes of the Deity, does not prove that prayers are actually efficacious: and in the want of that unequivocal testimony, which experience alone could afford to this point, but which we do not possess, and have seen good reason why we are not to expect, the light of nature leaves us to controverted probabilities, drawn from the impulse by which mankind have been almost universally prompted to devotion, and from some beneficial purposes, which, it is conceived, may be better answered by the audience of prayer, than by any other mode of communicating the same blessings. The revelations which we deem authentic, completely supply this defect of natural religion. They require prayer to God as a duty; and they contain positive assurances of its efficacy and acceptance. We could have no reasonable motive for the exercise of prayer, without believing that it may avail to the relief of our wants. This belief can only be founded, either in a sensible experience of the effect of prayer, or in promises of acceptance, signified by divine authority. Our knowledge would have come to us in the former way, less capable, indeed, of doubt, but subjected to the abuses and inconveniences briefly described above: in the latter way, that is, by authorized significations of God's general disposition to hear and answer the devout supplications of his creatures, we are encouraged to pray, but not to place such a dependence upon prayer, as might relax other obligations, or confound the order of events and human expectations.

The scriptures not only affirm the propriety of prayer in general, but furnish precepts or examples which justify some topics and modes of prayer that have been thought exceptionable. And as the whole subject rests so much upon the foundation of scripture, I shall put down at length texts applicable to the five following heads; to the duty and efficacy of prayer in general; of prayer for particular favours by name; for public national blessings; of intercession for others; of the repetition of unsuccessful prayers.

Texts injoining prayer in general; " Ask and it shall be " given you, seek and ye shall find——If ye, being evil, " know how to give good gifts unto your children, how " much more shall your father, which is in heaven, give good
" things

DUTY AND EFFICACY OF PRAYER.

"things to them that ask him." "Watch ye therefore, "and *pray always*, that ye may be accounted worthy to "escape all those things that shall come to pass, and to "stand before the son of man." "Serving the Lord, "rejoicing in hope, patient in tribulation, *continuing in-* "*stant in prayer*." "Be careful for nothing, but in every "thing *by prayer and supplication*, with thanksgiving let "your requests be made known unto God." "I will, "therefore, that men *pray every where*, lifting up holy "hands without wrath and doubting." "*Pray without* "*ceasing*." Mat. vii. 7, 9. Luke xxi. 36. Rom. xii. 12. Phil. iv. 6. 1 Thess. v. 17. 1 Tim. ii. 8. Add to these, that Christ's reproof of the ostentation and prolixity of pharisaical prayers, and his recommendation to his disciples of retirement and simplicity in theirs, together with his dictating a particular form of prayer, all presuppose prayer to be an acceptable and availing service.

Examples of prayer for particular favours by name: " For this thing (to wit, some bodily infirmity, which he calls " a thorn given him in the flesh") I besought the " Lord thrice that it might depart from me." " Night and " day praying exceedingly, that we *might see your face*, and " perfect that which is lacking in your faith." 2 Cor. xii. " 8. 1 Thess. iii. 10.

Directions to pray for national or public blessings: " *Pray* " *for the peace of Jerusalem*." " Ask ye of the Lord rain, " in the time of the latter rain; so the Lord shall make

" bright

"bright clouds, and give them showers of rain to every
"one grass in the field." "I exhort, therefore, that first of
"all, supplications, prayers, intercessions, and giving of
"thanks, be made for all men; for kings and for all that
"are in authority, that we may lead a quiet and peaceable
"life, in all godliness and honesty; for this is good and
"acceptable in the sight of God our Saviour." *Psalm*
cxxii. 6. *Zech.* x. 1. 1 *Tim.* ii. 1, 2, 3.

Examples of intercession, and exhortations to intercede for others: "And *Moses* besought the Lord his God, "and said, Lord, why doth thy wrath wax hot against "thy people?" "Remember *Abraham, Isaac,* and *Israel,* "thy servants." "And the Lord repented of the evil "which he thought to do unto his people." "*Peter* "therefore was kept in prison, but prayer was made with- "out ceasing, of the church unto God *for him.*" "For "God is my witness, that without ceasing *I make mention* "*of you always in my prayers.*" "Now I beseech you, "brethren, for the Lord Jesus Christ's sake, and for the "love of the spirit, that ye strive together with me, in "your *prayers for me.*" "Confess your faults one to ano- "ther, and *pray one for another,* that ye may be healed: "the effectual fervent prayer of a righteous man availeth "much." *Ex.* xxxii. 11. *Acts* xii. 5. *Rom.* i. 9. xv. 30. *James* v. 16.

Declarations and examples authorizing the repetition of unsuccessful prayers: "And he spoke a parable unto
"them,

"them, to this end, that men ought always to pray, and
"not to faint." "And he left them, and went away
"again, and prayed *the third time, saying the same words.*"
"For this thing I besought the Lord *thrice* that it might
"depart from me." *Luke* xviii. 1. *Mat.* xxvi. 44. 2 *Cor.*
xii. 8 *.

* The reformed churches of Christendom, sticking close in this article to their guide, have laid aside prayers for the dead, as authorized by no precept or precedent found in scripture. For the same reason they properly reject the invocation of saints; as also because such invocations suppose in the saints whom they address a knowledge which can perceive what passes in different regions of the earth at the same time. And they deem it too much to take for granted, without the smallest intimation of such a thing in scripture, that any created being possesses a faculty little short of that omniscience and omnipresence which they ascribe to the Deity.

CHAP. IV.

OF PRIVATE PRAYER, FAMILY PRAYER, AND PUBLIC WORSHIP.

CONCERNING these three descriptions of devotion, it is first of all to be observed, that they have each their separate and peculiar use; and therefore, that the exercise of one species of worship, however regular it be, does not supersede, or dispense with the obligation of either of the other two.

I. *Private prayer* is recommended for the sake of the following advantages:

Private wants cannot always be made the subjects of public prayer; but whatever reason there is for praying at all, there is the same for making the sore and grief of each man's own heart the business of his application to God. This must be the office of private exercises of devotion, being imperfectly, if at all, practicable in any other.

Private prayer is generally more hearty and in earnest than the share we are capable of taking in joint acts of worship; because it affords leisure and opportunity for the circumstantial recollection of those personal wants, by the remembrance and ideas of which, the warmth and earnestness of prayer is chiefly excited.

Private prayer, in proportion as it is usually accompanied with more actual thought and reflection of the petitioner's own, has a greater tendency than other modes of devotion to revive and fasten upon the mind the general impressions of religion. Solitude powerfully assists this effect. When a man finds himself alone in communication with his Creator, his imagination becomes filled with a conflux of aweful ideas concerning the universal agency, and invisible presence of that being; concerning what is likely to become of himself; and of the superlative importance of providing for the happiness of his future existence, by endeavours to please *him*, who is the arbiter of his destiny: reflexions, which, whenever they gain admittance, for a season overwhelm all others; and leave, when they depart, a solemnity upon the thoughts that will seldom fail, in some degree, to affect the conduct of life.

Private prayer, thus recommended by its own propriety, and by advantages not attainable in any form of religious communion, receives a superior sanction from the authority and example of Christ. " When thou prayest, enter " into thy closet; and when thou hast shut thy door, pray " to thy father which is in secret; and thy father, which seeth " in secret, shall reward thee openly." " And when he had " sent the multitudes away, he went up into a mountain " *apart to pray.*" Mat. vi. 6. xiv. 23.

II. *Family*

II. *Family prayer.*

The peculiar use of family piety consists in its influence upon servants, and the young members of a family, who want sufficient seriousness and reflection to retire of their own accord to the exercise of private devotion, and whose attention you cannot easily command in public worship. The example also and authority of a father and master act in this way with the greatest force; for his private prayers, to which his children and servants are not witnesses, act not at all upon them as examples; and his attendance upon public worship they will readily impute to fashion, to a care to preserve appearances, to a concern for decency and character, and to many motives beside a sense of duty to God. Add to this, that forms of public worship, in proportion as they are more comprehensive, are always less interesting than family prayers; and that the ardor of devotion is better supported, and the sympathy more easily propagated through a small assembly connected by the affections of domestic society, than in the presence of a mixed congregation.

III. *Public worship.*

If the worship of God be a duty of religion, public worship is a necessary institution; forasmuch as without it, the greater part of mankind would exercise no religious worship at all.

These

These assemblies afford also, at the same time, opportunities for moral and religious instruction to those who otherwise would receive none. In all protestant, and in most Christian countries, the elements of natural religion, and the important parts of the evangelic history, are familiar to the lowest of the people. This competent degree and general diffusion of religious knowledge amongst all orders of Christians, which will appear a great thing when compared with the intellectual condition of barbarous nations, can fairly, I think, be ascribed to no other cause, than the regular establishment of assemblies for divine worship; in which, either portions of scripture are recited and explained, or the principles of Christian erudition are so constantly taught in sermons, incorporated with liturgies, or expressed in extempore prayer, as to imprint, by the very repetition, some knowledge and memory of these subjects upon the most unqualified and careless hearer.

The two reasons above stated bind all the members of a community to uphold public worship by their presence and example, although the helps and opportunities which it affords may not be necessary to the devotion or edification of all; and to some may be useless: for it is easily foreseen, how soon religious assemblies would fall into contempt and disuse, if that class of mankind, who are above seeking instruction in them, and want not that their own piety should be assisted by either forms or society in devotion, were to withdraw their attendance; especially when it is considered, that all who please are at liberty to

rank

rank themselves of this class. This argument meets the following, and the only serious apology that is made for the absenting of ourselves from public worship. "Surely "I may be excused from going to church, so long as I pray "at home, and have no reason to doubt but that my prayers "are equally acceptable and efficacious in my closet, as in a "cathedral; still less can I think myself obliged to sit out "a tedious sermon, in order to hear what is known already, "or better learnt from books, or suggested by meditation." They, whose qualifications and habits best supply to themselves all the effect of public ordinances, will be the last to prefer this excuse, when they reflect upon the *general consequence* of setting up such an exemption, as well as the *turn* which is sure to be given in the neighbourhood to their absence from public worship. You stay from church, to employ the sabbath at home in exercises and studies suited to its proper business: your next neighbour stays from church, to spend the seventh day less religiously than he passed any of the six, in a sleepy, stupid rest, or at some rendezvous of drunkenness and debauchery, and yet thinks that he is only imitating you, because you both agree in not going to church. The same consideration should overrule many small scruples concerning the rigorous propriety of some things, which may be contained in the forms, or admitted into the administration of the public worship of our communion; for it seems impossible, that even "two or three should be gathered together," in any act of social worship, if each one require from the rest an implicit submission to his objections; and if no man will attend

tend upon a religious service, which in any point contradicts his opinion of truth, or falls short of his ideas of perfection.

Beside the direct necessity of public worship to the greater part of every Christian community, (supposing worship at all to be a Christian duty) there are other valuable advantages growing out of the use of religious assemblies, without being designed in the institution, or thought of by the individuals who compose them.

1. Joining in prayer and praises to their common Creator and Governor has a sensible tendency to unite mankind together, and to cherish and enlarge the generous affections.

So many pathetic reflections are awakened by every exercise of social devotion, that most men, I believe, carry away from public worship a better temper towards the rest of mankind, than they brought with them. Sprung from the same extraction, preparing together for the period of all worldly distinctions, reminded of their mutual infirmities and common dependency, imploring and receiving support and supplies from the same great source of power and bounty, having all one interest to secure, one Lord to serve, one judgment, the supreme object to all of their hopes and fears, to look towards, it is hardly possible, in this position, to behold mankind as strangers, competitors, or enemies; or not to regard them as children of the same family assembled before their common parent, and with some portion of the tenderness which belongs to the most endearing of our domestic relations. It is not to be expected, that any single effect of this kind should be considerable or lasting; but the frequent return of such sentiments as the presence of a devout congregation naturally suggests, will gradually melt down the ruggedness of many unkind passions, and may generate in time a permanent and productive benevolence.

2. Assemblies for the purpose of divine worship, placing men under impressions, by which they are taught to consider their relation to the Deity, and to contemplate those around them with a view to that relation, force upon their thoughts the natural equality of the human species, and thereby promote humility and condescension in the highest orders of the community, and inspire the lowest with a sense of their rights. The distinctions of civil life are almost always insisted upon too much, and urged too far. Whatever therefore conduces to restore the level, by qualifying the dispositions which grow out of great elevation or depression of rank, improves the character on both sides. Now things are made to appear little, by being placed beside what is great. In which manner, superiorities, which occupy the whole field of the imagination, will vanish, or shrink to their proper diminutiveness, when compared with the distance by which even the highest of men are removed from the supreme Being: and this comparison is naturally introduced by all acts of joint worship. If ever the poor man holds up his head, it is at church: if ever the rich man

man views him with respect, it is there: and both will be the better, and the public profited, the oftener they meet in a situation, in which the consciousness of dignity in the one is tempered and mitigated, and the spirit of the other erected and confirmed. We recommend nothing adverse to subordinations, which are established and necessary; but then it should be remembered, that subordination itself is an evil, being an evil to the subordinate, who are the majority, and therefore ought not to be carried a tittle beyond what the greater good, the peaceable government of the community, requires.

The public worship of Christians is a duty of divine appointment. "Where two or three," says Christ, " are " gathered together in my name, there am I in the midst " of them [*]." This invitation will want nothing of the force of a command with those, who respect the person and authority from which it proceeds. Again, in the Epistle to the *Hebrews*, " not forsaking the assembling of ourselves " together as the manner of some is," which reproof seems as applicable to the desertion of our public worship at this day, as to the forsaking the religious assemblies of Christians in the age of the Apostle. Independently of these passages of scripture, a disciple of Christianity will hardly think himself at liberty to dispute a practice set on foot by the inspired preachers of his religion, coeval with its institution, and retained by every sect into which it has been since divided.

[*] *Matt.* xviii. 20. *Heb.* x. 25.

CHAP. V.

OF FORMS OF PRAYER IN PUBLIC WORSHIP.

LITURGIES, or preconcerted forms of public devotion, being neither injoined nor forbidden in scripture, there can be no good reason either for receiving or rejecting them, but that of expediency; which expediency is to be gathered from a comparison of the advantages and disadvantages attending upon this mode of worship, with those which usually accompany extemporary prayer.

The advantages of a liturgy are these:

1. That it prevents absurd, extravagant, or impious addresses to God, which the folly and enthusiasm of many, in an order of men so numerous as the sacerdotal, must always be in danger of producing, where the conduct of the public worship is entrusted without restraint or assistance to the discretion and abilities of the officiating minister.

2. That it prevents the *confusion* of extemporary prayer, in which the congregation being ignorant of each petition before they hear it, and having little or no time to join in it after they have heard it, are confounded between their attention to the minister, and to their own devotion. The devotion of the hearer is necessarily suspended, until a petition be concluded; and before he can assent to it, or properly adopt it, that is, before he can address the same request to God for himself, and from himself, his attention is called off to keep pace with what succeeds. Add to this, that the mind of the hearer is held in continual expectation, and detained from its proper business by the very novelty with which it is gratified. A congregation may be pleased and affected with the prayers and devotion of their minister without joining in them, in like manner as an audience oftentimes are with the representation of devotion upon the stage, who, nevertheless, come away without being conscious of having exercised any act of devotion themselves. *Joint* prayer, which is the duty, and amongst all denominations of Christians the declared design of " coming together," is prayer in which all *join*; and not that which one alone in the congregation conceives and delivers, and of which the rest are merely hearers. This objection seems fundamental, and holds even where the minister's office is discharged with every possible advantage and accomplishment. The labouring recollection, and embarrassed or tumultuous delivery, of many extempore speakers, form an additional objection to this mode of public worship; for these imperfections are very general,

general, and give great pain to the serious part of a congregation, as well as afford a profane diversion to the levity of the other part.

These advantages of a liturgy are connected with two principal inconveniences; first, that forms of prayer composed in one age become unfit for another by the unavoidable change of language, circumstances, and opinions; secondly, that the perpetual repetition of the same form of words produces weariness and inattentiveness in the congregation. However, both these inconveniences are in their nature vincible. Occasional revisions of a liturgy may obviate the first, and devotion will supply a remedy for the second: or they may both subsist in a considerable degree, and yet be outweighed by the objections which are inseparable from extemporary prayer.

The Lord's prayer is a precedent, as well as a pattern for forms of prayer. Our Lord appears, if not to have prescribed, at least to have authorised the use of fixed forms, when he complied with the request of the disciple who said unto him, " Lord, teach us to pray, as *John* also taught his disciples." *Luke* xi. 1.

The properties required in a public liturgy are, that it be compendious; that it express just conceptions of the divine attributes; that it recite such wants as the congregation are likely to feel, and no other; and that it contain as few controverted propositions as possible.

1. That

1. That it be compendious.

It were no difficult task to contract the liturgies of most churches into half their present compass, and yet retain every distinct petition, as well as the substance of every sentiment, which can be found in them. But brevity may be studied too much. The composer of a liturgy must not sit down to his work with the hope, that the devotion of the congregation will be uniformly sustained throughout, or that every part will be attended to by every hearer. If this could be depended upon, a very short service would be sufficient for every purpose that can be answered or designed by social worship: but seeing the attention of most men is apt to wander and return at intervals, and by starts, he will admit a certain degree of amplification and repetition, of diversity of expression upon the same subject, and variety of phrase and form with little addition to the sense, to the end that the attention, which has been slumbering or absent during one part of the service, may be excited and recalled by another; and the assembly kept together until it may reasonably be presumed, that the most heedless and inadvertent have performed some act of devotion, and the most desultory attention been caught by some part or other of the public service. On the other hand, the too great length of church services is more unfavourable to piety, than almost any fault of composition can be. It begets in many an early and unconquerable dislike to the public worship of their country or communion. They come to church seldom; and enter the doors when they do come under the apprehension of a tedious attendance, which they prepare for at first, or soon after relieve, by compoſing themſelves to a drowſy forgetfulneſs of the place and duty, or by ſending abroad their thoughts in ſearch of more amuſing occupation. Although there may be ſome few of a diſpoſition not be wearied with religious exerciſes, yet, where a ritual is prolix, and the celebration of divine ſervice long, no effect is in general to be looked for, but that indolence will find in it an excuſe, and piety be diſconcerted by impatience.

The length and repetitions complained of in our liturgy are not ſo much the fault of the compilers as the effect of uniting into *one* ſervice, what was originally, but with very little regard to the conveniency of the people, diſtributed into *three*. Notwithſtanding that dread of innovations in religion, which ſeems to have become the *panic* of the age, few, I ſhould ſuppoſe, would be diſpleaſed with ſuch omiſſions, abridgements, or change in the arrangement, as the combination of ſeparate ſervices muſt neceſſarily require, even ſuppoſing each to have been faultleſs in itſelf. If together with theſe alterations, the Epiſtles and Goſpels, and Collects which precede them, were compoſed and ſelected with more regard to unity of ſubject and deſign; and the Pſalms and Leſſons, either left to the choice of the miniſter, or better accommodated to the capacity of the audience, and the edification of modern life; the church of *England* would be in poſſeſſion of a liturgy, in which thoſe who aſſent to her doctrines would have little to blame, and the

moſt

most dissatisfied must acknowledge many beauties. The style throughout is excellent; calm, without coldness; and, though every where sedate, oftentimes affecting. The pauses in the service are disposed at proper intervals. The transitions from one office of devotion to another, from confession to prayer, from prayer to thanksgiving, from thanksgiving to "hearing of the word," are contrived, like scenes in the drama, to supply the mind with a succession of diversified engagements. As much variety is introduced also into the form of praying as this kind of composition seems capable of admitting. The prayer at one time is continued; at another, broken by responses, or cast into short alternate ejaculations; and sometimes the congregation are called upon to take their share in the service, by being left to complete a sentence which the minister had begun. The enumeration of human wants and sufferings in the litany is almost complete. A Christian petitioner can have few things to ask of God, or deprecate, which he will not find there expressed, and for the most part with inimitable tenderness and simplicity.

II. That it express just conceptions of the divine attributes.

This is an article in which no care can be too great. The popular notions of God are formed, in a great measure, from the accounts which the people receive of his nature and character in their religious assemblies. An error here becomes the error of multitudes: and as it is a subject in which almost every opinion leads the way to some practical conclusion, the purity or depravation of public manners will be affected, amongst other causes, by the truth or corruption of the public forms of worship.

III. That it recite such wants as the congregation are likely to feel, and no other.

Of forms of prayer, which offend not egregiously against truth and decency, that has the most merit, which is best calculated to keep alive the devotion of the assembly. It were to be wished therefore, that every part of a liturgy were personally applicable to every individual in the congregation; and that nothing were introduced to interrupt the passion, or damp a flame which it is not easy to rekindle. Upon this principle, the *state prayers* in our liturgy should be fewer and shorter. Whatever may be pretended, the congregation do not feel that concern in the subject of these prayers, which must be felt, or ever prayer be made to God with earnestness. The *state style* likewise seems unseasonably introduced into these prayers, as ill-according with that annihilation of human greatness, of which every act that carries the mind to God presents the idea.

IV. That it contain as few controverted propositions as possible.

We allow to each church the truth of its peculiar tenets, and all the importance which zeal can ascribe to them.

We dispute not here the right or the expediency of framing creeds, or of imposing subscriptions. But why should every position which a church maintains be woven with so much industry into her forms of public worship? Some are offended, and some are excluded: this is an evil in itself, at least to *them:* and what advantage or satisfaction can be derived to the *rest*, from the separation of their brethren, it is difficult to imagine; unless it were a duty, to publish our system of polemic divinity, under the name of making confession of our faith, every time we worship God; or a sin, to agree in religious exercises with those, from whom we differ in some religious opinions. Indeed, where one man thinks it his duty constantly to worship a being, whom another cannot, with the assent of his conscience, permit himself to worship at all, there seems to be no place for comprehension, or any expedient left, but a quiet secession. All other differences may be compromised by silence. If sects and schisms be an evil, they are as much to be avoided by one side as the other. If sectaries are blamed for taking unnecessary offence, established churches are no less culpable for unnecessarily giving it; or bound at least to produce a command, or a reason of equivalent utility, for shutting out any from their communion, by mixing with divine worship doctrines, which, whether true or false, are unconnected, in their nature, with devotion.

CHAP. VI.

OF THE USE OF SABBATICAL INSTITUTIONS.

AN assembly cannot be collected, unless the time of assembling be fixed and known before hand; and if the design of the assembly require that it be held frequently, it is easiest that it should return at stated intervals. This produces a necessity of appropriating set seasons to the social offices of religion. It is also highly convenient, that the *same* seasons be observed throughout the country, that all may be employed, or all at leisure together; for, if the recess from worldly occupation be not general, one man's business will perpetually interfere with another man's devotion; the buyer will be calling at the shop when the seller is gone to church. This part, therefore, of the religious distinction of seasons, namely, a general intermission of labour and business during times previously set apart for the exercise of public worship, is founded in the reasons which make public worship itself a duty. But the celebration of divine service never occupies the whole day. What remains, therefore, of Sunday, beside the part of it employed at church, must be considered as a mere rest from the ordinary occupations of civil life; and he who would defend the institution, as it is required to be be observed in Christian countries, unless he can produce a command for a *Christian sabbath*, must point out the uses of it in that view.

First then, that interval of relaxation which Sunday affords to the laborious part of mankind contributes greatly to the comfort and satisfaction of their lives, both as it refreshes them for the time, and as it relieves their six days labour by the prospect of a day of rest always approaching; which could not be said of *casual* indulgences of leisure and rest, even were they more frequent than there is reason to expect they would be, if left to the discretion or humanity of interested task-masters. To this difference it may be added, that holydays which come seldom and unexpected are unprovided, when they do come with any duty or employment; and the manner of spending them being regulated by no public decency or established usage, they are commonly consumed in rude, if not criminal pastimes, in a stupid sloth or brutish intemperance. Whoever considers how much sabbatical institutions conduce, in this respect, to the happiness and civilization of the labouring classes of mankind, and reflects how great a majority of the human species these classes compose, will acknowledge the utility, whatever he may believe of the origin, of this distinction; and will, consequently, perceive it to be every man's duty to uphold the observation of Sunday when once established, let the establishment have proceeded from whom or what authority it will.

Nor is there any thing loft to the community by the intermiffion of public induftry one day in the week. For in countries tolerably advanced in population and the arts of civil life, there is always enough of human labour, and to fpare. The difficulty is not fo much to procure, as to employ it. The addition of the feventh day's labour to that of the other fix would have no other effect than to reduce the price. The labourer himfelf, who deferved and fuffered moft by the change, would gain nothing.

2. Sunday, by fufpending many public diverfions, and the ordinary rotation of employment, leaves to men of all ranks and profeffions fufficient leifure, and not more than what is fufficient, both for the external offices of Chriftianity, and the retired, but equally neceffary duties of religious meditation and enquiry. It is true, that many do not convert their leifure to this purpofe; but it is of moment, and is all which a public conftitution can effect, that to every one be allowed the opportunity.

3. They whofe humanity embraces the whole fenfitive creation will efteem it no inconfiderable recommendation of a weekly return of public reft, that it affords a refpite to the toil of brutes. Nor can we omit to recount this amongft the ufes, which the divine founder of the *Jewifh* fabbath exprefsly appointed a law of the inftitution.

We admit, that none of thefe reafons fhow why Sunday fhould be preferred to any other day in the week, or one day in seven to one day in six or eight: but these points, which in their nature are of arbitrary determination, being established to our hands, our obligation applies to the subsisting establishment, so long as we confess, that some such institution is necessary, and are neither able, nor attempt to substitute any other in its place.

CHAP. VII.

OF THE SCRIPTURE ACCOUNT OF SABBATICAL INSTITUTIONS.

THE subject, so far as it makes any part of Christian morality, is contained in two questions:

I. Whether the command, by which the *Jewish* sabbath was instituted, extend to Christians?

II. Whether any new command was delivered by Christ; or any other day substituted in the place of the *Jewish* sabbath by the authority or example of his Apostles?

In treating of the first question, it will be necessary to collect the accounts, which are preserved of the institution in the *Jewish* history; for the seeing these accounts together, and in one point of view, will be the best preparation

paration for the discussing or judging of any arguments on one side or the other.

In the second chapter of *Genesis*, the historian having concluded his account of the six days creation, proceeds thus: "And on the seventh day God ended his work "which he had made; and he rested on the seventh day "from all his work which he had made: and God *blessed* "the seventh day, and *sanctified it*, because that in it "he had rested from all his work which God created "and made." After this, we hear no more of the sabbath, or of the seventh day, as in any manner distinguished from the other six, until the history brings us down to the sojourning of the *Jews* in the wilderness, when the following remarkable passage occurs. Upon the complaint of the people for want of food, God was pleased to provide for their relief by a miraculous supply of manna, which was found every morning upon the ground about the camp when the dew went off; "and they gathered it every morning, "every man according to his eating; and when the sun "waxed hot, it melted: and it came to pass, that on "the sixth day they gathered twice as much bread, two "omers for one man; and all the rulers of the congre- "gation came and told *Moses;* and he said unto them, "this is that which the Lord hath said, *to-morrow is the* "*rest of the holy sabbath unto the Lord;* bake that which ye "will bake to day, and seeth that ye will seeth, and "that which remaineth over lay up for you, to be kept "until the morning; and they laid it up till the morn-
"ing,

SABBATICAL INSTITUTIONS.

"ing, as *Moses* bade, and it did not stink (as it had done
"before, when some of them left it till the morning,)
"neither was there any worm therein. And *Moses* said,
"Eat that to day; *for to day is a sabbath unto the Lord:*
"to day ye shall not find it in the field. Six days ye shall
"gather it, but on the seventh day, which is the sabbath,
"in it there shall be none. And it came to pass, that
"there went out some of the people on the seventh day
"for to gather, and they found none. And the Lord
"said unto *Moses*, how long refuse ye to keep my com-
"mandments and my laws? See, for *that the Lord hath
"given you the sabbath*, therefore he giveth you on the sixth
"day the bread of two days; abide ye every man in his
"place; let no man go out of his place on the seventh day:
"so the people rested on the seventh day." *Exodus*
xvi.

Not long after this, the sabbath, as is well known,
was established with great solemnity in the fourth commandment.

Now, in my opinion, the transaction in the wilderness,
above recited, was the first actual institution of the sabbath. For, if the sabbath had been instituted at the time of
the creation, as the words in *Genesis* may seem at first sight
to import, and observed all along, from that time to the
departure of the *Jews* out of *Egypt*, a period of about
two thousand five hundred years, it appears unaccountable,
that no mention of it, no occasion of even the obscurest al-
lusion

lusion to it, should occur either in the general history of the world before the call of *Abraham*, which contains, we admit, only a few memoirs of its early ages, and those extremely abridged; or, which is more to be wondered at, in that of the lives of the three first *Jewish* patriarchs, which, in many parts of the account, is sufficiently circumstantial and domestic. Nor is there, in the passage above quoted from the sixteenth chapter of *Exodus*, any intimation that the sabbath, then appointed to be observed, was only the revival of an ancient institution, which had been neglected, forgotten, or suspended; nor is any such neglect imputed either to the inhabitants of the old world, or to any part of the family of *Noah*; nor lastly, is any permission recorded to dispense with the institution during the captivity of the *Jews* in *Egypt*, or on any other public emergency.

The passage in the second chapter of *Genesis*, which creates the whole controversy upon the subject, is not inconsistent with this opinion; for as the seventh day was erected into a sabbath, on account of God's resting upon that day from the work of the creation, it was natural enough in the historian, when he had related the history of the creation, and of God's ceasing from it on the seventh day, to add, " and God blessed the seventh day, and sanctified it, because that on it he had rested from all his work which God created and made;" although the " blessing" and " sanctification," i. e. the religious distinction and appropriation of that day, was not actually made till many ages afterwards. The words do not affert, that God *then* "bleffed" and "fanctified" the feventh day, but that he bleffed and fanctified it *for that reafon*; and if any afk, why the fabbath, or fanctification of the feventh day, was *then* mentioned, if it was not *then* appointed, the anfwer is at hand, the order of connection, and not of time, introduced the mention of the fabbath, in the hiftory of the fubject which it was ordained to commemorate.

This interpretation is ftrongly fupported by a paffage in the prophet *Ezekiel*, where the fabbath is plainly fpoken of as *given*, and what elfe can that mean, but as *firft inftituted*, in the wildernefs? " Wherefore I caufed them " to go forth out of the land of *Egypt*, and brought them " into the wildernefs; and I gave them my ftatutes, and " fhewed them my judgments, which if a man do, he " fhall even live in them: moreover alfo *I gave them my* " *fabbaths*, to be a fign between me and them, that they " might know that I am the Lord that fanctify them." Ezek. xx. 10, 11, 12.

Nehemiah alfo recounts the promulgation of the fabbatic law amongft the tranfactions in the wildernefs; which fupplies another confiderable argument in aid of our opinion: " Moreover thou leddeft them in the day by a " cloudy pillar, and in the night by a pillar of fire, to " give them light in the way wherein they fhould go. " Thou cameft down alfo upon Mount *Sinai*, and fpakeft " with them from heaven, and gaveft them right judg-
" ments

"ments and true laws, good statutes and commandments, "*and madest known unto them thy holy sabbath*, and com-"mandedst them precepts, statutes and laws by the hand "of *Moses* thy servant, and gavest them bread from hea-"ven for their hunger, and broughtest forth water for "them out of the rock.*" *Nehem.* ix. 12.

If it be enquired, what duties were appointed for the *Jewish* sabbath, and under what penalties and in what manner it was observed amongst the ancient *Jews*; we find that, by the fourth commandment, a strict cessation from work was enjoined, not only upon *Jews* by birth, or religious profession, but upon all who resided within the limits of the *Jewish* state; that the same was to be permitted to their slaves and their cattle; that this rest was not to be violated under pain of death: " Whosoever "doeth any work in the sabbath day, he shall surely be "put to death." *Ex.* xxxi. 14. Beside which, the seventh day was to be solemnized by double sacrifices in the temple. "And on the sabbath day *two* lambs of the first year with-"out spot, and two tenth deals of floor for a meat of-

---

* From the mention of the sabbath in so close a connection with the descent of God upon mount *Sinai*, and the delivery of the law from thence, one would be inclined to believe, that *Nehemiah* referred solely to the fourth commandment. But the fourth commandment certainly did not first make known the sabbath. And it is apparent, that *Nehemiah* observed not the order of events, for he speaks of what passed upon mount *Sinai*, before he mentions the miraculous supplies of bread and water, though the *Jews* did not arrive at mount *Sinai* till some time after both these miracles were wrought.

"fering,

"fering, mingled with oil, and the drink offering thereof; this is the burnt offering of every sabbath, beside the continual burnt offering and his drink offering." *Numb.* xxviii. 9, 10. Also holy convocations, or assemblies for the purpose, we presume, of public worship or religious instruction, were directed to be held on the sabbath day; "the seventh day is a sabbath of rest, *an holy convocation.*" *Lev.* xxiii. 3.

And accordingly we read, that the sabbath was in fact observed amongst the *Jews*, by a scrupulous abstinence from every thing that, by any possible construction, could be deemed labour; as from dressing meat, from travelling beyond a sabbath day's journey, or about a single mile. In the *Maccabean* wars, they suffered a thousand of their number to be slain, rather than do any thing in their own defence on the sabbath day. In the final siege of *Jerusalem*, after they had so far overcome their scruples, as to defend their persons when attacked, they refused any operation on the sabbath day, by which they might have interrupted the enemy in filling up the trench. After the establishment of synagogues, (of the origin of which we have no account) it was the custom to assemble in them upon the sabbath day, for the purpose of hearing the law rehearsed and explained, and for the exercise, it is probable, of public devotion. "For *Moses* of old time hath in every city them that preach him, *being read in the synagogues every sabbath day.*" The seventh day is *Saturday*; and agreeably to the *Jewish* way of computing the day, the sabbath held from six o'clock on the Friday evening, to six o'clock on Saturday afternoon.——These observations being premised, we approach the main question, "Whether the command, by which the *Jewish* sabbath was instituted, extend to us?"

If the divine command was actually delivered at the creation, it was addressed, no doubt, to the whole human species alike, and continues, unless repealed by some subsequent revelation, binding upon all who come to the knowledge of it. If the command was published for the first time in the wilderness, then it was directed to the *Jewish* people alone; and something farther, either in the subject, or circumstances of the command, will be necessary to show, that it was designed for any other. It is on this account, that the question concerning the date of the institution was first to be considered. The former opinion precludes all debate about the extent of the obligation; the latter admits, and, *primâ facie*, induces a belief, that the sabbath ought to be considered as part of the peculiar law of the *Jewish* policy.

Which belief receives great confirmation from the following arguments.

The sabbath is described as a sign between God and the people of *Israel*: " Wherefore the children of *Israel* shall
" keep the sabbath, to observe the sabbath throughout
" their generations, for a perpetual covenant; *it is a sign*
" *between*

" *between me and the children of Israel for ever.*" Exodus
" xxxi. 16, 17. Again, " And I gave them my statutes,
" and shewed them my judgements, which, if a man do,
" he shall even live in them; *moreover also I gave them*
" *my sabbaths to be a sign between me and them,* that they
" might know that I am the Lord that sanctify them."
Ezek. xx. 12. Now it does not seem easy to understand
how the sabbath could be a *sign* between God and the
people of *Israel*, unless the observance of it was peculiar
to that people, and designed to be so.

The distinction of the sabbath is, in its nature, as much
a positive ceremonial institution, as that of many other
seasons which were appointed by the levitical law to be kept
holy, and to be observed by a strict rest; as the first and
seventh days of unleavened bread; the feast of pentecost;
the feast of tabernacles; and in the twenty third chapter of
Exodus the sabbath and these are recited together.

If the command by which the sabbath was instituted
be binding upon Christians, it must bind as to the day,
the duties, and the penalty; in none of which it is received.

The observation of the sabbath was not one of the articles enjoined by the Apostles, in the fifteenth chapter of
Acts, upon them, " which, from among the Gentiles, were
turned unto God."

St.

St. *Paul* evidently appears to have confidered the fabbath as part of the *Jewish* ritual, not binding upon Chriftians as fuch: " Let no man therefore judge you in meat or " in drink, or in refpect of an holy day, or of the new " moon, or *of the fabbath days*, which are a fhadow of " things to come, but the body is of Chrift." *Col.* ii. 16, 17.

I am aware of only two objections which can be oppofed to the force of thefe arguments: one is, that the reafon affigned in the fourth commandment for hallowing the feventh day, namely, " becaufe God refted on the fe- venth day from the work of the creation," is a reafon which pertains to all mankind; the other, that the com- mand, which enjoins the obfervation of the fabbath, is inferted in the decalogue, of which all the other precepts and prohibitions are of moral and univerfal obligation.

Upon the firft objection it may be remarked, that al- though in *Exodus* the commandment is founded upon God's reft from the creation, in *Deuteronomy* the commandment is repeated with a reference to a different event: " Six " days fhalt thou labour, and do all thy work; but the " feventh day is the fabbath of the Lord thy God; in it " thou fhalt not do any work, thou, nor thy fon, nor " thy daughter, nor thy man-fervant, nor thy maid-fer- " vant, nor thine ox, nor thine afs, nor any of thy " cattle, nor thy ftranger that is within thy gates, that " thy man-fervant and thy maid-fervant may reft as well
" as

" as thou; and remember that thou waſt a ſervant in the
" land of Egypt, and that the Lord thy God brought
" thee out thence, through a mighty hand, and by a
" ſtretched-out arm; *therefore* the Lord thy God com-
" manded thee to keep the ſabbath day." It is farther
obſervable, that God's reſt from the creation is propoſed
as the reaſon of the inſtitution, even where the inſtitution
itſelf is ſpoken of as peculiar to the Jews:—" Wherefore
" the children of Iſrael ſhall keep the ſabbath, to obſerve
" the ſabbath throughout their generations, for a perpe-
" tual covenant: it is a ſign between me and the children
" of Iſrael for ever; *for* in ſix days the Lord made heaven
" and earth, and on the ſeventh day he reſted and was
" refreſhed." The truth is, theſe different reaſons were
aſſigned to account for different circumſtances in the command. If a Jew enquired, why the *ſeventh day* was ſanc-
tified rather than the ſixth or eighth, his law told him
becauſe God reſted on the *ſeventh day* from the creation.
If he aſked, why was the ſame reſt indulged to *ſlaves*,
his law bid him remember, that he alſo was a *ſlave* in the
land of Egypt; and, " that the Lord his God brought
" him out thence," In this view, the two reaſons are perfectly compatible with each other, and with a third end
of the inſtitution, its being a *ſign* between God and the
people of Iſrael; but in this view they determine nothing
concerning the extent of the obligation. If the reaſon by
its proper energy had conſtituted a natural obligation,
or if it had been mentioned with a view to the extent of
the obligation, we ſhould ſubmit to the concluſion, that

all were comprehended by the command, who are concerned in the reason. But the sabbatic rest being a duty which results from the ordination and authority of a positive law, the reason can be alledged no farther than as it explains the design of the legislator; and if it appear to be recited with an intentional application to one part of the law, it can explain his design upon no other.

With respect to the second objection, that inasmuch as the other nine commandments are confessedly of moral and universal obligation, it may reasonably be presumed that this is of the same;—we answer, that this argument will have little weight, when it is considered, that the distinction between positive and natural duties, like other distinctions of modern ethics, was unknown to the simplicity of ancient language; and that there are various passages in scripture, in which duties of a political or ceremonial, or positive nature, and confessedly of partial obligation, are enumerated, and without any mark of discrimination, along with others which are natural and universal. Of this the following is an incontestible example: " But if a man be just, and do that which is lawful
" and right; and hath not eaten upon the mountains; nor
" hath lift up his eyes to the idols of the house of *Israel*; nei-
" ther hath defiled his neighbour's wife; *neither hath come*
" *near to a menstruous woman*; and hath not oppressed any,
" but hath restored to the debtor his pledge; hath spoiled
" none by violence; hath given his bread to the hungry,
" and hath covered the naked with a garment; *he that*
" hath

SABBATICAL INSTITUTIONS.

"*hath not given upon usury, neither hath taken any increase;*
"that hath withdrawn his hand from iniquity; hath exe-
"cuted true judgment between man and man; hath
"walked in my statutes, and hath kept my judgments to
"deal truly; he is just, he shall surely live, saith the
"Lord God." *Ezek.* xviii. 5—9. The same thing may
be observed of the apostolic decree recorded in the fifteenth
chapter of the *Acts*.—" It seemed good to the Holy Ghost
"and to us, to lay upon you no greater burden than these
"necessary things; that ye abstain from meats offered to
"idols, and from blood, and from things strangled, and
"*from fornication:* from which if ye keep yourselves,
"ye shall do well."

II. If the law by which the sabbath was instituted, was a law only to the *Jews*, it becomes an important question with the *Christian* enquirer, whether the founder of his religion delivered any new command upon the subject; or, if that should not appear to be the case, whether any day was appropriated to the service of religion, by the authority or example of his apostles?

The practice of holding religious assemblies upon the first day of the week, was so early and universal in the *Christian* church, that it carries with it considerable proof of having originated from some precept of *Christ* or of his apostles, though none such be now extant. It was upon the *first* day of the week that the disciples were assembled when *Christ* appeared to them for the first time after his

resurrection; "then the same day at evening, *being the first* "*day of the week*, when the doors were shut, where the "disciples were assembled, for fear of the *Jews*, came "*Jesus* and stood in the midst of them." *John* xx. 19. This, for any thing that appears in the account, might, as to the day, have been accidental: but in the 26th verse of the same chapter we read, "that after eight days," that is on the *first day* of the week *following*, "*again* the disciples were "within," which second meeting upon the same day of the week looks like an appointment and design to meet on that particular day. In the twentieth chapter of the Acts of the apostles we find the same custom in a *Christian* church at a great distance from *Jerusalem*:—" And we came unto "them to *Troas* in five days, where we abode seven days; "and *upon the first day of the week, when the disciples came* "*together to break bread, Paul* preached unto them." *Acts* xx. 6, 7. The manner in which the historian mentions "the disciples coming together to break bread on the *first* "day of the week," shews, I think, that the practice by this time was familiar and established. St. *Paul* to the *Corinthians* writes thus: "Concerning the collection for "the saints, as I have given order to the churches of *Ga-* "*latia*, even so do ye; *upon the first day of the week* let "every one of you lay by him in store as God hath pros- "pered him, that there be no gatherings when I come." 1. *Cor.* xvi. 1, 2. Which direction affords a probable proof, that the *first* day of the week was already, amongst the Christians both of *Corinth* and *Galatia*, distinguished from the rest, by some religious application or other. At the
time

time that St. *John* wrote the book of his revelation, the first day of the week had obtained the name of the *Lord's day*; I was in the spirit, says he, *on the Lord's day. Rev.* i. 10. Which name, and St. *John's* use of it, sufficiently denote the appropriation of this day to the service of religion, and that this appropriation was perfectly known to the churches of *Asia*. I make no doubt but that by the *Lord's* day was meant the *first* day of the week; for we find no footsteps of any distinction of days, which could entitle any other to that appellation. The subsequent history of Christianity corresponds with the accounts delivered on this subject, in scripture.

It will be remembered, that we are contending by these proofs, for no other duty upon the first day of the week, than that of holding and frequenting religious assemblies. A cessation upon that day from labour, beyond the time of attendance upon public worship, is not intimated in any passage of the New Testament. Nor did *Christ* or his Apostles deliver, that we know of, any command to their disciples for a discontinuance upon that day of the common offices of their professions. A reserve which none will see reason to wonder at, or to blame as a defect in the institution, who consider that in the primitive condition of Christianity, the observation of a new sabbath would have been useless, or inconvenient, or impracticable. During *Christ's* personal ministry his religion was preached to the *Jews* alone. They already had a sabbath, which, as citizens and subjects of that œconomy, they were obliged

to

to keep, and did keep. It was not therefore probable that *Chrift* would enjoin another day of reft in conjunction with this. When the new religion came forth into the Gentile world, converts to it were, for the moft part, made from thofe claffes of fociety who have not their time and labour at their own difpofal; and it was fcarcely to be expected, that unbelieving mafters and magiftrates, and they who directed the employment of others, would permit their flaves and labourers to reft from their work every feventh day; or that civil government, indeed, would have fubmitted to the lofs of a feventh part of the public induftry, and that too in addition to the numerous feftivals which the national religions indulged to the people: at leaft this would have been an incumbrance, which might have greatly retarded the reception of Chriftianity in the world. In reality, the inftitution of a weekly fabbath is fo connected with the functions of civil life, and requires fo much of the concurrence of civil laws in its regulation and fupport, that it cannot, perhaps, properly be made the ordinance of any religion, till that religion be received as the religion of the ftate.

The opinion that *Chrift* and his Apoftles meant to retain the duties of the *Jewifh* fabbath, fhifting only the day from the feventh to the firft, feems to prevail without fufficient proof; nor does any evidence remain in fcripture, (of what, however, is not improbable) that the firft day of the week was thus diftinguifhed in commemoration of our Lord's refurrection.

The

The conclusion from the whole enquiry, (for it is our business to follow the arguments to whatever probability they conduct us,) is this: the *assembling* upon the first day of the week for the purpose of public worship and religious instruction is a law of Christianity, of divine appointment; the *resting* on that day from our employments longer than we are detained fom them by attendance upon these assemblies, is to Christians, an ordinance of human institution; binding nevertheless upon the conscience of every individual of a country in which a weekly sabbath is established, for the sake of the beneficial purposes which the public and regular observation of it promotes; and recommended perhaps in some degree to the divine approbation, by the resemblance it bears to what God was pleased to make a solemn part of the law which he delivered to the people of *Israel*, and by its subserviency to many of the same uses.

CHAP. VIII.

BY WHAT ACTS AND OMISSIONS THE DUTY OF THE CHRISTIAN SABBATH IS VIOLATED.

SINCE the obligation upon Christians, to comply with the religious observation of Sunday, arises from the public uses of the institution, and the authority of the apostolic practice, the *manner* of observing it ought to be that, which best fulfils *these* uses, and conforms the nearest to *this* practice.

The uses proposed by the institution are,

1. To facilitate attendance upon public worship.

2. To meliorate the condition of the laborious classes of mankind, by regular and seasonable returns of rest.

3. By a general suspension of business and amusement, to invite and enable persons of every description, to apply their time and thoughts, to subjects appertaining to their salvation.

With the primitive Christians the peculiar, and probably for some time the only distinction of the first day of the week, was the holding of religious assemblies upon that day. We learn, however, from the testimony of a very early writer amongst them, that they also reserved the day for religious meditations. *Unusquisque nostrum*, saith *Irenæus, sabbatizat spiritualiter, meditatione legis gaudens, opificium Dei admirans.*

Wherefore the duty of the day is violated;

1st. By all such employments or engagements, as (though differing from our ordinary occupation) hinder our attendance upon public worship, or take up so much of our time, as not to leave a sufficient part of the day at leisure for religious reflection; as the going of journeys, the paying or receiving of visits which engage the whole day, or employing the time at home in writing letters, settling accounts, or in applying ourselves to studies, or the reading of books, which bear no relation to the business of religion.

2dly. By unnecessary encroachments upon the rest and liberty which Sunday ought to bring to the inferior orders of the community; as by keeping servants on that day confined and busied in preparations for the superfluous elegancies of our table, or dress.

3dly. By such recreations as are customarily forborne out of respect to the day; as hunting, shooting, fishing, public diversions, frequenting taverns, playing at cards or dice.

If it be asked, as it often has been, wherein consists the difference between walking out with your stick, or with your gun? between spending the evening at home, or in a tavern? between passing the Sunday afternoon at a game of cards, or in conversation not more edifying, nor always so inoffensive?—To these, and to the same question, under a variety of forms, and in a multitude of similar examples, we return the following answer:—That the religious observation of Sunday, if it ought to be retained at all, must be upheld by some public and visible distinctions—that draw the line of distinction where you will, many actions which are situated on the confines of the line, will differ very little, and yet lie on opposite sides of it—that every trespass upon that reserve, which public decency has established, breaks down the fence, by which the day is separated to the service of religion—that it is unsafe to trifle with scruples and habits that have a beneficial tendency, although founded merely in custom—that these liberties, however intended, will certainly be considered by those who observe them, not only as disrespectful to the day and institution, but as proceeding from a secret contempt of the Christian faith—that consequently they diminish a reverence for religion in others, so far as the authority of our opinion, or the efficacy of our example reaches; or rather, so far as either will serve for an excuse of negligence to those who are glad of any—that as to cards and dice, which put in their claim to be considered amongst the *harmless* occupations of a vacant hour, it may be observed, that few find any difficulty in refraining from *play* on Sunday, except they who sit down to it, with the views and eagerness of

gamesters;

gamesters;—that *gaming* is seldom innocent—that the anxiety and perturbations, however, which it excites, are inconsistent with the tranquillity and frame of temper, in which the duties and thoughts of religion should always both find, and leave us—and lastly, we shall remark, that the example of other countries, where the same or greater licence is *allowed*, affords no apology for irregularities in our own; because a practice which is tolerated by public order and usage, neither receives the same construction, nor gives the same offence, as where it is censured and prohibited by both.

CHAP. IX.

OF REVERENCING THE DEITY.

IN many perfons a ferioufnefs, and fenfe of awe, overfpread the imagination, whenever the idea of the Supreme Being is prefented to their thoughts. This effect, which forms a confiderable fecurity againft vice, is the confequence not fo much of reflection, as of habit; which habit being generated by the external expreffions of reverence, which we ufe ourfelves, and obferve in thofe about us, may be deftroyed by caufes oppofite to thefe, and efpecially, by that familiar levity with which fome learn to fpeak of the Deity, of his attributes, providence, revelations, or worfhip.

God hath been pleafed, no matter for what reafon, although probably for this, to forbid the vain mention of his name—" Thou fhalt not take the name of the Lord thy " God in vain." Now the mention is *vain*, when it is ufelefs; and it is ufelefs, when it is neither likely nor intended to ferve any good purpofe; as when it flows from the lips idle or unmeaning, or is applied upon occafions inconfiftent with any confideration of religion or devotion, to exprefs our anger, our earneftnefs, our courage, or our mirth; or indeed, when it is ufed at all, except in acts of religion, or in serious and seasonable discourse upon religious subjects.

The prohibition of the third commandment is recognized by *Christ*, in his sermon upon the mount, which sermon adverts to none but the moral parts of the *Jewish* law. " I say unto you swear not at all; but let your commu-
" nication be yea yea, nay nay; for whatsoever is more
" than these, cometh of evil." The *Jews* probably interpreted the prohibition as restrained to the name *Jehovah*, the name which the Deity had appointed and appropriated to himself. *Ex.* vi. 3. The words of *Christ* extend the prohibition beyond the *name* of God to every thing associated with the idea. " Swear not, neither by heaven, for it is God's
" throne; nor by the earth, for it is his foot-stool; neither
" by Jerusalem, for it is the city of the Great King."
Matt. v. 35.

The offence of profane swearing is aggravated by the consideration, that duty and decency are sacrificed thereby to the slenderest of temptations. Suppose the habit, either from affectation, or by negligence and inadvertency, to be already formed; it costs, one would think, little to relinquish the pleasure and honour which it confers, and it must always be within the power of the most ordinary resolution to correct it. Zeal, and a concern for duty, are in fact never strong, when the exertion requisite to vanquish a habit founded in no antecedent propensity, is thought too much, or too painful.

A contempt of pofitive duties, or rather of thofe duties for which the reafon is not fo plain as the command, indicates a difpofition upon which the authority of revelation has obtained little influence.—This remark is applicable to the offence of profane fwearing, and defcribes, perhaps, pretty exactly the general character of thofe who are moft addicted to it.

Mockery and ridicule, when exercifed upon the fcriptures, or even upon the places, perfons, and forms fet apart for the miniftration of religion, fall within the mifchief of the law, which forbids the profanation of God's name; efpecially as it is extended by Chrift's interpretation. They are moreover inconfiftent with a religious frame of mind; for as no one ever feels himfelf either difpofed to pleafantry, or capable of being diverted with the pleafantry of others, upon matters in which he is cordially interefted, fo a mind intent upon the attainment of heaven, rejects with indignation, every attempt to entertain it with jefts, calculated to degrade or deride fubjects, which it never recollects, but with ferioufnefs and anxiety—Nothing but ftupidity, or the moft frivolous diffipation of thought, can make even the inconfiderate forget the fupreme importance of every thing which relates to the expectation of a future exiftence. Whilft the infidel mocks at the fuperftitions of the vulgar, infults over their credulous fears, their childifh errors, and fantaftic rites, it does not occur to him to obferve, that the moft prepofterous device by which the weakeft devotee ever believed he was

fecuring

securing the happiness of a future life, is more rational, than unconcern about it. Upon this subject nothing is so absurd, as indifference—no folly so contemptible, as thoughtlessness and levity.

Finally, the knowledge of what is due to the solemnity of those interests, concerning which revelation professes to inform and direct us, may teach even those who are least inclined to respect the prejudices of mankind, to observe a decorum in the style and conduct of religious disquisitions, with the neglect of which, many adversaries of Christianity are justly chargeable. Serious arguments are fair on all sides. Christianity is but ill defended by refusing audience or toleration to the objections of unbelievers. But whilst we would have freedom of enquiry restrained by no laws, but those of decency, we are entitled to demand on behalf of a religion, which holds forth to mankind assurances of immortality, that its credit be assailed by no other weapons than those of sober discussion and legitimate reasoning—that the truth or falsehood of Christianity be never made a topic of raillery, a theme for the exercise of wit or eloquence, or a subject of contention for literary fame and victory—that the cause be tried upon its merits—that all applications to the fancy, passions, or prejudices of the reader, all attempts to pre-occupy, ensnare or perplex his judgment, by any art, influence, or impression whatsoever, extrinsic to the proper grounds and evidence upon which his assent ought to proceed, be rejected from a question, which involves in its determination,

the

the hopes, the virtue, and repose of millions—that the controversy be managed on both sides with sincerity, that is, that nothing be produced in the writings of either, contrary to, or beyond, the writer's own knowledge and persuasion—that objections and difficulties be proposed from no other motive, than an honest and serious desire to obtain satisfaction, or to communicate information which may promote the discovery and progress of truth—that in conformity with this design, every thing be stated with integrity, with method, precision and simplicity; and above all, that whatever is published in opposition to received and confessedly beneficial persuasions, be set forth under a form, which is likely to invite enquiry, and to meet examination. If with these moderate and equitable conditions, be compared, the manner in which hostilities have been waged against the Christian religion, not only the votaries of the prevailing faith, but every man who looks forward with anxiety to the destination of his being, will see much to blame, and to complain of. By *one unbeliever*, all the follies which have adhered, in a long course of dark and superstitious ages, to the popular creed, are assumed as so many doctrines of Christ and his Apostles, for the purpose of subverting the whole system, by the absurdities, which it is *thus* represented to contain. By *another*, the ignorance and vices of the sacerdotal order, their mutual dissensions and persecutions, their usurpations and incroachments upon the intellectual liberty and civil rights of mankind, have been displayed with no small triumph and invective, not so much to guard the Christian
laity

laity againſt a repetition of the ſame injuries, which is the only proper uſe to be made of the moſt flagrant examples of the paſt, as to prepare the way for an inſinuation, that the religion itſelf, is nothing elſe than a profitable fable, impoſed upon the fears and credulity of the multitude, and upheld by the frauds and influence of an intereſted and crafty prieſthood. And yet how remotely is the character of the clergy connected with the truth of Chriſtianity! what, after all, do the moſt diſgraceful pages of eccleſiaſtical hiſtory prove, but that the paſſions of our common nature are not altered or excluded by diſtinctions of name, and that the characters of men are formed much more by the temptations than the duties of their profeſſion? A *third* finds delight in collecting and repeating accounts of wars and maſſacres, of tumults and inſurrections, excited in almoſt every age of the Chriſtian æra by religious zeal; as though the vices of Chriſtians were parts of Chriſtianity; intolerance and extirpation precepts of the goſpel; or as if its ſpirit could be judged of, from the councils of princes, the intrigues of ſtateſmen, the pretences of malice and ambition, or the unauthorized cruelties of ſome gloomy and virulent ſuperſtition. By a *fourth*, the ſucceſſion and variety of popular religions; the viciſſitudes with which ſects and tenets have flouriſhed and decayed; the zeal with which they were once ſupported, the negligence with which they are now remembered; the little ſhare which reaſon and argument appear to have had in framing the creed, or regulating the religious conduct of the multitude; the indifference and ſubmiſſion with which the religion of the ſtate is generally received by the common people; the caprice and vehemence with which it is ſometimes oppoſed; the phrenzy with which men have been brought to contend for opinions and ceremonies, of which they knew neither the proof, the meaning, nor original: laſtly, the equal and undoubting confidence with which we hear the doctrines of *Chriſt* or of *Confucius*, the law of *Moſes* or of *Mahomet*, the *Bible*, the *Koran*, or the *Shaſter*, maintained or anathematized, taught or abjured, revered or derided, according as we live on this, or on that ſide of a river; keep within, or ſtep over the boundaries of a ſtate; or even in the ſame country, and by the ſame people, ſo often as the event of a battle, or the iſſue of a negociation delivers them to the dominion of a new maſter: points, I ſay, of this ſort are exhibited to the public attention, as ſo many arguments againſt the *truth* of the *Chriſtian* religion—and with ſucceſs. For theſe topics, being brought together, and ſet off with ſome aggravation of circumſtances, and with a vivacity of ſtyle and deſcription, familiar enough to the writings and converſation of free-thinkers, inſenſibly lead the imagination into a habit of claſſing Chriſtianity with the deluſions, that have taken poſſeſſion, by turns, of the public belief; and of regarding it, as what the ſcoffers of our faith repreſent it to be, *the ſuperſtition of the day*. But is this to deal honeſtly by the ſubject, or with the world? May not the ſame things be ſaid, may not the ſame prejudices be excited by theſe repreſentations, whether Chriſtianity be true or falſe, or by whatever proofs its truth be atteſted? May not truth as well

well as falsehood be taken upon credit? May not a religion be founded upon evidence, accessible and satisfactory to every mind competent to the enquiry, which yet, by the greatest part of its professors, is received upon authority?

But if the *matter* of these objections be reprehensible, as calculated to produce an effect upon the reader, beyond what their real weight and place in the argument deserve, still more shall we discover of management and disingenuousness in the *form* under which they are dispersed among the public. Infidelity is served up in every shape, that is likely to allure, surprise, or beguile the imagination; in a fable, a tale, a novel, a poem; in interspersed and broken hints; remote and oblique surmises; in books of travels, of philosophy, of natural history; in a word, in any form, rather than the right one, that of a professed and regular disquisition. And because the coarse buffoonery, and broad laugh of the old and rude adversaries of the Christian faith, would offend the taste, perhaps, rather than the virtue of this cultivated age, a graver irony, a more skilful and delicate banter is substituted in their place. An eloquent historian, besides his more direct, and therefore fairer attacks upon the credibility of the evangelic story, has contrived to weave into his narration one continued sneer upon the cause of Christianity, and upon the writings and characters of its ancient patrons. The knowledge which this author possesses of the frame and conduct of the human mind, must have led him to observe, that such attacks do their execution without enquiry. Who can refute a *fneer?* Who can compute the number, much lefs, one by one, fcrutinize the juftice of thofe difparaging infinuations, which crowd the pages of this elaborate hiftory? What reader fufpends his curiofity, or calls off his attention from the principal narrative, to examine references, to fearch into the foundation, or to weigh the reafon, propriety and force of every tranfient farcafm, and fly allufion, by which the Chriftian teftimony is depreciated and traduced? and by which, neverthelefs, he may find his faith afterwards unfettled and perplexed.

But the enemies of Chriftianity have purfued her with poifoned arrows. Obfcenity itfelf is made the vehicle of infidelity. The awful doctrines, if we be not permitted to call them the facred truths, of our religion, together with all the adjuncts and appendages of its worfhip and external profeffion, have been fometimes impudently profaned by an unnatural conjunction with impure and lafcivious images. The fondnefs for ridicule is almoft univerfal; and ridicule to many minds is never fo irrefiftible, as when feafoned with obfcenity, and employed upon religion. But in proportion as thefe noxious principles take hold of the imagination, they infatuate the judgment; for trains of ludicrous and unchafte affociations adhering to every fentiment and mention of religion, render the mind indifpofed to receive either conviction from its evidence, or impreffions from its authority. And this effect being exerted upon the fenfitive part of our frame, is altogether independent of argument, proof, or reafon; is as formidable

able to a true religion, as to a false one; to a well-grounded faith, as to a chimerical mythology, or fabulous tradition. Neither, let it be observed, is the crime or danger less, because impure ideas are exhibited under a veil, in covert and chastized language.

Seriousness, is not constraint of thought; nor levity, freedom. Every mind which wishes the advancement of truth and knowledge, in the most important of all human researches, must abhor this licentiousness as violating no less the laws of reasoning, than the rights of decency. There is but one description of men, to whose principles it ought to be tolerable, I mean that class of reasoners, who can see *little* in Christianity, even supposing it to be true. To such adversaries we address this reflection—Had *Jesus Christ* delivered no other declaration than the following: " The hour is coming, in the which all " that are in the graves shall hear his voice, and shall " come forth; they that have done good, unto the resur- " rection of life, and they that have done evil, unto the " resurrection of damnation;" he had pronounced a message of inestimable importance, and well worthy of that splendid apparatus of prophecy and miracles, with which his mission was introduced, and attested—a message, in which the wisest of mankind would rejoice to find an answer to their doubts, and rest to their enquiries. It is idle to say, that a future state had been discovered already—It had been discovered, as the *Copernican* system was

was—it was one guefs among many. He alone difcovers, who *proves;* and no man can prove this point, but the teacher who teftifies by miracles that his doctrine comes from God.

MORAL PHILOSOPHY.

BOOK VI.

ELEMENTS OF POLITICAL KNOWLEDGE.

CHAP. I.

OF THE ORIGIN OF CIVIL GOVERNMENT.

GOVERNMENT, at first, was either patriarchal or military; *that* of a parent over his family, or of a commander over his fellow warriors.

I. Paternal authority, and the order of domestic life, supplied the foundation of *civil government*. Did mankind spring out of the earth mature and independent, it would be found perhaps impossible, to introduce subjection and subordination among them; but the condition of human infancy

infancy prepares men for society, by combining individuals into small communities, and by placing them from the beginning under direction and control. A family contains the rudiments of an empire. The authority of one over many, and the disposition to govern and to be governed, are in this way incidental to the very nature, and coeval, no doubt, with the existence of the human species. Moreover, the constitution of families, not only assists the formation of civil government, by the dispositions which it generates, but also furnishes the first steps of the process by which empires have been actually reared. A parent would retain a considerable part of his authority after his children were grown up, and had formed families of their own. The obedience, of which they remembered not the beginning, would be considered as natural; and would scarcely, during the parent's life, be entirely or abruptly withdrawn. Here then we see the second stage in the progress of dominion. The first, was that of a parent over his young children: this that of an ancestor presiding over his adult descendants.

Although the original progenitor was the centre of union to his posterity, yet it is not probable that the association would be immediately or altogether dissolved by his death. Connected by habits of intercourse and affection, and by some common rights, necessities and interests, they would consider themselves as allied to each other in a nearer degree than to the rest of the species. Almost all would be sensible of an inclination to continue in the society in which

which they had been brought up; and experiencing, as they soon would do, many inconveniences from the absence of that authority which their common ancestor exercised, especially in deciding their disputes, and directing their operations in matters in which it was necessary to act in conjunction, they might be induced to supply his place by a formal choice of a successor, or rather might willingly, and almost imperceptibly, transfer their obedience to some one of the family, who by his age or services, or by the part he possessed in the direction of their affairs during the life-time of the parent, had already taught them to respect his advice, or to attend to his commands; or lastly, the prospect of these inconveniences might prompt the first ancestor to appoint a successor, and his posterity, from the same motive united with an habitual deference to his authority, might receive the appointment with submission. Here then we have a tribe or clan incorporated under one chief. Such communities might be increased by considerable numbers, and fulfil the purposes of civil union without any other or more regular convention, constitution, or form of government, than what we have described. Every branch which was slipped off from the primitive stock, and removed to a distance from it, would in like manner take root, and grow into a separate clan. Two or three of these clans were frequently, we may suppose, united into one. Marriage, conquest, mutual defence, common distress, or more accidental coalitions, might produce this effect.

II. A second source of personal authority, and which might easily extend, or sometimes perhaps supersede the patriarchal, is that, which results from military arrangement. In wars, either of aggression or defence, manifest necessity would prompt those who fought on the same side to array themselves under one leader. And although their *leader* was advanced to this eminence for the purpose only, and during the operations of a single expedition, yet his authority would not always terminate with the reasons for which it was conferred. A warrior who had led forth his tribe against their enemies with repeated success, would procure to himself even in the deliberations of peace, a powerful and permanent influence. If this advantage were added to the authority of the patriarchal chief, or favoured by any previous distinction of ancestry, it would be no difficult undertaking for the person who possessed it to obtain the almost absolute direction of the affairs of the community, especially if he was careful to associate to himself proper auxiliaries, and content to practice the obvious art of gratifying or removing those who opposed his pretensions.

But although we may be able to comprehend how by his personal abilities or fortune one man may obtain the rule over many, yet it seems more difficult to explain how empire became *hereditary*, or in what manner sovereign power, which is never acquired without great merit or management, learns to descend in a succession, which has no dependence upon any qualities, either of understanding, or activity. The causes which have introduced hereditary dominion into so general a reception in the world, are principally the following—the influence of association, which communicates to the son a portion of the same respect which was wont to be paid to the virtues, or station of the father—the mutual jealousy of other competitors—the greater envy, with which all behold the exaltation of an equal, than the continuance of an acknowledged superiority—a reigning prince leaves behind him many adherents, who can preserve their own importance only by supporting the succession of his children—Add to these reasons, that elections to the supreme power having upon some occasions produced the most destructive contentions, many states would take refuge from a return of the same calamities, in a rule of succession; and no rule presents itself so obvious, certain, and intelligible, as consanguinity of birth.

The ancient state of society in most countries, and the modern condition of some uncivilized parts of the world, exhibit that appearance, which this account of the original of civil government would lead us to expect. The earliest histories of *Palestine, Greece, Italy, Gaul, Britain,* inform us, that these countries were occupied by many small independent nations, not much perhaps unlike those which are found at present amongst the savage inhabitants of *North America,* and upon the coast of *Africa.* These nations, I consider, as the amplifications of so many single families; or as derived from the junction of two or three families,

families, whom society in war, or the approach of common danger had united. Suppose a country to have been first peopled by shipwreck on its coasts, or by emigrants or exiles from some neighbouring country, the new settlers having no enemy to provide against, and occupied with the care of their personal subsistence, would think little of digesting a system of laws, of contriving a form of government, or indeed of any political union whatever; but each settler would remain at the head of his own family, and each family would include all of every age and generation who were descended from him. So many of these families as were holden together after the death of the original ancestor, by the reasons, and in the method above recited, would wax as the individuals were multiplied, into tribes, clans, hords, or nations, similar to those into which the ancient inhabitants of many countries are known to have been divided, and which are still found, wherever the state of society and manners is immature and uncultivated.

Nor need we be surprized at the early existence in the world of some vast empires, or at the rapidity with which they advanced to their greatness, from comparatively small and obscure originals. Whilst the inhabitants of so many countries were broken into numerous communities, unconnected, and oftentimes contending with each other; before experience had taught these little states to see their own danger in their neighbour's ruin; or had instructed them in the necessity of resisting the aggrandizement of an aspiring power, by alliances and timely preparations; in this

this condition of civil policy, a particular tribe who by any means had got the start of the rest in strength, or discipline, and happened to fall under the conduct of an ambitious chief, by directing their first attempts to the part where success was most secure, and by assuming, as they went along, those whom they conquered, into a share of their future enterprizes, might soon gather a force, which would infallibly overbear any opposition, that the divided power and unprovided state of such enemies could make to the progress of their victories.

Lastly, our theory affords a presumption, that the earliest governments were monarchies, because the government of families, and of armies, from which, according to our account civil government derived its institution, and probably its form, is universally monarchical.

CHAP. II.

HOW SUBJECTION TO CIVIL GOVERNMENT IS MAINTAINED.

COULD we view our own species from a diftance, and regard mankind with the fame fort of obfervation, with which we read the natural hiftory or remark the *manners* of any other animal, there is nothing in the human character which would more furprize us, than the almoft univerfal fubjugation of ftrength to weaknefs—than to fee many millions perhaps of robuft men, in the complete ufe and exercife of their perfonal faculties, and without any defect of courage, waiting upon the will of a child, a woman, a driveller, or a lunatic. And although when we fuppofe a vaft empire in abfolute fubjection to one perfon, and that one depreffed beneath the level of his fpecies by infirmities, or vice, we fuppofe perhaps an extreme cafe, yet in all cafes, even in the moft popular forms of civil government, *the phyfical ftrength refides in the governed*. In what manner opinion thus prevails over ftrength, or how power, which naturally belongs to fuperior force, is maintained in oppofition to it, in other words, by what motives the many are induced to fubmit to the few, becomes an enquiry which lies at the root of
almoft

almoft every political fpeculation. It removes, indeed, but does not refolve the difficulty, to fay, that civil governments are now-a-days almoft univerfally upheld by ftanding armies, for the queftion ftill returns, how are thefe armies themfelves kept in fubjection, or made to obey the directions, and carry on the defigns, of the prince, or ftate which employs them.

Now although we fhould look in vain for any *fingle* reafon which will account for the general fubmiffion of mankind to civil government, yet it may not be difficult to affign for every clafs and character in the community, confiderations powerful enough to diffuade each from any attempts to refift eftablifhed authority. Every man has his motive, though not the fame. In this as in other inftances, the conduct is fimilar, but the principles which produce it, extremely various.

There are three principal diftinctions of character, into which the fubjects of a ftate may be divided; into thofe who obey from prejudice; thofe who obey from reafon; and thofe who obey from felf-intereft.

1. They who obey from prejudice, are determined by an opinion of *right*, in their governors; which opinion is founded upon *prefcription*. In monarchies and ariftocracies which are hereditary, the prefcription operates in favour of particular families; in republics and elective offices, in favour of particular forms of government, or *conftitutions*.

Nor is it to be wondered at, that mankind should reverence authority founded in prescription, when they observe that prescription confers a title to almost every thing else. The whole course, and all the habits of civil life, favour this prejudice. Upon what other foundation stands any man's right to his estate? The right of primogeniture, the succession of kindred, the descent of property, the inheritance of honours, the demand of tythes, tolls, rents, or services from the estates of others, the right of way, the powers of office and magistracy, the privileges of nobility, the immunities of the clergy, upon what are they all founded, in the apprehension at least of the multitude, but upon prescription? To what else, when the claims are contested, is the appeal made? It is natural to transfer the same principle to the affairs of government, and to regard those exertions of power, which have been long exercised and acquiesced in, as so many *rights* in the sovereign; and to consider obedience to his commands, within certain accustomed limits, as enjoined by that rule of conscience, which requires us to render to every man his due.

In hereditary monarchies, the *prescriptive title* is corroborated, and its influence considerably augmented, by an accession of religious sentiments, and by that sacredness which men are wont to ascribe to the persons of princes. Princes themselves have not failed to take advantage of this disposition, by claiming a superior dignity, as it were, of nature, or a peculiar delegation from the Supreme Being. For this purpose were introduced the titles of

sacred

of God's anointed, representative, vicegerent, together with the ceremonies of investitures and coronations, which are calculated not so much to recognize the authority of sovereigns, as to consecrate their persons. Where a fabulous religion permitted it, the public veneration has been challenged by bolder pretensions. The Roman emperors usurped the titles, and arrogated the worship of gods. The mythology of the heroic ages, and of many barbarous nations, was easily converted to this purpose. Some princes, like the heroes of Homer, and the founder of the Roman name, derived their birth from the gods: others, with Numa, pretended a secret but supernatural communication with some divine being: and others again, like the Incas of Peru, and the ancient Saxon kings, extracted their descent from the deities of their country. The *Lama* of *Thibet*, at this day, is held forth to his subjects, not as the offspring or successor of a divine race of princes, but as the immortal God himself, the object at once of civil obedience and religious adoration. This instance is singular, and may be accounted the farthest point to which the abuse of human credulity has ever been carried. But in all these instances the purpose was the same—to engage the reverence of mankind, by an application to their religious principles.

The reader will be careful to observe, that in this article we denominate every opinion a *prejudice*, which, whether true or false, is not founded upon argument, in the mind of the person who entertains it.

II. They

II. They who obey from *reason*, that is to say, from conscience as instructed by reasonings and conclusions of their own, are determined, by the consideration of the necessity of some government or other; the certain mischief of civil commotions; and the danger of resettling the government of their country better, or at all, if once subverted or disturbed.

III. They who obey from *self-interest*, are kept in order by want of leisure; by a succession of private cares, pleasures, and engagements; by contentment, or a sense of the ease, plenty, and safety, which they enjoy; or lastly and principally, by fear, foreseeing that they would bring themselves by resistance into a worse situation than their present, inasmuch as the strength of government, each discontented subject reflects, is greater than his own, and he knows not that others would join him. This last consideration has often been called *opinion of power*.

This account of the principles by which mankind are retained in their obedience to civil government, may suggest the following cautions:

1. Let civil governors learn from hence to respect their subjects; let them be admonished, that *the physical strength resides in the governed*; that this strength wants only to be felt and roused, to lay prostrate the most ancient and confirmed dominion; that civil authority is founded in opinion; that general opinion therefore ought always to be

treated

treated with deference, and managed with delicacy and circumspection.

2. *Opinion of right* always following *the custom*, being for the most part founded in nothing else, and lending one principal support to government, every innovation in the constitution, or, in other words, in the custom of governing, diminishes the stability of government. Hence some absurdities are to be retained, and many small inconveniences endured in every country, rather than that the usage should be violated, or the course of public affairs diverted from their old and smooth channel. Even *names* are not indifferent. When the multitude are to be dealt with, there is a *charm* in sounds. It was upon this principle, that several statesmen of those times advised *Cromwell* to assume the title of King, together with the ancient style and insignia of royalty. The minds of many, they contended, would be brought to acquiesce in the authority of a King, who suspected the office, and were offended with the administration of a Protector. Novelty reminded them of usurpation. The adversaries of this design opposed the measure, from the same persuasion of the efficacy of names and forms, jealous lest the veneration paid to these, should add an influence to the new settlement, which might ensnare the liberty of the commonwealth.

3. *Government may be too secure.* The greatest tyrants have been those, whose titles were the most unquestioned. Whenever therefore the opinion of right becomes too pre-

dominant and superstitious, it is abated by *breaking the custom.* Thus the Revolution broke the *custom of succession,* and thereby moderated both in the prince and in the people, those lofty notions of hereditary right, which in the one were become a continual temptation to tyranny, and disposed the other to invite servitude, by undue compliances and dangerous concessions.

4. As ignorance of union and want of communication appear amongst the principal preservatives of civil authority, it behoves every state to keep its subjects in this want and ignorance, not only by vigilance in guarding against actual confederacies and combinations, but by a timely care to prevent great collections of men of any separate party or religion, or of like occupation or profession, or in any way connected by a participation of interest or passion, from settling in the same vicinity. A protestant establishment in this country may have little to fear from its popish subjects, scattered as they are throughout the kingdom, and intermixed with the protestant inhabitants, which yet might think them a formidable body, if they were gathered together into one county. The most frequent and desperate riots are those, which break out amongst men of the same profession, as weavers, miners, sailors. This circumstance makes a mutiny of soldiers more to be dreaded than any other insurrection. Hence also one danger of an overgrown metropolis, and of those great cities and crowded districts, into which the inhabitants of trading countries are commonly collected. The worst effect of

popular

popular tumults confifts in this, that they difcover to the infurgents the fecret of their own ftrength, teach them to depend upon it againft a future occafion, and both produce and diffufe fentiments of confidence in one another, and affurances of mutual fupport. Leagues thus formed and ftrengthened, may over-awe, or over-fet the power of any ftate; and the danger is greater, in proportion, as from the propinquity of habitation and intercourfe of employment, the paffions and counfels of the party can be circulated with eafe and rapidity. It is by thefe means, and in fuch fituations, that the minds of men are fo affected and prepared, that the moft dreadful uproars often arife from the flighteft provocations.—When the train is laid, a fpark will produce the explofion.

CHAP. III.

THE DUTY OF SUBMISSION TO CIVIL GOVERNMENT EXPLAINED.

THE subject of this chapter is sufficiently distinguished from the subject of the last, as the motives which actually produce civil obedience, may be, and often are, very different from the reasons which make that obedience a duty.

In order to prove civil obedience to be a moral duty, and an obligation upon the conscience of the subject, it hath been usual with many political writers, at the head of whom we find the venerable name of *Locke*, to state a compact between the citizen and the state, as the ground and cause of the relation between them; which compact binding the parties, for the same general reason that private contracts do, resolves the duty of submission to civil government into the universal obligation of fidelity in the performance of promises. This compact is two-fold;

First, *An express* compact by the primitive founders of the state, who are supposed to have convened for the declared purpose of settling the terms of their political union, and a future constitution of government. The whole body is supposed, in the first place, to have unanimously consented, to be bound by the refolutions of the majority; that majority, in the next place, to have fixed certain fundamental regulations; and then to have conftituted, either in one perfon, or in an affembly (the rule of fucceffion or appointment being at the fame time determined) a *ftanding legiflature*, to whom, under thefe pre-eftablifhed reftrictions, the government of the ftate was thenceforward committed, and whofe laws the feveral members of the convention were, by their firft undertaking, thus perfonally engaged to obey.—This tranfaction is fometimes called the *focial compact*, and thefe fuppofed original regulations compofe what are meant by the *conftitution*, the *fundamental laws of the conftitution*; and form on one fide, the *inherent indefeafible prerogative of the crown*; and on the other, the unalienable *birthright* of the fubject.

Secondly, A *tacit* or *implied* compact, by all fucceeding members of the ftate, who, by accepting its protection, confent to be bound by its laws; in like manner as whoever *voluntarily enters* into a private fociety, is underftood, without any other or more explicit ftipulation, to promife a conformity with the rules, and obedience to the government of that fociety, as the known conditions, upon which he is admitted to a participation of its privileges.

This account of the fubject, although fpecious, and patronized by names the moft refpectable, appears to labour under the following objections; that it is founded upon a

fuppofition

supposition false in fact; and leading to dangerous conclusions.

No social compact, similar to what is here described, was ever made or entered into in reality; no such original convention of the people was ever actually held, or in any country could be held, antecedent to the existence of civil government in that country. It is to suppose it possible to call savages out of caves and deserts, to deliberate and vote upon topics, which the experience, and studies, and refinements of civil life alone suggest. Therefore no government in the universe *began* from this original. Some imitation of a social compact may have taken place at a *Revolution*. The present age has been witness to a transaction, which bears the nearest resemblance to this political idea, of any of which history has preserved the account or memory. I refer to the establishment of the united states of *North America*. We saw the *people* assembled to elect deputies, for the avowed purpose of framing the constitution of a new empire. We saw this deputation of the people deliberating and resolving upon a form of government, erecting a permanent legislature, distributing the functions of sovereignty, establishing and promulging a code of fundamental ordinances, which were to be considered by succeeding generations, not merely as laws and acts of the state, but as the very terms and conditions of the confederation; as binding not only upon the subjects and magistrates of the state, but as limitations of power, which were to controul and regulate the

the future legislature. Yet even here much was presupposed. In settling the constitution many important parts were presumed to be already settled. The qualifications of the constituents who were admitted to vote in the election of members of Congress, as well as the mode of electing the representatives, were taken from the old forms of government. That was wanting from which every social union should set off, and which alone makes the resolutions of the society the act of the individual, the unconstrained consent of all to be bound by the decision of the majority; and yet, without this previous consent, the revolt, and the regulations which followed it, were compulsory upon dissentients.

But the original compact, we are told, is not proposed as a *fact*, but as a fiction, which furnishes a commodious explication of the mutual rights and duties of sovereigns and subjects. In answer to this representation of the matter we observe, that the original compact, if it be not a fact, is nothing; can confer no actual authority upon laws or magistrates, nor afford any foundation to rights, which are supposed to be real and existing. But the truth is, that in the books, and in the apprehension of those who deduce our civil rights and obligations *a pactis*, the original convention is appealed to and treated of as a reality. Whenever the disciples of this system speak of the constitution; of the fundamental articles of the constitution; of laws being constitutional or unconstitutional; of inherent, unalienable, inextinguishable rights, either in the prince, or the people; or indeed of any laws, usages, or civil rights, as transcending the authority of the subsisting legislature, or possessing a force and sanction superior to what belong to the modern acts and edicts of the legislature, they secretly refer us to what passed at the original convention. They would teach us to believe, that certain rules and ordinances were established by the people, at the same time that they settled the charter of government, and the powers as well as the form of the future legislature; which legislature consequently, deriving its commission and existence from the consent and act of the primitive assembly, (of which indeed it is only the standing deputation,) continues subject in the exercise of its offices, and as to the extent of its power, to the rules, reservations, and limitations which the same assembly then made and prescribed to it.

" As the first members of the state were bound by
" express stipulation to obey the government which they
" had erected, so the succeeding inhabitants of the same
" country are understood to promise allegiance to the con-
" stitution and government they find established, by ac-
" cepting its protection, claiming its privileges, and ac-
" quiescing in its laws; more especially, by the purchase
" or inheritance of lands, to the possession of which, alle-
" giance to the state is annexed, as the very service and
" condition of the tenure." Smoothly as this train of argument proceeds, little of it will endure examination. The native subjects of modern states are not conscious of any stipulation with their sovereigns, of ever exercising an
election

election whether they will be bound or not by the acts of the legislature, of any alternative being proposed to their choice, of a promise either required or given; nor do they apprehend that the validity or authority of the laws depends at all upon *their* recognition or consent. In all stipulations, whether they be expressed or implied, private or public, formal or constructive, the parties stipulating must both possess the liberty of assent and refusal, and also be conscious of this liberty; which cannot with truth be affirmed of the subjects of civil government, as government is now, or ever was actually administered. This is a defect, which no arguments can excuse or supply: all presumptions of consent, without this consciousness, or in opposition to it, are vain and erroneous. Still less is it possible to reconcile with any idea of stipulation the practice in which all *European* nations agree, of founding allegiance upon the circumstance of nativity, that is, of claiming and treating as subjects all those who are born within the confines of their dominions, although removed to another country in their youth or infancy. In this instance certainly, the state does not presume a compact. Also if the subject be bound only by his own consent, and if the voluntary abiding in a country be the proof and intimation of that consent, by what arguments shall we defend the right, which sovereigns universally assume, of prohibiting, when they please, the departure of their subjects out of the realm?

Again, when it is contended that the taking and holding possession of land amounts to an acknowledgment of the sovereign, and a virtual promise of allegiance to his laws, it is necessary to the validity of the argument to prove, that the inhabitants, who first composed and constituted the state, collectively possessed a right to the soil of the country—a right to parcel it out to whom they pleased, and to annex to the donation what conditions they thought fit. How came they by this right? An agreement amongst themselves would not confer it: that could only adjust what already belonged to them. A society of men vote themselves to be the owners of a region of the world;—does that vote, unaccompanied especially with any culture, inclosure, or proper act of occupation, make it theirs? does it entitle them to exclude others from it, or to dictate the conditions upon which it shall be enjoyed? Yet this original collective right and ownership, is the foundation of all the reasoning, by which the duty of allegiance is inferred from the possession of land.

The theory of government which affirms the existence and the obligation of a social compact, would, after all, merit little discussion, and however groundless and unnecessary, should receive no opposition from us, did it not appear to lead to conclusions unfavourable to the improvement, and to the peace, of human society.

1st. Upon the supposition that government was first erected by, and that it derives all its just authority from, resolutions entered into by a convention of the people, it is capable of being presumed, that many points were settled by that convention, anterior to the establishment of the subsisting legislature, and which the legislature, consequently, has no right to alter, or interfere with. These points are called the *fundamentals* of the constitution; and as it is impossible to determine how many, or what they are, the suggesting of any such, serves extremely to embarrass the deliberations of the legislature, and affords a dangerous pretence for disputing the authority of the laws. It was this sort of reasoning (so far as reasoning of any kind was employed in the question) that produced in this nation the doubt, which so much agitated the minds of men in the reign of the *second Charles*, whether an Act of Parliament could of right alter or limit the succession of the Crown.

2dly. If it be by virtue of a compact, that the subject owes obedience to civil government, it will follow, that he ought to abide by the form of government which he finds established, be it ever so absurd, or inconvenient. He is bound by his bargain. It is not permitted to any man to retreat from his engagement, merely because he finds the performance disadvantageous, or because he has an opportunity of entering into a better. This law of contracts is universal: and to call the relation between the sovereign and the subject a contract, yet not to apply to it the rules, or allow of the effects of a contract, is an arbitrary use of names, and an unsteadiness in reasoning, which can teach nothing. Resistance to the encroachments of the supreme magistrate may be justified upon this principle; recourse
to

to arms, for the purpose of bringing about an amendment of the constitution, never can. No form of government contains a provision for its own dissolution; and few governors will consent to the extinction, or even to any abridgement of their own power. It does not therefore appear, how despotic governments can ever in consistency with the obligation of the subject be changed, or mitigated. Despotism is the constitution of many states: and whilst a despotic prince exacts from his subjects the most rigorous servitude, according to this account, he is only holding them to their agreement. They may vindicate, by force, the rights which the constitution has left them; but every attempt to narrow the prerogative of the crown, by *new* limitations, and in opposition to the will of the reigning prince, whatever opportunities may invite, or success follow it, must be condemned as an infraction of the compact between the sovereign and the subject.

3dly. *Every violation of the compact on the part of the governor releases the subject from his allegiance, and dissolves the government.* I do not perceive how we can avoid this consequence, if we found the duty of allegiance upon compact, and confess any analogy between the social compact and other contracts. In private contracts, the violation or non-performance of the conditions, by one of the parties, vacates the obligation of the other. Now the terms and articles of the social compact being no where extant or expressed; the rights and offices of the administrator of an empire being so many and various; the imaginary and
con-

controverted line of his prerogative being so liable to be overstepped in one part or other of it: the position that every such transgression amounts to a forfeiture of the government, and consequently authorizes the people to withdraw their obedience and provide for themselves by a new settlement, would endanger the stability of every political fabric in the world, and has in fact always supplied the disaffected with a topic of seditious declamation. If occasions have arisen, in which this plea has been resorted to with justice and success, they have been occasions, in which a revolution was defensible upon other and plainer principles. The plea itself, is at all times captious and unsafe.

Wherefore, rejecting the intervention of a compact, as unfounded in its principle, and dangerous in the application, we assign for the only ground of the subjects' obligation, THE WILL OF GOD AS COLLECTED FROM EXPEDIENCY.

The steps by which the argument proceeds are few and direct. " It is the will of God that the happiness of hu-
" man life be promoted;"—this is the first step, and the foundation not only of this but of every moral conclusion. " Civil society conduces to that end;"—this is the second proposition. " Civil societies cannot be upheld, unless
" in each, the interest of the whole society be binding
" upon every part and member of it;"—this is the third
step,

step, and conducts us to the conclusion, namely, "that so long as the interest of the whole society requires it, that is, so long as the established government cannot be resisted or changed without public inconveniency, it is the will of God (which *will* universally determines our duty) that the established government be obeyed,"— and no longer.

This principle being admitted, the justice of every particular case of resistance, is reduced to a computation of the quantity of the danger and grievance on the one side, and of the probability and expence of redressing it on the other.

But who shall judge of this? We answer, "Every man for himself." In contentions between the sovereign and the subject, the parties acknowledge no common arbitrator; and it would be absurd to commit the decision to *those* whose conduct has provoked the question, and whose own interest, authority, and fate, are immediately concerned in it. The danger of error and abuse, is no objection to the rule of expediency, because every other rule is liable to the same or greater; and every rule that can be propounded upon the subject (like all rules which appeal to, or bind, the conscience) must in the application depend upon private judgment. It may be observed, however, that it ought equally to be accounted the exercise of a man's private judgment, whether he be determined by reasonings and conclusions of his own, or submit to be directed by the advice of others, provided he be free to choose his guide.

We proceed to point out some easy but important inferences, which result from the substitution of *public expediency* into the place of all implied compacts, promises, or conventions whatsoever.

I. It may be as much a duty, at one time, to resist government, as it is at another, to obey it—to wit, whenever more advantage will, in our opinion, accrue to the community from resistance, than mischief.

II. The lawfulness of resistance, or the lawfulness of a revolt, does not depend alone upon the grievance which is sustained or feared, but also upon the probable expence and event of the contest. They who concerted the Revolution in *England* were justifiable in their counsels, because from the apparent disposition of the nation, and the strength and character of the parties engaged, the measure was likely to be brought about with little mischief or bloodshed; whereas, it might have been a question with many friends of their country, whether the injuries then endured and threatened would have authorized the renewal of a doubtful civil war.

III. Irregularity in the first foundation of a state, or subsequent violence, fraud, or injustice in getting possession of the supreme power, are not sufficient reasons for resistance, after the government is once peaceably settled. No subject of the *British* empire conceives himself engaged to vindicate the justice of the *Norman* claim or conquest, or apprehends that his duty in any manner depends upon that controversy. So likewise if the House of *Lancaster*, or even the posterity of *Cromwell* had been at this day seated upon the throne of *England*, we should have been as little concerned to enquire how the founder of the family came there. No civil contests are so futile, although none have been so furious and sanguinary, as those which are excited by a disputed succession.

IV. Not every invasion of the subject's rights, or liberty, or of the constitution; not every breach of promise, or of oath; not every stretch of prerogative, abuse of power, or neglect of duty by the chief magistrate, or by the whole or any branch of the legislative body, justifies resistance, unless these crimes draw after them public consequences of sufficient magnitude to outweigh the evils of civil disturbance. Nevertheless, every violation of the constitution ought to be watched with jealousy, and resented as *such*, beyond what the quantity of estimable damage would require or warrant; because a known and settled usage of governing affords the best security against the enormities of uncontrolled dominion, and because this security is weakened by every encroachment which is made without opposition, or opposed without effect.

V. No usage, law, or authority whatever, is so binding, that it need or ought to be continued, when it may be changed

changed with advantage to the community. The family of the prince, the order of succession, the prerogative of the crown, the form and parts of the legislature, together with the respective powers, office, duration, and mutual dependency of the several parts, are all only so many *laws*, mutable like other laws, whenever expediency requires, either by the ordinary act of the legislature, or, if the occasion deserve it, by the interposition of the people. These points are wont to be approached with a kind of awe; they are represented to the mind as principles of the constitution settled by our ancestors, and being settled, to be no more committed to innovation or debate; as foundations never to be stirred; as the terms and conditions of the social compact, to which every citizen of the state has engaged his fidelity, by virtue of a promise, which he cannot now recall. Such reasons have no place in our system: to us, if there be any good reason for treating these with more deference and respect than other laws, it is, either the advantage of the present constitution of government (which reason must be of different force in different countries), or because in all countries, it is of importance, that the form and usage of governing be acknowledged and understood, as well by the governors as the governed, and because the seldomer it is changed, the more it will be respected by both sides.

VI. As all civil obligation is resolved into expediency, what, it may be asked, is the difference between the obligation of an Englishman and a Frenchman? or, why is a

Frenchman bound in conscience to bear any thing from his King, which an Englishman would not be bound to bear, since the obligation of both is founded in the same reason? Their conditions may differ, but their *rights*, according to this account should seem to be equal; and yet we are accustomed to speak of the *rights* as well as of the happiness of a free people, compared with what belong to the subjects of absolute monarchies: how, you will say, can this comparison be explained, unless we refer to a difference in the compacts, by which they are respectively bound?—This is a fair question, and the answer to it will afford a further illustration of our principles. We admit then that there are many things which a Frenchman is bound in conscience, as well as by coercion, to endure at the hands of his prince, to which an Englishman would not be obliged to submit; but we assert, that it is for these two reasons alone: *first*, because the same act of the prince is not the same grievance where it is agreeable to the constitution, as where it infringes it: *secondly*, because redress in the two cases is not equally attainable. Resistance cannot be attempted with equal hopes of success, or with the same prospect of receiving support from others, where the people are reconciled to their sufferings, as where they are alarmed by innovation. In this way, and no otherwise, the subjects of different states possess different civil rights; the duty of obedience is defined by different boundaries, and the point of justifiable resistance placed at different parts of the *scale* of suffering—all which is sufficiently intelligible without a social compact.

VII. " The

VII. "The interest of the whole society is binding upon "every part of it." No rule, short of this, will provide for the stability of civil government, or for the peace and safety of social life. Wherefore, as individual members of the state are not permitted to pursue their private emolument to the prejudice of the community, so is it equally a consequence of this rule, that no particular colony, province, town, or district, can justly concert measures for their separate interest, which shall appear at the same time to diminish the *sum* of public prosperity. I do not mean, that it is necessary to the justice of a measure, that it profit each and every part of the community; for as the happiness of the whole may be increased, whilst that of some parts is diminished, it is possible, that the conduct of one part of an empire, may be detrimental to some other part, and yet just, provided one part gain more in happiness, than the other part loses, so that the common weal be augmented by the change: but what I affirm is, that those counsels can never be reconciled with the obligations resulting from civil union, which cause the *whole* happiness of the society to be impaired for the conveniency of a *part*. This conclusion is applicable to the question of right between *Great Britain* and her revolted colonies. Had I been an *American*, I should not have thought it enough to have had it even demonstrated, that a separation from the parent state would produce effects beneficial to *America*; my relation to that state imposed upon me a further enquiry, namely, whether the whole happiness of the empire was likely to be promoted by such a measure?—Not indeed the happiness

ness of every part, that was not necessary, nor to be expected—but whether what *Great Britain* would lose by the separation was likely to be compensated to the joint stock of happiness, by the advantages which *America* would receive from it. The contested claims of sovereign states, and their remote dependencies, may be submitted to the adjudication of this rule with mutual safety. A public advantage, is measured by the advantage, which each individual receives, and by the number of those who receive it. A public evil is compounded of the same proportions. Whilst, therefore, a colony is small, or a province thinly inhabited, if a competition of interests arise between the original country and their acquired dominions, the former ought to be preferred, because it is fit, that, if one must necessarily be sacrificed, the less give place to the greater: but when, by an increase of population, the interest of the provinces begins to bear a considerable proportion to the *entire* interest of the community, it is possible that they may suffer so much by their subjection, that not only their's, but the whole happiness of the empire may be obstructed by their union. The rule and principle of the calculation being still the same, the *result* is different; and this difference begets a new situation, which entitles the subordinate parts of the state to more equal terms of confederation, and, if these be refused, to independency.

CHAP. IV.

OF THE DUTY OF CIVIL OBEDIENCE AS STATED IN THE CHRISTIAN SCRIPTURES.

WE affirm, that as to the *extent* of our civil rights and obligations, *Christianity* hath left us where she found us; that she hath neither altered, nor ascertained it; that the New Testament contains not one passage, which fairly interpreted, affords either argument or objection applicable to any conclusions upon the subject, that are deduced from the law and religion of nature.

The only passages which have been seriously alledged in the controversy, or which it is necessary for us to state and examine, are the two following; the one extracted from St. *Paul's* Epistle to the *Romans*, the other from the First General Epistle of St. *Peter*.

ROMANS xiii. 1—7.

" Let every soul be subject unto the higher powers.
" For there is no power but of God; the powers that be,
" are ordained of God. Whosoever therefore resisteth the
" power, resisteth the ordinance of God: and they that
" resist,

"refist, shall receive to themselves damnation. For rulers "are not a terror to good works, but to the evil. Wilt "thou then not be afraid of the power? Do that which "is good, and thou shalt have praise of the same: for he "is the minister of God to thee for good. But if thou do "that which is evil be afraid; for he beareth not the "sword in vain: for he is the minister of God, a revenger "to *execute* wrath upon him that doeth evil. Wherefore "ye must needs be subject, not only for wrath, but also "for conscience sake. For, for this cause pay you tribute "also: for they are God's ministers, attending continually "upon this very thing. Render therefore to all their "dues: tribute to whom tribute is due, custom to whom "custom, fear to whom fear, honour to whom honour."

1. PETER, ii. 13—18.

"Submit yourselves to every ordinance of man for the "Lord's sake: whether it be to the King as supreme; or "unto Governors, as unto them that are sent by him for "the punishment of evil doers, and for the praise of them "that do well. For so is the will of God, that with well- "doing ye may put to silence the ignorance of foolish "men: as free, and not using your liberty for a cloak of "maliciousness, but as the servants of God."

To comprehend the proper import of these instructions, let the reader reflect, that upon the subject of civil obedience there are two questions; the first, whether to obey government be a moral duty and obligation upon the
conscience

confcience at all; the fecond, how far, and to what cafes, that obedience ought to extend;—that thefe two queftions are fo diftinguifhable in the imagination, that it is poffible to treat of the one, without any thought of the other; and laftly, that if expreffions which relate to one of thefe queftions be transferred and applied to the other, it is with great danger of giving them a fignification very different from the author's meaning. This diftinction is not only poffible, but natural. If I met with a perfon, who appeared to entertain doubts, whether civil obedience were a moral duty which ought to be voluntarily difcharged, or whether it were not a mere fubmiffion to force, like that, which we yield to a robber, who holds a piftol to our breaft; I fhould reprefent to him the ufe and offices of civil government, the end and the neceffity of civil fubjection; or, if I preferred a different theory, I fhould explain to him the focial compact, urge him with the obligation and the equity of his implied promife and tacit confent to be governed by the laws of the ftate from which he received protection; or I fhould argue, perhaps, that Nature herfelf dictated the law of fubordination, when fhe planted within us an inclination to affociate with our fpecies, and framed us with capacities fo various and unequal.—From whatever principle I fet out, I fhould labour to infer from it this conclufion, " That obedience to the ftate, is to be " numbered amongft the relative duties of human life, " for the tranfgreffion of which, we fhall be accountable at " the tribunal of divine juftice, whether the magiftrate " be able to punifh us for it or not;" and being arrived at this conclusion, I should stop, having delivered the conclusion itself, and throughout the whole argument expressed the obedience, which I inculcated, in the most general and unqualified terms, all reservations and restrictions being superfluous, and foreign to the doubts I was employed to remove.

If in a short time afterwards, I should be accosted by the same person, with complaints of public grievances, of exorbitant taxes, of acts of cruelty and oppression, of tyrannical encroachments upon the ancient or stipulated rights of the people, and should be consulted whether it were lawful to revolt, or justifiable to join in an attempt to shake off the yoke by open resistance; I should certainly consider myself as having a case and question before me very different from the former. I should now define and discriminate. 'I should reply, that if public expediency be the foundation, it is also the measure of civil obedience; that the obligation of subjects and sovereigns is reciprocal; that the duty of allegiance, whether it be founded in utility or compact, is neither unlimited nor unconditional; that peace may be purchased too dear; that patience becomes culpable pusillanimity, when it serves only to encourage our rulers to increase the weight of our burthen, or to bind it the faster; that the submission, which surrenders the liberty of a nation, and entails slavery upon future generations, is enjoined by no law of rational morality: finally, I should instruct him to compare

pare the peril and expence of his enterprize, with the effects it was expected to produce, and to make choice of the alternative, by which not his own prefent relief or profit, but the whole and permanent intereft of the ftate was likely to be beft promoted. If any one who had been prefent at both thefe converfations fhould upbraid me with change or inconfiftency of opinion, fhould retort upon me the paffive doctrine I before taught, the large and abfolute terms in which I then delivered leffons of obedience and fubmiffion, I fhould account myfelf unfairly dealt with. I fhould reply, that the only difference which the language of the two converfations prefented was, that I added now many exceptions and limitations, which were omitted or unthought of then; that this difference arofe naturally from the two occafions, fuch exceptions being as neceffary to the fubject of our prefent conference, as they would have been fuperfluous and unfeafonable in the former. Now the difference in thefe two converfations is precifely the diftinction to be taken in interpreting thofe paffages of Scripture, concerning which we are debating. They inculcate the *duty*, they do not defcribe the *extent* of it. They enforce the obligation by the proper fanctions of Chriftianity, without intending either to enlarge or contract, without confidering indeed the limits by which it is bounded. This is alfo the method, in which the fame Apoftles enjoin the duty of fervants to their mafters, of children to their parents, of wives to their hufbands. " Servants be fubject to your mafters."— " Children " obey your parents in all things.— " Wives fubmit "yourselves unto your own husbands." The same concise and absolute form of expression occurs in all these precepts; the same silence, as to any exceptions or distinctions; yet no one doubts, but that the commands of masters, parents, and husbands, are often so immoderate, unjust, and inconsistent with other obligations, that they both may and ought to be resisted. In letters or dissertations written professedly upon separate articles of morality, we might with more reason have looked for a precise delineation of our duty, and some degree of modern accuracy in the rules which were laid down for our direction; but in those short collections of practical maxims, which compose the conclusion, or some small portion, of a doctrinal or perhaps controversial epistle, we cannot be surprized to find the author more solicitous to impress the duty, than curious to enumerate exceptions.

The consideration of this distinction, is alone sufficient to vindicate these passages of Scripture, from any explanation, which may be put upon them, in favour of an unlimited passive obedience. But if we be permitted to assume a supposition, which many commentators proceed upon as a certainty, that the first Christians privately cherished an opinion, that their conversion to Christianity entitled them to new immunities, to an exemption as of *right* (however they might give way to necessity) from the authority of the *Roman* sovereign, we are furnished with a still more apt and satisfactory interpretation of the Apostles' words. The two passages apply with great propriety to the refutation of of this error; they teach the Chriſtian convert to obey the magiſtrate "for the Lord's ſake,"—"not only for wrath, "but for conſcience ſake."—"That there is no power but "of God;"—"that the powers that be," even the preſent rulers of the *Roman* empire, though heathens and uſurpers, ſeeing they are in poſſeſſion of the actual and neceſſary authority of civil government "are ordained of God," and conſequently, entitled to receive obedience from thoſe who profeſs themſelves the peculiar ſervants of God, in a greater (certainly not in a leſs) degree, than from any others. They briefly deſcribe the office of civil governors, "the puniſhment of evil doers, and the praiſe of them that do well;" from which deſcription of the uſe of government, they juſtly infer the duty of ſubjection, which duty being as extenſive, as the reaſon upon which it is founded, belongs to Chriſtians no leſs than to the heathen members of the community. If it be admitted, that the two Apoſtles wrote with a view to this particular queſtion, it will be confeſſed, that their words cannot be transferred to a queſtion totally different from this, with any certainty of carrying along with us their authority and intention. There exiſts no reſemblance between the caſe of a primitive convert who diſputed the juriſdiction of the *Roman* government over a diſciple of Chriſtianity, and *his*, who acknowledging the general authority of the ſtate over all its ſubjects, doubts, whether that authority be not in ſome important branch of it, ſo ill conſtituted or abuſed, as to warrant the endeavours of the people to bring about a reformation by force: Nor can we judge what reply the

Apostles would have made to this *second* question, if it had been proposed to them, from any thing they have delivered upon the *first*; any more than in the two consultations above described, it could be known beforehand, what I would say in the latter, from the answer which I gave to the former.

The only defect in this account is, that neither the Scriptures, nor any subsequent history of the early ages of the church, furnish any direct attestation of the existence of such disaffected sentiments amongst the primitive converts. They supply indeed some circumstances, which render probable the opinion, that extravagant notions of the political rights of the Christian state were at that time entertained by many proselytes to the religion. From the question proposed to Christ, " Is it lawful to give tribute " unto Cæsar?" it may be presumed that doubts had been started in the *Jewish* schools concerning the obligation, or even the lawfulness of submission to the *Roman* yoke. The accounts delivered by *Josephus*, of various insurrections of the *Jews*, of that, and the following age, excited by this principle, or upon this pretence, confirm the presumption. For as the *Christians* were at first chiefly taken from the *Jews*, confounded with them by the rest of the world, and from the affinity of the two religions, apt to intermix the doctrines of both, it is not to be wondered at, that a tenet, so flattering to the self-importance of those who embraced it, should have been communicated to the new institution. Again, the teachers of Christianity,

amongst

amongst the privileges which their religion conferred upon its professors, were wont to extoll the "*liberty* into "which they were called,"—"in which Christ had made "them free." This liberty, which was intended of a deliverance from the various servitude, in which they had heretofore lived, to the domination of sinful passions, to the superstition of the *Gentile* idolatry, or the incumbered ritual of the *Jewish* dispensation, might by some be interpreted to signify an emancipation from all restraint which was imposed by an authority merely human. At least they might be represented by their enemies as maintaining notions of this dangerous tendency. To some error or calumny of this kind, the words of St. *Peter* seem to allude: "For so is the will of God, that with well-doing ye may "put to silence the ignorance of foolish men: as free, "and not using your liberty for a cloak of maliciousness, "(i. e. sedition) but as the servants of God." After all, if any one think this conjecture too feebly supported by testimony, to be relied upon in the interpretation of scripture, he will then revert to the considerations alledged in the preceding part of this chapter.

After so copious an account of what we apprehend to be the general design and doctrine of these much agitated passages, little need be added in explanation of particular clauses. St. *Paul* has said, "whosoever resisteth the "power, resisteth the ordinance of God." This phrase, "the ordinance of God," is by many so interpreted as to authorize the most exalted and superstitious ideas of the

regal

regal character. But surely, such interpreters have sacrificed truth to adulation. For in the first place, the expression, as used by St. *Paul*, is just as applicable to one kind of government, and to one kind of succession as to another—to the elective magistrates of a pure republic, as to an absolute hereditary monarch: in the next place, it is not affirmed of the supreme magistrate exclusively, that *he* is the ordinance of God; the title, whatever it imports, belongs to every inferior officer of the state as much as to the highest. The divine right of *Kings*, is, like the divine right of *Constables*,—the law of the land, or even actual and quiet possession of their office; a right, ratified, we humbly presume, by the divine approbation, so long as obedience to their authority appears to be necessary or conducive to the common welfare. Princes are ordained of God by virtue only of that general decree, by which he assents, and adds the sanction of his will, to every law of society, which promotes his own purpose, the communication of human happiness: according to which idea of their origin and constitution, and without any repugnancy to the words of St. *Paul*, they are by St. *Peter* denominated the *ordinance of man*.

CHAP. V.

OF CIVIL LIBERTY.

CIVIL Liberty is the not being restrained by any Law, but what conduces in a greater degree to the public welfare.

To do what we will is natural liberty; to do what we will, consistently with the interest of the community to which we belong, is civil liberty; that is to say, the only liberty to be desired in a state of civil society.

I should wish, no doubt, to be allowed to act in every instance as I pleased, but I reflect that the rest also of mankind would then do the same; in which state of universal independence and self-direction I should meet with so many checks and obstacles to my own will, from the interference and opposition of other men's, that not only my happiness, but my liberty, would be less, than whilst the whole community were subjected to the dominion of equal laws.

The boasted liberty of a state of nature exists only in a state of solitude. In every kind and degree of union and intercourse with his species, the liberty of the individual is augmented by the very laws which restrain it; because he gains more from the limitation of other men's freedom than he suffers by the diminution of his own. Natural liberty is the right of common upon a waste; civil liberty is the safe, exclusive, unmolested enjoyment of a cultivated inclosure.

The definition of civil liberty above laid down, imports that the laws of a free people impose no restraints upon the private will of the subject, which do not conduce in *a greater degree* to the public happiness: by which it is intimated, 1st, that restraint itself is an evil; 2dly, that this evil ought to be overbalanced by some public advantage; 3dly, that the proof of this advantage lies upon the legislature; 4thly, that a law being found to produce no sensible good effects, is a sufficient reason for repealing it, as adverse and injurious to the rights of a free citizen, without demanding specific evidence of its bad effects.—This maxim might be remembered with advantage in a revision of many laws of this country; especially the game laws—the poor laws, so far as they lay restrictions upon the poor them-

themselves—the laws against papists and dissenters: and amongst a people enamoured to excess and jealous of their liberty, it seems a matter of surprize that this principle has been so imperfectly attended to.

The degree of actual liberty always bearing, according to this account of it, a reversed proportion to the number and severity of the *restrictions* which are either useless, or the utility of which does not outweigh the evil of the restraint; it follows that every nation possesses some, no nation perfect liberty; that this liberty may be enjoyed under every form of government; that it may be impaired indeed, or increased, but that it is neither gained, nor lost, nor recovered, by any single regulation, change, or event whatever; that consequently, those popular phrases which speak of a free people; of a nation of slaves; which call one revolution the æra of liberty; or another the loss of it; with many expressions of a like absolute form, are intelligible only in a comparative sense.

Hence also we are enabled to apprehend the distinction between *personal* and *civil* liberty. A citizen of the freest republic in the world may be imprisoned for his crimes; and though his personal freedom be restrained by bolts and fetters, so long as his confinement is the effect of a beneficial public law, his civil liberty is not invaded. If this instance appear dubious, the following will be plainer. A passenger from the Levant, who, upon his return to England, should be conveyed to a lazaretto by an order of quarantine,

quarantine, with whatever impatience he might defire his enlargement, and though he faw a guard placed at the door to oppofe his efcape, or even ready to deftroy his life if he attempted it, would hardly accufe government of incroaching upon his civil freedom; nay, might, perhaps, rather congratulate himfelf that he had at length fet his foot again in a land of liberty. The manifeft expediency of the meafure not only juftifies it, but reconciles the moft odious confinement with the perfect poffeffion, and the loftieft notions of civil liberty. And if this be true of the coercion of a prifon, that it is compatible with a ftate of *civil* freedom; it cannot with reafon be difputed of thofe more moderate conftraints which the ordinary operation of government impofes upon the will of the individual. It is not the rigour, but the inexpediency of laws and acts of authority, which makes them tyrannical.

There is another idea of civil liberty, which, though neither fo fimple, nor fo accurate as the former, agrees better with the fignification, which the ufage of common difcourfe, as well as the example of many refpectable writers upon the fubject, has affixed to the term. This idea places liberty in fecurity; making it to confift not merely in an actual exemption from the conftraint of ufelefs and noxious laws and acts of dominion, but in being free from the *danger* of having any fuch hereafter impofed or exercifed. Thus, fpeaking of the political ftate of modern Europe, we are accuftomed to fay of Sweden, that fhe hath loft her *liberty* by the revolution which lately took place in

that

that country; and yet we are affured that the people continue to be governed by the fame laws as before, or by others which are wifer, milder, and more equitable. What then have they loft? They have loft the power and functions of their diet; the conftitution of their ftates and orders, whofe deliberation and concurrence were required in the formation and eftablifhment of every public law; and thereby have parted with the fecurity which they poffeffed againft any attempts of the crown to harrafs its fubjects, by oppreffive and ufelefs exertions of prerogative. The lofs of this fecurity we denominate the lofs of liberty. They have changed not their laws, but their legiflature; not their enjoyment, but their fafety; not their prefent burthens, but their profpects of future grievances: and this we pronounce a change from the condition of freemen to that of flaves. In like manner, in our own country, the act of parliament, in the reign of Henry the Eighth, which gave to the king's proclamation the force of law, has properly been called a complete and formal furrender of the liberty of the nation; and would have been fo, although no proclamation were iffued in purfuance of thefe new powers, or none but what was recommended by the higheft wifdom and utility. The fecurity was gone. Were it probable, that the welfare and accommodation of the people would be as ftudioufly, and as providently, confulted in the edicts of a defpotic prince, as by the refolutions of a popular affembly, then would an abfolute form of government be no lefs free than the pureft democracy. The different degree of care and knowledge of the public intereft which may

reafonably

reasonably be expected from the different form and composition of the legislature, constitutes the distinction, in respect of liberty, as well between these two extremes, as between all the intermediate modifications of civil government.

The definitions which have been framed of civil liberty, and which have become the subject of much unnecessary altercation, are most of them adapted to this idea. Thus one political writer makes the very essence of the subject's liberty to consist in his being governed by no laws but those to which he hath actually consented; another is satisfied with an indirect and virtual consent; another again places civil liberty in the separation of the legislative and executive offices of government; another in the being governed by *law*, that is, by known, preconstituted, inflexible rules of action and adjudication; a fifth in the exclusive right of the people to tax themselves by their own representatives; a sixth in the freedom and purity of elections of representatives; a seventh in the control which the democratic part of the constitution possesses over the military establishment. Concerning which, and some other similar accounts of civil liberty, it may be observed, that they all labour under one inaccuracy, viz. that they describe not so much liberty itself, as the safeguards and preservatives of liberty: for example, a man's being governed by no laws, but those to which he has given his consent, were it practicable, is no otherwise necessary to the enjoyment of civil liberty, than as it affords a probable security against the

the dictation of laws, imposing superfluous restrictions upon his private will. This remark is applicable to the rest. The diversity of these definitions will not surprize us, when we consider that there is no contrariety or opposition amongst them whatever; for by how many different provisions and precautions civil liberty is fenced and protected, so many different accounts of liberty itself, all sufficiently consistent with truth and with each other, may, according to this mode of explaining the term, be framed and adopted.

Truth cannot be offended by a definition, but propriety may. In which view those definitions of liberty ought to be rejected, which by making that essential to civil freedom which is unattainable in experience, inflame expectations that can never be gratified, and disturb the public content with complaints, which no wisdom or benevolence of government can remove.

It will not be thought extraordinary, that an idea, which occurs so much oftener as the subject of panegyric and careless declamation, than of just reasoning or correct knowledge, should be attended with uncertainty and confusion; or that it should be found impossible to contrive a definition, which may include the numerous, unsettled, and ever varying significations, which the term is made to stand for, and at the same time accord with the condition and experience of social life.

Of the two ideas that have been stated of civil liberty, whichever we assume, and whatever reasoning we found upon them, concerning its extent, nature, value and preservation, this is the conclusion:—that *that* people, government, and constitution, is the *freest*, which makes the best provision for the enacting of expedient and salutary laws.

CHAP. VI.

OF DIFFERENT FORMS OF GOVERNMENT.

AS a series of appeals must be finite, there necessarily exists in every government a power from which the constitution has provided no appeal; and which power, for that reason, may be termed absolute, omnipotent, uncontrollable, arbitrary, despotic; and is alike so in all countries.

The person, or assembly, in whom this power resides, is called the *sovereign*, or the supreme power of the state.

Since to the same power universally appertains the office of establishing public laws, it is called also the *legislature* of the state.

A government receives its denomination from the form of the legislature; which form is likewise what we commonly mean by the *constitution* of a country.

Political writers enumerate three principal forms of government, which, however, are to be regarded rather as the simple forms, by some combination and intermixture of which all actual governments are composed, than as any where existing in a pure and elementary state. These forms are,

I. Despotism, or absolute MONARCHY, where the legislature is in a single person.

II. An ARISTOCRACY, where the legislature is in a select assembly, the members of which, either fill up by election the vacancies in their own body, or succeed to their places in it by inheritance, property, tenure of certain lands, or in respect of some personal right, or qualification.

III. A REPUBLIC, or democracy, where the people at large, either collectively, or by representation, constitute the legislature.

The separate advantages of MONARCHY, are unity of council, activity, decision, secrecy, dispatch; the military strength and energy which result from these qualities of government; the exclusion of popular and aristocratical contentions; the preventing, by a known rule of succession, of all competition for the supreme power; and thereby repressing the hopes, intrigues, and dangerous ambition of aspiring citizens.

The

The mischiefs, or rather the dangers of MONARCHY, are tyranny, expence, exaction, military domination; unnecessary wars waged to gratify the passions of an individual; risk of the character of the reigning prince; ignorance in the governors of the interests and accommodation of the people, and a consequent deficiency of salutary regulations; want of constancy and uniformity in the rules of government, and, proceeding from thence, insecurity of person and property.

The separate advantage of an ARISTOCRACY consists in the wisdom which may be expected from experience and education—a permanent council naturally possesses experience; and the members, who succeed to their places in it by inheritance, will, probably, be trained and educated with a view to the stations, which they are destined by their birth to occupy.

The mischiefs of an ARISTOCRACY are, dissensions in the ruling order of the state, which, from the want of a common superior, are liable to proceed to the most desperate extremities; oppression of the lower orders by the privileges of the higher, and by laws partial to the separate interests of the law makers.

The advantages of a REPUBLIC are, liberty, or exemption from needless restrictions; equal laws; regulations adapted to the wants and circumstances of the people; public spirit, frugality, averseness to war; the opportunities which democratic assemblies afford to men of every description, of producing their abilities and councils to public observation, and the exciting thereby, and calling forth to the service of the commonwealth, the faculties of its best citizens.

The evils of a REPUBLIC are, dissensions, tumults, faction; the attempts of powerful citizens to possess themselves of the empire; the confusion, rage, and clamour which are the inevitable consequences of assembling multitudes, and of propounding questions of state to the discussion of the people; the delay and disclosure of public councils and designs; and the imbecility of measures retarded by the necessity of obtaining the consent of members: lastly, the oppression of the provinces which are not admitted to a participation in the legislative power.

A *mixed* government is composed by the combination of two or more of the simple forms of government above described—and, in whatever proportion each form enters into the constitution of a government, in the same proportion may both the advantages and evils, which we have attributed to that form, be expected; that is, those are the uses to be maintained and cultivated in each part of the constitution, and these are the dangers to be provided against in each. Thus, if secrecy and dispatch be truly enumerated amongst the separate excellencies of regal government; then a mixed government, which retains monarchy in one part of its constitution, should be careful

ful that the other estates of the empire do not, by an officious and inquisitive interference with the executive functions, which are, or ought to be, reserved to the administration of the prince, interpose delays, or divulge what it is expedient to conceal. On the other hand, if profusion, exaction, military domination, and needless wars, be justly accounted natural properties of monarchy, in its simple unqualified form; then are these the objects to which, in a mixed government, the aristocratic and popular parts of the constitution ought to direct their vigilance; the dangers against which they should raise and fortify their barriers: these are departments of sovereignty, over which a power of inspection and control ought to be deposited with the people.

The same observation may be repeated of all the other advantages and inconveniences which have been ascribed to the several simple forms of government; and affords a rule whereby to direct the construction, improvement, and administration of mixed governments, subjected however to this remark, that a quality sometimes results from the conjunction of two simple forms of government, which belongs not to the separate existence of either: thus corruption, which has no place in an absolute monarchy, and little in a pure republic, is sure to gain admission into a constitution, which divides the supreme power between an executive magistrate and a popular council.

An *hereditary* MONARCHY is universally to be preferred to an *elective* monarchy. The confession of every writer upon

upon the subject of civil government, the experience of ages, the example of Poland, and of the papal dominion, seem to place this amongst the few indubitable maxims which the science of politics admits of. A crown is too splendid a prize to be conferred upon merit. The passions or interests of the electors exclude all consideration of the qualities of the competitors. The same observation holds concerning the appointment to any office which is attended with a great share of power or emolument. Nothing is gained by a popular choice worth the dissensions, tumults, and interruption of regular industry, with which it is inseparably attended. Add to this, that a king, who owes his elevation to the event of a contest, or to any other cause than a fixed rule of succession, will be apt to regard one part of his subjects as the associates of his fortune, and the other as conquered foes. Nor should it be forgotten, amongst the advantages of an *hereditary* monarchy, that as plans of national improvement and reform are seldom brought to maturity by the exertions of a single reign, a nation cannot attain to the degree of happiness and prosperity to which it is capable of being carried unless an uniformity of councils, a consistency of public measures and designs be continued through a succession of ages. This benefit of a consistent scheme of government may be expected with greater probability, where the supreme power descends in the same race, and where each prince succeeds, in some sort, to the aim, pursuits, and disposition of his ancestor, than if the crown, at every change, devolve upon a stranger, whose first care will commonly

commonly be to pull down what his predecessor had built up; and to substitute systems of administration, which must, in their turn, give way to the more favourite novelties of the next successor.

Aristocracies are of two kinds, first, where the power of the nobility belongs to them in their collective capacity alone; that is, where although the government reside in an assembly of the order, yet the members of that assembly separately and individually possess no authority or privilege beyond the rest of the community:—this describes the constitution of Venice. Secondly, where the nobles are severally invested with great personal power and immunities, and where the power of the senate is little more than the aggregated power of the individuals who compose it:—this is the constitution of Poland. Of these two forms of government, the first is more tolerable than the last; for although the members of a senate should many, or even all of them, be profligate enough to abuse the authority of their stations in the prosecution of private designs, yet, not being all under a temptation to the same injustice, not having all the same end to gain, it would still be difficult to obtain the consent of a majority, to any specific act of oppression, which the iniquity of an individual might prompt him to propose: or if the will were the same, the power is more confined; one tyrant, whether the tyranny reside in a single person, or a senate, cannot exercise oppression at so many places at the same time, as it may be carried on by the dominion of a numerous nobility over

their

their respective vassals and dependents. Of all species of domination this is the most odious: the freedom and satisfaction of private life are more constrained and harrassed by it, than by the most vexatious laws, or even by the lawless will of an arbitrary monarch; from whose knowledge, and from whose injustice, the greatest part of his subjects are removed by their distance, or concealed by their obscurity.

Europe exhibits more than one modern example, where the people, aggrieved by the exactions, or provoked by the enormities, of their immediate superiors, have joined with the reigning prince in the overthrow of the aristocracy, deliberately exchanging their condition for the miseries of despotism. About the middle of the last century, the commons of Denmark, weary of the oppressions which they had long suffered from the nobles, and exasperated by some recent insults, presented themselves at the foot of the throne, with a formal offer of their consent to establish unlimited dominion in the king. The revolution in Sweden, still more lately brought about with the acquiescence, not to say the assistance of the people, owed its success to the same cause, namely, to the prospect of deliverance, that it afforded, from the tyranny which their nobles exercised under the old constitution. In England the people behold the depression of the Barons, under the house of Tudor, with satisfaction, although they saw the crown ascending thereby to a height of power which no limitations, that the constitution had then provided, were likely to confine. The lesson to be drawn

drawn from such events is this, that a mixed government, which admits a patrician order into its constitution, ought to circumscribe the personal privileges of the nobility, especially claims of hereditary jurisdiction and local authority, with a jealousy equal to the solicitude with which it provides for its own preservation. For nothing so alienates the minds of the people, from the government under which they live, by a perpetual sense of annoyance and inconveniency; or so prepares them for the practices of an enterprising prince, or a factious demagogue, as the abuse which almost always accompanies the existence of separate immunities.

Amongst the inferior, but by no means inconsiderable advantages of a DEMOCRATIC constitution, or of a constitution in which the people partake of the power of legislation, the following should not be neglected.

I. The direction which it gives to the education, studies and pursuits of the superior orders of the community. The share which this has in forming the public manners and national character is very important. In countries, in which the gentry are excluded from all concern in the government, scarce any thing is left which leads to advancement, but the profession of arms. They who do not addict themselves to this profession, (and miserable must that country be, which constantly employs the military service of a great proportion of any order of its subjects,) are commonly lost by the mere want of object and destination; that is, they fall, without reserve, into the most sottish habits of animal gratification, or entirely devote themselves to the attainment of those futile arts and decorations, which compose the business and recommendation of a court: on the other hand, where the whole, or any effective portion of civil power is possessed by a popular assembly, more serious pursuits will be encouraged, purer morals and a more intellectual character will engage the public esteem; those faculties, which qualify men for deliberation and debate, and which are the fruit of sober habits, of early and long continued application, will be roused and animated by the reward, which, of all others, most readily awakens the ambition of the human mind, political dignity and importance.

II. Popular elections procure to the common people courtesy from their superiors. That contemptuous and overbearing insolence, with which the lower orders of the community are wont to be treated by the higher, is greatly mitigated where the people have something to give. The assiduity, with which their favour is sought upon these occasions, serves to generate settled habits of condescension and respect; and as human life is more embittered by affronts than injuries, whatever contributes to procure mildness and civility of manners towards those who are most liable to suffer from a contrary behaviour, corrects, with the pride, in a great measure the evil of inequality, and deserves to be accounted amongst the most generous institutions of social life.

III. The

III. The satisfaction which the people in free governments derive from the knowledge and agitation of political subjects; such as the proceedings and debates of the senate; the conduct and character of ministers; the revolutions, intrigues, and contentions of parties; and, in general, from the discussion of public measures, questions, and occurrences. Subjects of this sort excite just enough of interest and emotion, to afford a moderate engagement to the thoughts, without rising to any painful degree of anxiety, or ever leaving a fixed oppression upon the spirits—and what is this, but the aim and end of all those amusements, which compose so much of the business of life and of the value of riches? For my part, and I believe it to be the case with most men, who are arrived at the middle age, and occupy the middle classes of life; had I all the money, which I pay in taxes to government, at liberty to lay out upon amusement and diversion, I know not whether I could make choice of any, in which I should find greater pleasure, than what I receive from expecting, hearing, and relating public news; reading parliamentary debates, and proceedings; canvassing the political arguments, projects, predictions, and intelligence, which are conveyed, by various channels, to every corner of the kingdom. These topics, exciting universal curiosity, and being such as almost every man is ready to form, and prepared to deliver an opinion about, greatly promote, and, I think, improve conversation. They render it more rational and more innocent. They supply a substitute for drinking, gaming, scandal and obscenity. Now the secrecy, the jealousy, the solitude and precipitation of despotic governments exclude all this. But the loss, you say, is trifling. I know that it is possible to render even the mention of it ridiculous, by representing it as the idle employment of the most insignificant part of the nation, the folly of village-statesmen, and coffee-house politicians: but I allow nothing to be a trifle, which ministers to the harmless gratification of multitudes; nor any order of men to be insignificant, whose number bears a respectable proportion to the sum of the whole community.

We have been accustomed to an opinion, that a REPUBLICAN form of government suits only with the affairs of a small state: which opinion is founded in the consideration, that unless the people, in every district of the empire, be admitted to a share in the national representation, the government is not, as to *them*, a republic; that elections, where the constituents are numerous, and dispersed through a wide extent of country, are conducted with difficulty, or rather, indeed, managed by the intrigues, and combination of a few, who are situated near the place of election, each voter considering his single suffrage as too minute a portion of the general interest to deserve his care or attendance, much less to be worth any opposition to influence and application; that whilst we contract the representation within a compass small enough to admit of orderly debate, the interest of the constituent becomes too small, of the representative too great. It is difficult also to maintain any connection between them. He who represents

sents two hundred thousand, is necessarily a stranger to the greatest part of those who elect him: and when his interest amongst them ceases to depend upon an acquaintance with their persons and character, or a care and knowledge of their affairs; when such a representative finds the treasures and honours of a great empire at the disposal of a few, and himself one of the few, there is little reason to hope that he will not prefer to his public duty, those temptations of personal aggrandizement which his situation offers, and which the price of his vote will always purchase. All appeal to the people is precluded by the impossibility of collecting a sufficient proportion of their force and numbers. The factions, and the unanimity of the senate are equally dangerous. Add to these considerations, that in a democratic constitution the mechanism is too complicated, and the motions too slow for the operations of a great empire; whose defence and government require execution and dispatch, in proportion to the magnitude, extent, and variety of its interests and concerns. There is weight, no doubt, in these reasons; but much of the objection seems to be done away by the contrivance of a *federal* republic, which, distributing the country into districts of a commodious extent, and leaving to each its internal legislation, reserves to a convention of the states, the adjustment of their relative claims; the levying, direction and government of the common force of the confederacy; the requisition of subsidies for the support of this force; the making of peace and war; the entering into treaties; the regulation of foreign commerce; the equalization of duties upon imports, so as to prevent the defrauding of the revenue of one province by smuggling articles of taxation from the borders of another; and likewise, so as to guard against undue partialities in the encouragement of trade. To what limits such a republic might, without inconveniency, enlarge its dominions, by assuming neighbouring provinces into the confederation; or how far it is capable of uniting the liberty of a small commonwealth, with the safety of a powerful empire; or whether, amongst co-ordinate powers, dissensions and jealousies would not be likely to arise, which, for want of a common superior, might proceed to fatal extremities, are questions, upon which the records of mankind do not authorize us to decide with tolerable certainty.—The experiment is about to be tried in America upon a large scale.

CHAP. VII.

OF THE BRITISH CONSTITUTION.

BY the CONSTITUTION of a country is meant so much of its law, as relates to the designation and form of the legislature; the rights and functions of the several parts of the legislative body; the construction, office, and jurisdiction of courts of justice. The constitution is one principal division, section, or title of the code of public laws; distinguished from the rest only by the superior importance of the subject of which it treats. Therefore the terms *constitutional* and *unconstitutional*, mean legal and illegal. The distinction and the ideas, which these terms denote, are founded in the same authority with the law of the land upon any other subject; and to be ascertained by the same inquiries. In England the system of public jurisprudence is made up of acts of parliament, of decisions of courts of law, and of immemorial usages: consequently, these are the principles of which the English constitution itself consists; the sources from which all our knowledge of its nature and limitations is to be deduced,

and

and the authorities to which all appeal ought to be made, and by which every conſtitutional doubt and queſtion can alone be decided. This plain and intelligible definition is the more neceſſary to be preſerved in our thoughts, as ſome writers upon the ſubject abſurdly confound what is conſtitutional, with what is expedient; pronouncing forthwith a meaſure to be unconſtitutional, which they adjudge in any reſpect to be detrimental or dangerous: whilſt others again, aſcribe a kind of tranſcendent authority, or myſterious ſanctity, to the conſtitution, as if it were founded in ſome higher original than that which gives force and obligation to the ordinary laws and ſtatutes of the realm, or were inviolable on any other account than its intrinſic utility. An act of parliament, in England, can never be unconſtitutional, in the ſtrict and proper acceptation of the term; in a lower ſenſe it may, viz. when it militates with the ſpirit, contradicts the analogy, or defeats the proviſion of other laws, made to regulate the form of government. Even that flagitious abuſe of their truſt, by which a parliament of Henry the Eighth conferred upon the king's proclamation the authority of law, was unconſtitutional only in this latter ſenſe.

Moſt of thoſe who treat of the Britiſh conſtitution, conſider it as a ſcheme of government formally planned and contrived by our anceſtors, in ſome certain æra of our national hiſtory, and as ſet up in purſuance of ſuch regular plan and deſign. Something of this ſort is ſecretly ſuppoſed

poſed, or referred to, in the expreſſions of thoſe who ſpeak of the " principles of the conſtitution," of bringing back the conſtitution to its " firſt principles," of reſtoring it to its " original purity," or primitive model." Now this appears to me an erroneous conception of the ſubject. No ſuch plan was ever formed, conſequently no ſuch firſt principles, original model, or ſtandard exiſt. I mean there never was a date, or point of time in our hiſtory, when the government of England was to be ſet up anew, and when it was referred to any ſingle perſon, or aſſembly, or committee, to frame a charter for the future government of the country; or when a conſtitution, ſo prepared and digeſted, was by common conſent received and eſtabliſhed. In the time of the civil wars, or rather between the death of Charles the Firſt, and the reſtoration of his ſon, many ſuch projects were publiſhed, but none were carried into execution. The great charter, and the bill of rights, were wiſe and ſtrenuous efforts to obtain ſecurity againſt certain abuſes of regal power, by which the ſubject had been formerly aggrieved; but theſe were, either of them, much too partial modifications of the conſtitution to give it a new original. The conſtitution of England, like that of moſt countries in Europe, hath grown out of occaſion and emergency; from the various policy of different ages; from the contentions, ſucceſſes, intereſts, and opportunities of different orders and parties of men in the community. It reſembles one of thoſe old manſions, which, inſtead of being built all at once, after a regular plan, and according to the rules of architecture at present established, has been reared in different ages of the art, has been altered from time to time, and has been continually receiving additions and repairs suited to the taste, fortune, or conveniency of its successive proprietors. In such a building we look in vain for the elegance and proportion, for the just order and correspondence of parts, which we expect in a modern edifice; and which external symmetry, after all, contributes much more perhaps to the amusement of the beholder, than the accommodation of the inhabitant.

In the British, and possibly in all other constitutions, there exists a wide difference between the actual state of the government and the theory. The one results from the other; but still they are different. When we contemplate the *theory* of the British government, we see the King invested with the most absolute personal impunity; with a power of rejecting laws, which have been resolved upon by both houses of parliament; of conferring by his charter, upon any set or succession of men he pleases, the privilege of sending representatives into one house of parliament, as by his immediate appointment he can place whom he will in the other. What is this, a foreigner might ask, but a more circuitous despotism? Yet, when we turn our attention from the legal existence to the actual exercise of royal authority in England, we see these formidable prerogatives dwindled into mere ceremonies; and in their stead, a sure and commanding influence, of which

which the constitution, it seems, is totally ignorant, growing out of that enormous patronage, which the increased extent, and opulence of the empire has placed in the disposal of the executive magistrate.

Upon questions of reform the habit of reflection to be encouraged, is a sober comparison of the constitution under which we live, not with models of speculative perfection, but with the actual chance of obtaining a better. This turn of thought will generate a political disposition, equally removed from that puerile admiration of present establishments which sees no fault, and can endure no change, and that distempered sensibility, which is alive only to perceptions of inconveniency, and is too impatient to be delivered from the uneasiness which it feels, to compute either the peril, or expence of the remedy. Political innovations commonly produce many effects beside those that are intended. The direct consequence is often the least important. Incidental, remote, and unthought of evils or advantages frequently exceed the good that is designed, or the inconveniency that is foreseen. It is from the silent and unobserved operation; from the obscure progress of causes, set at work for different purposes, that the greatest revolutions take their rise. When Elizabeth, and her immediate successor, applied themselves to the encouragement and regulation of trade by many wise laws, they knew not, that, together with wealth and industry, they were diffusing a consciousness of strength and independency, which would not long endure, under the forms of a mixed government, the dominion of arbitrary princes. When it was debated whether the mutiny act, the law by which the army is governed and maintained, should be temporary or perpetual, little else, probably, occurred to the advocates of an annual bill, than the expediency of retaining a control over the most dangerous prerogative of the crown—the direction and command of a standing army: whereas, in its effect, this single reservation has altered the whole frame and quality of the British constitution. For since, in consequence of the military system, which prevails in neighbouring and rival nations, as well as on account of the internal exigencies of government, a standing army has become essential to the safety and administration of the empire, it enables parliament, by discontinuing this necessary provision, so to enforce its resolutions upon any other subject, as to render the king's dissent to a law, which has received the approbation of both houses, too dangerous an experiment any longer to be advised. A contest between the king and parliament, cannot now be persevered in, without a dissolution of the government. Lastly, when the constitution conferred upon the crown the nomination to all employments in the public service, the authors of this arrangement were led to it, by the obvious propriety of leaving to a master the choice of his servants; and by the manifest inconveniency of engaging the national council, upon every vacancy, in those personal contests which attend elections to places of honour and emolument.

Our

Our anceſtors did not obſerve that this diſpoſition added an influence to the regal office, which, as the number and value of public employments increaſed, would ſuperſede in a great meaſure the forms, and change the character of the ancient conſtitution. They knew not, what the experience and reflection of modern ages has diſcovered, that patronage univerſally is power; that he who poſſeſſes in a ſufficient degree the means of gratifying the deſires of mankind after wealth and diſtinction, by whatever checks and forms his authority may be limited or diſguiſed, will direct the management of public affairs. Whatever be the mechaniſm of the political engine, he will guide the motion. Theſe inſtances are adduced to illuſtrate the propoſition we laid down, that, in politics, the moſt important and permanent effects have, for the moſt part, been incidental, and unforeſeen: and this propoſition we inculcate, for the ſake of the caution which it teaches, that changes ought not be adventured upon without a *comprehenſive* diſcernment of the conſequences,—without a knowledge, as well of the remote tendency, as of the immediate deſign. The courage of a ſtateſman ſhould reſemble that of a commander, who, however regardleſs of perſonal danger, never forgets, that with his own he commits the lives and fortunes of a multitude; and who does not conſider it as any proof of zeal or valour, to ſtake the ſafety of *other* men, upon the ſucceſs of a perilous or deſperate enterprize.

There is one end of civil government peculiar to a good constitution, namely, the happiness of its subjects; there is another end essential to a good government, but common to it with many bad ones,—its own preservation. Observing that the best form of government would be defective, which did not provide for its own permanency, in our political reasonings we consider all such provisions as expedient; and are content to accept as a sufficient reason for a measure, or law, that it is necessary or conducive to the preservation of the constitution. Yet, in truth, such provisions are absolutely expedient, and such an excuse final, only whilst the constitution is worth preserving; that is, until it can be exchanged for a better. I premise this distinction, because many things in the English, as in every constitution, are to be vindicated and accounted for, solely from their tendency to maintain the government in its present state, and the several parts of it in possession of the powers which the constitution has assigned to them; and because I would wish it to be remarked that such a consideration is always subordinate to another—the value and usefulness of the constitution itself.

The Government of England, which has been sometimes called a mixed government, sometimes a limited monarchy, is formed by a combination of the three regular species of government; the monarchy, residing in the King; the aristocracy, in the House of Lords; and the republic being represented by the House of Commons. The perfection intended by such a scheme of government is, to unite the advantages of the several simple forms, and to exclude the inconveniencies. To what degree this purpose is attained or attainable in the British constitution; wherein it is lost sight of or neglected; and by what means it may in any part be promoted with better success, the reader will be enabled to judge, by a separate recollection of these advantages and inconveniencies, as enumerated in the preceding chapter, and a distinct application of each to the political condition of this country. We will present our remarks upon the subject in a brief account of the expedients by which the British constitution provides.

1st, For the interest of its subjects.

2dly, For its own preservation.

The contrivances for the first of these purposes are the following:

In order to promote the establishment of salutary public laws, every citizen of the state is capable of becoming a member of the senate; and every senator possesses the right of propounding to the deliberation of the legislature whatever law he pleases.

Every district of the empire enjoys the privilege of choosing representatives, informed of the interests and circumstances and desires of their constituents, and entitled by their situation to communicate that information to the national council. The meanest subject has some one whom he can call upon to bring forward his complaints and requests to public attention.

By annexing the right of voting for members of the House of Commons to different qualifications in different places, each order and profession of men in the community, become virtually represented; that is, men of all orders and professions, statesmen, courtiers, country gentlemen, lawyers, merchants, manufacturers, soldiers, sailors, interested in the prosperity, and experienced in the occupation of their respective professions, obtain seats in parliament.

The elections, at the same time, are so connected with the influence of landed property as to afford a certainty that a considerable number of men of great estates will be returned to parliament; and are also so modified, that men the most eminent and successful in their respective professions, are the most likely, by their riches, or the weight of their stations, to prevail in these competitions.

The number, fortune, and quality of the members; the variety of interests and characters amongst them; above all, the temporary duration of their power, and the change of men which every new election produces, are so many securities to the public, as well against the subjection of their judgments to any external dictation, as
against

against the formation of a junto in their own body, sufficiently powerful to govern their decisions.

The representatives are so intermixed with the constituents, and the constituents with the rest of the people, that they cannot, without a partiality too flagrant to be endured, impose any burden upon the subject, in which they do not share themselves; nor scarcely can they adopt an advantageous regulation, in which their own interests will not participate of the advantage.

The proceedings and debates of parliament, and the parliamentary conduct of each representative, are known by the people at large.

The representative is so far dependent upon the constituent, and political importance upon public favour, that a senator most effectually recommends himself to eminence and advancement in the state, by contriving and patronizing laws of public utility.

When intelligence of the condition, wants, and occasions of the people, is thus collected from every quarter, when such a variety of invention, and so many understandings are set at work upon the subject, it may be presumed, that the most eligible expedient, remedy or improvement, will occur to some one or other: and when a wise council, or beneficial regulation is once suggested, it may be expected, from the disposition of an assembly so conſtituted as the Britiſh houſe of commons is, that it cannot fail of receiving the approbation of the majority.

To prevent thoſe deſtructive contentions for the ſupreme power, which are ſure to take place, where the members of the ſtate do not live under an acknowledged head, and a known rule of ſucceſſion; to preſerve the people in tranquillity at home, by a ſpeedy and vigorous execution of the laws; to protect their intereſt abroad, by ſtrength and energy in military operations, by thoſe advantages of deciſion, ſecrecy and diſpatch, which belong to the reſolutions of monarchical councils;—for theſe purpoſes, the conſtitution has committed the executive government to the adminiſtration and limited authority of an hereditary King.

In the defence of the empire; in the maintenance of its power, dignity, and privileges, with foreign nations; and in the providing for the general adminiſtration of municipal juſtice, by a proper choice and appointment of magiſtrates, the inclination of the king and of the people uſually coincide: in this part, therefore, of the regal office, the conſtitution entruſts the prerogative with ample powers.

The dangers principally to be apprehended from regal government, relate to the two articles, of *taxation* and *puniſhment*. In every form of government, from which the people are excluded, it is the intereſt of the governors to get as much, and of the governed to give as little as they can: the power alfo of punifhment, in the hands of an arbitrary prince oftentimes becomes an engine of extortion, jealoufy, and revenge. Wifely, therefore, hath the Britifh conftitution guarded the fafety of the people, in thefe two points, by the moft ftudious precautions.

Upon that of *taxation;* every law, which, by the remoteft conftruction, may be deemed to levy money upon the property of the fubject, muft originate, that is, muft firft be propofed and affented to, in the Houfe of Commons: by which regulation, accompanying the weight which that affembly poffeffes in all its functions, the levying of taxes is almoft exclufively referved to the popular part of the conftitution, who, it is prefumed, will not tax themfelves, nor their fellow fubjects, without being firft convinced of the neceffity of the aids which they grant.

The application alfo of the public fupplies, is watched with the fame circumfpection, as the affeffment. Many taxes are annual; the produce of others is mortgaged, or appropriated to fpecific fervices; the expenditures of all of them, is accounted for to the houfe of commons; as computations of the charge of the purpofe, for which they are wanted, are previoufly fubmitted to the fame tribunal.

In the infliction of *punifhment,* the power of the crown, and of the magiftrate appointed by the crown, is confined by the moſt preciſe limitations: the guilt of the offender muſt be pronounced by twelve men of his own order, indifferently choſen out of the county where the offence was committed: the puniſhment, or the limits to which the puniſhment may be extended, are aſcertained and affixed to the crime, by laws which knew not the perſon of the criminal.

And whereas, the arbitrary or clandeſtine ſeizure and confinement of the perſon is the injury moſt to be dreaded from the ſtrong hand of the executive government, becauſe it deprives the priſoner at once of protection and defence, and delivers him into the power, and to the malicious or intereſted deſigns of his enemies; the conſtitution has provided againſt this danger with extreme ſolicitude. The ancient writ of habeas corpus, the habeas corpus act of Charles the Second, and the practice and determinations of our ſovereign courts of juſtice founded upon theſe laws, afford a complete remedy for every conceivable caſe of illegal impriſonment.*

Treaſon

---

* Upon complaint in writing by, or on behalf of any perſon in confinement, to any of the four courts of Weſtminſter Hall, in term time, or to the Lord Chancellor, or one of the Judges, in the vacation; and upon a probable reaſon being ſuggeſted to queſtion the legality of the detention, a writ is iſſued, to the perſon in whoſe cuſtody the complainant is alledged to be, commanding him within a certain limited and ſhort time to produce the body of the priſoner, and the authority under which he is detained. Upon the return of the writ, ſtrict and inſtantaneous obedience to which is enforced by very ſevere penalties,

if

Treason being that charge, under colour of which the destruction of an obnoxious individual is often sought; and government being at all times more immediately a party in the prosecution; the law, beside the general care with which it watches over the safety of the accused, in this case, sensible of the unequal contest in which the subject is engaged, has assisted his defence with extraordinary indulgencies. By two statutes, enacted since the revolution, every person indicted for high treason shall have a copy of his indictment, a list of the witnesses to be produced, and of the jury impanelled, delivered to him ten days before the trial; he is also permitted to make his defence by counsel—privileges which are not allowed to the prisoner, in a trial for any other crime: and what is of more importance to the party than all the rest, the testimony of two witnesses, at the least, is required to convict a person of treason; whereas, one positive witness is sufficient in almost every other species of accusation.

if no lawful cause of imprisonment appear, the court or judge, before whom the prisoner is brought, is authorized and bound to discharge him; even though he may have been committed by a secretary, or other high officer of state, by the privy council, or by the King in person: so that no subject of this realm can be held in confinement, by any power, or under any pretence whatever, provided he can find means to convey his complaint to one of the four courts of Westminster Hall, or, during their recess, to any of the Judges of the same, unless all these several tribunals agree in determining his imprisonment to be legal. He may make application to them, in succession; and if one out of the number be found, who thinks the prisoner entitled to his liberty, that one possesses authority to restore it to him.

We

We proceed, in the second place, to enquire in what manner the constitution has provided for its own preservation; that is, in what manner each part of the legislature is secured in the exercise of the powers assigned to it, from the incroachment of the other parts. This security is sometimes called the *balance of the constitution*; and the political equilibrium, which this phrase denotes, consists in two contrivances,—a balance of power, and a balance of interest. By a balance of power is meant, that there is no power possessed by one part of the legislature, the abuse, or excess of which is not checked by some antagonist power, residing in another part. Thus the power of the two houses of parliament to frame laws is checked by the king's negative; that if laws subversive of regal government should obtain the consent of parliament, the reigning prince, by interposing his prerogative, may save the necessary rights and authority of his station. On the other hand, the arbitrary application of this negative is checked by the privilege which parliament possesses, of refusing supplies of money to the exigencies of the King's administration. The constitutional maxim, " that the king " can do no wrong," is balanced by another maxim, not less constitutional, " that the illegal commands of the king " do not justify those who assist, or concur, in carrying " them into execution;" and by a second rule, subsidiary to this, " that the acts of the crown acquire not any legal " force, until authenticated by the subscription of some of " its great officers." The wisdom of this contrivance is worthy of observation. As the King could not be punished,

without

without a civil war, the constitution exempts his person from trial or account; but, lest this impunity should encourage a licentious exercise of dominion, various obstacles are opposed to the private will of the sovereign, when directed to illegal objects. The pleasure of the crown must be announced with certain solemnities, and attested by certain officers of state. In some cases, the royal order must be signified by a secretary of state; in others, it must pass under the privy seal, and in many, under the great seal. And when the king's command is regularly published, no mischief can be achieved by it, without the ministry and compliance of those to whom it is directed. Now all who either concur in an illegal order, by authenticating its publication with their seal or subscription, or who assist in carrying it into execution, subject themselves to prosecution and punishment, for the part they have taken; and are not permitted to plead or produce the command of the king, in justification of their obedience. And, that the crown may not protect its servants, in a criminal submission to their master's desires, by the power, which in general belongs to its authority, of pardoning offences, and of remitting the sentence of the law, prosecutions by impeachment, which is the usual way of proceeding against offenders of this sort, are excepted out of that prerogative.* But farther; the power of

---

* Amongst the checks, which parliament holds over the administration of public affairs, I forbear to mention the practice of addressing the King, to know by whose advice he resolved upon a particular measure, and of punishing the authors

of the crown to direct the military force of the kingdom, is balanced by the annual necessity of resorting to parliament for the maintenance and government of that force. The power of the king to declare war, is checked by the privilege of the house of commons, to grant or withhold the supplies by which the war must be carried on. The king's choice of his ministers is controlled by the obligation he is under of appointing those men to offices in the state, who are found capable of managing the affairs of his government, with the two houses of parliament. Which consideration imposes such a necessity upon the crown, as hath in a great measure subdued the influence of favouritism; insomuch, that it is become no uncommon spectacle in this country, to see men promoted by the king to the highest offices, and richest preferments, which he has in power to bestow, who have been distinguished by their opposition to his personal inclinations.

By the *balance of interest*, which accompanies and gives efficacy to the *balance of power*, is meant this, that the respective interests of the three estates of the empire are so disposed and adjusted, that whichever of the three shall

---

authors of that advice, for the counsel they had given. Not because I think this method either unconstitutional or improper, but for this reason, that it does not so much subject the king to the controll of parliament, as it supposes him to be already in subjection. For if the king were so far out of the reach of the resentment of the house of commons, as to be able, with safety, to refuse the information requested, or to take upon himself the responsibility inquired after, there must be an end of all proceedings founded in this mode of application.

attempt any encroachment, the other two will unite in refisting it. If the king should endeavour to extend his authority, by contracting the power and privileges of the commons, the house of lords would see their own dignity endangered by every advance which the crown made to independency upon the resolutions of parliament. The admission of arbitrary power is no less formidable to the grandeur of the aristocracy, than it is fatal to the liberty of the republic; that is, it would reduce the nobility from the hereditary share they possess in the national councils, in which their real greatness consists, to the being made a part of the empty pageantry of a despotic court. On the other hand, if the house of commons should intrench upon the distinct province, or usurp the established prerogative of the crown, the house of lords would receive an instant alarm from every new stretch of popular power. In every contest in which the king may be engaged with the representative body, in defence of his established share of authority, he will find a sure ally in the collective power of the nobility. An attachment to the monarchy, from which they derive their own distinction; the allurements of a court, in the habits and with the sentiments of which they have been brought up; their hatred of equality, and of all levelling pretensions, which may ultimately affect the privileges, or even the existence of their order; in short, every principle and every prejudice which are wont to actuate human conduct, will determine their choice, to the side and support of the crown. Lastly, if the nobles themselves should attempt to revive the superiorities, which their ancestors exercised under the feudal constitution, the king and the people would alike remember, how the one had been insulted, and the other enslaved, by that barbarous tyranny. They would forget the natural opposition of their views and inclinations, when they saw themselves threatened with the return of a domination, which was odious and intolerable to both.

The reader will have observed, that in describing the British constitution little notice has been taken of the house of lords. The proper use and design of this part of the constitution, are the following: First, to enable the king, by his right of bestowing the peerage, to reward the servants of the public, in a manner most grateful to them, and at a small expence to the nation; secondly, to fortify the power and to secure the stability of regal government, by an order of men naturally allied to its interests; and, thirdly, to answer a purpose, which though of superior importance to the other two, does not occur so readily to our observation; namely, to stem the progress of popular fury. Large bodies of men are subject to sudden phrenzies. Opinions are sometimes circulated amongst a multitude without proof or examination, acquiring confidence and reputation merely by being repeated from one to another; and passions founded upon these opinions, diffusing themselves with a rapidity that can neither be accounted for nor resisted, may agitate a country with the most violent commotions. Now the only way to stop the fermentation,

mentation, is to divide the mafs; that is, to erect different orders in the community, with feparate prejudices and interefts. And this may, occafionally, become the ufe of an hereditary nobility, invefted with a fhare of legiflation. Averfe to the prejudices which actuate the minds of the vulgar; accuftomed to contemn the clamour of the populace; difdaining to receive laws and opinions from their inferiors in rank, they will oppofe refolutions, which are founded in the folly and violence of the lower part of the community. Was the voice of the people always dictated by reflection; did every man, or even one man in an hundred think for himfelf, or actually confider the meafure he was about to approve or cenfure; or even were the common people tolerably ftedfaft in the judgment which they formed, I fhould hold the interference of a fuperior order, not only fuperfluous, but wrong: for, when every thing is allowed to difference of rank and education, which the actual ftate of thefe advantages deferves, that, after all, is moft likely to be right and expedient, which appears to be fo to the feparate judgment and decifion of a great majority of the nation; at leaft, that, in general, is right *for them*, which is agreeable to their fixed opinions and defires. But when we obferve what is urged as the public opinion, to be, in truth, the opinion only, or perhaps the feigned profeffions of a few crafty leaders; that the numbers who join in the cry, ferve only to fwell and multiply the found, without any acceffion of judgment, or exercife of underftanding; and that oftentimes the wifeft counfels have been thus overborne by tumult and uproar,—we may conceive occafions to arife, in which the commonwealth may be faved by the reluctance of the nobility to adopt the caprices, or to yield to the vehemence of the common people. In expecting this advantage from an order of nobles, we do not fuppofe the nobility to be more unprejudiced than others; we only fuppofe that their prejudices will be different from, and may occafionally counteract thofe of others.

If the perfonal privileges of the peerage, which are ufually fo many injuries to the reft of the community, be reftrained, I fee little inconveniency in the increafe of its number; for it is only dividing the fame quantity of power amongft more hands, which is rather favourable to public freedom, than otherwife.

The admiffion of a fmall number of ecclefiaftics into the houfe of lords, is but an equitable compenfation to the clergy for the exclufion of their order from the houfe of commons. They are a fet of men confiderable by their number and property, as well as by their influence, and the duties of their ftation; yet, whilft every other profeffion has thofe amongft the national reprefentatives, who, being converfant in the fame occupation, are able to ftate, and naturally difpofed to fupport the rights and interefts of the clafs and calling to which they belong, the clergy alone are deprived of this advantage. Which hardfhip is made up to them by introducing the prelacy into parliament; and if bifhops, from gratitude or expectation,

tion be more obsequious to the will of the crown, than those who possess great temporal inheritances, they are properly inserted into that part of the constitution, from which much or frequent resistance to the measures of government is not expected.

I acknowledge, that I perceive no sufficient reason for exempting the persons of members of either house of parliament from arrest for debt. The counsels or suffrage of a single senator, especially of one who in the management of his own affairs may justly be suspected of a want of prudence or honesty, can seldom be so necessary to those of the public, as to justify a departure from that wholesome policy, by which the laws of a commercial state punish and stigmatize insolvency. But whatever reason may be pleaded for their *personal* immunity, when this privilege of parliament is extended to domestics and retainers, or when it is permitted to impede or delay the course of judicial proceedings, it becomes an absurd sacrifice of equal justice to imaginary dignity.

There is nothing, in the British constitution, so remarkable, as the irregularity of the popular representation. The house of commons consists of five hundred and forty eight members, of whom, two hundred are elected by seven thousand constituents: so that a majority of these seven thousand, without any reasonable title to superior weight and influence in the state, may, under certain circumstances, decide a question against the opinion of as many millions.

millions. Or, to place the same object in another point of view; if my estate be situated in one county of the kingdom, I possess the ten thousandth part of a single representative; if in another, the thousandth; if in a particular district, I may be one in twenty who choose two representatives; if in a still more favoured spot, I may enjoy the right of appointing two myself. If I have been born, or dwell, or have served an apprenticeship in one town, I am represented in the national assembly by two deputies, in the choice of whom, I exercise an actual and sensible share of power; if accident has thrown my birth, or habitation, or service into another town, I have no representive at all, nor more power or concern in the election of those who make the laws, by which I am governed, than if I was a subject of the Grand Seignior—and this partiality subsists without any pretence whatever of merit or of propriety, to justify the preference of one place to another. Or, thirdly, to describe the state of national representation as it exists in reality; it may be affirmed, I believe, with truth, that about one half of the house of commons obtain their seats in that assembly by the election of the people, the other half by purchase, or by the nomination of single proprietors of great estates.

This is a flagrant incongruity in the constitution; but it is one of those objections which strike most forcibly at first sight. The effect of all reasoning upon the subject is to diminish the first impression: on which account it deserves the more attentive examination, that we may be assured,

assured, before we adventure upon a reformation, that the magnitude of the evil justifies the danger of the experiment. In the few remarks that follow, we would be understood, in the first place, to decline all conference with those who wish to alter the form of government of these kingdoms. The reformers with whom we have to do, are they, who, whilst they change this part of the system, would retain the rest. If any Englishman expect more happiness to his country under a republic, he may very consistently recommend a new modelling of elections to parliament; because, if the king and house of lords were laid aside, the present disproportionate representation would produce nothing but a confused and ill-digested oligarchy. In like manner we wave a controversy with those writers who insist upon representation as a *natural* right*: we consider it so far only as a right at all, as it conduces to public utility; that is, as it contributes to the establishment of good laws, or as it secures to the people the just administration of these laws. These effects depend upon the disposition and abilities of the national counsellors. Wherefore, if men the most likely by their qualifications to know and to promote the public interest, be

---

* If this right be *natural*, no doubt it must be equal, and the right, we may add, of one sex, as well as of the other. Whereas every plan of representation, that we have heard of, begins, by excluding the votes of women: thus cutting off, at a single stroke, one half of the public from a right which is asserted to be inherent in all; a right too, as some represent it, not only universal, but unalienable and indefeasible.

actually returned to parliament, it signifies little who return them. If the properest persons be elected, what matters it by whom they are elected? At least, no prudent statesman would subvert long established or even settled rules of representation, without a prospect of procuring wiser or better representatives. This then being well observed, let us, before we seek to obtain any thing more, consider duly what we already have. We *have* a house of commons composed of five hundred and forty-eight members, in which number are found, the most considerable landholders and merchants of the kingdom; the heads of the army, the navy, and the law; the occupiers of great offices in the state; together with many private individuals, eminent by their knowledge, eloquence, or activity. Now, if the country be not safe in such hands, in whose may it confide its interests? If such a number of such men be liable to the influence of corrupt motives, what assembly of men will be secure from the same danger? Does any new scheme of representation promise to collect together more wisdom, or to produce firmer integrity? In this view of the subject, and attending not to ideas of order and proportion, (of which many minds are much enamoured,) but to effects alone, we may discover just excuses for those parts of the present representation, which appear to a hasty observer most exceptionable and absurd. It should be remembered as a maxim extremely applicable to this subject, that no order or assembly of men whatever can long maintain their place and authority in a mixed government, of which the members do not

indivi-

individually possess a respectable share of personal importance. Now, whatever may be the defects of the present arrangement, it infallibly secures a great weight of property to the house of commons, by rendering many seats in that house accessible to men of large fortunes, and to such men alone. By which means those characters are engaged in the defence of the separate rights and interests of this branch of the legislature, that are best able to support its claims. The constitution of most of the small boroughs, especially the burgage tenure, contributes, though undesignedly, to the same effect; for the appointment of the representatives we find commonly annexed to certain great inheritances. Elections purely popular are in this respect uncertain: in times of tranquillity, the natural ascendency of wealth will prevail; but when the minds of men are inflamed by political dissentions, this influence often yields to more impetuous motives.—The variety of tenures and qualifications, upon which the right of voting is founded, appears to me a recommendation of the mode which now subsists, as it tends to introduce into parliament a corresponding mixture of characters and professions. It has been long observed that conspicuous abilities are most frequently found with the representatives of small boroughs. And this is nothing more than what the laws of human conduct might teach us to expect: when such boroughs are set to sale, those men are likely to become purchasers who are enabled by their talents to make the best of their bargain: when a seat is not sold, but given by the opulent proprietor of a burgage tenure, the patron finds his own intereſt conſulted, by the reputation and abilities of the member whom he nominates. If certain of the nobility hold the appointment of ſome part of the houſe of commons, it ſerves to maintain that alliance between the two branches of the legiſlature, which no good citizen would wiſh to ſee diſſevered: it helps to keep the government of the country in the houſe of commons, in which, it would not perhaps long continue to reſide, if ſo powerful and wealthy a part of the nation as the peerage compoſe, were excluded from all ſhare and intereſt in its conſtitution. If there be a few boroughs ſo circumſtanced as to lie at the diſpoſal of the crown, whilſt the number of ſuch is known and ſmall, they may be tolerated with little danger. For where would be the impropriety, or the inconveniency, if the king at once ſhould nominate a limited number of his ſervants to ſeats in parliament; or, what is the ſame thing, if ſeats in parliament were annexed to the poſſeſſion of certain of the moſt efficient and reſponſible offices in the ſtate? The preſent repreſentation, after all theſe deductions, and under the confuſion in which it confeſſedly lies, is ſtill in ſuch a degree popular; or rather the repreſentatives are ſo connected with the maſs of the community, by a ſociety of intereſts and paſſions, that the will of the people, when it is determined, permanent, and general, almoſt always at length prevails.

Upon the whole, in the ſeveral plans which have been ſuggeſted, of an equal or a reformed repreſentation,

tion, it will be difficult to difcover any propofal that has a tendency to throw more of the bufinefs of the nation into the houfe of commons, or to collect a fet of men more fit to tranfact that bufinefs, or in general more interefted in the national happinefs and profperity. One confequence, however, may be expected from thefe projects, namely, " lefs flexibility to the influence of the " crown." And fince the diminution of this influence, is the declared, and perhaps the fole defign of the various fchemes that have been produced, whether for regulating the elections, contracting the duration, or for purifying the conftitution of parliament by the exclufion of placemen and penfioners; it is obvious and of importance to remark, that the more apt and natural, as well as the more fafe and quiet way of attaining the fame end, would be, by a direct reduction of the patronage of the crown, which might be effected to a certain extent without hazarding farther confequences. Superfluous and exorbitant emoluments of office may not only be fuppreffed for the prefent; but provifions of law be devifed, which fhould for the future reftrain within certain limits, the number and value of the offices in the donation of the king.

But whilft we difpute concerning different fchemes of reformation, all directed to the fame end, a previous doubt occurs in the debate, whether the end itfelf be good, or fafe—whether the influence fo loudly complained of can be deftroyed, or even diminifhed, without danger to the ftate. Whilft the zeal of fome men beholds this influence with a jealoufy, which nothing but its abolition can appeafe, many wife and virtuous politicians deem a confiderable portion of it to be as neceffary a part of the Britifh conftitution, as any other ingredient in the compofition—to be that, indeed, which gives cohefion and folidity to the whole. Were the meafures of government, fay they, oppofed from nothing but principle, government ought to have nothing but the rectitude of its meafures to fupport them; but fince oppofition fprings from other motives, government muft poffefs an influence to counteract that oppofition—to produce, not a bias of the paffions, but a neutrality: it muft have fome weight to caft into the fcale to fet the balance even. It is the nature of power always to prefs upon the boundaries which confine it. Licentioufnefs, faction, envy, impatience of control or inferiority; the fecret pleafure of mortifying the great, or the hope of difpoffeffing them; a conftant willingnefs to queftion and thwart whatever is dictated or even propofed by another; a difpofition common to all bodies of men to extend the claims and authority of their order; above all, that love of power, and of fhowing it, which refides more or lefs in every human breaft, and which, in popular affemblies, is inflamed, like every other paffion, by communication and encouragement: thefe motives, added to private defigns and refentments, cherifhed alfo by popular acclamation, and operating upon the great fhare of power already poffeffed by the houfe of commons, might induce a majority, or at leaft a large party of men in that affembly, to unite in endeavouring to draw to themfelves the whole government

government of the ſtate; or at leaſt ſo to obſtruct the conduct of public affairs, by a wanton and perverſe oppoſition, as to render it impoſſible for the wifeſt ſtateſman to carry forwards the buſineſs of the nation in parliament, with ſucceſs or ſatisfaction.

Some paſſages of our national hiſtory afford grounds for theſe apprehenſions. Before the acceſſion of James the Firſt, or, at leaſt, during the reigns of his three immediate predeceſſors, the government of England was a government by force; that is, the king carried his meaſures in parliament by *intimidation*. A ſenſe of perſonal danger kept the members of the houſe of commons in ſubjection. A conjunction of fortunate cauſes delivered at laſt the parliament and nation from ſlavery. That overbearing ſyſtem, which had declined in the hands of James, expired early in the reign of his ſon. After the reſtoration there ſucceeded in its place, and ſince the revolution has been methodically purſued, the more ſucceſsful expedient of *influence*. Now we remember what paſſed between the loſs of terror, and the eſtabliſhment of influence. The tranſactions of that interval, whatever we may think of their occaſion or effect, no friend of regal government would wiſh to ſee revived. —But the affairs of this kingdom afford a more recent atteſtation to the ſame doctrine. In the Britiſh colonies of North America, the late aſſemblies poſſeſſed much of the power and conſtitution of our houſe of commons. The king and government of Great Britain held no patronage in the country, which could create attachment and influence,

ence, sufficient to counteract that restless, arrogating spirit, which in popular assemblies, when left to itself, will never brook an authority, that checks and interferes with its own. To this cause, excited perhaps by some unseasonable provocations, we may attribute, as to their true and proper original, we will not say the misfortunes, but the changes that have taken place in the British empire. The admonition, which such examples suggest, will have its weight with those, who are content with the general frame of the English constitution; and who consider stability amongst the first perfections of any government.

We protest however against any construction, by which what is here said shall be attempted to be applied to the justification of bribery, or of any clandestine reward or solicitation whatever. The very secrecy of such negotiations confesses or begets a consciousness of guilt; which, when the mind is once taught to endure without uneasiness, the character is prepared for every compliance. And there is the greater danger in these corrupt practices, as the extent of their operation is unlimited and unknown. Our apology relates solely to that influence, which results from the acceptance or expectation of public preferments. Nor does the influence, which we defend, require any sacrifice of personal probity. In political, above all other subjects, the arguments, or rather the conjectures on each side of a question, are often so equally poized, that the wisest judgments may be held in suspense. These I call subjects of *indifference*. But again, when the subject is not

indifferent

indifferent in itself, it will appear such to a great part of those to whom it is proposed, for want of information, or reflection, or experience, or of capacity to collect and weigh the reasons by which either side is supported. These are subjects of *apparent indifference*. This indifference occurs still more frequently in personal contests; in which, we do not often discover any reason of public utility, for the preference of one competitor to another. These cases compose the province of influence; that is, the decision in these cases will inevitably be determined by influence of some sort or other. The only doubt is, what influence shall be admitted. If you remove the influence of the crown, it is only to make way for influence from a different quarter. If motives of expectation and gratitude be withdrawn, other motives will succeed in their place, acting probably in an opposite direction, but equally irrelative and external to the proper merits of the question. There exist, as we have seen, passions in the human heart, which will always make a strong party against the executive power of a mixed government. According as the disposition of parliament is friendly or adverse to the recommendation of the crown in matters which are really or apparently indifferent, as indifference hath been now explained, the business of empire will be transacted with ease and convenience, or embarrassed with endless contention and difficulty. Nor is it a conclusion founded in justice or warranted by experience, that, because men are induced by views of interest to yield their consent to measures, concerning which their judgment decides nothing,

they

they may be brought by the same influence, to act in deliberate opposition to knowledge and duty. Whoever reviews the operations of government in this country since the revolution, will find few even of the most questionable measures of administration, about which the best instructed judgment might not have doubted at the time; but of which he may affirm with certainty, that they were *indifferent* to the greatest part of those who concurred in them. From the success or the facility, with which they who dealt out the patronage of the crown carried measures like these, ought we conclude, that a similar application of honours and emoluments would procure the consent of parliament to councils evidently detrimental to the common welfare? Is there not, on the contrary, more reason to fear, that the prerogative, if deprived of influence, would not be long able to support itself? For when we reflect upon the power of the house of commons to extort a compliance with its resolutions from the other parts of the legislature; or to put to death the constitution by a refusal of the annual grants of money, to the support of the necessary functions of government—when we reflect also, what motives there are, which, in the vicissitudes of political interests and passions, may one day arm and point this power against the executive magistrate—when we attend to these considerations, we shall be led perhaps to acknowledge, that there is not more of paradox than of probability, in that important, but much decried apothegm, " that an independent parliament is incompatible with the " existence of the monarchy."

CHAP. VIII.

OF THE ADMINISTRATION OF JUSTICE.

THE first maxim of a free state is, that the laws be made by one set of men, and administered by another; in other words, that the legislative and judicial characters be kept separate. When these offices are united in the same person or assembly, particular laws are made for particular cases, springing oftentimes from partial motives, and directed to private ends: whilst they are kept separate, general laws are made by one body of men, without foreseeing whom they may affect; and when made, must be applied by the other, let them affect whom they will.

For the sake of illustration, let it be supposed, in this country, either that, parliaments being laid aside, the courts of Westminster-Hall made their own laws; or that the two houses of parliament, with the king at their head, tried, and decided causes at their bar: it is evident, in the first place, that the decisions of such a judicature would be so many laws; and, in the second place, that, when the parties and the interests to be affected by the law were known, the inclinations of the law-makers would inevitably attach on one fide or the other; and that, where there was neither any fixed rules to regulate their determinations, nor any fuperior power to control their proceedings, thefe inclinations would interfere with the integrity of public juftice. The confequence of which muft be, that the fubjects of fuch a conftitution would live either without any conftant laws, that is, without any known pre-eftablifhed rules of adjudication whatever; or under laws made for particular cafes and particular perfons, and partaking of the contradictions and iniquity of the motives, to which they owed their origin,

Which dangers, by the divifion of the legiflative and judicial functions, are effectually provided againft. Parliament knows not the individuals upon whom its acts will operate; it has no cafes or parties before it; no private defigns to ferve: confequently its refolutions will be fuggefted by the confideration of univerfal effects and tendencies, which always produces impartial, and commonly advantageous regulations. When laws are made, courts of juftice, whatever be the difpofition of the judges, muft abide by them; for the legiflative being neceffarily the fupreme power of the ftate, the judicial and every other power is accountable to that; and it cannot be doubted, but that the perfons, who poffefs the fovereign authority of government, will be tenacious of the laws which they themfelves prefcribe, and fufficiently jealous

jealous of the assumption of dispensing and legislative powers by any others.

This fundamental rule of civil jurisprudence is violated in the case of acts of attainder or confiscation, in bills of pains and penalties, and in all *ex post facto* laws whatever, in which parliament exercises the double office of legislature and judge. And whoever either understands the value of the rule itself, or collects the history of those instances, in which it has been invaded, will be induced, I believe, to acknowledge, that it had been wiser and safer never to have departed from it. He will confess at least, that nothing but the most manifest and immediate peril of the commonwealth will justify a repetition of these dangerous examples. If the laws in being do not punish an offender, let him go unpunished; let the legislature, admonished of the defect of the laws, provide against the commission of future crimes of the same sort. The escape of one delinquent can never produce so much harm to the community, as may arise from the infraction of a rule, upon which the purity of public justice, and the existence of civil liberty essentially depend.

The next security for the impartial administration of justice, especially in decisions to which government is a party, is the independency of the judges. As protection against every illegal attack upon the rights of the subject by the servants of the crown is to be sought for from these tribunals, the judges of the land become not unfrequently the arbitrators between the king and the people. On which account they ought to be independent of either; or, what is the same thing, equally dependent upon both; that is, if they be appointed by the one, they should be removeable only by the other. This was the policy, which dictated that memorable improvement in our constitution, by which the judges, who, before the revolution, held their offices during the pleasure of the king, can now only be deprived of them by an address from both houses of parliament; as the most regular, solemn, and authentic way, by which the dissatisfaction of the people can be expressed. To make this independency of the judges complete, the public salaries of their office ought not only to be certain both in amount and continuance, but so liberal as to secure their integrity from the temptation of secret bribes: which liberality will answer also the farther purpose of preserving their jurisdiction from contempt, and their characters from suspicion; as well as of rendering the station worthy of the ambition of men of eminence in their profession.

A third precaution to be observed in the formation of courts of justice, is, that the number of the judges be small. For, beside that the violence and tumult inseparable from large assemblies are inconsistent with the patience, method, and attention requisite in judicial investigations; beside that all passions and prejudices act with augmented force upon a collected multitude; beside these objections, judges when they are numerous *divide* the shame of an unjust determination; they shelter themselves under one another's example; each man thinks his own character hid in the crowd: for which reason the judges ought always to be so few, as that the conduct of each may be conspicuous to public observation; that each may be responsible in his separate and particular reputation for the decisions in which he concurs. The truth of the above remark has been exemplified in this country, in the effects of that wise regulation which transferred the trial of parliamentary elections from the house of commons at large, to a select committee of that house composed of thirteen members. This alteration, simply by reducing the number of the judges, and, in consequence of that reduction, exposing the judicial conduct of each to public animadversion, has given to a judicature, which had been long swayed by interest and solicitation, the solemnity and virtue of the most upright tribunals.—I should prefer an even to an odd number of judges, and four to almost any other number; for in this number, beside that it sufficiently consults the idea of separate responsibility, nothing can be decided but by a majority of three to one. And when we consider that every decision establishes a perpetual precedent, we shall allow that it ought to proceed from an authority not less than this. If the court be equally divided, nothing is done; things remain as they were; with some inconveniency, indeed, to the parties, but without the danger to the public of a hasty precedent.

A fourth requisite in the constitution of a court of justice, and equivalent to many checks upon the discretion of of judges, is that its proceedings be carried on in public; *apertis foribus*; not only before a promiscuous concourse of by-standers, but in the audience of the whole profession of the law. The opinion of the Bar concerning what passes will be impartial; and will commonly guide that of the public. The most corrupt judge will fear to indulge his dishonest wishes in the presence of such an assembly: he must encounter what few can support, the censure of his equals and companions, together with the indignation and reproaches of his country.

Something is also gained to the public by appointing two or three courts of concurrent jurisdiction, that it may remain in the option of the suitor to which he will resort. By this means a tribunal which may happen to be occupied by ignorant or suspected judges, will be deserted for others, that possess more of the confidence of the nation.

But, lastly, if several courts co-ordinate to, and independent of each other, subsist together in the country, it seems necessary that the appeals from all of them should meet and terminate in the same judicature; in order that one supreme tribunal, by whose final sentence all others are bound and concluded, may superintend and preside over the rest. This constitution is necessary for two purposes —to preserve an uniformity in the decisions of inferior courts, and to maintain to each the proper limits of its jurisdiction. Without a common superior, different courts might establish contradictory rules of adjudication, and the contradiction be final and without remedy; the same question might receive opposite determinations, according as it was brought before one court or another, and the determination in each be ultimate and irreversible. A common appellant jurisdiction prevents or puts an end to this confusion. For when the judgments upon appeals are consistent, which may be expected, whilst it is the same court which is at last resorted to, the different courts, from which the appeals are brought will be reduced to a like consistency with one another. Moreover, if questions arise between courts independent of each other, concerning the extent and boundaries of their respective jurisdiction, as each will be desirous of enlarging its own, an authority which both acknowledge can alone adjust the controversy. Such a power, therefore, must reside somewhere, lest the rights and repose of the country be distracted, by the endless opposition and mutual encroachments of its courts of justice.

There are two kinds of judicature; the one, where the office of the judge is permanent in the same person, and consequently where the judge is appointed and known long before the trial; the other, where the judge is determined by lot at the time of the trial, and for that turn only. The one may be called a *fixed*, the other a *casual* judicature. From the former may be expected those qualifications, which are preferred and sought for in the choice of judges, and that knowledge and readiness which result from experience in the office. But then, as the judge is known before-hand, he is accessible to the parties;

there exifts a poffibility of fecret management and undue practices: or, in contefts between the crown and the fubject, the judge appointed by the crown may be fufpected of partiality to his patron; or of entertaining inclinations favourable to the authority from which he derives his own. The advantage attending the fecond kind of judicature is indifferency; the defect, the want of that legal fcience, which produces uniformity and juftice in legal decifions. The conftruction of Englifh courts of law, in which caufes are tried by a jury with the affiftance of a judge, combines the two fpecies together with peculiar fuccefs. This admirable contrivance unites the wifdom of a fixed with the integrity of a cafual judicature, and avoids, in a great meafure, the inconveniencies of both. The judge imparts to the jury the benefit of his erudition and experience; the jury, by their difintereftednefs, check any corrupt partialities which previous application may have produced in the judge. If the determination was left to the judge, the party might fuffer under the fuperior intereft of his adverfary: if it was left to an uninftructed jury, his rights would be in ftill greater danger from the ignorance of thofe who were to decide upon them. The prefent wife admixture of chance and choice in the conftitution of the court, in which his caufe is tried, guards him equally againft the fear of injury from either of thefe caufes.

In proportion to the acknowledged excellency of this mode of trial, every deviation from it ought to be watched with

with vigilance, and admitted by the legiflature with caution and reluctance. Summary convictions before juftices of the peace, efpecially for offences againft the game laws; courts of confcience; extending the jurifdiction of courts of equity; urging too far the diftinction between queftions of law and matters of fact, are all fo many infringements upon this great charter of public fafety.

Neverthelefs, the trial by jury is fometimes found inadequate to the adminiftration of equal juftice. This imperfection takes place chiefly in difputes, in which fome popular paffion or prejudice intervenes; as where a particular order of men advance claims upon the reft of the community, which is the cafe of the clergy contending for tythes; or where an order of men are obnoxious by their profeffion, as are officers of the revenue, bailiffs, bailiffs followers, and other low minifters of the law; or where one of the parties has an intereft in common with the general intereft of the jurors, and that of the other is oppofed to it, as in contefts between landlords and tenants, between lords of manors and the holders of eftates under them; or, laftly, where the minds of men are inflamed by political diffenfions or religious hatred. Thefe prejudices act moft powerfully upon the common people, of which order juries are made up. The force and danger of them are alfo increafed by the very circumftance of taking juries out of the county in which the fubject of difpute arifes. In the neighbourhood of the parties the caufe is often prejudged: and thefe fecret decifions of the mind proceed commonly more upon fentiments of favour or hatred; upon fome opinion concerning the fect, family, profeffion, character, connections, or circumftances of the parties, than upon any knowledge or difcuffion of the proper merits of the queftion. More exact juftice would, in many inftances, be rendered to the fuitors, if the determination were left entirely to the judges; provided we could depend upon the fame purity of conduct, when the power of thefe magiftrates was enlarged, which they have long manifefted in the exercife of a mixed and reftrained authority. But this is an experiment too big with public danger to be hazarded. The effects, however, of fome local prejudices might be fafely obviated, by a law empowering the court, in which the action is brought, to fend the caufe to trial in a diftant county: the expences attending the change of place always falling upon the party who applied for it.

There is a fecond divifion of courts of juftice, which prefents a new alternative of difficulties. Either one, two, or a few fovereign courts may be erected in the metropolis, for the whole kingdom to refort to; or courts of local jurifdiction may be fixed in the various provinces and diftricts of the empire. Great, though oppofite inconveniences attend each arrangement. If the court be remote and folemn, it becomes, by thefe very qualities, expenfive and dilatory: the expence is unavoidably increafed when witneffes, parties, and agents muft be brought to attend from diftant parts of the country: and, where the whole judicial bufinefs of a large nation is collected into a

few

few superior tribunals, it will be found impossible, even if the prolixity of forms which retards the progress of causes were removed, to give a prompt hearing to every complaint, or an immediate answer to any. On the other hand, if to remedy these evils, and to render the administration of justice cheap and speedy, domestic and summary tribunals be erected in each neighbourhood, the advantage of such courts will be accompanied with all the dangers of ignorance and partiality, and with the certain mischief of confusion and contrariety in their decisions. The law of England, by its circuit or itinerary courts, contains a provision for the distribution of private justice in a great measure relieved from both these objections. As the presiding magistrate comes into the country a stranger to its prejudices, rivalships, and connections, he brings with him none of those attachments and regards, which are so apt to pervert the course of justice, when the parties and the judges inhabit the same neighbourhood. Again, as this magistrate is usually one of the judges of the supreme tribunals of the kingdom, and has past his life in the study and administration of the laws, he possesses, it may be presumed, those professional qualifications, which befit the dignity and importance of his station. Lastly, as both he, and the advocates who accompany him in his circuit, are employed in the business of those superior courts, (to which also their proceedings are amenable,) they will naturally conduct themselves by the rules of adjudication, which they have applied, or learnt there; and by this means maintain, what constitutes a principal perfection of civil government, one law of the land in every part and diſtrict of the empire.

Next to the conſtitution of courts of juſtice, we are naturally led to conſider the maxims which ought to guide their proceedings: and upon this ſubject, the chief enquiry will be, how far, and for what reaſons, it is expedient to adhere to former determinations; or, whether it be neceſſary for judges to attend to any other conſideration than the apparent and particular equity of the caſe before them. Now although to aſſert, that precedents eſtabliſhed by one ſet of judges, ought to be incontrovertible by their ſucceſſors in the ſame juriſdiction, or by thoſe who exerciſe a higher, would be to attribute to the ſentence of thoſe judges, all the authority we aſcribe to the moſt ſolemn acts of the legiſlature: yet, the general ſecurity of private rights, and of civil life, requires, that ſuch precedents, eſpecially if they have been confirmed by repeated adjudications, ſhould not be overthrown without a detection of manifeſt error, or without ſome imputation of diſhoneſty upon the court by whoſe judgment the queſtion was firſt decided. And this deference to prior deciſions is founded upon two reaſons; firſt, that the diſcretion of judges may be bound down by poſitive rules; and, ſecondly, that the ſubject upon every occaſion, in which his legal intereſt is concerned, may know beforehand how to act, and what to expect. To ſet judges free from any obligation to conform themſelves to the deciſions of their predeceſſors would be to lay open a latitude of judging, with which no deſcription

scription of men can safely be entrusted: it would be to allow space for the exercise of those concealed partialities, which, since they cannot by any human policy be excluded, ought to be confined by boundaries and land-marks. It is in vain to alledge, that the superintendency of parliament is always at hand to control and punish abuses of judicial discretion. By what rules can parliament proceed? How shall they pronounce a decision to be wrong, where there exists no acknowledged measure or standard of what is right, which, in a multitude of instances, would be the case, if prior determinations were no longer to be appealed to?

Diminishing the danger of partiality, is one thing gained by adhering to precedents; but not the principal thing. The subject of every system of laws must expect that decision in his own case, which he knows that others have received in cases similar to his. If he expect not this, he can expect nothing. There exists no other rule or principle of reasoning, by which he can foretell, or even conjecture the event of a judicial contest. To remove therefore the ground of this expectation, by rejecting the force and authority of precedents, is to entail upon the subject the worst property of slavery—to have no assurance of his rights, or knowledge of his duty. But the quiet of the country, as well as the confidence and satisfaction of each man's mind, requires uniformity in judicial proceedings. Nothing quells a spirit of litigation, like despair of success; therefore, nothing so completely puts an end to litigation as a rigid adherence to known rules of adjudication.

Whilst

Whilst the event is uncertain, which it ever must be, whilst it is uncertain whether former determinations upon the same subject will be followed or not, law-suits will be endless and innumerable: men will continually engage in them, either from the hope of prevailing in their claims, which the smallest chance is sufficient to encourage; or with the design of intimidating their adversary by the terrors of a dubious litigation. When justice is rendered to the parties, but half the business of a court of justice is done: the more important part of its office remains—to put an end, for the future, to every fear, and quarrel, and expence upon the same point; and so to regulate its proceedings, that not only a doubt once decided may be stirred no more, but that the whole train of law-suits, which issue from one uncertainty, may die with the parent question. Now this advantage can only be attained by considering each decision as a direction to succeeding judges. And it should be observed, that every departure from former determinations, especially if they have been often repeated, or long submitted to, shakes the stability of all legal title. It is not fixing a point anew; it is leaving every thing unfixed. For by the same stretch of power, by which the present race of judges take upon them to contradict the judgment of their predecessors, those who try the question next, may set aside theirs.

From an adherence however to precedents, by which so much is gained to the public, two consequences arise which are often lamented; the hardship of particular determinations, and the intricacy of the law as a science. To the first of these complaints, we must apply this reflection, "that uniformity is of more importance than "equity, in proportion as general uncertainty would be a "greater evil than particular injustice." The second is attended with no greater inconveniency than that of erecting the practice of the law into a separate profession: which this reason, we allow, makes necessary; for if we attribute so much authority to precedents, it is expedient that they be known in every cause, both to the advocates and to the judge: this knowledge cannot be general, since it is the fruit oftentimes of laborious research, or demands a memory stored with long-collected erudition.

To a mind revolving upon the subject of human jurisprudence, there frequently occurs this question; why, since the maxims of natural justice are few and evident, do there arise so many doubts and controversies in the application? Or, in other words, how comes it to pass, that although the principles of the law of nature be simple, and for the most part sufficiently obvious, there should exist nevertheless, in every system of municipal laws, and in the actual administration of relative justice, numerous uncertainties and acknowledged difficulty? Whence, it may be asked, so much room for litigation, and so many subsisting disputes, if the rules of human duty be neither obscure nor dubious? If a system of morality, containing both the precepts of revelation, and the deductions of reason, may
be

be comprised within the compass of one moderate volume; and the moralist be able, as he pretends, to describe the rights and obligations of mankind, in all the different relations they may hold to one another; what need of those codes of positive and particular institutions, of those tomes of statutes and reports, which require the employment of a long life even to peruse? And this question is immediately connected with the argument which has been discussed in the preceding paragraph; for unless there be found some greater uncertainty in the law of nature, or what may be called natural equity, when it comes to be applied to real cases and to actual adjudication, than what appears in the rules and principles of the science, as delivered in the writings of those who treat of the subject, it were better that the determination of every cause should be left to the conscience of the judge, unfettered by precedents and authorities; since the very purpose, for which these are introduced, is to give a certainty to judicial proceedings, which such proceedings would want without them.

Now to account for the existence of so many sources of litigation, notwithstanding the clearness and perfection of natural justice, it should be observed, in the first place, that treatises of morality always suppose facts to be ascertained; and not only so, but the intention likewise of the parties to be known and laid bare. For example, when we pronounce that promises ought to be fulfilled in that sense in which the promiser apprehended, at the time of making the promise, the other party received and understood it, the apprehension of one side,

and

and the expectation of the other, must be discovered before this rule can be reduced to practice, or applied to the determination of any actual dispute. Wherefore the discussion of facts, which the moralist supposes to be settled; the discovery of intentions, which he presumes to be known, still remain to exercise the enquiry of courts of justice. And as these facts and intentions are often to be inferred or rather conjectured, from obscure indications, from suspicious testimony, or from a comparison of opposite and contending probabilities, they afford a never-failing supply of doubt and litigation. For which reason, as hath been observed in a former part of this work, the science of morality is to be considered rather as a direction to the parties, who are conscious of their own thoughts, and motives, and designs, and to which consciousness the teacher of morality constantly appeals; than as a guide to the judge, or to any third person, whose arbitration must proceed upon rules of evidence, and maxims of credibility, with which the moralist has no concern.

Secondly, there exist a multitude of cases, in which the law of nature, that is, the law of public expediency, prescribes nothing, except that some certain rule be adhered to, and that the rule actually established be preserved; it either being indifferent what rule obtains, or out of many rules, no one being so much more advantageous than the rest, as to recompence the inconveniency of an alteration. In all such cases the law of nature sends us to the law of the land. She directs either that some fixed rule be introduced

troduced by an act of the legiflature, or that the rule which accident, or cuftom, or common confent hath already eftablifhed, be fteadily maintained. Thus, in the defcent of lands or the inheritance of perfonals from inteftate proprietors, whether the kindred of the grandmother, or of the great grandmother, fhall be preferred in the fucceffion; whether the degrees of confanguinity fhall be computed through the common anceftor, or from him; whether the widow fhall take a third or a moiety of her hufband's fortune; whether fons fhall be preferred to daughters, or the elder to the younger; whether the diftinction of age fhall be regarded amongft fifters, as well as between brothers; in thefe, and in a great variety of queftions which the fame fubject fupplies, the law of nature determines nothing. The only anfwer fhe returns to our enquiries is, that fome certain and general rule be laid down by public authority; be obeyed when laid down; and that the quiet of the country be not difturbed, nor the expectation of heirs fruftrated by capricious innovations. This filence or neutrality of the law of nature, which we have exemplified in the cafe of inteftacy, holds concerning a great part of the queftions that relate to the right or acquifition of property. Recourfe then muft neceffarily be had to ftatutes, or precedents, or ufage, to fix what the law of nature has left loofe. The interpretation of thefe ftatutes, the fearch after precedents, the inveftigation of cuftoms, compofe therefore an unavoidable, and at the fame time a large and intricate portion of forenfic bufinefs. Pofitive conftitutions or judicial

cial authorities are, in like manner, wanted to give precision to many things, which are in their nature *indeterminate*. The age of legal discretion; at what time of life a person shall be deemed competent to the performance of any act, which may bind his property; whether at twenty, or twenty one, or earlier or later, or at some point of time between these years, can only be ascertained by a positive rule of the society to which the party belongs. The line has not been drawn by nature; the human understanding advancing to maturity by insensible degrees, and its progress varying in different individuals. Yet it is necessary, for the sake of mutual security, that a precise age be fixed, and that what is fixed be known to all. It is on these occasions that the intervention of law supplies the inconstancy of nature. Again, there are other things which are perfectly *arbitrary*, and capable of no certainty but what is given to them by positive regulation. It is necessary that a limited time should be assigned to defendants, to plead to the complaints alledged against them; and also that the default of pleading within a certain time, should be taken for a confession of the charge: but to how many days or months that term should be extended, though necessary to be known with certainty, cannot be known at all, by any information which the law of nature affords. And the same remark seems applicable to almost all those rules of proceeding, which constitute what is called the practice of the court: as they cannot be traced out by reasoning, they must be settled by authority.

Thirdly,

Thirdly, in contracts, whether expreſs or implied, which involve a great number of conditions, as in thoſe which are entered into between maſters and ſervants, principals and agents; many alſo of merchandize, or for works of art; ſome likewiſe which relate to the negociation of money or bills, or to the acceptance of credit or ſecurity; the original deſign and expectation of the parties was, that both ſides ſhould be guided by the courſe and cuſtom of the country in tranſactions of the ſame ſort. Conſequently, when theſe contracts come to be diſputed, natural juſtice can only refer to that cuſtom. But as ſuch cuſtoms are not always ſufficiently uniform or notorious, but often to be collected from the production and compariſon of inſtances and accounts repugnant to one another; and each cuſtom being only that, after all, which amongſt a variety of uſages ſeems to predominate, we have *here* alſo ample room for doubt and conteſt.

Fourthly, as the law of nature, founded in the very conſtruction of human ſociety, which is formed to endure through a ſeries of periſhing generations, requires that the juſt engagements a man enters into, ſhould continue in force beyond his own life; it follows that the private rights of perſons frequently depend upon what has been tranſacted, in times remote from the preſent, by their anceſtors or predeceſſors, by thoſe under whom they claim, or to whoſe obligations they have ſucceeded. Thus the queſtions which uſually ariſe between lords of manors and their tenants, between the king and thoſe who claim royal

franchiſes

franchises, or between them and the persons affected by these franchises, depend upon the terms of the original grant. In like manner every dispute concerning tythes, in which an exemption or composition is pleaded, depends upon the agreement which took place between the predecessor of the claimant, and the ancient owner of the land. The appeal to these grants and agreements is dictated by natural equity, as well as by the municipal law: but concerning the existence, or the conditions of such old covenants, doubts will perpetually occur, to which the law of nature affords no solution. The loss or decay of records, the perishableness of living memory, the coruption and carelessness of tradition, all conspire to multiply uncertainties upon this head; what cannot be produced or proved, must be left to loose and fallible presumption. Under the same head may be included another topic of altercation; the tracing out of boundaries, which time, or neglect, or unity of possession, or mixture of occupation have founded or obliterated. To which should be added a difficulty which often presents itself in disputes concerning rights of *way*, both public and private, and of those easements which one man claims in another mans property; namely, that of distinguishing, after a lapse of years, the use of an indulgence from the exercise of a right.

Fifthly, The quantity or extent of an injury, even when the cause and author of it are known, is often dubious and undefined. If the injury consist in the loss of some specific right, the value of the right measures the amount of the injury: but what a man may have suffered in his person, from an assault; in his reputation, by slander; or in the comfort of his life, by the seduction of a wife or daughter; or what sum of money shall be deemed a reparation for the damage, cannot be ascertained by any rules which the law of nature supplies. The law of nature commands that reparation be made; and adds to her command, that when the aggressor and the sufferer disagree, the damage be assessed by authorized and indifferent arbitrators. Here then recourse must be had to courts of law, not only with the permission, but in some measure, by the direction of natural justice.

Sixthly, When controversies arise in the interpretation of written laws, they, for the most part, arise upon some contingency which the composer of the law did not foresee or think of. In the adjudication of such cases, this dilemma presents itself: if the laws be permitted to operate only upon the cases, which were actually contemplated by the law makers, they will always be found defective: if they be extended to every case, to which the reasoning and spirit and expediency of the provision seem to belong, without any farther evidence of the intention of the legislature, we shall allow to the judges a liberty of applying the law, which will fall very little short of the power of making it. If a literal construction be adhered to, the law will often fail of its end: if a loose and vague exposition be admitted, the law might as well have never been enacted; for this

licence

licenfe will bring back into the fubject all the uncertainty which it was the defign of the legiflature to take away. Courts of juftice are, and always muft be embarraffed by thefe oppofite difficulties: and as it can never be known beforehand, in what degree either confideration may prevail in the mind of the judge, there remains an unavoidable caufe of doubt, and a place for contention.

Seventhly, the deliberations of courts of juftice upon every *new* queftion are incumbered with additional difficulties, in confequence of the authority which the judgment of the court poffeffes, as a precedent to future judicatures: which authority appertains not only to the conclufions the court delivers, but to the principles and arguments upon which they are built. The view of this effect makes it neceffary for a judge to look beyond the cafe before him; and, befide the attention he owes to the truth and juftice of the caufe between the parties, to reflect whether the principles, and maxims, and reafoning, which he adopts and authorizes, can be applied with fafety to all cafes, which admit of a comparifon with the prefent. The decifion of the caufe, were the effects of the decifion to ftop there, might be eafy: but the confequence of eftablifhing the principle, which fuch a decifion affumes, may be difficult, though of the utmoft importance, to be forefeen and regulated.

Finally, after all the certainty and reft that can be given to points of law, either by the interpofition of the legiflature,

ture, or the authority of precedents, one principal source of disputation, and into which indeed the greater part of legal controversies may be resolved, will remain still, namely, "the competition of opposite analogies." When a point of law has been once adjudged, neither that question, nor any which completely and in all its circumstances corresponds with *that*, can be brought a second time into dispute: but questions arise, which resemble this only indirectly and in part, in certain views and circumstances, and which may seem to bear an equal or a greater affinity to other adjudged cases; questions, which can be brought within any affixed rule only by analogy, and which hold a relation by analogy to different rules. It is by the urging of these different analogies that the contention of the bar is carried on: and it is in the comparison, adjustment, and reconciliation of them with one another; in the discerning of such distinctions, and in the framing of such a determination, as may either save the various rules alledged in the cause, or, if that be impossible, may give up the weaker analogy to the stronger, that the sagacity and wisdom of the court are seen and exercised. Amongst a thousand instances of this, we may cite one of general notoriety in the contest that has lately been agitated concerning literary property. The personal industry, which an author expends upon the composition of his work, bears so near a resemblance to that, by which every other kind of property is earned, or deserved, or acquired; or rather there exists such a correspondency between what is created by the study of a man's mind, and the production of his labour in any other way of applying it, that he feems entitled to the fame exclufive, affignable, and perpetual right in both; and that right to the fame protection of law. This was the analogy contended for on one fide. On the other hand, a book, as to the author's right in it, appears fimilar to an invention of art, as a machine, an engine, a medicine. And fince the law permits thefe to be copied, or imitated, except where an exclufive ufe or fale is referved to the inventor by patent, the fame liberty fhould be allowed in the publication and fale of books. This was the analogy maintained by the advocates of an open trade. And the competition of thefe oppofite analogies conftituted the difficulty of the cafe, as far as the fame was argued, or adjudged upon principles of common law.—One example may ferve to illuftrate our meaning; but whoever takes up a volume of reports, will find moft of the arguments it contains capable of the fame analyfis; although the analogies, it muft be confeffed, are fometimes fo entangled as not to be eafily unravelled, or even perceived.

Doubtful and obfcure points of law are not however nearly fo numerous, as they are apprehended to be. Out of the multitude of caufes, which in the courfe of each year are brought to trial in the metropolis, or upon the circuits, there are few in which any point is referved for the judgment of fuperior courts. Yet thefe few contain all the doubts, with which the law is chargeable: for as to the rest, the uncertainty, as hath been shown above, is not in the law, but in the means of human information.

There are two peculiarities in the judicial constitution of this country, which do not carry with them that evidence of their propriety, which recommends almost every other part of the system. The first of these is the rule, which requires that juries be *unanimous* in their verdicts. To expect that twelve men, taken by lot out of a promiscuous multitude, should agree in their opinion upon points confessedly dubious; and upon which oftentimes the wisest judgments might be held in suspense; or to suppose that any real *unanimity*, or change of opinion in the dissenting jurors, could be procured by confining them until they all consented to the same verdict; bespeaks more of the conceit of a barbarous age, than of the policy which could dictate such an institution as that of juries. Nevertheless, the effects of this rule are not so detrimental, as the rule itself is unreasonable: in criminal prosecutions it operates considerably in favour of the prisoner; for if a juror find it necessary to surrender to the obstinacy of others, he will much more readily resign his opinion on the side of mercy, than of condemnation: in civil suits it adds weight to the direction of the judge; for when a conference with one another does not seem likely to produce, in the jury, the agreement that is necessary, they will naturally close their disputes by a common submission to the opinion delivered from the bench. However, there seems to be less of the concurrence of separate judgments in in the same conclusion; consequently, less assurance that the conclusion is founded in reasons of apparent truth and justice, than if the decision were left to a plurality, or to some certain majority of voices.

The second circumstance in our constitution, which, however it may succeed in practice, does not seem to have been suggested by any intelligible fitness in the nature of the thing, is the choice that is made of the *House of Lords*, as a court of appeal from every civil court of judicature in the kingdom; and of the last also and highest appeal, to which the subject can resort. There appears to be nothing in the constitution of that assembly; in the education, habits, character, or professions of the members who compose it; in the mode of their appointment, or the right by which they succeed to their places in it, that should qualify them for this arduous office: except, perhaps, that the elevation of their rank and fortune affords a security against the offer and influence of small bribes. Officers of the army and navy, courtiers, ecclesiastics; young men who have just attained the age of twenty-one, and who have passed their youth in the dissipation and pursuits which commonly accompany the possession or inheritance of great fortunes; country gentlemen occupied in the management of their estates, or in the care of their domestic concerns and family interests; the greater part of the assembly born to their station, that is, placed in it by chance; most of the rest advanced to the peerage, for services, and from motives utterly unconnected with legal erudition—these men compose the tribunal, to which the Constitution entrusts the interpretation of her laws, and the ultimate decision of every dispute between her subjects. These are the men assigned to review judgments of law, pronounced by sages of the profession, who have spent their lives in the study and practice of the jurisprudence of their country. Such is the order which our ancestors have established. The effect only proves the truth of this maxim, " that when a single " institution is extremely dissonant from other parts of the " system to which it belongs, it will always find some way " of reconciling itself to the analogy which governs and " pervades the rest." By constantly placing in the House of Lords some of the most eminent and experienced lawyers in the kingdom; by calling to their aid the advice of the judges, when any abstract question of law awaits their determination; by the almost implicit and undisputed deference, which the uninformed part of the house find it necessary to pay to the learning of their colleagues, the appeal to the House of Lords becomes in truth an appeal to the collected wisdom of our supreme courts of justice: receiving indeed solemnity, but little perhaps of direction or assistance, from the presence of the assembly in which it is heard and determined.

These, however, even if real, are minute imperfections. A politician, who should sit down to delineate a plan for the dispensation of public justice, guarded against all access to influence and corruption, and bringing together the separate

rate advantages of knowledge and impartiality, would find, when he had done, that he had been tranfcribing the judicial conftitution of England. And it may teach the moft difcontented amongft us to acquiefce in the government of his country, to reflect, that the pure, and wife, and equal adminiftration of the laws, forms the firft end and blefling of focial union; and that this blefling is enjoyed by him in a perfection, which he will feek in vain, in any other nation of the world.

CHAP. IX.

OF CRIMES AND PUNISHMENTS.

THE proper end of human punishment is, not the satisfaction of justice, but the prevention of crimes. By the satisfaction of justice, I mean the retribution of so much pain for so much guilt; which is the dispensation we expect at the hand of God, and which we are accustomed to consider as the order of things that perfect justice dictates and requires. In what sense, or whether with truth in any sense, justice may be said to demand the punishment of offenders I do not now enquire; but I assert that this *demand* is not the motive or occasion of human punishment. What would it be to the magistrate that offences went altogether unpunished, if the impunity of the offenders were followed by no danger or prejudice to the commonwealth? The fear lest the escape of the criminal should encourage him, or others by his example, to repeat the fame crime, or to commit different crimes, is the fole confideration which authorizes the infliction of punifhment by human laws. Now that, whatever it be, which is the caufe and end of the punifhment, ought undoubtedly to regulate the meafure of its feverity. But this caufe appears to be founded, not in the guilt of the offender, but in the neceffity of preventing the repetition of the offence. And from hence refults the reafon, that crimes are not by any government punifhed in proportion to their guilt, nor in all cafes ought to be fo, but in proportion to the difficulty and the neceffity of preventing them. Thus the ftealing of goods privately out of a fhop, may not, in its moral quality, be more criminal than the ftealing of them out of a houfe; yet, being equally neceffary, and more difficult to be prevented, the law, in certain circumftances, denounces againft it a feverer punifhment. The crime muft be prevented by fome means or other; and confequently, whatever means appear neceffary to this end, whether they be proportionable to the guilt of the criminal or not, are adopted rightly, becaufe they are adopted upon the principle which alone juftifies the infliction of punifhment at all. From the fame confideration it alfo follows, that punifhment ought not to be employed, much lefs rendered fevere, when the crime can be prevented by any other means. Punifhment is an evil to which the magiftrate reforts only from its being neceffary to the prevention of a greater. This neceffity does not exift, when the end may be attained, that is, when the public may be defended from the effects of the crime

by

by any other expedient. The sanguinary laws which have been made against counterfeiting or diminishing the gold coin of the kingdom might be just, until the method of detecting the fraud, by weighing the money, was introduced into general usage. Since that precaution was practised, these laws have slept: and an execution under them would be deemed, at this day, a measure of unjustifiable severity. The same principle accounts for a circumstance, which has been often censured as an absurdity in the penal laws of this, and of most modern nations, namely, that breaches of trust are either not punished at all, or punished with less rigour than other frauds.—Wherefore is it, some have asked, that a violation of confidence, which increases the guilt, should mitigate the penalty. This lenity, or rather forbearance of the laws, is founded in the most reasonable distinction. A due circumspection in the choice of the persons whom they trust; caution in limiting the extent of that trust; or the requiring of sufficient security for the faithful discharge of it, will commonly guard men from injuries of this description: and the law will not interpose its sanctions, to protect negligence and credulity, or to supply the place of domestic care and prudence. To be convinced that the law proceeds entirely upon this consideration, we have only to observe, that, where the confidence is unavoidable, where no practicable vigilance could watch the offender, as in the case of theft committed by a servant in the shop or dwelling-house of his master, or upon property to which he must necessarily have access, the sentence
of

tence of the law is not lefs fevere, and its execution commonly more certain and rigorous, than if no truſt at all had intervened.

It is in purfuance of the fame principle, which pervades indeed the whole fyſtem of penal jurifprudence, that the facility with which any fpecies of crimes is perpetrated, has been generally deemed a reafon for aggravating the puniſhment. Thus, ſheep-ſtealing, horfe-ſtealing, the ſtealing of cloth from tenters, or bleaching grounds, by our laws, fubject the offenders to fentence of death: not that thefe crimes are in their nature more heinous, than many fimple felonies which are puniſhed by imprifonment or tranfportation, but becaufe the property being more expofed, requires the terror of capital puniſhment to protect it. This feverity would be abfurd and unjuſt, if the guilt of the offender were the immediate caufe and meafure of the puniſhment; but is a confiſtent and regular confequence of the fuppofition, that the right of puniſhment refults from the neceffity of preventing the crime: for if this be the end propofed, the feverity of the puniſhment muſt be increafed in proportion to the expediency and the difficulty of attaining this end; that is, in a proportion compounded of the mifchief of the crime, and of the eafe with which it is executed. The difficulty of difcovery is a circumſtance to be included in the fame confideration. It conſtitutes indeed, with refpect to the crime, the facility we fpeak of. By how much therefore the detection of an offender is more rare and uncertain, by fo much the more fevere must be the punishment, when he is detected. Thus the writing of incendiary letters, though in itself a pernicious and alarming injury, calls for a more condign and exemplary punishment, by the very obscurity with which the crime is committed.

From the justice of God we are taught to look for a gradation of punishment, exactly proportioned to the guilt of the offender; when therefore, in assigning the degrees of human punishment, we introduce considerations distinct from that guilt, and a proportion so varied by external circumstances, that equal crimes frequently undergo unequal punishments, or the less crime the greater; it is natural to demand the reason why a different measure of punishment should be expected from God, and observed by man; why that rule, which befits the absolute and perfect justice of the Deity, should not be the rule which ought to be pursued and imitated by human laws. The solution of this difficulty must be sought for in those peculiar attributes of the divine nature, which distinguish the dispensations of supreme wisdom from the proceedings of human judicature. A Being whose knowledge penetrates every concealment; from the operation of whose will no art or flight can escape; and in whose hands punishment is sure; such a Being may conduct the moral government of his creation, in the best and wisest manner, by pronouncing a law that every crime shall finally receive a punishment proportioned to the guilt which it contains, abstracted from any foreign consideration whatever;

ever: and may teftify his veracity to the fpectators of his judgments, by carrying this law into ftrict execution. But when the care of the public fafety is entrufted to men, whofe authority over their fellow creatures is limited by defects of power and knowledge; from whofe utmoft vigilance and fagacity the greateft offenders often lie hid; whofe wifeft provifions and fpeedieft purfuit may be eluded by artifice or concealment; a different neceffity, a new rule of proceeding refults from the very imperfection of their faculties. In their hands the uncertainty of punifhment muft be compenfated by the feverity. The eafe with which crimes are committed or concealed, muft be counteracted by additional penalties and increafed terrors, The very end for which human government is eftablifhed, requires that its regulations be adapted to the fuppreffion of crimes. This end, whatever it may do in the plans of infinite wifdom, does not in the defignation of temporal penalties, always coincide with the proportionate punifhment of guilt.

There are two methods of adminiftring penal juftice.

The firft method affigns capital punifhments to few offences, and inflicts it invariably.

The fecond method affigns capital punifhments to many kinds of offences, but inflicts it only upon a few examples of each kind.

The latter of which two methods has been long adopted in this country, where, of those who receive sentence of death, scarcely one in ten is executed. And the preference of this to the former method seems to be founded in the consideration, that the selection of proper objects for capital punishment principally depends upon circumstances, which, however easy to perceive in each particular case, after the crime is committed, it is impossible to enumerate or define beforehand; or to ascertain however with that exactness, which is requisite in legal descriptions. Hence, although it be necessary to fix by precise rules of law, the boundary on one side, that is, the limit to which the punishment may be extended, and also that nothing less than the authority of the whole legislature be suffered to determine that boundary and assign these rules; yet the mitigation of punishment, the exercise of lenity, may, without danger, be entrusted to the executive magistrate, whose discretion will operate upon those numerous, unforeseen, mutable, and indefinite circumstances, both of the crime and the criminal, which constitute or qualify the malignity of each offence. Without the power of relaxation lodged in a living authority, either some offenders would escape capital punishment, whom the public safety required to suffer; or some would undergo this punishment, where it was neither deserved nor necessary. For if judgment of death were reserved for one or two species of crimes only, which would probably be the case, if that judgment was intended to be executed without exception, crimes might occur of the most dangerous example, and accompanied

accompanied with circumstances of heinous aggravation, which did not fall within *any* description of offences that the laws had made capital, and which consequently could not receive the punishment their own malignity and the public safety required. What is worse, it would be known beforehand, that such crimes might be committed without danger to the offender's life. On the other hand, if, to reach these possible cases, the whole class of offences to which they belong be subjected to pains of death, and no power of remitting this severity remain any where, the execution of the laws will become more sanguinary than the public compassion would endure, or than is necessary to the general security.

The law of England is constructed upon a different and a better policy. By the number of statutes creating capital offences, it sweeps into the net every crime, which under any possible circumstances may merit the punishment of death: but when the execution of this sentence comes to be deliberated upon, a small proportion of each class are singled out, the general character, or the peculiar aggravations of whose crimes, render them fit examples of public justice. By this expedient few actually suffer death, whilst the dread and danger of it hang over the crimes of many. The tenderness of the law cannot be taken advantage of. The life of the subject is spared, as far as the necessity of restraint and intimidation permits, yet no one will adventure upon the commission of any enormous crime, from a knowledge that the laws have not provided for its punishment. The wisdom and humanity of this
design

design furnish a just excuse for the multiplicity of capital offences, which the laws of England are accused of creating beyond those of other countries. The charge of cruelty is answered by observing, that these laws were never meant to be carried into indiscriminate execution; that the legislature, when it establishes its last and highest sanctions, trusts to the benignity of the crown to relax their severity, as often as circumstances appear to palliate the offence, or even as often as those circumstances of aggravation are wanting, which rendered this rigorous interposition necessary. Upon this plan it is enough to vindicate the lenity of the laws, that *some* instances are to be found in each class of capital crimes, which require the restraint of capital punishment; and that this restraint could not be applied, without subjecting the whole class to the same condemnation.

There is however one species of crimes, the making of which capital can hardly, I think, be defended, even upon the comprehensive principle just now stated; I mean that of privately stealing from the person. As every degree of force is excluded by the description of the crime, it will be difficult to assign an example, where either the amount or circumstances of the theft place it upon a level with those dangerous attempts, to which the punishment of death should be confined. It will be still more difficult to shew, that, without gross and culpable negligence on the part of the sufferer, such examples can ever become so frequent, as to make it necessary to constitute a class of capital offences, of very wide and large extent.

The

The prerogative of pardon is properly reserved to the chief magistrate. The power of suspending the laws is a privilege of too high a nature to be committed to many hands, or to those of any inferior officer in the state. The king also can best collect the advice by which his resolutions should be governed; and is at the same time removed at the greatest distance from the influence of private motives. But let this power be deposited where it will, the exercise of it ought to be regarded, not as the gift of a favour to be yielded to solicitation, granted to friendship, or, least of all, to be made subservient to the conciliating or gratifying of political attachments, but as a judicial act; as a deliberation to be conducted with the same character of impartiality, with the same exact and diligent attention to the proper merits and reasons and circumstances of the case, as that which the judge upon the bench was expected to maintain and show in the trial of the prisoner's guilt. The questions whether the prisoner be guilty, and whether, being guilty, he ought to be executed, are equally questions of public justice. The adjudication of the latter question is as much a function of magistracy as the trial of the former. The public welfare is interested in both. The conviction of an offender should depend upon nothing but the proof of his guilt, nor the execution of the sentence upon any thing beside the quality and circumstances of his crime. It is necessary to the good order of society, and to the reputation and authority of government, that this be known and believed to be the case in each part of the proceeding. Which reflections show, that the admission of extrinsic or oblique considerations, in dispensing with the power of pardon, is a crime in the authors and advisers of such unmerited partiality, of the same nature with that of corruption in a judge.

Aggravations which ought to guide the magistrate in the selection of objects of condign punishment are principally these three—repetition, cruelty, combination. The two first, it is manifest, add to every reason upon which the justice or the necessity of rigorous measures can be founded; and, with respect to the last circumstance, it may be observed that when thieves and robbers are once collected into gangs, their violence becomes more formidable, the confederates more desperate, and the difficulty of defending the public against their depredations much greater, than in the case of solitary adventurers. Which several considerations compose a distinction, that is properly adverted to, in deciding upon the fate of convicted malefactors.

In crimes however, which are perpetrated by a multitude, or by a gang, it is proper to separate, in the punishment, the ring-leader from his followers, the principal from his accomplices, and even the person who struck the blow, broke the lock, or first entered the house, from those who joined him in the felony; not so much on account of any distinction in the guilt of the offenders, as for the sake of casting an obstacle in the way of such confederacies, by rendering it difficult for the confederates to settle who shall begin the attack, or to find a man amongst their number willing to expose himself to greater danger than his associates.
This

This is another instance in which the punishment, which expediency directs, does not pursue the exact proportion of the crime.

Injuries effected by terror and violence, are those which it is the first and chief concern of legal government to repress; because, their extent is unlimited; because, no private precaution can protect the subject against them; because, they endanger life and safety, as well as property; and lastly, because, they render the condition of society wretched, by a sense of personal insecurity. These reasons do not apply to frauds, which circumspection may prevent; which must wait for opportunity; which can proceed only to certain limits; and, by the apprehension of which, although the business of life be incommoded, life itself is not made miserable. The appearance of this distinction has led some humane writers to express a wish, that capital punishments might be confined to crimes of violence.

In estimating the comparative malignancy of crimes of violence, regard is to be had, not only to the proper and intended mischief of the crime, but to the fright occasioned by the attack, to the general alarm excited by it in others, and to the consequences which may attend future attempts of the same kind. Thus in affixing the punishment of burglary, or of breaking into dwelling-houses by night, we are to consider not only the peril to which the most valuable property is exposed by this crime, and which may be called the direct mischief of it, but the danger also of murder, in case of resistance, or for the sake of preventing discovery, and the universal dread with which the silent and defenceless hours of rest and sleep must be disturbed, were attempts of this sort to become frequent; and which dread alone, even without the mischief which is the object of it, is not only a public evil, but almost of all evils the most insupportable. These circumstances place a difference between the breaking into a dwelling-house by day, and by night; which difference obtains in the punishment of the offence by the law of Moses, and is probably to be found in the judicial codes of most countries, from the earliest ages to the present.

Of frauds, or of injuries which are effected without force, the most noxious kinds are forgeries, counterfeiting or diminishing of the coin, and the stealing of letters in the course of their conveyance; inasmuch as these practices tend to deprive the public of accommodations, which not only improve the conveniencies of social life, but are essential to the prosperity, and even the existence of commerce. Of these crimes it may be said, that, although they seem to affect property alone, the mischief of their operation does not terminate there. For let it be supposed, that the remissness or lenity of the laws should, in any country, suffer offences of this sort to grow into such a frequency, as to render the use of money, the circulation of bills, or the public conveyance of letters no longer safe or practicable; what would follow, but that every species of trade and of activity must decline under these discouragements; the sources of subsistence fail, by which the inhabitants of the country

country are supported; the country itself, where the intercourse of civil life was so endangered and defective, be deserted; and that, beside the distress and poverty, which the loss of employment would produce to the industrious and valuable part of the existing community, a rapid depopulation must take place, each generation becoming less numerous than the last, till solitude and barrenness overspread the land; until a desolation similar to what obtains in many countries of Asia, which were once the most civilized and frequented parts of the world, succeed in the place of crowded cities, of cultivated fields, of happy and well-peopled regions. When we carry forwards therefore our views to the more distant, but not less certain consequences of these crimes, we perceive that, though no living creature be destroyed by them, yet human life is diminished; that an offence, the particular consequence of which deprives only an individual of a small portion of his property, and which even in its general tendency seems only to obstruct the enjoyment of certain public conveniencies, may nevertheless, by its ultimate effects, conclude in the laying waste of human existence. This observation will enable those, who regard the divine rule of " life for " life, and blood for blood," as the only authorized and justifiable measure of capital punishment, to perceive, with respect to the effects and quality of the actions, a greater resemblance than they suppose to exist, between certain atrocious frauds, and these crimes which attack personal safety.

In the case of forgeries there appears a substantial difference, between the forging of bills of exchange, or of securities

rities which are circulated, and of which the circulation and currency are found to ferve and facilitate valuable purpofes of commerce, and the forging of bonds, leafes, mortgages, or of inftruments which are not commonly transferred from one hand to another; becaufe, in the former cafe credit is neceffarily given to the fignature, and, without that credit, the negociation of fuch property could not be carried on, nor the public utility fought from it be attained; in the other cafe, all poffibility of deceit might be precluded, by a direct communication between the parties, or by due care in the choice of their agents, with little interruption to bufinefs, and without deftroying, or much incumbering, the ufes for which thefe inftruments are calculated. This diftinction, I apprehend, to be not only real, but precife enough to afford a line of divifion between forgeries, which, as the law now ftands, are almoft univerfally capital, and punifhed with undiftinguifhing feverity.

Perjury is another crime of the fame clafs and magnitude. And, when we confider what reliance is neceffarily placed upon oaths; that all judicial decifions proceed upon teftimony; that confequently, there is not a right, that a man poffeffes, of which falfe witneffes may not deprive him; that reputation, property, and life itfelf lie open to the attempts of perjury; that it may often be committed without a poffibility of contradiction or difcovery; that the fuccefs and prevalency of this vice tend to introduce the moft grievous and fatal injuftice into the adminiftration of human affairs, or fuch a diftruft of teftimony as muft create

create universal embarrassment and confusion; when we reflect upon these mischiefs, we shall be brought, probably, to agree with the opinion of those, who contend that perjury, in its punishment, especially that which is attempted in solemn evidence, and in the face of a court of justice, should be placed upon a level with the most flagitious frauds.

The obtaining of money by secret threats, whether we regard the difficulty with which the crime is traced out, the odious imputations to which it may lead, or the profligate conspiracies that are sometimes formed to carry it into execution, deserves to be reckoned amongst the worst species of robbery.

The frequency of capital executions in this country, owes its necessity to three causes—much liberty, great cities, and the want of a punishment, short of death, possessing a sufficient degree of terror. And if the taking away of the life of malefactors be more rare in other countries than in ours, the reason will be found in some difference in these articles. The liberties of a free people, and still more the jealousy with which these liberties are watched, and by which they are preserved, permit not those precautions and restraints, that inspection, scrutiny, and control, which are exercised with success in arbitrary governments. For example, neither the spirit of the laws, nor of the people, will suffer the detention or confinement of suspected persons, without proofs of their guilt, which it is often impossible to obtain; nor will they allow that masters of families be obliged to record and render up a description
of

of the strangers or inmates whom they entertain; nor that an account be demanded, at the pleasure of the magistrate, of each man's time, employment, and means of subsistence; nor securities to be required when these accounts appear unsatisfactory or dubious; nor men to be apprehended upon the mere suggestion of idleness or vagrancy; nor to be confined to certain districts; nor the inhabitants of each district to be made responsible for one another's behaviour; nor passports to be exacted from all persons entering or leaving the kingdom: least of all will they tolerate the appearance of an armed force, or of military law; or suffer the streets and public roads to be guarded and patrolled by soldiers; or, lastly, entrust the police with such discretionary powers, as may make sure of the guilty, however they involve the innocent. These expedients, although arbitrary and rigorous, are many of them effectual; and in proportion as they render the commission or concealment of crimes more difficult, they substract from the necessity of severe punishment. *Great cities* multiply crimes by presenting easier opportunities and more incentives to libertinism, which in low life is commonly the introductory stage to other enormities; by collecting thieves and robbers into the same neighbourhood, which enables them to form communications and confederacies, that increase their art and courage, as well as strength and wickedness; but principally by the refuge they afford to villainy, in the means of concealment, and of subsisting in secrecy, which crowded towns supply to men of every description. These temptations and facilities can only be coun-

counteracted by adding to the number of capital punishments. But a *third* cause, which increases the frequency of capital executions in England, is a defect of the laws in not being provided with any other punishment than that of death, sufficiently terrible to keep offenders in awe. Transportation, which is the sentence second in the order of severity, appears to me to answer the purpose of example very imperfectly; not only because exile is in reality a slight punishment to those, who have neither property, nor friends, nor reputation, nor regular means of subsistence at home; and because their situation becomes little worse by their crime, than it was before they committed it; but because the punishment, whatever it be, is unobserved and unknown. A transported convict may suffer under his sentence, but his sufferings are removed from the view of his countrymen; his misery is unseen; his condition strikes no terror into the minds of those, for whose warning and admonition it was intended. This chasm in the scale of punishment produces also two farther imperfections in the administration of penal justice: the first is, that the same punishment is extended to crimes of very different character and malignancy; the second, that punishments separated by a great interval, are assigned to crimes hardly distinguishable in their guilt and mischief.

The end of punishment is two-fold, *amendment* and *example*. In the first of these, the *reformation* of criminals, little has ever been effected, and little I fear is practicable. From every species of punishment that has hitherto been devised, from imprisonment and exile, from pain and infamy, malefactors return more hardened in their crimes, and more instructed. If there be any thing that shakes the soul of a confirmed villain, it is the expectation of approaching death. The horrors of this situation may cause such a wrench in the mental organs, as to give them a holding turn: and I think it probable, that many of those who are executed, would, if they were delivered at the point of death, retain such a remembrance of their sensations, as might preserve them, unless urged by extreme want, from relapsing into their former crimes. But this is an experiment that from its nature cannot be repeated often.

Of the *reforming* punishments which have not yet been tried, none promises so much success as that of *solitary* imprisonment, or the confinement of criminals in separate apartments. This improvement would augment the terror of the punishment; would seclude the criminal from the society of his fellow prisoners, in which society the worse are sure to corrupt the better; would wean him from the knowledge of his companions, and from the love of that turbulent, precarious life, in which his vices had engaged him; would raise up in him reflections on the folly of his choice, and dispose his mind to such bitter and continued penitence, as might produce a lasting alteration in the principles of his conduct.

As aversion to labour is the cause, from which half of the vices of low life deduce their origin and continuance, punishments ought to be contrived with a view to the conquering of this disposition. Two opposite expedients have been recommended for this purpose; the one solitary confinement with hard labour; the other solitary confinement, with nothing to do. Both expedients seek the same end—to reconcile the idle to a life of industry. The former hopes to effect this by making labour habitual; the latter by making idleness irksome and insupportable: and the preference of one method to the other depends upon the question, whether a man is more likely to betake himself, of his own accord, to work, who has been accustomed to employment, or who has been distressed by the want of it. When jails are once provided for the *separate* confinement of prisoners, which both proposals require, the choice between them may soon be determined by experience. If labour be exacted, I would leave the whole or a portion of the profit to the prisoner's use, and I would debar him from any other provision or supply; that his subsistence, however coarse or penurious, may be proportioned to his diligence, and that he may taste the advantage of industry, together with the toil. I would go farther; I would measure the confinement, not by duration of time, but by quantity of work, in order both to excite industry, and to render it more voluntary. But the principal difficulty remains still; namely, how to dispose of criminals after their enlargement. By a rule of life, which is perhaps too invariably and indiscriminately adhered to, no one will receive a man or woman out of a jail, into any service or employment whatever. This is the common misfortune of public punishments, that they preclude the offender from all honest means of future support.* It seems incumbent upon the state to secure a maintenance to those who are willing to work for it; and yet it is absolutely necessary to divide criminals as far asunder from one another as possible. Whether male prisoners might not, after the term of their confinement was expired, be distributed in the country, detained within certain limits, and employed upon the public roads; and females be remitted to the overseers of country parishes, to be there furnished with dwellings, and with the materials and implements of occupation; whether by these or by what other methods, it may be possible to effect the two purposes of *employment* and *dispersion*, well merits the attention of all who are anxious to perfect the internal regulation of their country.

Torture is applied, either to obtain confessions of guilt, or to exasperate or prolong the pains of death. No bodily punishment, however excruciating or long continued, receives the name of torture, unless it be designed to kill the criminal by a more lingering death, or to extort from him the discovery of some secret, which is supposed to lie concealed in his breast. *The question by torture* appears to be equivocal in its effects; for, since extremity of pain, and not any consciousness of remorse in the mind, produces

---

* Until this inconvenience be remedied, small offences had, perhaps, better go unpunished; I do not mean that the laws should exempt them from punishment, but that private persons should be tender in prosecuting them.

those effects, an innocent man may sink under the torment, as soon as the guilty. The latter has as much to fear from yielding as the former. The instant and almost irresistible desire of relief may draw from one sufferer false accusations of himself or others, as it may sometimes extract the truth out of another. This ambiguity renders the use of torture, as a means of procuring information in criminal proceedings, liable to the risk of grievous and irreparable injustice. For which reason, though recommended by ancient and general example, it has been properly exploded from the mild and cautious system of penal jurisprudence established in this country.

Barbarous spectacles of human agony are justly found fault with, as tending to harden and deprave the public feelings, and to destroy that sympathy with which the sufferings of our fellow creatures ought always to be seen; or if no effect of this kind follow from them, they counteract in some measure their own design, by sinking men's abhorrence of the crime in their commiseration of the criminal. But if a mode of execution could be devised, which would augment the horror of the punishment, without offending or impairing the public sensibility by cruel or unseemly exhibitions of death, it might add something to the efficacy of the example; and by being reserved for a few atrocious crimes, might also enlarge the scale of punishment, an addition to which seems wanting; for, as the matter remains at present, you hang a malefactor for a simple robbery, and can do no more to the villain who has poifoned his father. Somewhat of the fort we have been defcribing was the propofal not long fince fuggefted, of cafting murderers into a den of wild beafts, where they would perifh in a manner dreadful to the imagination, yet concealed from the view.

Infamous punifhments are mifmanaged in this country, with refpect both to the crimes and the criminals. In the firft place, they ought to be confined to offences, which are held in undifputed and univerfal deteftation. To condemn to the pillory the author or editor of a libel againft the ftate, who has rendered himfelf the favourite of a party, if not of the people, by the very act for which he ftands there, is to gratify the offender, and to expofe the laws to mockery and infult. In the fecond place, the delinquents who receive this fentence are for the moft part fuch as have long ceafed either to value reputation, or to fear fhame; of whofe happinefs, and of whofe enjoyments character makes no part. Thus the low minifters of libertinifm, the keepers of bawdy or diforderly houfes. are threatened in vain with a punifhment that affects a fenfe which they have not; that applies folely to the imagination, to the virtue and the pride of human nature. The pillory or any other infamous diftinction might be employed rightly, and with effect, in the punifhment of fome offences of higher life ; as of frauds and peculation in office; of collufions and connivances, by which the public treafury is defrauded; of breaches of truft, of perjury, and fubornation of perjury; of the clandeftine

and

and forbidden fale of places; of flagrant abufes of authority, or neglect of duty; and laftly, of corruption in the exercife of confidential, or judicial offices. In all which the more elevated was the ftation of the criminal, the more fignal and confpicuous would be the triumph of juftice.

The *certainty* of punifhment is of more confequence than the feverity. Criminals do not fo much flatter themfelves with the lenity of the fentence, as with the hope of efcaping. They are not fo apt to compare what they gain by the crime with what they may fuffer from the punifhment, as to encourage themfelves with the chance of concealment or flight. For which reafon a vigilant magiftracy, an accurate police, a proper diftribution of force and intelligence, together with due rewards for the difcovery and apprehenfion of malefactors, and an undeviating impartiality in carrying the laws into execution, contribute more to the reftraint and fuppreffion of crimes, than any violent exacerbations of punifhment. And for the fame reafon, of all contrivances directed to this end, thofe perhaps are moft effectual which facilitate the conviction of criminals. The offence of counterfeiting the coin could not be checked by all the terrors and the utmoft feverity of law, whilft the act of coining was neceffary to be eftablifhed by fpecific proof. The ftatute which made the poffeffion of the implements of coining capital, that is, which conftituted that poffeffion complete evidence of the offender's guilt, was the firft thing

thing that gave force and efficacy to the denunciations of law upon this subject. The statute of James the First, relative to the murder of bastard children, which ordains that the concealment of the birth should be deemed incontestible proof of the charge, though a harsh law, was in like manner with the former, well calculated to put a stop to the crime.

It is upon the principle of this observation, that I apprehend much harm to have been done to the community, by the over-strained scrupulousness, or weak timidity of juries, which demands often such proof of a prisoner's guilt, as the nature and secrecy of his crime scarce possibly admit of; and which holds it the part of a *safe* conscience not to condemn any man, whilst there exists the minutest possibility of his innocence. Any story they may happen to have heard or read, whether real or feigned, in which courts of justice have been misled by presumptions of guilt, is enough, in their minds, to found an acquittal upon, where positive proof is wanting. I do not mean that juries should indulge conjectures, magnify suspicions into proofs, or even that they should weigh probabilities in *gold scales*; but when the preponderation of evidence is so manifest, as to persuade every private understanding of the prisoner's guilt, when it furnishes that degree of credibility, upon which men decide and act in all other doubts, and which experience hath shown that they may decide and act upon with sufficient safety; to reject such proof, from an insinuation of of uncertainty that belongs to all human affairs, and from a general dread left the charge of innocent blood should lie at their doors, is a conduct which, however natural to a mind studious of its own quiet, is authorized by no considerations of rectitude or utility. It counteracts the care and damps the activity of government: it holds out public encouragement to villainy, by confessing the impossibility of bringing villains to justice; and that species of encouragement, which, as hath been just now observed, the minds of such men are most apt to entertain and dwell upon.

There are two popular maxims, which seem to have a considerable influence in producing the injudicious acquittals of which we complain. One is, " that circumstantial evidence falls short of positive proof." This assertion, in the unqualified sense in which it is applied, is not true. A concurrence of well-authenticated circumstances composes a stronger ground of assurance than positive testimony, unconfirmed by circumstances, usually affords. Circumstances cannot lie. The conclusion also which results from them, though deduced by only probable inference, is commonly more to be relied upon than the veracity of an unsupported solitary witness. The danger of being deceived is less; the actual instances of deception are fewer in the one case than the other. What is called positive proof in criminal matters, as where a man swears to the person of the prisoner, and that he actually saw him commit the crime with which he is charged, may be founded in

the

the mistake or perjury of a single witness. Such mistakes, and such perjuries, are not without many examples. Whereas, to impose upon a court of justice, a chain of *circumstantial* evidence in support of a fabricated accusation, requires such a number of false witnesses as seldom meet together; an union also of skill and wickedness which is still more rare; and after all, this species of proof lies much more open to discussion, and is more likely, if false, to be contradicted, or to betray itself by some unforeseen inconsistency, than that direct proof, which being confined within the knowledge of a single person, which appealing to, or standing connected with no external or collateral circumstances, is incapable, by its very simplicity, of being confronted with opposite probabilities.

The other maxim which deserves a similar examination is this, " that it is better that ten guilty persons escape, than " that one innocent man should suffer." If by saying it is *better*, be meant that it is more for the public advantage, the proposition, I think, cannot be maintained. The security of civil life, which is essential to the value and the enjoyment of every blessing it contains, and the interruption of which is followed by universal misery and confusion, is protected chiefly by the dread of punishment. The misfortune of an individual, for such may the sufferings, or even the death of an innocent person be called, when they are occasioned by no evil intention, cannot be placed in competition with this object. I do not contend that the life or safety of the meanest subject ought, in any case, to be
knowingly

knowingly sacrificed. No principle of judicature, no end of punishment can ever require *that*. But when certain rules of adjudication must be pursued, when certain degrees of credibility must be accepted, in order to reach the crimes with which the public are infested; courts of justice should not be deterred from the application of these rules by *every* suspicion of danger, or by the mere possibility of confounding the innocent with the guilty. They ought rather to reflect, that he who falls by a mistaken sentence, may be considered as falling for his country; whilst he suffers under the operation of these rules, by the general effect and tendency of which the welfare of the community is maintained and upheld.

CHAP. X.

OF RELIGIOUS ESTABLISHMENTS, AND OF TOLERATION.

"A Religious establishment is no part of Christianity, it is only the means of inculcating it." Amongst the Jews, the rights and offices, the order, family, and succession of the priesthood were marked out by the authority which declared the law itself. These, therefore, were *parts* of the Jewish religion, as well as the means of transmitting it. Not so with the new institution.—It cannot be proved that any form of church government was laid down in the Christian, as it had been in the Jewish scriptures, with a view of fixing a constitution for succeeding ages; and which constitution, consequently, the disciples of Christianity would, every where, and at all times, by the very law of their religion, be obliged to adopt. Certainly no command for this purpose was delivered by Christ himself; and if it be shewn that the apostles ordained bishops and presbyters amongst their first converts, it must be remembered that deacons also and deaconesses were appointed by them, with functions very dissimilar to any which obtain in the church

church at present. The truth seems to have been, that such offices were at first erected in the Christian church, as the good order, the instruction, and the exigencies of the society at that time required, without any intention, at least, without any declared design, of regulating the appointment, authority, or the distinction of Christian ministers under future circumstances. This reserve, if we may so call it, in the Christian Legislator, is sufficiently accounted for by two considerations: First, that no precise constitution could be framed, which would suit with the condition of Christianity in its primitive state, and with that which it was to assume, when it should be advanced into a national religion. Secondly, that a particular designation of office or authority amongst the ministers of the new religion might have so interfered with the arrangements of civil policy, as to have formed, in some countries, a considerable obstacle to the progress and reception of the religion itself.

The authority therefore of a church establishment is founded in its utility: and whenever, upon this principle, we deliberate concerning the form, propriety, or comparative excellency of different establishments, the single view, under which we ought to consider any one of them, is that of " a scheme of instruction:" the single end we ought to propose by them is, " the preservation and " communication of religious knowledge." Every other idea, and every other end that have been mixed with this, as the making of the church an engine, or even *an ally* of the state; converting it into the means of strengthening or of diffusing influence; or regarding it as a support of regal in opposition to popular forms of government, have served only to debase the institution, and to introduce into it numerous corruptions and abuses.

The notion of a religious establishment comprehends three things; a clergy, or an order of men secluded from other professions to attend upon the offices of religion; a legal provision for the maintenance of the clergy; and the confining of that provision to the teachers of a particular sect of Christianity. If any one of these three things be wanting; if there be no clergy, as amongst the quakers; or, if the clergy have no other provision than what they derive from the voluntary contribution of their hearers; or, if the provision which the laws assign to the support of religion be extended to various sects and denominations of Christians, there exists no national religion or established church, according to the sense which these terms are usually made to convey. He, therefore, who would defend ecclesiastical establishments, must show the separate utility of these three essential parts of their constitution.

1. The question first in order upon the subject, as well as the most fundamental in its importance, is, whether the knowledge and profession of Christianity can be maintained in a country, without a class of men set apart by public authority to the study and teaching of religion, and to the conducting of public worship; and for these purposes

purposes secluded from other employments. I add this last circumstance, because in it consists, as I take it, the substance of the controversy. Now it must be remembered that Christianity is an historical religion, founded in facts which are related to have passed, upon discourses which were held, and letters which were written, in a remote age, and distant country of the world, as well as under a state of life and manners, and during the prevalency of opinions, customs and institutions, very unlike any which are found amongst mankind at present. Moreover, this religion, having been first published in the country of Judea, and being built upon the more ancient religion of the Jews, is necessarily and intimately connected with the sacred writings, with the history and polity of that singular people; to which must be added, that the records of both revelations are preserved in languages which have long ceased to be spoken in any part of the world. Books which come down to us from times so remote, and under so many causes of unavoidable obscurity, cannot, it is evident, be understood without study and preparation. The languages must be learnt. The various writings which these volumes contain must be carefully compared with one another, and with themselves. What remains of cotemporary authors, or of authors connected with the age, the country, or the subject of our scriptures, must be perused and consulted, in order to interpret doubtful forms of speech, and to explain allusions which refer to objects or usages that no longer exist. Above all, the modes of expression, the habits of reasoning

ing and argumentation, which were then in ufe, and to which the difcourfes even of infpired teachers were neceffarily adapted, muft be fufficiently known, and can only be known at all, by a due acquaintance with ancient literature. And, laftly, to eftablifh the genuinenefs and integrity of the canonical fcriptures themfelves, a feries of teftimony, recognizing the notoriety and reception of thefe books, muft be deduced from times near to thofe of their firft publication, down the fucceffion of ages through which they have been tranfmitted to us. The qualifications neceffary for fuch refearches demand, it is confeffed, a degree of leifure, and a kind of education, inconfiftent with the exercife of any other profeffion; but how few are there amongft the clergy, from whom any thing of this fort can be expected? How fmall a proportion of their number, who feem likely either to augment the fund of facred literature, or even to collect what is already known!—To this objection it may be replied, that we fow many feeds to raife one flower. In order to produce a *few* capable of improving and continuing the flock of Chriftian erudition, leifure and opportunity muft be afforded to great numbers. Original knowledge of this kind can never be univerfal; but it is of the utmoft importance, and it is enough, that there be, at all times, found *fome* qualified for fuch enquiries, and in whofe concurring and independent conclufions upon each fubject, the reft of the Chriftian community may fafely confide: whereas, without an order of clergy educated for the purpofe, and led to the profecu-
tion

tion of these studies by the habits, the leisure, and the object of their vocation, it may well be questioned whether the learning itself would not have been lost, by which the records of our faith are interpreted and defended. We contend, therefore, that an order of clergy is necessary to perpetuate the evidences of revelation, and to interpret the obscurities of these ancient writings, in which the religion is contained. But beside this, which forms, no doubt, one design of their institution, the more ordinary offices of public teaching, and of conducting public worship, call for qualifications not usually to be met with amidst the employments of civil life. It has been acknowledged by some, who cannot be suspected of making unnecessary concessions in favour of establishments, " to be barely *possible* that a person who was never " educated for the office should acquit himself with decency " as a public teacher of religion." And that surely must be a very defective policy, which trusts to *possibilities* for success, when provision is to be made for regular and general instruction. Little objection to this argument can be drawn from the example of the quakers, who, it may be said, furnish an experimental proof that the worship and profession of Christianity may be upheld, without a separate clergy. These sectaries every where subsist in conjunction with a regular establishment. They have access to the writings, they profit by the labours of the clergy, in common with other Christians. They participate in that general diffusion of religious knowledge, which the constant teaching of a more regular ministry keeps up in the country:

with such aids, and under such circumstances, the defects of a plan may not be much felt, although the plan itself be altogether unfit for general imitation.

2. If then an order of clergy be necessary, if it be necessary also to seclude them from the employments and profits of other professions, it is evident they ought to be enabled to derive a maintenance from their own. Now this maintenance must either depend upon the voluntary contributions of their hearers, or arise from revenues assigned by authority of law. To the scheme of voluntary contribution there exists this insurmountable objection, that few would ultimately contribute any thing at all. However the zeal of a sect, or the novelty of a change, might support such an experiment for a while, no reliance could be placed upon it as a general and permanent provision. It is at all times a bad constitution which presents temptations of interest in opposition to the duties of religion; or which makes the offices of religion expensive to those who attend upon them; or which allows pretences of conscience to be an excuse for not sharing in a public burthen. If, by declining to frequent religious assemblies, men could save their money, at the same time that they indulged their indolence, and their disinclination to exercises of seriousness and reflection; or if, by dissenting from the national religion, they could be excused from contributing to the support of the ministers of religion, it is to be feared that many would take advantage of the option which was thus imprudently left

left open to them, and that this liberty might finally operate to the decay of virtue, and an irrecoverable forgetfulness of all religion in the country. Is there not too much reason to fear, that, if it were referred to the discretion of each neighbourhood, whether they would maintain amongst them a teacher of religion or not, many districts would remain unprovided with any; that with the difficulties which incumber every measure, requiring the co-operation of numbers, and where each individual of the number has an interest secretly pleading against the success of the measure itself, associations for the support of Christian worship and instruction would neither be numerous nor long continued? The devout and pious might lament in vain the want or the distance of a religious assembly: they could not form or maintain one, without the concurrence of neighbours who felt neither their zeal nor their liberality.

From the difficulty with which congregations would be established and upheld upon the *voluntary* plan, let us carry our thoughts to the condition of those who are to officiate in them. Preaching, in time, would become a mode of begging. With what sincerity, or with what dignity, can a preacher dispense the truths of Christianity, whose thoughts are perpetually solicited to the reflection how he may increase his subscription? His eloquence, if he possess any, resembles rather the exhibition of a player who is computing the profits of his theatre, than the simplicity of a man, who, feeling himself the awful expectations

tions of religion, is seeking to bring others to such a sense and understanding of their duty as may save their souls. Moreover, a little experience of the disposition of the common people will in every country inform us, that it is one thing to edify them in Christian knowledge, and another to gratify their taste for vehement impassioned oratory; that he, not only whose success, but whose subsistence depends upon collecting and pleasing a crowd, must resort to other arts than the acquirement and communication of sober and profitable instruction. For a preacher to be thus at the mercy of his audience, to be obliged to adapt his doctrines to the pleasure of a capricious multitude, to be continually affecting a style and manner neither natural to him, nor agreeable to his judgment, to live in constant bondage to tyrannical and insolent directors, are circumstances so mortifying, not only to the pride of the human heart, but to the virtuous love of independency, that they are rarely submitted to without a sacrifice of principle, and a depravation of character—at least it may be pronounced, that a ministry, so degraded, would soon fall into the lowest hands; for it would be found impossible to engage men of worth and ability, in so precarious and humiliating a profession.

If in deference then to these reasons, it be admitted that a legal provision for the clergy, compulsory upon those who contribute to it, is expedient; the next question will be, whether this provision should be confined to one sect of Christianity, or extended indifferently to all. Now it should be observed, that this question never *can* offer itself where the people are agreed in their religious opinions; and that it never *ought* to arise, where a system may be framed of doctrines and worship wide enough to comprehend their disagreement; and which might satisfy all by uniting all in the articles of their common faith, and in a mode of divine worship, that omits every subject of controversy or offence. Where such a comprehension is practicable, the comprehending religion ought to be made that of the state. But if this be despaired of; if religious opinions exist, not only so various, but so contradictory, as to render it impossible to reconcile them to each other, or to any one confession of faith, rule of discipline, or form of worship; if, consequently, separate congregations and different sects must unavoidably continue in the country: under such circumstances, whether the laws ought to establish one sect in preference to the rest, that is, whether they ought to confer the provision assigned to the maintenance of religion upon the teachers of one system of doctrines alone, becomes a question of necessary discussion and of great importance. And whatever we may determine concerning speculative rights and abstract proprieties, when we set about the framing of an ecclesiastical constitution adapted to real life, and to the actual state of religion in the country, we shall find this question very nearly related to, and principally indeed dependent upon another; namely, " in what way, or by whom ought the ministers " of religion to be *appointed?*" If the species of patronage be retained to which we are accustomed in this country, and which allows private individuals to nominate teachers of religion for districts and congregations to which they are absolute strangers; without some test proposed to the persons nominated, the utmost discordancy of religious opinions might arise between the several teachers and their respective congregations. A popish patron might appoint a priest to say mass to a congregation of protestants; an episcopal clergyman be sent to officiate in a parish of presbyterians; or a presbyterian divine to inveigh against the errors of popery before an audience of papists. The requisition then of subscription, or any other test by which the national religion is guarded, may be considered merely as a restriction upon the exercise of private patronage. The laws speak to the private patron thus: " Of those " whom we have previously pronounced to be fitly qualified " to teach religion, we allow you to select one; but we do " not allow you to decide what religion shall be established " in a particular district of the country; for which decision " you are in no wise fitted by any qualifications which, as a " private patron, you may happen to possess. If it be ne- " cessary that the point be determined for the inhabitants " by any other will than their own, it is surely better that it " should be determined by the deliberate resolution of the " legislature, than by the casual inclination of an individual, " by whom the right is purchased, or to whom it devolves " as a mere secular inheritance." Wheresoever, therefore, this constitution of patronage is adopted, a national religion, or the legal preference of one particular religion to all others, muſt almoſt neceſſarily accompany it. But, ſecondly, let it be ſuppoſed that the appointment of the miniſter of religion was in every pariſh left to the choice of the pariſhioners, might not this choice, we aſk, be ſafely exerciſed without its being limited to the teachers of any particular ſect? The effect of ſuch a liberty muſt be, that a papiſt, or a preſbyterian, a methodiſt, a moravian, or an anabaptiſt, would ſucceſſively gain poſſeſſion of the pulpit, according as a majority of the party happened at each election to prevail. Now with what violence the conflict would upon every vacancy be renewed; what bitter animoſities would be revived, or rather be conſtantly fed and kept alive in the neighbourhood; with what unconquerable averſion the teacher and his religion would be received by the defeated party, may be foreſeen by thoſe who reflect with how much paſſion every diſpute is carried on, in which the name of religion can be made to mix itſelf; much more where the cauſe itſelf is concerned ſo immediately as it would be in this. Or thirdly, if the ſtate appoint the miniſters of religion, this conſtitution will differ little from the eſtabliſhment of a national religion; for the ſtate will, undoubtedly, appoint thoſe, and thoſe alone, whoſe religious opinions, or rather whoſe religious denomination agrees with its own: unleſs it be thought that any thing would be gained to religious liberty by transferring the choice of the national religion from the legiſlature of the country, to the magiſtrate who adminiſters the executive government. The only plan which seems to render the legal maintenance of a clergy practicable, without the legal preference of one sect of Christians to others, is that of an experiment which is said to be attempted or designed in some of the new states of North America. The nature of the plan is thus described. A tax is levied upon the inhabitants for the general support of religion; the collector of the tax goes round with a register in his hand, in which are inserted, at the head of so many distinct columns, the names of the several religious sects, that are professed in the country. The person, who is called upon for the assessment, as soon as he has paid his quota, subscribes his name in which of the columns he pleases: and the amount of what is collected in each column is paid over to the minister of that denomination. In this scheme it is not left to the option of the subject, whether he will contribute, or how much he shall contribute to the maintenance of a Christian ministry; it is only referred to his choice to determine by what sect his contribution shall be received. The above arrangement is, undoubtedly, the best that has been proposed upon this principle: it bears the appearance of liberality and justice; it may contain some solid advantages; nevertheless, it labours under inconveniences which will be found, I think, upon trial, to over-balance all its recommendations. It is scarcely compatible with that, which is the first requisite in an ecclesiastical establishment, the division of the country into parishes of a commodious extent. If the parishes be small, and ministers of every denomination be

stationed

stationed in each, which the plan seems to suppose, the expence of their maintenance will become too burthensome a charge for the country to support. If, to reduce the expence, the districts be enlarged, the place of assembling will oftentimes be too far removed from the residence of the persons who ought to resort to it. Again, the making the pecuniary success of the different teachers of religion to depend upon the number and wealth of their respective followers, would naturally generate strifes, and indecent jealousies amongst them, as well as produce a polemical and proselyting spirit, founded in or mixed with views of private gain, which would both deprave the principles of the clergy, and distract the country with endless contentions.

The argument, then, by which ecclesiastical establishments are defended, proceeds by these steps. The knowledge and profession of Christianity cannot be upheld without a clergy; a clergy cannot be supported without a legal provision; a legal provision for the clergy cannot be constituted without the preference of one sect of Christians to the rest: and the conclusion will be satisfactory in the degree in which the truth of these several propositions can be made out.

If it be deemed expedient to establish a national religion, that is to say, one sect in preference to all others; some *test*, by which the teachers of that sect may be distinguished from the teachers of different sects, appears

pears to be an indepenſible conſequence. The exiſtence of ſuch an eſtabliſhment ſuppoſes it: the very notion of a national religion includes that of a teſt. But this neceſſity, which is real, hath, according to the faſhion of human affairs, furniſhed to almoſt every church a pretence for extending, multiplying and continuing ſuch teſts beyond what the occaſion juſtified. For though ſome purpoſes of order and tranquillity may be anſwered by the eſtabliſhment of creeds and confeſſions, yet they are all at times attended with ſerious inconveniencies. They check enquiry; they violate liberty; they enſnare the conſciences of the clergy by holding out temptations to prevarication; however they may expreſs the perſuaſion, or be accomodated to the controverſies, or to the fears of the age in which they are compoſed, in proceſs of time, and by reaſon of the changes which are wont to take place in the judgment of mankind upon religious ſubjects, they come at length to contradict the actual opinions of the church, whoſe doctrines they profeſs to contain; and they often perpetuate the proſcription of ſects and tenets, from which any danger has long ceaſed to be apprehended.

It may not follow from theſe objections that teſts and ſubſcriptions ought to be aboliſhed, but it follows that they ought to be made as ſimple and eaſy as poſſible; that they ſhould be adapted from time to time to the varying ſentiments and circumſtances of the church in which they are received; and that they ſhould at no time
advance

advance one step farther than some subsisting necessity requires. If, for instance, promises of conformity to the rites, liturgy and offices of the church, be sufficient to prevent confusion and disorder in the celebration of divine worship, then such promises ought to be accepted in the place of stricter subscriptions. If articles of *peace*, as they are called, that is, engagements not to preach certain doctrines, nor to revive certain controversies, would exclude indecent altercations amongst the national clergy, as well as secure to the public teaching of religion as much of uniformity and quiet as is necessary to edification; then confessions of *faith* ought to be converted into articles of peace. In a word, it ought to be held a sufficient reason for relaxing the terms of subscription, or for dropping any or all of the articles to be subscribed, that no *present* necessity requires the strictness which is complained of, or that it should be extended to so many points of doctrine.

The division of the country into districts, and the stationing in each district a teacher of religion, forms the substantial part of every church establishment. The varieties that have been introduced into the government and discipline of different churches are of inferior importance, when compared with this, in which they all agree. Of these œconomical questions, none seems more material than that which has been long agitated in the reformed churches of Christendom, whether a parity amongst the clergy, or a distinction of orders in the ministry, be more conducive to the general ends of the inftitution. In favour of that fyftem which the laws of this country have preferred, we may alledge the following reafons; that it fecures tranquillity and fubordination amongft the clergy themfelves; that it correfponds with the gradations of rank in civil life, and provides for the edification of each rank, by ftationing in each an order of clergy of their own clafs and quality; and laftly, that the fame fund produces more effect, both as an allurement to men of talents to enter into the church, and as a ftimulus to the induftry of thofe who are already in it, when diftributed into prizes of different value, than when divided into equal fhares.

After the ftate has once eftablifhed a particular fyftem of faith as a national religion, a queftion will foon occur, concerning the treatment and toleration of thofe who *diffent* from it. This queftion is properly preceded by another, concerning the right which the civil magiftrate poffeffes to interfere in matters of religion at all: for although this right be acknowledged whilft he is employed folely in providing means of public inftruction, it will probably be difputed, indeed it ever has been, when he proceeds to inflict penalties, to impofe reftraints or incapacities, on the account of religious diftinctions. They who acknowledge no other juft original of civil government, than what is founded in fome ftipulation with its fubjects, are at liberty to contend that the concerns of religion were excepted out of the focial compact; that in an affair which can only be tranfacted between God and a man's own confcience, no commission or authority was ever delegated to the civil magistrate, or could indeed be transferred from the person himself to any other. We, however, who have rejected this theory, because we cannot discover any actual contract between the state and the people, and because we cannot allow an arbitrary fiction to be made the foundation of real rights and of real obligations, find ourselves precluded from this distinction. The reasoning which deduces the authority of civil government from the will of God, and which collects that will from public expediency alone, binds us to the unreserved conclusion, that the jurisdiction of the magistrate is limited by no consideration but that of general utility: in plainer terms, that whatever be the subject to be regulated, it is lawful for him to interfere, whenever his interference, in its general tendency, appears to be conducive to the common interest. There is nothing in the nature of religion, as *such*, which exempts it from the authority of the legislator, when the safety or welfare of the commmunity requires his interposition. It has been said indeed, that religion, pertaining to the interests of a life to come, lies beyond the province of civil government, the office of which is confined to the affairs of this life. But in reply to this objection, it may be observed, that when the laws interfere even in religion, they interfere only with temporals: their effects terminate, their power operates only upon those rights and interests, which confessedly belong to their disposal. The acts of the legislature, the edicts of the prince, the sentence of the judge cannot effect my salvation;

nor do they, without the moſt abſurd arrogance, pretend to any ſuch power: but they may deprive me of liberty, of property, and even of life itſelf on account of my religion; and however I may complain of the injuſtice of the ſentence, by which I am condemned, I cannot alledge, that the magiſtrate has tranſgreſſed the boundaries of his juriſdiction; becauſe the property, the liberty, and the life of the ſubject, *may* be taken away by the authority of the laws, for any reaſon, which, in the judgment of the legiſlature, renders ſuch a meaſure neceſſary to the common welfare. Moreover, as the precepts of religion may regulate all the offices of life, or may be ſo conſtrued as to extend to all, the exemption of religion from the control of human laws might afford a plea, which would exclude civil government from every authority over the conduct of its ſubjects. Religious liberty is like civil liberty, not an immunity from reſtraint, but the being reſtrained by no law, but what in a greater degree conduces to the public welfare.

Still it is right " to obey God rather than man." Nothing that we have ſaid encroaches upon the truth of this ſacred and undiſputed maxim: the right of the magiſtrate to ordain, and the obligation of the ſubject to obey, in matters of religion, may be very different; and will be ſo as often as they flow from oppoſite apprehenſions of the divine will. In affairs that are properly of a civil nature; in " the things that are Cæſar's," this difference ſeldom happens. The law authorizes the act which it enjoins;

revelation being either silent upon the subject, or referring to the laws of the country, or requiring only that men act by some fixed rule, and that this rule be established by competent authority. But when human laws interpose their direction in matters of religion, by dictating, for example, the object or the mode of divine worship; by prohibiting the profession of some articles of faith, and by exacting that of others, they are liable to clash with what private persons believe to be already settled by precepts of revelation, or to contradict what God himself, they think, hath declared to be true. In this case, on whichever side the mistake lies, or whatever plea the state may alledge to justify its edict, the subject can have none to excuse his compliance. The same consideration also points out the distinction, as to the authority of the state between temporals and spirituals. The magistrate is not to be obeyed in one, any more than in the other, where any repugnancy is perceived between his commands, and certain credited manifestations of the divine will; but such repugnancies are much less likely to arise in one case than the other.

When we grant that it is lawful for the magistrate to interfere in religion as often as his interference appears to him to conduce, in its general tendency, to the public happiness; it may be argued from this concession, that since salvation is the highest interest of mankind, and since consequently to advance *that* is to promote the public happiness in the best way, and in the greatest degree, in which it can be promoted; it follows, that it is not only the
right

right, but the duty of every magistrate, invested with supreme power, to enforce upon his subjects the reception of that religion, which he deems most acceptable to God; and to enforce it by such methods as may appear most effectual for the end proposed. A popish king, for example, who should believe that salvation is not attainable out of the precincts of the Romish church, would derive a right, from our principles, (not to say that he would be bound by them) to employ the power with which the constitution entrusted him, and which power, in absolute monarchies, commands the lives and fortunes of every subject of the empire, in reducing his people within that communion. We confess that this consequence is inferred from the principles we have laid down concerning the foundation of civil authority, not without the resemblance of a regular deduction: we confess also that it is a conclusion which it behoves us to dispose of: because if it really follows from our theory of government, the theory itself ought to be given up. Now it will be remembered, that the terms of our proposition are these: " That it is lawful for the magistrate to interfere in the affairs of religion, whenever his interference appears to him to conduce, by its general tendency, to the public happiness." The clause of " general tendency," when this rule comes to be applied, will be found a very significant part of the direction. It obliges the magistrate to reflect, not only whether the religion which he wishes to propagate amongst his subjects, be that which will best secure their eternal welfare; not only, whether the methods he employs

ploys be likely to effectuate the establishment of that religion; but also upon this further question, whether the kind of interference, which he is about to exercise, if it were adopted as a common maxim amongst states and princes, or received as a general rule for the conduct of government in matters of religion, would, upon the whole, and in the mass of instances, in which his example might be imitated, conduce to the furtherance of human salvation. If the magistrate, for example, should think, that, although the application of his power, might in the instance concerning which he deliberates, advance the true religion, and together with it the happiness of his people, yet that the same engine, in other hands, who might assume the right to use it with the like pretensions of reason and authority that he himself alledges, would more frequently shut out truth, and obstruct the means of salvation; he would be bound by this opinion, and still admitting public utility to be the supreme rule of his conduct, to refrain from expedients, which, whatever particular effects *he* may expect from them, are in their general operation dangerous or hurtful. If there be any difficulty in the subject it arises from that, which is the cause of every difficulty in morals, the competition of particular and general consequences—or what is the same thing, the submission of one general rule to another rule which is still more general.

Bearing then in mind that it is the *general* tendency of the measure, or in other words, the effects which would arise

arise from the measure being *generally* adopted, that fixes upon it the character of rectitude or injustice; we proceed to enquire what is the degree and the sort of interference of secular laws in matters of religion, which are likely to be beneficial to the public happiness. There are two maxims which will in a great measure regulate our conclusions upon this head. The first is, that any form of Christianity is better than no religion at all: the second, that of different systems of faith, that is the best, which is the truest. The first of these positions will hardly be disputed, when we reflect, that every sect and modification of Christianity holds out the happiness and misery of another life, as depending chiefly upon the practice of virtue or of vice in this; and that the distinctions of virtue and vice are nearly the same in all. A person who acts under the impression of these hopes and fears, though combined with many errors and superstitions, is more likely to advance both the public happiness and his own, than one who is destitute of all expectation of a future account. The latter proposition is founded in the consideration that the principal importance of religion consists in its influence upon the fate and condition of a future existence. This influence belongs only to that religion which comes from God. A political religion may be framed, which shall embrace the purposes, and describe the duties of political society perfectly well; but if it be not delivered by God, what assurance does it afford, that the decisions of the divine judgment will have any regard to the rules which it contains? By a man who acts with
a view

a view to a future judgment, the authority of a religion is the firſt thing enquired after; a religion which wants authority, with him wants every thing. Since then this authority appertains not to the religion which is moſt commodious, to the religion which is moſt ſublime and efficacious, to the religion which ſuits beſt with the conſtitution, or ſeems moſt calculated to uphold the power and ſtability of civil government but only to that religion which comes from God; we are juſtified in pronouncing the *true* religion, by its very *truth*, and independently of all conſiderations of tendencies, aptneſſes, or any other internal qualities whatever, to be univerſally the beſt.

From the firſt propoſition follows this inference, that when the ſtate enables its ſubjects to learn *ſome* form of Chriſtianity, by diſtributing teachers of a religious ſyſtem throughout the country, and by providing for the maintenance of theſe teachers at the public expence; that is, in fewer terms, when the laws *eſtabliſh* a national religion, they exerciſe a power and an interference, which are likely, in their general tendency, to promote the intereſt of mankind; for even ſuppoſing the ſpecies of Chriſtianity which the laws patronize to be erroneous and corrupt, yet when the option lies between this religion and no religion at all, which would be the conſequence of leaving the people without any public means of inſtruction, or any regular celebration of the offices of Chriſtianity, our propoſition teaches us that the former alternative is conſtantly to be preferred.

But after the right of the magistrate to establish a particular religion has been, upon this principle, admitted; a doubt sometimes presents itself, whether the religion which he ought to establish be that which he himself professes, or that which he observes to prevail amongst the majority of the people. Now when we consider this question with a view to the formation of a general rule upon the subject, which view alone can furnish a just solution of the doubt, it must be assumed to be an equal chance whether of the two religions contain more of truth, that of the magistrate, or that of the people. The chance then that is left to truth being equal upon both suppositions, the remaining consideration will be, from which arrangement more efficacy can be expected—from an order of men appointed to teach the people their own religion, or to convert them to another. In my opinion the advantage lies on the side of the former scheme; and this opinion, if it be assented to, makes it the duty of the magistrate, in the choice of the religion which he establishes, to consult the faith of the nation rather than his own.

The case also of dissenters must be determined by the principles just now stated. *Toleration* is of two kinds: the allowing to dissenters the unmolested profession and exercise of their religion, but with an exclusion from offices of trust and emolument in the state, which is a *partial* toleration; and the admitting them, without distinction, to all the civil privileges and capacities of other citizens, which is a *complete* toleration. The expediency of toleration, and consequently the right of every citizen to demand it, as far as relates to liberty of conscience, and the claim of being protected in the free and safe profession of his religion, is deducible from the *second* of those propositions, which we have delivered as the grounds of our conclusions upon the subject. That proposition asserts truth, and truth in the abstract, to be the supreme perfection of every religion. The advancement, consequently, and discovery of truth, is that end to which all regulations concerning religion ought principally to be adapted. Now every species of intolerance which enjoins suppression and silence; and every species of persecution which enforces such injunctions, is adverse to the progress of truth; forasmuch as it causes that to be fixed by one set of men, at one time, which is much better, and with much more probability of success, left to the independent and progressive enquiries of separate individuals. Truth results from discussion and from controversy: is investigated by the labours and researches of private persons. Whatever therefore prohibits these, obstructs that industry and that liberty, which it is the common interest of mankind to promote. In religion, as in other subjects, truth, if left to itself, will almost always obtain the ascendency. If different religions be professed in the same country, and the minds of men remain unfettered and unawed by intimidations of law, that religion which is founded in maxims of reason and credibility, will gradually gain over the other to it. I do not mean that men will formally renounce their ancient religion, but that they will adopt into it the more rational doctrines, the improvements and discoveries of the neighbouring sect; by which means the worse religion, without the ceremony of a reformation, will insensibly assimulate itself to the better. If popery, for instance, and protestantism were permitted to dwell quietly together, papists might not become protestants, (for the name is commonly the last thing that is changed*) but they would become more enlightened and informed; they would by little and little incorporate into their creed many of the tenets of protestantism, as well as imbibe a portion of its spirit and moderation.

The justice and expediency of toleration we found primarily in its conduciveness to truth, and in the superior value of truth to that of any other quality which a religion can possess: this is the principal argument, but there are some auxiliary considerations too important to be omitted. The confining of the subject to the religion of the state, is a needless violation of natural liberty, and in an instance in which constraint is always grievous. Persecution produces no sincere conviction, nor any real change of opinion; on the contrary it vitiates the public morals by driving men to prevarication, and commonly ends in a general though secret infidelity, by imposing, under the name of revealed religion, systems of doctrine which men cannot believe, and dare not examine: finally,

---

* Would we let the *name* stand, we might often attract men, without their perceiving it, much nearer to ourselves, than, if they did perceive it, they would be willing to come.

it difgraces the character, and wounds the reputation of Chriftianity itfelf, by making it the author of oppreffion, cruelty, and bloodfhed.

Under the idea of religious toleration I include the toleration of all books of ferious argumentation; but I deem it no infringement of religious liberty to reftrain the circulation of ridicule, invective and mockery upon religious fubjects; becaufe this fpecies of writing applies folely to the paffions, weakens the judgment, and contaminates the imagination of its readers; has no tendency whatever to affift either the inveftigation or the impreffion of truth; on the contrary, whilft it ftays not to diftinguifh the character or authority of different religions, it deftroys alike the influence of all.

Concerning the admiffion of diffenters from the eftablifhed religion to offices and employments in the public fervice, which is neceffary to render toleration *complete*, doubts have been entertained with fome appearance of reafon. It is poffible that fuch religious opinions may be holden as are utterly incompatible with the neceffary functions of civil government; and which opinions confequently difqualify thofe who maintain them, from exercifing any fhare in its adminiftration. There have been enthufiafts who held that Chriftianity has abolifhed all diftinction of property, and that fhe enjoins upon her followers a community of goods. With what tolerable propriety could one of this fect be appointed a judge or a magiftrate, magistrate, whose office it is to decide upon questions of private right, and to protect men in the exclusive enjoyment of their property. It would be equally absurd to entrust a military command to a quaker, who believes it to be contrary to the Gospel to take up arms. This is possible; therefore it cannot be laid down as an universal truth, that religion is not in its nature a cause which will justify exclusion from public employments. When we examine, however, the sects of Christianity which actually prevail in the world, we must confess, that with the single exception of refusing to bear arms, we find no tenet in any of them, which incapacitates men for the service of the state. It has indeed been asserted that discordancy of religions, even supposing each religion to be free from any errors that affect the safety or the conduct of government, is enough to render men unfit to act together in public stations. But upon what argument, or upon what experience is this assertion founded? I perceive no reason why men of different religious persuasions may not sit upon the same bench, deliberate in the same council, or fight in the same ranks, as well as men of various or opposite opinions upon any controverted topic of natural philosophy, history, or ethics.

There are two cases in which test laws are wont to be applied, and in which, if in any, they may be defended. One is where two or more religions are contending for establishment; and where there appears no way of putting an end to the contest, but by giving to one religion such a decided

decided superiority in the legislature and government of the country, as to secure it against danger from any other. I own that I should assent to this precaution with many scruples. If the dissenters from the establishment become a majority of the people, the establishment itself ought to be altered or qualified. If there exist amongst the different sects of the country such a parity of numbers, interest and power, as to render the preference of one sect to the rest, and the choice of that sect, a matter of hazardous success, and of doubtful election; some plan similar to that which is meditated in North America, and which we have described in a preceding part of the present chapter, may perhaps suit better with this divided state of public opinions, than any constitution of a national church whatever. In all other situations, the establishment will be strong enough to maintain itself. However, if a test be applicable with justice upon this principle at all, it ought to be applied in regal governments to the chief magistrate himself, whose power might otherwise overthrow or change the established religion of the country, in opposition to the will and sentiments of the people.

The second case of *exclusion*, and in which, I think, the measure is more easily vindicated, is that of a country in which some disaffection to the subsisting government happens to be connected with certain religious distinctions. The state undoubtedly has a right to refuse its power and its confidence to those who seek its destruction. Wherefore, if the generality of any religious sect entertain dispositions hostile to the constitution, and if government have no other way of knowing its enemies than by the religion they profess, the professors of that religion may justly be excluded from offices of trust and authority. But even *here* it should be observed, that it is not against the religion that government shuts its doors, but against those political principles, which, however independent they may be of any article of religious faith, the members of that communion are found in fact to hold. Nor would the legislator make religious tenets the test of men's inclinations towards the state, if he could discover any other that was equally certain and notorious. Thus if the members of the Romish church, for the most part adhere to the interests, or maintain the right of a foreign pretender to the crown of these kingdoms; and if there be no way of distinguishing those who do from those who do not retain such dangerous prejudices; government is well warranted in fencing out the whole sect from situations of trust and power. But even in this example, it is not to popery that the laws object, but to popery as the mark of jacobitism; an equivocal indeed and fallacious mark, but the best, and perhaps the only one that can be devised. But then it should be remembered, that as the connection between popery and jacobitism, which is the sole cause of suspicion, and the sole justification of those severe and jealous laws which have been enacted against the professors of that religion, was accidental in its origin, so probably it will be temporary in its duration; and that these restrictions ought not to continue one day longer,

longer, than some visible danger renders them necessary to the preservation of public tranquillity.

After all, it may be asked, why should not the legislator direct his test against the political principles themselves which he wishes to exclude, rather than encounter them through the medium of religious tenets, the only crime and the only danger of which consist in their presumed alliance with the former? Why, for example, should a man be required to renounce transubstantiation, before he be admitted to an office in the state, when it might seem to be sufficient that he abjure the pretender? There are but two answers that can be given to the objection which this question contains: first, that it is not opinions which the laws fear, so much as inclinations, and that political inclinations are not so easily detected by the affirmation or denial of any abstract proposition in politics, as by the discovery of the religious creed with which they are wont to be united: secondly, that when men renounce their religion, they commonly quit all connection with the members of the church which they have left; that church no longer expecting assistance or friendship from them: whereas particular persons might insinuate themselves into offices of trust and authority, by subscribing political assertions, and yet retain their predilection for the interests of the religious sect to which they continued to belong. By which means government would sometimes find, though it could not accuse the individual, whom it had received into its service, of disaffection to the civil establishment, yet that, through him, it had communicated the aid and influence of a powerful station to a party who were hostile to the constitution. These answers, however, we propose, rather than defend. The measure certainly cannot be defended at all, except where the suspected union between certain obnoxious principles in politics, and certain tenets in religion, is nearly universal: in which case it makes little difference to the subscriber, whether the test be religious or political; and the state is somewhat better secured by the one than the other.

The result of our examination of those general tendencies, by which every interference of civil government in matters of religion ought to be tried, is this: " That a " comprehensive national religion, guarded by a few arti- " cles of peace and conformity, together with a legal pro- " vision for the clergy of that religion; and with a *complete* " toleration of all dissenters from the established church, " without any other limitation or exception, than what arises " from the conjunction of dangerous political dispositions " with certain religious tenets, appears to be, not only the " most just and liberal, but the wisest and safest system, which " a state can adopt: inasmuch as it unites the several per- " fections which a religious constitution ought to aim at— " liberty of conscience, with means of instruction; the " progress of truth, with the peace of society; the right " of private judgment, with the care of the public safety."

CHAP. XI.

OF POPULATION AND PROVISION; AND OF AGRICULTURE AND COMMERCE, AS SUBSERVIENT THERETO.

THE final view of all rational politics is to produce the greatest quantity of happiness in a given tract of country. The riches, strength, and glory of nations, the topics which history celebrates, and which alone almost engage the praises, and possess the admiration of mankind, have no value farther than as they contribute to this end. When they interfere with it, they are evils, and not the less real for the splendour that surrounds them.

Secondly, although we speak of communities as of sentient beings; although we ascribe to them happiness and misery, desires, interests and passions, nothing really exists or feels but *individuals*. The happiness of a people is made up of the happiness of single persons; and the quantity of happiness can only be augmented by increasing the number of the percipients, or the pleasures of their perceptions.

Thirdly, notwithstanding that diversity of condition, especially different degrees of plenty, freedom, and security, greatly vary the quantity of happiness enjoyed by the same number of individuals; and notwithstanding that extreme cases may be found, of human beings so galled by the rigours of slavery, that the increase of numbers is only the amplification of misery; yet, within certain limits, and within those limits to which civil life is diversified, under the temperate governments that obtain in Europe, it may be affirmed, I think, with certainty, that the quantity of happiness produced in any given district, *so far* depends upon the number of inhabitants, that, in comparing adjoining periods, in the same country, the collective happiness will be nearly in the exact proportion of the numbers, that is, twice the number of inhabitants will produce double the quantity of happiness; in distant periods, and different countries, under great changes or great dissimilitude of civil condition, although the proportion of enjoyment may fall much short of that of the numbers, yet still, any considerable excess of numbers will usually carry with it a preponderation of happiness; that at least, it may, and ought to be assumed in all political deliberations, that a larger portion of happiness is enjoyed amongst *ten* persons, possessing the means of healthy subsistence,

than

than can be produced by *five* persons, under every advantage of power, affluence, and luxury.

From these principles it follows, that the quantity of happiness in a given district, although it is possible it may be increased, the number of inhabitants remaining the same, is chiefly and most naturally affected by alteration of the numbers: that, consequently, the decay of population is the greatest evil that a state can suffer; and the improvement of it the object which ought, in all countries, to be aimed at, in preference to every other political purpose whatsoever.

The importance of population, and the superiority of *it* to every other national advantage, are points necessary to be inculcated, and to be well understood; inasmuch as false estimates, or fantastic notions of national grandeur, are perpetually drawing the attention of statesmen and legislators from the care of this, which is, at all times, the true and absolute interest of a country: for which reason, we have stated these points with unusual formality. We will confess, however, that a competition can seldom arise between the advancement of population and any measure of sober utility; because, in the ordinary progress of human affairs, whatever, in any way, contributes to make a people happier, tends to render them more numerous.

In the fecundity of the human, as of every other species of animals, nature has provided for an indefinite multiplication.

cation. Mankind have increased to their present number from a single pair: the offspring of early marriages, in the ordinary course of procreation, do more than replace the parents: in countries, and under circumstances very favourable to subsistence, the population has been doubled in the space of twenty years: the havock occasioned by wars, earthquakes, famine, or pestilence, is usually repaired in a short time. These indications sufficiently demonstrate the tendency of nature in the human species to a continual increase of its numbers. It becomes therefore a question that may reasonably be propounded, what are the causes which confine or check the natural progress of this multiplication? And the answer which first presents itself to the thoughts of the enquirer is, that the population of a country must stop when the country can maintain no more, that is, when the inhabitants are already so numerous as to exhaust all the provision which the soil can be made to produce. This however, though an insuperable bar, will seldom be found to be *that* which actually checks the progress of population in any country of the world; because the number of the people have seldom, in any country, arrived at this limit, or even approached to it. The fertility of the ground, in temperate regions, is capable of being improved by cultivation to an extent which is unknown; much, however, beyond the state of improvement in any country in Europe. In our own, which holds almost the first place in the knowledge and encouragement of agriculture, let it only be supposed that every field in England of the same original

quality

quality with those in the neighbourhood of the metropolis, and consequently capable of the same fertility, were by a like management made to yield an equal produce, and it may be asserted, I believe, with truth, that the quantity of human provision raised in the island would be increased fivefold. The two principles, therefore, upon which population seems primarily to depend, the fecundity of the species, and the capacity of the soil, would in most, perhaps in all countries, enable it to proceed much farther than it has yet advanced. The number of marriageable women, who, in each country, remain unmarried, afford a computation how much the agency of nature in the diffusion of human life is cramped and contracted; and the quantity of waste, neglected, or mismanaged surface, together with a comparison, like the preceding, of the crops raised from the soil in the neighbourhood of populous cities, and under a perfect state of cultivation, with those, which lands of equal or superior quality yield in different situations, will show in what proportion the indigenous productions of the earth are capable of being farther augmented.

The fundamental proposition upon the subject of *population*, which must guide every endeavour to improve it, and from which every conclusion concerning it may be deduced, is this: " Wherever the commerce between
" the sexes is regulated by marriage, and a provision for
" that mode of subsistence, to which each class of the com-
" munity is accustomed, can be procured with ease and
" certainty,

"certainty, there the number of the people will increase;
"and the rapidity, as well as the extent of the increase,
"will be proportioned to the degree in which these causes
"exist."

This proposition we will draw out into the several principles which it contains.

1. First, the proposition asserts the "necessity of confining the intercourse of the sexes to the marriage union." It is only in the marriage union that this intercourse is sufficiently prolific. Beside which, family establishments alone are fitted to perpetuate a succession of generations. The offspring of a vague and promiscuous concubinage are not only few, and liable to perish by neglect, but are seldom prepared for, or introduced into situations suited to the raising of families of their own. Hence the advantages of marriage. Now nature, in the constitution of the sexes, has provided a stimulus which will infallibly secure the frequency of marriages, with all their beneficial effects upon the state of population, provided the male part of the species be prohibited from irregular gratifications. This impulse, which is sufficient to surmount almost every impediment to marriage, will operate in proportion to the difficulty, expence, danger, or infamy, the sense of guilt, or the fear of punishment, which attend licentious indulgencies. Wherefore, in countries in which subsistence is become scarce, it behoves the state to watch over the
public

AGRICULTURE, AND COMMERCE.

public morals with increased solicitude; for nothing but the instinct of nature, under the restraint of chastity, will induce men to undertake the labour, or consent to the sacrifice of personal liberty and indulgence, which the support of a family, in such circumstances, requires.

II. The second requisite which the proposition states, as necessary to the success of population, is, "The ease "and certainty with which a provision can be procured for "that mode of subsistence to which each class of the com- "munity is accustomed." It is not enough that men's *natural* wants be supplied, that a provision adequate to the actual exigencies of human life be attainable: habitual superfluities become real wants; opinion and fashion convert articles of ornament and luxury into necessaries of life. And it must not be expected from men in general, at least in the present relaxed state of morals and discipline, that they will enter into marriages which degrade their condition, reduce their mode of living, deprive them of the accommodations to which they have been accustomed, or even of those ornaments or appendages of rank and station, which they have been taught to regard as belonging to their birth, or class, or profession, or place in society. The same consideration, namely, a view to their *accustomed* mode of life, which is so apparent in the superior orders of the people, has no less influence upon those ranks which compose the mass of the community. The kind and quality of food and liquor, the species of habitation, furniture, and cloathing, to which the common people of each country are habituated, must be attainable with ease and certainty before marriages will be sufficiently early and general, to carry the progress of population to its just extent. It is in vain to alledge, that a more simple diet, ruder habitations, or coarser apparel, would be sufficient for the purposes of life and health, or even of physical ease and pleasure. Men will not marry with this encouragement. For instance, when the common people of a country are accustomed to eat a large proportion of animal food, to drink wine, spirits, or beer, to wear shoes and stockings, to dwell in stone houses, they will not marry to live in clay cottages, upon roots and milk, with no other cloathing than skins, or what is necessary to defend the trunk of the body from the effects of cold, although these last may be all that the sustentation of life and health requires, or that even contribute much to animal comfort and enjoyment.

The ease then, and certainty, with which the means can be procured, not barely of subsistence, but of that mode of subsisting, which custom hath in each country established, form the point upon which the state and progress of population chiefly depend. Now, there are three causes which evidently regulate this point. The mode itself of subsisting which prevails in the country; the quantity of provision suited to that mode of subsistence, which is either raised in the country, or imported into it; and lastly, the distribution of that provision.

These three caufes merit diftinct confiderations.

I. The mode of living which actually obtains in a country. In China, where the inhabitants frequent the fea fhore, and fubfift in a great meafure upon fifh, the population is defcribed to be exceffive. This peculiarity arifes, not probably from any civil advantages, any care or policy, any particular conftitution, or fuperior wifdom of government, but fimply from hence, that the fpecies of food, to which cuftom hath reconciled the defires and inclinations of the inhabitants, is that which, of all others, is procured in the greateft abundance, with the moft eafe, and ftands in need of the leaft preparation. The natives of Indoftan, being confined, by the laws of their religion, to the ufe of vegetable food, and requiring little except rice, which the country produces in plentiful crops; and food, in warm climates, compofing the only want of life; thefe countries are populous, under all the injuries of a defpotic, and the agitations of an unfettled government. If any revolution, or what would be called perhaps refinement of manners, fhould generate in thefe people a tafte for the flefh of animals, fimilar to what prevails amongft the Arabian hordes; fhould introduce flocks and herds into grounds which are now covered with corn; fhould teach them to account a certain portion of this fpecies of food amongft the neceffaries of life; the population, from this fingle change, would fuffer in a few years a great diminution: and this diminution would follow, in fpite of every effort of the laws, or even of any improvement that might take place in their civil condition. In Ireland, the simplicity of living alone maintains a considerable degree of population, under great defects of police, industry, and commerce.

Under this head, and from a view of these considerations, may be understood the true evil and proper danger of *luxury*. Luxury, as it quickens circulation, as it supplies employment, and promotes industry, assists population. But then, there is another consequence attending it, which counteracts, and often overbalances these advantages. When, by introducing more superfluities into general reception, luxury has rendered the usual accommodations of life more expensive, artificial, and elaborate, the difficulty of maintaining a family, conformably with the established mode of living, becomes greater, and what each man has to spare from his personal consumption, proportionably less: the effect of which is, that marriages grow less frequent, agreeably to the maxim above laid down, and which must be remembered as the foundation of all our reasoning upon the subject, that men will not marry to *sink* their place or condition in society, or to forego those indulgencies, which their own habits, or what they observe amongst their equals, have rendered necessary to their satisfaction. This principle is applicable to every article of diet and dress, to houses, furniture, attendance; and this effect will be felt in every class of the community. For instance, the custom of wearing broad cloth and fine linen repays the shepherd and flax-

flax-grower, feeds the manufacturer, enriches the merchant, gives not only support, but existence to multitudes of families: hitherto, therefore, the effects are beneficial: and were these the only effects, such elegancies, or, if you please to call them so, such luxuries, could not be too universal. But here follows the mischief; when once fashion hath annexed the use of these articles of dress to any certain class, to the middling ranks, for example, of the community, each individual of that rank finds them to be *necessaries* of life; that is, finds himself obliged to comply with the example of his equals, and to maintain that appearance which the custom of society requires. This obligation creates such a demand upon his income, and withal adds so much to the cost and burthen of a family, as to put it out of his power to marry, with the prospect of continuing his habits, or of maintaining his place and situation in the world. We see, in this description, the cause which induces men to waste their lives in a barren celibacy; and this cause, which impairs the very source of population, is justly placed to the account of luxury.

It appears then, that *luxury*, considered with a view to population, acts by two opposite effects; and it seems probable, that there exists a point in the scale, to which luxury may ascend, or, to which the wants of mankind may be multiplied, with advantage to the community, and beyond which the prejudicial effects begin to preponderate. The determination of this point, though it assume the form of an arithmetical problem, depends upon circumstances too numerous, intricate, and undefined, to admit of a precise solution. However, from what has been observed concerning the tendency of luxury to diminish marriages, in which tendency, the evil of it resides, the following general conclusions may be established.

1st. That, of different kinds of luxury, those are the most innocent, which afford employment to the greatest number of artists and manufacturers; or those, in other words, in which the price of the work bears the greatest proportion to that of the raw material. Thus, luxury in dress or furniture is universally preferable to luxury in eating, because the articles which constitute the one, are more the production of human art and industry, than those which supply the other.

2dly. That it is the *diffusion*, rather than the *degree* of luxury, which is to be dreaded as a national evil. The mischief of luxury consists, as we have seen, in the obstruction that it forms to marriage. Now, it is only a small part of the people that the higher ranks in any country compose; for which reason, the facility, or the difficulty of supporting the expence of *their* station, and the consequent increase or diminution of marriages amongst *them*, will influence the state of population but little. So long as the prevalency of luxury is confined to a few of elevated rank, much of the benefit is felt,
and

and little of the inconveniency. But when the imitation of the same manners descends, as it always will do, into the mass of the people; when it advances the requisites of living beyond what it adds to men's abilities to purchase them, then it is, that luxury checks the formation of families, in a degree that ought to alarm the public fears.

3dly. That the condition most favourable to population is that of a laborious frugal people, ministring to the demands of an opulent, luxurious nation; because this situation, whilst it leaves them every advantage of luxury, exempts them from the evils which naturally accompany its admission into any country.

II. Next to the mode of living, we are to consider " The quantity of provision suited to that mode, which " is either raised in the country, or imported into it." For this is the order in which we assigned the causes of population, and undertook to treat of them. Now, if we measure the quantity of provision by the number of human bodies it will support in due health and vigour, this quantity, the extent and quality of the soil from which it is raised being given, will depend greatly upon the *kind*. For instance, a piece of ground capable of supplying animal food sufficient for the subsistence of ten persons, would sustain, at least, the double of that number with grain, roots, and milk. The first resource of savage life is in the flesh of wild animals; hence the numbers amongst savage nations,

compared

compared with the tract of country which they occupy, are universally small, because this species of provision is, of all others, supplied in the slenderest proportion. The next step was the invention of pasturage, or the rearing of flocks and herds of tame animals. This alteration added to the stock of provision much: but the last and principal improvement was to follow, namely, tillage, or the artificial production of corn, esculent plants, and roots. This discovery, whilst it changed the quality of human food, augmented the quantity in a vast proportion. So far as the state of population is governed and limited by the quantity of provision, perhaps, there is no single cause that affects it so powerfully, as the kind and quality of food, which chance or usage hath introduced into a country. In England, notwithstanding the produce of the soil has been, of late, considerably increased, by the inclosure of wastes, and the adoption, in many places, of a more successful husbandry, yet, we do not observe a corresponding addition to the number of inhabitants; the reason of which appears to me to be the more general consumption of animal food amongst us. Many ranks of people, whose ordinary diet was, in the last century, prepared almost entirely from milk, roots, and vegetables, now require every day a considerable portion of the flesh of animals. Hence, a great part of the richest lands of the country are converted to pasturage. Much also of the bread corn, which went directly to the nourishment of human bodies, now only contributes to it, by fattening the flesh of sheep and oxen.

oxen. The mass and volume of provisions are hereby diminished; and what is gained in the melioration of the soil is lost in the quality of the produce. This consideration teaches us, that tillage, as an object of national care and encouragement, is universally preferable to pasturage; because, the *kind* of provision, which it yields, goes much farther in the sustentation of human life. Tillage is also recommended by this additional advantage, that it affords employment to a much more numerous peasantry. Indeed, pasturage seems to be the art of a nation, either imperfectly civilized, as are many of the tribes which cultivate it in the internal parts of Asia; or of a nation, like Spain, declining from its summit by luxury and inactivity.

The kind and quality of provision, together with the extent and capacity of the soil, from which it is raised, being the same; the quantity procured will principally depend upon two circumstances, the *ability* of the occupier, and the *encouragement* which he receives. The greatest misfortune of a country is an indigent tenantry. Whatever be the native advantages of the soil, or even the skill and industry of the occupier, the want of a sufficient capital confines every plan, as well as cripples and weakens every operation of husbandry. This evil is felt, where agriculture is accounted a servile or mean employment: where farms are extremely subdivided, and badly furnished with habitations; where leases are unknown, or are of short or precarious duration. With respect to the

encouragement

encouragement of hufbandry; in this, as in every other employment, the true reward of induftry is in the price and fale of the produce. The exclufive right to the produce is the only incitement which acts conftantly and univerfally; the only fpring which keeps human labour in motion. All therefore that the laws can do, is to fecure this right to the occupier of the ground, that is, to conftitute fuch a fyftem of tenure, that the full and entire advantage of every improvement go to the benefit of the improver; that every man work for himfelf, and not for another; and that no one fhare in the profit who does not affift in the production. By the *occupier* I here mean, not fo much the perfon who performs the work, as him who procures the labour and directs the management; and I confider the whole profit as *received* by the occupier, when the occupier is benefited by the whole value of what is produced, which is the cafe with the tenant who pays a fixed rent for the ufe of land, no lefs than with the proprietor who holds it as his own. The one has the fame intereft in the produce, and in the advantage of every improvement, as the other. Likewife the proprietor, though he grant out his eftate to farm, may be confidered as the *occupier*, in fo much as he regulates the occupation by the choice, fuperintendency, and encouragement of his tenants, by the difpofition of his lands, by erecting buildings, providing accommodations, by prefcribing conditions, or fupplying implements and materials of improvement; and is entitled, by the rule of public expediency above-mentioned, to receive,

receive, in the advance of his rent, a share of the benefit which arises from the encreased produce of his estate. The violation of this fundamental maxim of agrarian policy constitutes the chief objection to the holding of lands by the state, by the king, by corporate bodies, by private persons in right of their offices or benefices. The inconveniency to the public arises not so much from the unalienable quality of lands thus holden in perpetuity, as from hence, that proprietors of this description seldom contribute much either of attention or expence to the cultivation of their estates, yet claim, by the rent, a share in the profit of every improvement that is made upon them. This complaint can only be obviated by " long leases at a fixed rent," which convey a large portion of the interest to those who actually conduct the cultivation. The same objection is applicable to the holding of lands by foreign proprietors, and in some degree, to estates of too great extent being placed in the same hands.

III. Beside the *production* of provision, there remains to be considered the DISTRIBUTION.—It is in vain that provisions abound in the country, unless I be able to obtain a share of them. This reflexion belongs to every individual. The plenty of provision produced, the quantity of the public stock, affords subsistence to individuals, and encouragement to the formation of families, only in proportion as it is *distributed*, that is, in proportion as these individuals are allowed to draw from it a supply of their own wants. The *distribution*, therefore, becomes of equal consequence to population with the *production*. Now, there is but one principle of distribution that can ever become universal, namely, the principle of " exchange;" or in other words, that every man have something to give in return for what he wants. Bounty, however it may come in aid of another principle, however it may occasionally qualify the rigour, or supply the imperfection of an established rule of distribution, can never itself become that rule or principle; because men will not work to give the produce of their labour away. Moreover, the only equivalents that can be offered in exchange for provision are *power* and *labour*. All property is *power*. What we call property in land is the power to use it, and to exclude others from the use. Money is the representative of *power*, because it is convertible into power: the value of it consists in its faculty of procuring *power* over things and persons. But *power* which results from civil conventions, and of this kind are what we call a man's fortune or estate, is necessarily confined to a few, and is withal soon exhausted: whereas the capacity of *labour* is every man's natural possession, and composes a constant and renewing fund. The hire, therefore, or produce of personal industry is that, which the bulk of every community must bring to market, in exchange for the means of subsistence; in other words, employment must, in every country, be the medium of distribution, and the source of supply to individuals. But when we consider the *production* and *distribution* of provision, as distinct from, and independent of each other; when

supposing

suppofing the fame quantity to be produced, we enquire in what way, or according to what rule, it may be *diftributed*, we are led to a conception of the fubject not at all agreeable to truth and reality; for, in truth and reality, though provifion muft be produced, before it be diftributed, yet the production depends, in a great meafure upon the diftribution. The quantity of provifion raifed out of the ground, fo far as the raifing of it requires human art or labour, will evidently be regulated by the demand; the demand, or, in other words, the price and fale, being that which alone rewards the care, or excites the diligence of the hufbandman. But the fale of provifion depends upon the number, not of thofe who want, but of thofe who have fomething to offer in return for what they want; not of thofe who would confume, but of thofe who can buy: that is, upon the number of thofe who have the fruits of fome other kind of induftry to tender in exchange for what they ftand in need of from the productions of the foil.

We fee, therefore, the connection between population and *employment*. Employment affects population " directly," as it affords the only medium of diftribution, by which individuals can obtain from the common ftock a fupply for the wants of their families: it affects population " indirectly," as it augments the ftock itfelf of provifion, in the only way by which the production of it can be effectually encouraged, by furnifhing purchafers. No man can purchafe without an equivalent, and that equivalent,

by

by the generality of the people, must, in every country, be derived from employment.

And upon this basis is founded the public benefit of *trade*, that is to say, its subserviency to population, in which its only real utility consists. Of that industry and of those arts and branches of trade, which are employed in the production, conveyance, and preparation of any principal species of human food, as of the business of the husbandman, the butcher, baker, brewer, corn-merchant, &c. we aknowledge the necessity: likewise of those manufactures which furnish us with warm cloathing, convenient habitations, domestic utensils, as of the weaver, taylor, smith, carpenter, &c. we perceive, (in climates, however, like ours, removed at a distance from the sun,) the conduciveness to population, by their rendering human life more healthy, vigorous, and comfortable. But not one half of the occupations, which compose the trade of Europe, fall within either of these descriptions. Perhaps two thirds of the manufacturers of England are employed upon articles of confessed luxury, ornament, or splendour; in the superfluous embellishment of some articles which are useful in their kind, or upon others which have no conceivable use or value, but what is founded in caprice or fashion. What can be less necessary, or less connected with the sustentation of human life, than the whole produce of the silk, lace, and plate manufactory? yet what multitudes labour in the different branches of these arts! What can be imagined

gined more capricious than the fondness for tobacco and snuff? yet, how many various occupations, and how many thousands in each, are set at work, in administring to this frivolous gratification! Concerning trades of this kind, and this kind comprehends more than half of the trades that are exercised, it may fairly be asked, " how, " since they add nothing to the stock of provision, do " they tend to increase the number of the people." We are taught to say of trade, " that it maintains multitudes;" but by what means does it *maintain* them, when it produces nothing upon which the support of human life depends?—In like manner with respect to foreign commerce; of that merchandize which brings the necessaries of life into a country, which imports, for example, corn, or cattle, or cloth or fuel, we allow the tendency to advance population, because it encreases the stock of provision, by which the people are subsisted. But this effect of foreign commerce is so little seen in our own country, that, I believe, it may be affirmed of Great Britain, what Bishop *Berkley* said of a neighbouring island, that if it was encompassed with a wall of brass fifty cubits high, the country might maintain the same number of inhabitants, that find subsistence in it at present; and that every necessary, and even every real comfort and accommodation of human life might be supplied in as great abundance as they are now. Here, therefore, as before, we may fairly ask, by what operation it is, that foreign commerce, which brings into the country no one article of human subsistence, promotes the multiplication of human life?

The answer to this enquiry will be contained in the discussion of another; viz.

Since the soil will maintain many more than it can employ, what must be done, supposing the country to be full, with the remainder of the inhabitants? They, who, by the rules of partition, (and some such must be established in every country,) are entitled to the land; and they who, by their labour upon the soil, acquire a right in its produce, will not part with their property for nothing; or rather, they will no longer raise from the soil what they can neither use themselves, nor exchange for what they want. Or, lastly, if these were willing to distribute what they could spare of the provision which the ground yielded, to others who had no share or concern in the property or cultivation of it, yet still, the must enormous mischiefs would ensue from great numbers remaining unemployed. The idleness of one half of the community would overwhelm the whole with confusion and disorder. One only way presents itself of removing the difficulty which this question states, and which is simply this; that they, whose work is not wanted, nor can be employed in the raising of provision out of the ground, convert their hands and ingenuity to the fabrication of articles which may gratify and requite those who are so employed, or who, by the division of lands

lands in the country, are entitled to the exclusive possession of certain parts of them. By this contrivance all things proceed well. The occupier of the ground raises from it the utmost that he can procure, because he is repaid for what he can spare by something else, which he wants, or with which he is pleased: the artist and manufacturer, though he have neither any property in the soil, nor any concern in its cultivation, is regularly supplied with the produce, because he gives, in exchange for what he stands in need of, something, upon which the receiver places an equal value: and the community is kept quiet, whilst both sides are engaged in their respective occupations.

It appears then, that the business of one half of mankind is, to set the other half at work; that is, to provide articles, which, by tempting the desires, may stimulate the industry, and call forth the activity of those, upon the exertion of whose industry, and the application of whose faculties, the production of human provision depends. A certain portion only of human labour is, or can be *productive;* the rest is *instrumental*—both equally necessary, though the one have no other object than to excite the other. It appears also, that it signifies nothing as to the main purpose of trade, how superfluous the articles which it furnishes are; whether the want of them be real or imaginary, founded in nature, or in opinion, in fashion, habit, or emulation: it is enough that they be actually desired and sought after. Flourishing cities are raised and supported by trading in tobacco: populous towns subsist by the manufactory of ribbons. A watch may be a very unneceffary appendage to the drefs of a peafant, yet if the peafant will till the ground in order to obtain a watch, the true defign of trade is anfwered; and the watchmaker, whilft he polifhes the cafe, or files the wheels of his machine, is contributing to the production of corn as effectually, though not fo directly, as if he handled the fpade, or held the plough. The ufe of tobacco has been mentioned already as an acknowledged fuperfluity, and as affording a remarkable example of the caprice of human appetite: yet, if the fifherman will ply his nets, or the mariner fetch rice from foreign countries, in order to procure to himfelf this indulgence, the market is fupplied with two important articles of provifion, by the inftrumentality of a merchandize, which has no other apparent ufe, than the gratification of a vitiated palate.

But it may come to pafs that the hufbandman, land-owner, or whoever he be, that is entitled to the produce of the foil, will no longer exchange it for what the manufacturer has to offer. He is already fupplied to the extent of his defires. For inftance, he wants no more cloth; he will no longer therefore give the weaver corn, in return for the produce of his looms; but he would readily give it for tea, or for wine. When the weaver finds this to be the cafe, he has nothing to do but to fend his cloth abroad in exchange for tea or for wine, which he may barter for that provifion, which the offer of his cloth will no longer procure. The circulation is thus revived; and the benefit of the difcovery is, that whereas the number

number of weavers, who could find subsistence from their employment, was before limited by the consumption of cloth in the country, that number is now augmented, in proportion to the demand for tea and for wine. This is the principle of *foreign* commerce. In the magnitude and complexity of the machine, the principle of motion is sometimes lost or unobserved; but it is always simple and the same, to whatever extent it may be diversified and enlarged in its operation.

The effect of trade upon agriculture, the process of which we have been endeavouring to describe, is visible in the neighbourhood of trading towns, and in those districts which carry on a communication with the markets of trading towns. The husbandmen are busy and skilful; the peasantry laborious; the lands are managed to the best advantage, and double the quantity of corn or herbage, (articles which are ultimately converted into human provision,) raised from it, of what the same soil yields in remoter and more neglected parts of the country. Wherever a thriving manufactory finds means to establish itself, a new vegetation springs up around it. I believe it is true that agriculture never arrives at any considerable, much less at its highest degree of perfection, where it is not connected with trade, that is, where the demand for the produce is not increased by the consumption of trading cities. *Let* it be remembered then, that agriculture is the immediate source of human provision; that trade conduces to the production of provision only as it promotes agriculture; that the whole fyftem of commerce, vaft and various as it is, hath no other public importance than its fubferviency to this end.

We return to the propofition we laid down, "that "employment univerfally promotes population." From this propofition it follows, that the comparative utility of different branches of national commerce is meafured by the number which each branch *employs*. Upon which principle a fcale may eafily be conftructed, which fhall affign to the feveral kinds and divifions of foreign trade, their refpective degrees of public importance. In this fcale the *firft* place belongs to the exchange of wrought goods for raw materials, as of broad cloth for raw filk; cutlery for wool; clocks or watches for iron, flax, or furs; becaufe this traffic provides a market for the labour that has already been expended, at the fame time that it fupplies materials for new induftry. Population always flourifhes where this fpecies of commerce obtains to any confiderable degree. It is the caufe of employment, or the certain indication. As it takes off the manufactures of the country, it promotes employment; as it brings in raw materials, it fuppofes the exiftence of manufactories in the country, and a demand for the article when manufactured. The *fecond* place is due to that commerce, which barters one fpecies of wrought goods for another, as ftuffs for calicoes, fuftians for cambrics, leather for paper; or wrought goods for articles which require no farther preparation, as for wine, oil, tea, fugar, &c.

&c. This also assists employment, because when the country is stocked with one kind of manufacture, it renews the demand by converting it into another; but it is inferior to the former, as it promotes this end by one side only of the bargain—by what it carries out. The *last*, the lowest, and most disadvantageous species of commerce, is the exportation of raw materials in return for wrought goods; as when wool is sent abroad to purchase velvets; hinds or peltry to procure shoes, hats, or linen cloth. This trade is unfavourable to population, because it leaves no room or demand for employment, either in what it takes out of the country, or in what it brings into it. Its operation on both sides is noxious. By its exports it diminishes the very subject upon which the industry of the inhabitants ought to be exercised; by its imports it lessens the encouragement of that industry, in the same proportion that it supplies the consumption of the country with the produce of foreign labour. Of different branches of *manufactory*, those are, in their nature, the most beneficial, in which the price of the wrought article exceeds in the highest proportion that of the raw material; for this excess measures the quantity of employment, or, in other words, the number of manufacturers which each branch sustains. The produce of the ground is never the most advantageous article of foreign commerce. Under a perfect state of public œconomy, the soil of the country should be applied solely to the raising of provision for the inhabitants, and its trade be supplied by their industry, A nation will never reach its proper extent of population, so long as its principal commerce confifts in the exportation of corn or cattle; or even of wine, oil, tobacco, madder, indigo, timber; becaufe thefe laft articles take up that furface, which ought to be covered with the materials of human fubfiftence.

It muft be here however noticed, that we have all along confidered the inhabitants of a country as maintained by the produce of the country; and that what we have faid is applicable with ftrictnefs to this fuppofition alone. The reafoning, neverthelefs, may eafily be adapted to a different cafe; for when provifion is not produced, but imported, what has been affirmed concerning provifion, will be, in a great meafure, true of that article, whether it be money, produce, or labour, which is exchanged for provifion. Thus, when the Dutch raife madder, and exchange it for corn; or when the people of America plant tobacco, and fend it to Europe for cloth; the cultivation of madder and tobacco become as neceffary to the fubfiftence of the inhabitants, and, by confequence, will affect the ftate of population in thefe countries as fenfibly, as the actual production of food, or the manufactory of raiment. In like manner, when the fame inhabitants of Holland earn money by the carriage of the produce of one country to another, and with that money purchafe the provifion from abroad, which their own land is not extenfive enough to fupply, the increafe or decline of this trade will influence the numbers of the people no lefs less than similar changes would do in the cultivation of the soil.

The few principles already established will enable us to describe the effects upon population, which may be expected from the following important articles of national conduct and œconomy.

I. EMIGRATION. *Emigration* may be either the overflowing of a country, or the desertion. As the increase of the species is indefinite, and the number of inhabitants, which any given tract of surface can support, finite, it is evident that great numbers may be constantly leaving a country, and yet the country remain constantly full. Or whatever be the cause which invincibly limits the population of a country, when the number of the people have arrived at that limit, the progress of generation, beside continuing the succession, will supply multitudes for foreign emigration. In these two cases, emigration neither indicates any political decay, nor, in truth, diminishes the number of the people; nor ought to be prohibited or discouraged. But emigrants may relinquish their country from a sense of insecurity, oppression, annoyance, and inconveniency. Neither, again, *here* is it emigration which wastes the people, but the evils that occasion it. It would be in vain, if it were practicable, to confine the inhabitants at home; for the same causes which drive them out of the country, would prevent their multiplication if they remained in it. Lastly, men may be tempted to change their situation by the allurement of a better climate, of a more refined or luxurious manner of living, by the prospect of wealth, or, sometimes, by the mere nominal advantage of higher wages and prices. This class of emigrants, with whom alone the laws can interfere with effect, will never, I think, be numerous. With the generality of a people, the attachment of mankind to their homes and country, the irksomeness of seeking new habitations, and of living amongst strangers, will outweigh, so long as men possess the necessaries of life in safety, or, at least, so long as they can obtain a provision for that mode of subsistence, which the class of citizens, to which they belong, are accustomed to enjoy, all the inducements that the advantages of a foreign land can offer. There appear, therefore, to be few cases in which emigration can be prohibited with advantage to the state; it appears also that emigration is an equivocal symptom, which will probably accompany the decline of the political body, but which *may* likewise attend a condition of perfect health and vigour.

II. COLONIZATION. The only view under which our subject will permit us to consider *colonization*, is in its tendency to augment the population of the parent state. Suppose a fertile, but empty island, to lie within the reach of a country, in which arts and manufactures are already established: suppose a colony sent out from such a country to take possession of the island, and to live there under

under the protection and authority of their native government; the new settlers will naturally convert their labour to the cultivation of the vacant soil, and, with the produce of that soil, will draw a supply of manufactures from their countrymen at home. Whilst the inhabitants continue few, and the lands cheap and fresh, the colonists will find it easier and more profitable to raise corn, or rear cattle, and with corn and cattle to purchase woollen cloth, for instance, or linen, than to spin or weave these articles for themselves. The mother country, meanwhile, derives from this connection an increase both of provision and employment. It promotes at once the two great requisites, upon which the facility of subsistence, and, by consequence, the state of population depends, *production* and *distribution*: and this in a manner the most direct and beneficial. No situation can be imagined more favourable to population, than that of a country which works up goods for others, whilst these others are cultivating new tracts of land for them. For as, in a genial climate, and from a fresh soil, the labour of one man will raise provision enough for ten, it is manifest that, where all are employed in agriculture, much the greater part of the produce will be spared from the consumption; and that three out of four, at least, of those who are maintained by it, will reside in the country which receives the redundancy. When the new country does not remit *provision* to the old one, the advantage is less; but still the exportation of wrought goods, by whatever return they are paid for, advances population in that fecondary way, in which thofe trades promote it that are not employed in the production of provifion. Whatever prejudice, therefore, fome late events have excited againft fchemes of colonization, the fyftem itfelf is founded in apparent national utility, and, what is more, upon principles favourable to the common intereft of human nature: for it does not appear, by what other method newly difcovered and unfrequented countries can be peopled, or, during the infancy of their eftablifhment, be protected or fupplied. The error which we of this nation at prefent lament, feems to have confifted not fo much in the original formation of colonies, as in the fubfequent management; in impofing reftrictions too rigorous, or in continuing them too long; in not perceiving the point of time, when the irrefiftible order and progrefs of human affairs demanded a change of laws and policy.

III. MONEY. Where *money* abounds the people are generally numerous: yet, gold and filver neither feed nor clothe mankind; nor are they in all countries converted into provifion by purchafing the neceffaries of life at foreign markets; nor do they, in any country, compofe thofe articles of perfonal or domeftic ornament, which certain orders of the community have learnt to regard as neceffaries of life, and without the means of procuring which they will not enter into family eftablifhments—at leaft this property of the precious metals obtains in a very fmall degree. The effect of money upon the number of the people, though visible to observation, is not explained without some difficulty. To understand this connection properly, we must return to the proposition, with which we concluded our reasoning upon the subject, "that "population is chiefly promoted by employment." Now of employment money is partly the indication, and partly the cause. The only way in which money regularly and spontaneously *flows into* a country, is in return for the goods that are sent out of it, or the work that is performed by it; and the only way in which money is *retained* in a country is, by the country supplying, in a great measure, its own consumption of manufactures. Consequently, the quantity of money found in a country, denotes the amount of labour and employment: but still, employment, not money, is the cause of population; the accumulation of money being merely a collateral effect of the same cause, or a circumstance which accompanies the existence, and measures the operation of that cause. And this is true of money, only whilst it is acquired by the industry of the inhabitants. The treasures, which belong to a country by the possession of mines, or by the exaction of tribute from foreign dependencies, afford no conclusion concerning the state of population. The influx from these sources may be immense, and yet the country remain poor and ill peopled; of which we see an egregious example in the condition of Spain, since the acquisition of its South American dominions.

But, secondly, money may become also a real and an operative *cause* of population, by acting as a stimulus to industry, and by facilitating the means of subsistence. The ease of subsistence, and the encouragement of industry, depend neither upon the price of labour, nor upon the price of provision, but upon the proportion which the one bears to the other. Now the influx of money into a country naturally tends to advance this proportion; that is, every fresh accession of money raises the price of labour before it raises the price of provision. When money is brought from abroad, the persons, be they who they will, into whose hands it first arrives, do not buy up provision with it, but apply it to the purchase and payment of labour. If the state receive it, the state dispenses what it receives amongst soldiers, sailors, artificers, engineers, ship-wrights, workmen; if private persons bring home treasures of gold and silver, they usually expend them in the building of houses, the improvement of estates, the purchase of furniture, dress, equipage, in articles of luxury or splendour: if the merchant be enriched by returns of his foreign commerce, he applies his increased capital to the enlargement of his business at home. The money erelong comes to market for provision, but it comes thither through the hands of the manufacturer, the artist, the husbandman, and labourer. Its effect, therefore, upon the price of art and labour will *precede* its effect upon the price of provision; and, during the interval between one effect and the other, the means of subsistence will be multiplied and facilitated, as well as industry be excited by new rewards. When the greater plenty of money in circulation has produced an advance in the price of provision, corresponding to the advanced price of labour, its effect ceases. The labourer no longer gains any thing by the increase of his wages. It is not, therefore, the quantity of specie collected into a country, but the continual increase of that quantity, from which the advantage arises to employment and population. It is only the *accession* of money which produces the effect, and it is only by money constantly flowing into a country, that the effect can be constant. Now whatever consequence arises to the country from the influx of money, the contrary may be expected to follow from the diminution of its quantity; and accordingly we find, that whatever cause drains off the specie of a country, faster than the streams, which feed it, can supply, not only impoverishes the country, but depopulates it. The knowledge and experience of this effect has given occasion to a phrase which occurs in almost every discourse upon commerce or politics. The *balance of trade* with any foreign nation is said to be against or in favour of a country simply as it tends to carry money out, or to bring it in; that is, according as the price of the imports exceeds or falls short of the price of the exports. So invariably is the increase or diminution of the specie of a country regarded as a test of the public advantage or detriment, which arises from any branch of its commerce.

IV. TAXATION. As *taxes* take nothing out of a country; as they do not diminish the public stock, only vary the distribution of it, they are not necessarily prejudicial

dicial to population. If the state exact money from certain members of the community, she dispenses it also amongst other members of the same community. They who contribute to the revenue, and they who are supported or benefited by the expences of government, are to be placed one against the other; and whilst what the subsistence of one part is profited by receiving, compensates for what that of the other suffers by paying, the common fund of the society is not lessened. This is true: but it must be observed that although the sum distributed by the state be always *equal* to the sum collected from the people, yet the gain and loss to the means of subsistence may be very *unequal*; and the balance will remain on the wrong or the right side of the account, according as the money passes by taxation from the industrious to the idle, from the many to the few, from those who want to those who abound, or in a contrary direction. For instance, a tax upon coaches, to be laid out in the repair of roads, would probably improve the population of a neighbourhood; a tax upon cottages, to be ultimately expended in the purchase and support of coaches, would certainly diminish it. In like manner, a tax upon wine or tea, distributed in bounties to fishermen or husbandmen, would augment the provision of a country; a tax upon fisheries and husbandry, however indirect or concealed, to be converted, when raised, to the procuring of wine or tea for the idle and opulent, would naturally impair the public stock. The effect, therefore, of taxes upon the means of subsistence depends not so much upon the amount of the sum levied, as upon the object of the tax, and the application. Taxes likewise may be so adjusted as to conduce to the restraint of luxury, and the correction of vice; to the encouragement of industry, trade, agriculture, and marriage. Taxes thus contrived, become rewards and penalties; not only sources of revenue, but instruments of police. Vices indeed themselves cannot be taxed without holding forth such a conditional toleration of them as to destroy men's perception of their guilt; a tax comes to be considered as a commutation; the materials, however, and incentives of vice may. Although, for instance, drunkenness would be, on this account, an unfit object of taxation, yet public-houses and spirituous liquors are very properly subjected to heavy imposts.

Nevertheless, although it may be true, that taxes cannot be pronounced to be detrimental to population, by any absolute necessity in their nature; and though, under some modifications, and when urged only to a certain extent, they may even operate in favour of it; yet it will be found, in a great plurality of instances, that their tendency is noxious. Let it be supposed that nine families inhabit a neighbourhood, each possessing barely the means of subsistence, or of that mode of subsistence which custom hath established amongst them; let a tenth family be quartered upon these, to be supported by a tax raised from the nine; or rather let one of the nine have his income augmented by a similar deduction from the incomes of the rest: in either of these

these cases, it is evident that the whole district would be broken up. For as the entire income of each is supposed to be barely sufficient for the establishment which it maintains, a deduction of any part destroys that establishment. Now it is no answer to this objection, it is no apology for the grievance, to say, that nothing is taken out of the neighbourhood; that the stock is not diminished. The mischief is done by deranging the distribution. Nor, again, is the luxury of one family, or even the maintenance of an additional family, a recompence to the country for the ruin of nine others. Nor, lastly, will it alter the effect, though it may conceal the cause, that the contribution, instead of being levied directly upon each day's wages, is mixed up in the price of some article of constant use and consumption; as in a tax upon candles, malt, leather, or fuel. This example illustrates the tendency of taxes to obstruct subsistence; and the minutest degree of this obstruction will be felt in the formation of families. The example, indeed, forms an extreme case: the evil is magnified, in order to render its operation distinct and visible. In real life, families may not be broken up, or forced from their habitation, houses be quitted, or countries suddenly deserted, in consequence of any new imposition whatever; but marriages will become gradually less frequent.

It seems necessary, however, to distinguish between the operation of a new tax, and the effect of taxes which have been long established. In the course of circulation the money may flow back to the hands from which it was

was taken. The proportion between the supply and the expence of subsistence, which had been disturbed by the tax, may at length recover itself again. In the instance just now stated, the addition of a tenth family to the neighbourhood, or the enlarged expences of one of the nine, may, in some shape or other, so advance the profits, or increase the employment of the rest, as to make full restitution for the share of their property, of which it deprives them: or, what is more likely to happen, a reduction may take place in their mode of living, suited to the abridgment of their incomes. Yet still the ultimate and permanent effect of taxation, though distinguishable from the impression of a new tax, is generally adverse to population. The *proportion* above spoken of, can only be restored by one side or other of the following alternative; by the people either contracting their wants, which at the same time diminishes consumption and employment; or by raising the price of labour, which necessarily adding to the price of the productions and manufactures of the country, checks their sale at foreign markets. A nation, which is burthened with taxes, must always be undersold by a nation which is free from them, unless the difference be made up by some singular advantage of climate, soil, skill, or industry. This quality belongs to all taxes which affect the mass of the community, even when imposed upon the properest objects, and applied to the fairest purposes. But abuses are inseparable from the disposal of public money. As government is usually administered, the produce of public taxes is expended upon a train of gentry, in the maintaining of pomp, or in the purchafe of influence. The converfion of property, which taxes effectuate, when they are employed in this manner, is attended with obvious evils. It takes from the induftrious to give to the idle; it increafes the number of the latter; it tends to accumulation; it facrifices the conveniency of many to the luxury of a few; it makes no return to the people, from whom the tax is drawn, that is fatisfactory or intelligible; it encourages no activity which is ufeful or productive.

The fum to be raifed being fettled, a wife ftatefman will contrive his taxes principally with a view to their effect upon *population*, that is, he will fo adjuft them, as to give the leaft poffible obftruction to thofe means of fubfiftence by which the mafs of the community are maintained. We are accuftomed to an opinion that a tax, to be juft, ought to be accurately proportioned to the circumftances of the perfons who pay it. But upon what, it might be afked, is this opinion founded; unlefs it could be fhown that fuch a proportion interferes the leaft with the general conveniency of fubfiftence: whereas I fhould rather believe, that a tax, conftructed with a view to that conveniency, ought to rife upon the different claffes of the community, in a much higher ratio than the fimple proportion of their incomes. The point to be regarded, is not what men have, but what they can fpare; and it is evident that a man, who poffeffes a thoufand pounds a year, can more eafily give up a hundred, than a man
with

with a hundred pounds a year can part with ten; that is, those habits of life which are reasonable and innocent, and upon the ability to continue which the formation of families depends, will be much less affected by the one deduction than the other: it is still more evident, that a man of a hundred pounds a year would not be so much distressed in his subsistence, by a demand from him of ten pounds, as a man of ten pounds a year would be by the loss of one: to which we must add, that the population of every country being replenished by the marriages of the lowest ranks of the society, their accommodation and relief becomes of more importance to the state, than the conveniency of any higher but less numerous order of its citizens. But whatever be the proportion which public expediency directs, whether the simple, the duplicate, or any higher or intermediate proportion of men's incomes, it can never be attained by any *single* tax; as no single object of taxation can be found, which measures the ability of the subject with sufficient generality and exactness. It is only by a system and variety of taxes mutually balancing and equalizing one another, that a due proportion can be preserved. For instance, if a tax upon lands press with greater hardship upon those who live in the country, it may be properly counterpoised by a tax upon the rent of houses, which will affect principally the inhabitants of large towns. Distinctions may also be framed in some taxes, which shall allow abatements or exemptions to married persons; to the parents of a certain number of legitimate children; to improvers of the soil; to particular modes of cultivation, as to tillage in preference to pasturage; and in general to that industry which is immediately *productive*, in preference to that which is only *instrumental*; but above all, which may leave the heaviest part of the burthen upon the methods, whatever they be, of acquiring wealth without industry, or even of subsisting in idleness.

V. EXPORTATION OF BREAD-CORN. Nothing seems to have a more positive tendency to reduce the number of the people, than the sending abroad part of the provision by which they are maintained; yet this has been the policy of legislators very studious of the improvement of their country. In order to reconcile ourselves to a practice, which apears to militate with the chief interest, that is, with the population of the country that adopts it, we must be reminded of a maxim which belongs to the productions both of nature and art, " that it is impossible " to have enough without a superfluity." The point of sufficiency cannot, in any case, be so exactly hit upon, as to have nothing to spare, yet never to want. This is peculiarly true of bread-corn, of which the annual increase is extremely variable. As it is necessary that the crop be adequate to the consumption in a year of scarcity, it must, of consequence, greatly exceed it in a year of plenty. A redundancy therefore will occasionally arise from the very care that is taken to secure the people against the danger of want; and it is manifest that the exportation of this redundancy substracts nothing from

the

the number that can regularly be maintained by the produce of the foil. Moreover, as the exportation of corn, under thefe circumftances, is attended with no direct injury to population, fo the benefits, which indirectly arife to population from foreign commerce, belong to this in common with other fpecies of trade; together with the peculiar advantage of prefenting a conftant incitement to the fkill and induftry of the hufbandman, by the promife of a certain fale and an adequate price, under every contingency of feafon and produce. There is another fituation, in which corn may not only be exported, but in which the people can thrive by no other means; that is, of a newly fettled country with a fertile foil. The exportation of a large proportion of the corn which a country produces, proves, it is true, that the inhabitants have not yet attained to the number which the country is capable of maintaining; but it does not prove but that they may be haftening to this limit with the utmoft practicable celerity, which is the perfection to be fought for in a young eftablifhment. In all cafes except thefe two, and in the former of them to any greater degree than what is neceffary to take off occafional redundancies, the exportation of corn is either itfelf noxious to population, or argues a defect of population arifing from fome other caufe.

VI. ABRIDGMENT OF LABOUR. It has long been made a queftion whether thofe mechanical contrivances, which *abridge labour*, by performing the fame work by fewer hands,

hands, be detrimental or not to the population of a country. From what has been delivered in preceding parts of the prefent chapter it will be evident, that this queftion is equivalent to another, whether fuch contrivances diminifh or not the quantity of employment. Their firft and moft obvious effect undoubtedly is this; becaufe if one man be made to do what three men did before, two are immediately difcharged: but if, by fome more general and remoter confequence, they increafe the demand for work, or, what is the fame thing, prevent the diminution of that demand, in a greater proportion than they contract the number of hands by which it is performed, the quantity of employment, upon the whole, will gain an addition. Upon which principle it may be obferved, firftly, that whenever a mechanical invention fucceeds in one place, it is neceffary that it be imitated in every other, where the fame manufacture is carried on; for it is manifeft, that he, who has the benefit of a concifer operation, will foon outvie and underfell a competitor who continues to ufe a more circuitous labour. It is alfo true, in the fecond place, that whoever *firft* difcover or adopt a mechanical improvement will, for fome time, draw to themfelves an increafe of employment; and that this preference may continue even after the improvement has become general: for, in every kind of trade, it is not only a great but permanent advantage, to have once preoccupied the public reputation. Thirdly, after every fuperiority which might be derived from the poffeffion of a fecret has ceafed, it may be well queftioned, whether even then any

any loſs can accrue to employment. The ſame money will be ſpared to the ſame article ſtill. Wherefore, in proportion as the article can be afforded at a lower price, by reaſon of an eaſier or ſhorter proceſs in the manufacture, it will either grow into more general uſe, or an improvement will take place in the quality and fabric which will demand a proportionable addition of hands. The number of perſons employed in the manufactory of ſtockings has not, I apprehend, decreaſed, ſince the invention of ſtocking mills. The amount of what is expended upon the article after ſubſtracting from it the price of the raw material, and conſequently what is paid for work in this branch of our manufactories, is not leſs than it was before. Goods of a finer texture are worn in the place of coarſer. This is the change which the invention has produced, and which compenſates to the manufactory for every other inconveniency. Add to which, that in the above, and in almoſt every inſtance, an improvement which conduces to the recommendation of a manufactory, either by the cheapneſs or the quality of the goods, draws up after it many dependent employments, in which no abbreviation has taken place.

From the reaſoning that has been purſued, and the various conſiderations ſuggeſted in this chapter, a judgment may, in ſome ſort, be formed, how far regulations of law are in their nature capable of contributing to the ſupport and advancement of population. I ſay *how far:* for, as in many
ſubjects,

subjects, so especially in those which relate to commerce, to plenty, to riches, and to the number of the people, more is wont to be expected from laws, than laws can do. Laws can only imperfectly restrain that dissoluteness of manners, which, by diminishing the frequency of marriages, impairs the very source of population. Laws cannot regulate the wants of mankind, their mode of living, or their desire of those superfluities, which fashion, more irresistable than laws, has once introduced into general usage, or, in other words, has erected into necessaries of life. Laws cannot induce men to enter into marriages, when the expences of a family must deprive them of that system of accommodation, to which they have habituated their expectations. Laws by their protection, by assuring to the labourer the fruit and profit of his labour, may help to make a people industrious; but without industry, the laws cannot provide either subsistence, or employment: laws cannot make corn grow without toil and care; or trade flourish without art and diligence. In spite of all laws, the expert, laborious, honest workman will be *employed*, in preference to the lazy, the unskilful, the fraudulent, and evasive: and this is not more true of two inhabitants of the same village, than it is of the people of two different countries, which communicate either with each other, or with the rest of the world. The natural basis of trade is rivalship of quality and price; or, which is the same thing, of skill and industry. Every attempt to *force* trade by operation of law, that is, by compelling persons to buy goods at one market, which they can obtain

cheaper

cheaper and better from another, is sure to be either eluded by the quick-sightedness and incessant activity of private interest, or to be frustrated by retaliation. One half of the commercial laws of many states are calculated merely to counteract the restrictions which have been imposed by other states. Perhaps the only way, in which the interposition of law is salutary in trade, is in the prevention of frauds.

Next to the indispensible requisites of internal peace and security, the chief advantage, which can be derived to population from the interference of law, appears to me to consist in the encouragement of *agriculture*. This, at least, is the direct way of increasing the number of the people; every other mode being effectual only by its influence upon this. Now the principal expedient by which such a purpose can be promoted, is to adjust the laws of property, as nearly as possible, to the two following rules: firstly, " to give to the occupier all the power over the " soil which is necessary for its perfect cultivation;"—secondly, " to assign the whole profit of every improvement " to the persons by whose activity it is carried on." What we call property in land, as hath been observed above, is power over it. Now it is indifferent to the public in whose hands this power resides, if it be rightly used: it matters not to whom the land belongs, if it be well cultivated. When we lament that great estates are often united in the same hand, or complain that one man possesses what would be sufficient for a thousand, we suffer ourselves to be misled by words. The owner of ten thousand pounds a year *consumes* little more of the produce of the soil than the owner of ten pounds a year. If the cultivation be equal, the estate, in the hands of one great lord, affords subsistence and employment to the same number of persons, as it would do, if it were divided amongst a hundred proprietors. In like manner, we ought to judge of the effect upon the public interest, which may arise from lands being holden by the king, or by the subject; by private persons, or by corporations; by lay men, or ecclesiastics; in fee, or for life; by virtue of office, or in right of inheritance. I do not mean that these varieties make no difference, but I mean, that all the difference they do make respects the cultivation of the lands which are so holden.

There exist in this country conditions of tenure, which condemn the land itself to perpetual sterility. Of this kind is the right of *common*, which precludes each proprietor from the improvement, or even the convenient occupation of his estate, without, what seldom can be obtained, the consent of many others. This tenure is also usually embarrassed by the interference of *manorial* claims, under which it often happens that the surface belongs to one owner and the soil to another; so that neither owner can stir a clod without the concurrence of his partner in the property. In many manors, the tenant is restrained from granting leases beyond a short term of years; which renders every plan of solid and permanent improvement impracticable. In these cases the owner wants,

wants, what the first rule of rational policy requires, " sufficient power over the soil for its perfect cultivation." This power ought to be extended to him by some easy and general law of enfranchisement, partition, and inclosure, which, though compulsory upon the lord, or the rest of the tenants, whilst it has in view the melioration of the soil, and tenders an equitable compensation for every right that it takes away, is neither more arbitrary, nor more dangerous to the stability of property, than that which is done in the construction of roads, bridges, embankments, navigable canals, and, indeed, in almost every public work, in which private owners of land are obliged to accept that price for their property which an indifferent jury may award. It may here however be proper to observe, that although the inclosure of wastes and pastures be generally beneficial to population, yet the inclosure of lands in tillage, in order to convert them into pastures, is as generally hurtful.

But secondly, agriculture is discouraged by every constitution of landed property, which lets in those, who have no concern in the improvement, to a participation of the profit. This objection is applicable to all such customs of manors as subject the proprietor, upon the death of the lord or tenant, or the alienation of the estate, to a fine apportioned to the improved value of the land. But of all institutions, which are, in this way, adverse to cultivation and improvement, none is so noxious as that of *tithes*. A claimant here enters into the produce who contributed no affiftance whatever to the production. When years, perhaps, of care and toil have matured an improvement; when the hufbandman fees new crops ripening to his fkill and induftry, the moment he is ready to put his fickle to the grain, he finds himfelf compelled to divide his harveft with a ftranger. Tithes are a tax not only upon induftry, but upon that induftry which feeds mankind; upon that fpecies of exertion, which it is the aim of all wife laws to cherifh and promote; and to uphold and excite which, compofes, as we have feen, the main benefit that the community receives from the whole fyftem of trade, and the fuccefs of commerce. And together with the more general inconveniency that attends the exaction of tithes, there is this additional evil, in the mode at leaft according to which they are collected at prefent, that they operate as a bounty upon pafturage. The burthen of the tax falls with its chief, if not with its whole weight, upon tillage; that is to fay, upon that precife mode of cultivation, which, as hath been fhown above, it is the bufinefs of the ftate to relieve and remunerate, in preference to every other. No meafure of fuch extenfive concern appears to me fo practicable, nor any fingle alteration fo beneficial, as the converfion of tithes into corn rents. This commutation, I am convinced, might be fo adjufted, as to fecure to the tithe-holder a complete and perpetual equivalent for his intereft, and to leave to induftry its full operation and entire reward.

CHAP. XII.

OF WAR, AND OF MILITARY ESTABLISHMENTS.

BECAUSE the Christian scriptures describe wars, as what they are, as crimes or judgments, some have been led to believe that it is unlawful for a Christian to bear arms. But it should be remembered, that it may be necessary for individuals to unite their force, and, for this end, to resign themselves to the direction of a common will; and yet it may be true, that that will is often actuated by criminal motives, and often determined to destructive purposes. Hence, although the origin of wars be ascribed in scripture to the operation of lawless and malignant passions;* and though war itself be enumerated amongst the sorest calamities with which a land can be visited,

---

* James iv. 1.

visited, the profession of a soldier is no where forbidden or condemned. When the "soldiers demanded of John "the Baptist, and what shall we do?" he said unto them, "do violence to no man, neither accuse any falsely, and be "content with your wages."* In which answer we do not find that, in order to prepare themselves for the reception of the kingdom of God, it was required of soldiers to relinquish their profession, but only that they should beware of the vices, of which that profession, it may be presumed, was justly accused. The precept, "be con- "tent with your wages," supposed them to continue in their situation. It was of a Roman centurion that Christ pronounced that memorable eulogy, " I have not found so "great faith no not in Israel."† The first ‡ gentile convert who was received into the Christian church, and to whom the gospel was imparted by the immediate and especial direction of Heaven, held the same station: and, in the history of this transaction, we discover not the smallest intimation, that Cornelius, upon becoming a Christian, quitted the service of the Roman legion; that his profession was objected to, or his continuance in it considered as, in any wise, inconsistent with his new character.

In applying the principles of morality to the affairs of nations, the difficulty which meets us arises from hence, "that "the particular consequence, sometimes, appears to exceed

* Luke iii. 14. † Luke vii. 9. ‡ Acts x. 1.

the value of the general rule." In this circumstance is founded the only distinction that exists between the case of independent states, and of independent individuals. In the transactions of private persons, no advantage, that results from the breach of a general law of justice, can compensate to the public for the violation of the law: in the concerns of empire, this may sometimes be doubted. Thus, that the faith of promises ought to be maintained, as far as is lawful, and as far as was intended by the parties, whatever inconveniency either of them may suffer by his fidelity, in the intercourse of private life is seldom disputed; because it is evident to almost every man who reflects upon the subject, that the common happiness gains more by the preservation of the rule, than it could do by the removal of the inconveniency. But when the adherence to a public treaty would enslave a whole people, would block up seas, rivers, or harbours; depopulate cities, condemn fertile regions to eternal desolation, cut off a country from its sources of provision, or deprive it of those commercial advantages, to which its climate, produce, or situation naturally entitle it; the magnitude of the particular evil induces us to call in question the obligation of the general rule. Moral philosophy furnishes no precise solution to these doubts. She cannot pronounce that any rule of morality is so rigid as to bend to no exceptions; nor, on the other hand, can she comprize these exceptions within any previous description. She confesses that the obligation of every law depends upon its ultimate utility; that this utility

having

having a finite and determinate value, situations may be feigned, and consequently may possibly arise, in which the general tendency is outweighed by the enormity of the particular mischief: but she recalls, at the same time, to the consideration of the enquirer, the almost inestimable importance, as of other general rules of relative justice, so especially of national and personal fidelity; the unseen, if not unbounded extent of the mischief, which must follow from the want of it; the danger of leaving it to the sufferer to decide upon the comparison of particular and general consequences, and the still greater danger of such decisions being drawn into future precedents. If treaties, for instance, be no longer binding than whilst they are convenient, or until the inconveniency ascend to a certain point, which point must be fixed by the judgment, or rather by the feelings of the complaining party; or if such an opinion, after being authorized by a few examples, come at length to prevail; one and almost the only method of averting or closing the calamities of war, of either preventing, or putting a stop to the destruction of mankind, is lost to the world for ever. We do not say that no evil can exceed this, nor any possible advantage compensate it; but we say that a loss, which affects *all*, will scarcely be made up to the common stock of human happiness, by any benefit that can be procured to a single nation, which, however respectable when compared with any other single nation, bears an inconsiderable proportion to the whole. These, however, are the principles upon which the calculation is to be be formed. It is enough, in this place, to remark the cause which produces the hesitation that we sometimes feel, in applying the rules of personal probity to the conduct of nations.

As between individuals it is found impossible to ascertain every duty by an immediate reference to public utility, not only because such reference is oftentimes too remote or obscure for the direction of private consciences, but because a multitude of cases arise, in which it is indifferent to the general interest by what rule men act, though it be absolutely necessary that they act by some constant and known rule or other; and as for these reasons certain positive constitutions are wont to be established in every society, which, when established, become as obligatory as the original principles of natural justice themselves; so, likewise, it is between independent communities. Together with those maxims of universal equity which are common to states and to individuals, and by which the rights and conduct of the one as well as of the other ought to be adjusted, when they fall within the scope and application of such maxims; there exists also amongst sovereigns a system of artificial jurisprudence, under the name of the *law of nations*. In this code are found the rules which determine the right to vacant or newly discovered countries; those which relate to the protection of fugitives, the privileges of ambassadors, the condition and duties of neutrality, the immunities of neutral ships, ports, and coasts, the distance from shore to which these immunities extend, the distinction between free and contraband goods, and a variety of subjects of the same kind. Concerning which examples, and indeed the principal part of what is called the *jus gentium*, it may be observed, that the rules derive their moral force, by which I mean the regard that ought to be paid to them by the consciences of sovereigns, not from their internal reasonableness or justice, for many of them are perfectly arbitrary; nor yet from the authority by which they were established, for the greater part have grown insensibly into usage, without any public compact, formal acknowledgment, or even known original; but simply from the fact of their being established, and the general duty of conforming to established rules upon questions, and between parties, where nothing but positive regulations can prevent disputes, and where disputes are followed by such destructive consequences. The first of the instances, which we have just now enumerated, may be selected for the illustration of this remark. The nations of Europe consider the sovereignty of newly discovered countries as belonging to the prince or state whose subject makes the discovery; and, in pursuance of this rule, it is usual for a navigator, who falls upon an unknown shore, to take possession of it, in the name of his sovereign at home, by erecting his standard, or displaying his flag upon a desert coast. Now nothing can be more fanciful, or less substantiated by any considerations of reason or justice, than the right which such discovery, or the transient occupation and idle ceremony that accompany it, confer upon the country of the discoverer. Nor can

any

any stipulation be produced, by which the rest of the world have bound themselves to submit to this pretension. Yet when we reflect that the claims to newly discovered countries can hardly be settled, between the different nations that frequent them, without some positive rule or other; that such claims, if left unsettled, would prove sources of ruinous and fatal contentions; that the rule already proposed, however arbitrary, possesses one principal quality of a rule—determination and certainty; above all that it is acquiesced in, and that no one has power to substitute another, however he might contrive a better in its place: when we reflect upon these properties of the rule, or rather upon these consequences of rejecting its authority, we are led to ascribe to it the virtue and obligation of a precept of natural justice, because we perceive in it, that which is the foundation of justice itself, public importance and utility. And a prince who should dispute this rule, for the want of regularity in its formation, or of intelligible justice in its principle, and by such disputes should disturb the tranquillity of nations, and at the same time lay the foundation of future disturbances, would be little less criminal, than he who breaks the public peace by a violation of engagements to which he had himself consented, or by an attack upon those national rights, which are founded immediately in the law of nature, and in the first perceptions of equity. The same thing may be repeated of the rules which the law of nations prescribes in the other instances that were mentioned, namely, that the obscurity of their origin, or the arbitrariness of their principle, subtracts nothing from the respect that is due to them, when once established.

War may be considered with a view to its *causes* and to its *conduct*.

The *justifying* causes of war are deliberate invasions of right, and the necessity of maintaining such a balance of power amongst neighbouring nations, as that no single state, or confederacy of states, be strong enough to overwhelm the rest. The objects of just war are precaution, defence, or reparation. In a larger sense, every just war is a *defensive* war, inasmuch as every just war supposes an injury perpetrated, attempted, or feared.

The *insufficient* causes, or *unjustifiable* motives of war, are the family alliances, the personal friendships, or the personal quarrels of princes; the internal disputes which are carried on in other nations; the justice of other wars; the extension of territory, or of trade; the misfortunes or accidental weakness of a neighbouring or rival nation.

There are *two* lessons of rational and sober policy, which, if it were possible to inculcate into the councils of princes, would exclude many of the motives of war, and allay that restless ambition which is constantly stirring up one part of mankind against another. The first of these lessons admonishes princes to " place their glory and their " emulation, not in extent of territory, but in raising the
" greatest

"greatest quantity of happiness out of a given territory." The enlargement of territory by conquest is not only not a just object of war, but in the greater part of the instances in which it is attempted, not even desireable. It is certainly not desireable where it adds nothing to the numbers, the enjoyments, or the security of the conquerors. What commonly is gained to a nation, by the annexing of new dependencies, or the subjugation of other countries to its dominion, but a wider frontier to defend; more interfering claims to vindicate; more quarrels; more enemies; more rebellions to encounter; a greater force to keep up by sea and land; more services to provide for, and more establishments to pay? And, in order to draw from these acquisitions something that may make up for the charge of keeping them, a revenue is to be extorted, or a monopoly to be enforced and watched, at an expence which costs half their produce. Thus the provinces are oppressed, in order to pay for being ill governed; and the original state is exhausted in maintaining a feeble authority over discontented subjects. No assignable portion of country is benefited by the change; and if the sovereign appear to himself to be enriched or strengthened, when every part of his dominion is made poorer and weaker than it was, it is probable that he is deceived by appearances. Or were it true that the grandeur of the prince is magnified by those exploits; the glory which is purchased, and the ambition which is gratified by the distress of one country, without adding to the happiness of another, which, at the same time enslaves the new, and impoverishes the ancient part of the empire, by whatever names it may be known or flattered, is an object of universal execration; and not more so to the vanquished, than it is oftentimes to the very people whose armies or whose treasures have atchieved the victory.

There are, indeed, two cases in which the extension of territory may be of real advantage, and to both parties. The first is, where an empire thereby reaches to the natural boundaries which divide it from the rest of the world. Thus we account the British channel the natural boundary which separates the nations of England and France: and if France possessed any counties on this, or England any cities or provinces on that side of the sea, the recovery of such towns and districts to what may be called their natural sovereign, though it might not be a just reason for commencing war, would be a proper use to make of victory. The other case is, where neighbouring states, being severally too small and weak to defend themselves against the dangers that surround them, can only be safe by a strict and constant junction of their strength: here conquest will effect the purposes of confederation and alliance: and the union which it produces is often more close and permanent than that which results from voluntary association. Thus, if the heptarchy had continued in England, the different kingdoms of it might have separately fallen a prey to foreign invasion; and although the interest and danger of one part of the island was in truth common to every other part, it might have been difficult to have circulated this persuasion

sion amongst independent nations; or to have united them in any regular or steady opposition to their continental enemies, had not the valour and fortune of an enterprising prince incorporated the whole into a single monarchy. Here the conquered gained as much by the revolution as the conquerors. In like manner, and for the same reason, when the two royal families of Spain were met together in one race of princes, and the several provinces of France had devolved into the possession of a single sovereign, it became unsafe for the inhabitants of Great Britain any longer to remain under separate governments. The union of England and Scotland, which transformed two quarrelsome neighbours into one powerful empire, and which was first brought about by the course of succession, and afterwards completed by amicable convention, would have been a fortunate conclusion of hostilities, had it been effected by the operations of war. These two cases being admitted, namely, the obtaining of natural boundaries and barriers, and the including under the same government those who have a common danger, and a common enemy to guard against; I know not whether a third can be thought of, in which the extension of empire by conquest is useful even to the conquerors.

The second rule of prudence which ought to be recommended to those who conduct the affairs of nations is, " never to pursue national *honour* as distinct from national " *interest.*" This rule acknowledges that it is often necessary
to

to affert the honour of a nation for the fake of its intereft. The fpirit and courage of a people are fupported by flattering their pride. Conceffions which betray too much of fear or weaknefs, though they relate to points of mere ceremony, invite demands and attacks of more ferious importance. Our rule allows all this, and directs only that, when points of honour become fubjects of contention between fovereigns, or are likely to be made the occafions of war, they be eftimated with a reference to utility, and not *by themfelves.* " The dignity of his crown, the " honour of his flag, the glory of his arms," in the mouth of a prince, are ftately and impofing terms; but the ideas they infpire are infatiable. It may be always glorious to conquer, whatever be the juftice of the war, or the price of the victory. The dignity of a fovereign may not permit him to recede from claims of homage and refpect, at whatever expence of national peace and happinefs they are to be maintained, however unjuft they may have been in their original, or, in their continuance, however ufelefs to the poffeffor, or mortifying and vexatious to other ftates. The purfuit of honour, when let loofe from the admonitions of prudence, becomes in kings a wild and romantic paffion; eager to engage, and gathering fury in its progrefs, it is checked by no difficulties, repelled by no dangers: it forgets or defpifes thofe confiderations of fafety, eafe, wealth, and plenty, which, in the eye of true public wifdom, compofe the objects, to which the renown of arms, the fame of victory, are only inftrumental and fubordinate. The purfuit of intereft, on the other hand,

is

is a sober principle; computes costs and consequences; is cautious of entering into war; stops in time; when regulated by those universal maxims of relative justice which belong to the affairs of communities, as well as of private persons, it is the right principle for nations to proceed by; even when it trespasses upon these regulations, it is much less dangerous, because much more temperate than the other.

II. The conduct of war.—If the cause and end of war be justifiable, all the means that appear necessary to the end are justifiable also. This is the principle which defends those extremities, to which the violence of war usually proceeds; for since war is a contest by *force* between parties who acknowledge no common superior, and since it includes not in its idea the supposition of any convention which should place limits to the operations of force, it has naturally no boundary, but that in which force terminates, the destruction of the life against which the force is directed. Let it be observed however, that the licence of war authorizes no acts of hostility but what are necessary or conducive to the end and object of the war. Gratuitous barbarities borrow no excuse from this plea. Of which kind is every cruelty and every insult that serves only to exasperate the sufferings, or to incense the hatred of an enemy, without weakening his strength, or in any manner tending to procure his submission; such as the slaughter of captives, the subjecting of them to indignities or torture, the violation of women, the profanation of temples, the demolition of public buildings, libraries, statues, and in general the destruction or defacing of works that conduce nothing to annoyance or defence. These enormities are prohibited not only by the practice of civilized nations, but by the law of nature itself; as having no proper tendency to accelerate the termination, or accomplish the object of the war; and as containing that, which in peace and war is equally unjustifiable, ultimate and gratuitous mischief.

There are other restrictions imposed upon the conduct of war, not by the law of nature primarily, but by the *laws of war* first, and by the law of nature as seconding, and ratifying the laws of war. The laws of war are part of the law of nations; and founded, as to their authority, upon the same principle with the rest of that code, namely, upon the fact of their being established, no matter when or by whom; upon the expectation of their being mutually observed, in consequence of that establishment; and upon the general utility which results from such observation. The binding force of these rules is the greater, because the regard that is paid to them must be universal or none. The breach of the rule can only be punished by the subversion of the rule itself. On which account the whole mischief, that ensues from the loss of those salutary restrictions, which such rules prescribe, is justly chargeable upon the first aggressor. To this consideration may be referred the duty of refraining in war from poison and from assassination. If the law of

nature

nature simply be consulted, it may be difficult to distinguish between these and other methods of destruction, which are practised without scruple by nations at war. If it be lawful to kill an enemy at all, it seems lawful to do so by one mode of death as well as by another; by a dose of poison, as by the point of a sword; by the hand of an assassin, as by the attack of an army: for if it be said that one species of assault leaves to an enemy the power of defending himself against it, and that the other does not, it may be answered that we possess at least the same right to cut off an enemy's defence, that we have to seek his destruction. In this manner might the question be debated, if there existed no rule or law of war upon the subject. But when we observe that such practices are at present excluded by the usage and opinions of civilized nations; that the first recourse to them would be followed by instant retaliation; that the mutual licence which such attempts must introduce, would fill both sides with the misery of continual dread and suspicion, without adding to the strength or success of either; that when the example came to be more generally imitated, which it soon would be, after the sentiment that condemns it had been once broken in upon, it would greatly aggravate the horrors and calamities of war, yet procure no superiority to any of the nations engaged in it: when we view these effects, we join in the public reprobation of such fatal expedients, as of the admission amongst mankind of new and enormous evils without necessity or advantage. The law of nature, we see at length,

length, forbids thefe innovations as fo many tranfgreffions of a beneficial general rule, actually fubfifting.

The licenfe of war then acknowledges *two* limitations: it authorizes no hoftilities which have not an apparent tendency to effectuate the object of the war; it refpects thofe pofitive laws which the cuftom of nations hath fanctified, and which, whilft they are mutually conformed to, mitigate the calamities of war without weakening its operations, or diminifhing the power or fafety of belligerent ftates.

Long and various experience feems to have convinced the nations of Europe that nothing but a *ftanding army* can oppofe a ftanding army, where the numbers on each fide bear any moderate proportion to one another. The firft ftanding army that appeared in Europe after the fall of the Roman legion, was that which was erected in France by Charles VII. about the middle of the fifteenth century. And that the inftitution hath fince become general, can only be attributed to the fuperiority and fuccefs which are every where obferved to attend it. The truth is, the clofenefs, regularity, and quicknefs of their movements; the unreferved, inftantaneous, and almoft mechanical obedience to orders; the fenfe of perfonal honour, and the familiarity with danger, which belong to a difciplined, veteran, and embodied foldiery, give fuch firmnefs and intrepidity to their approach, fuch weight and execution to their attack, as are not to be withftood by by loose ranks of occasional and newly levied troops, who are liable by their inexperience to disorder and confusion, and in whom fear is constantly augmented by novelty and surprize. It is possible that a *militia*, with a great excess of numbers, and a ready supply of recruits, may sustain a defensive or a flying war against regular troops: it is also true that any service, which keeps soldiers for a while together, and inures them by little and little to the habits of war and the dangers of action, transforms them in effect into a standing army: but upon this plan it may be necessary for almost a whole nation to go out to war to repel an invader; beside that, a people so unprepared must always have the seat, and with it the miseries of war, at home, being utterly incapable of carrying their operations into a foreign country.

From the acknowledged superiority of standing armies, it follows, not only that it it is unsafe for a nation to disband its regular troops, whilst neighbouring kingdoms retain theirs, but also that regular troops provide for the public service at the least possible expence. I suppose a certain quantity of military strength to be necessary, and I say that a standing army costs the community less than any other establishment which presents to an enemy the same force. The constant drudgery of low employments is not only incompatible with any great degree of perfection or expertness in the profession of a soldier, but the profession of a soldier almost always unfits men for the business of regular occupations. Of three inhabitants of a

village,

village, it is better that one should addict himself entirely to arms, and the other two stay constantly at home to cultivate the ground, than that all the three should mix the avocations of a camp with the business of husbandry. By the former arrangement the country gains one complete soldier, and two industrious husbandmen; from the latter it receives three raw militia-men, who are at the same time three idle and profligate peasants. It should be considered also, that the emergencies of war wait not for seasons. Where there is no standing army ready for immediate service, it may be necessary to call the reaper from the fields in harvest, or the ploughman in seed-time; and the provision of a whole year may perish by the interruption of one month's labour. A standing army, therefore, is not only a more effectual, but a cheaper method of providing for the public safety, than any other, because it adds more than any other to the common strength, and takes less from that, which composes the wealth of a nation, its stock of productive industry.

There is yet another distinction between standing armies and militias, which deserves a more attentive consideration than any that has been mentioned. When the state relies for its defence upon a militia, it is necessary that arms be put into the hands of the people at large. The militia itself must be numerous, in proportion to the want or inferiority of its discipline, and the imbecilities or defects of its constitution. Moreover, as such a militia must be supplied by rotation, allotment, or some mode

mode of succession, whereby they, who have served a certain time, are replaced by fresh draughts from the country, a much greater number will be instructed in the use of arms, and will have been occasionally embodied together, than are actually employed, or than are supposed to be wanted at the same time. Now what effects upon the civil condition of the country may be looked for from this general diffusion of the military character, becomes an enquiry of great importance and delicacy. To me it appears doubtful, whether any government can be long secure, where the people are acquainted with the use of arms, and accustomed to resort to them. Every faction will find itself at the head of an army. Every disgust will excite commotion, and every commotion become a civil war. Nothing perhaps can govern a nation of armed citizens but that which governs an army—despotism. I do not mean that a regular government would become despotic by training up its subjects to the knowledge and exercise of arms, but that it would ere long be forced to give way to despotism in some other shape; and that the country would be liable to what is even worse than a settled and constitutional despotism, to perpetual rebellions, and to perpetual revolutions; to short and violent usurpations; to the successive tyranny of governors, rendered cruel and jealous by the danger and instability of their situation.

The same purposes of strength and efficacy which make a standing army necessary at all, make it necessary, in mixt governments, that this army be submitted to the management and direction of the prince. For however well a popular council may be qualified for the offices of legislation, it is altogether unfit for the conduct of war; in which success usually depends upon vigour and enterprize, upon secresy, dispatch, and unanimity, upon a quick perception of opportunities, and the power of seizing every opportunity immediately. It is likewise necessary that the obedience of an army be as prompt and active as possible; for which reason it ought to be made an obedience of will and emulation. Upon this consideration is founded the expediency of leaving to the prince not only the government and destination of the army, but the appointment and promotion of its officers; because a design is then alone likely to be executed with zeal and fidelity, when the person who issues the order, chooses the instruments, and rewards the service. To which we may subjoin that, in governments like ours, if the direction and *officering* of the army were placed in the hands of the democratic part of the constitution, this power, added to what they already possess, would so overbalance all that would be left of regal prerogative, that little would remain of monarchy in the constitution, but the name and expence; nor would they probably remain long.

Whilst we describe, however, the advantages of standing armies, we must not conceal the danger. These properties of their constitution, the soldiery being separated in a great a great degree from the reſt of the community, their being cloſely linked amongſt themſelves by habits of ſociety and ſubordination, and the dependency of the whole chain upon the will and favour of the prince, however eſſential they may be to the purpoſes for which armies are kept up, give them an aſpect in no wiſe favourable to public liberty. The danger however is diminiſhed by maintaining, upon all occaſions, as much alliance of intereſt, and as much intercourſe of ſentiment, between the military part of the nation and the other orders of the people, as are conſiſtent with the union and diſcipline of an army. For which purpoſe the officers of the army, upon whoſe diſpoſition towards the commonwealth a great deal may depend, ſhould be taken from the principal families of the country, and at the ſame time alſo be encouraged to eſtabliſh in it families of their own, as well as be admitted to ſeats in the ſenate, to hereditary diſtinctions, and to all the civil honours and privileges that are compatible with their profeſſion: which circumſtances of connection and ſituation will give them ſuch a ſhare in the general rights of the people, and ſo engage their inclinations on the ſide of public liberty, as to afford a reaſonable ſecurity that they cannot be brought, by any promiſes of perſonal aggrandizement, to aſſiſt in the execution of meaſures which might enſlave their poſterity, their kindred, and their country.——

F I N I S.

www.ingramcontent.com/pod-product-compliance
Lightning Source LLC
Chambersburg PA
CBHW081141230426
43664CB00018B/2769